ORIGIN AND AUTHORITY IN SEVENTEENTH-
CENTURY ENGLAND: BACON, MILTON, BUTLER

ALVIN SNIDER

Origin and Authority in Seventeenth-Century England: Bacon, Milton, Butler

UNIVERSITY OF TORONTO PRESS
Toronto Buffalo London

© University of Toronto Press Incorporated 1994
Toronto Buffalo London
Printed in Canada

ISBN 0-8020-2865-9

Printed on acid-free paper

Canadian Cataloguing in Publication Data

Snider, Alvin
  Origin and authority in seventeenth-century England :
Bacon, Milton, Butler

  Includes index.
  ISBN 0-8020-2865-9
  1. Bacon, Francis, 1561–1626. Novum organum.
  2. Milton, John, 1608–1674. Paradise lost.
  3. Butler, Samuel, 1612–1680. Hudibras.
  4. Beginning – History – 17th century. 5. English poetry –
Early modern, 1500–1700 – History and criticism. I. Title.
  B1131.S55 1994   121   C94-930166-3

Contents

ACKNOWLEDGMENTS vii

A NOTE ON TEXTS ix

Introduction: Origin, Error, Ideology 3

PART ONE
Francis Bacon: Organon and Origin

1 'Pure and Uncorrupted Natural Knowledge' 21
2 Writing Error in the *Novum Organum* 37
3 Authorizing Aphorism 55
4 Legitimation and the Origin of Restoration Science 69

PART TWO
Seeing Double in *Paradise Lost*

5 Beginning Late 91
6 Who Himself Beginning Knew? 117
7 The Figure in the Mirror 139

PART THREE
Butler's *Hudibras:* The Post-Epic Condition

8 'As *Aeneas* Bore His Sire' 163
9 Metaphysick Wit 183
10 A Babylonish Dialect 201
11 By Equivocation Swear 215

NOTES 245

INDEX 279

Acknowledgments

In writing this book I have benefited from the apparently limitless generosity of family, friends, colleagues, and students. Formal expressions of gratitude can only begin to suggest the real extent of my indebtedness.

Thanks are due to Jacqueline Krivel, Allan Megill, Mary Janell Metzger, and James Shapiro for their comments on individual chapters. Herman Rapaport read all of the chapters and responded with characteristic insight, generosity, and wisdom. Marlon Ross also read the entire unrevised manuscript, and tactfully prompted me to rethink some basic issues. Janel Mueller and John Wallace first encouraged me, as a graduate student, to pursue many of the questions raised here. I cannot imagine this book existing without their example, support, and advice. Over the past few years I have learned a great deal from conversations with graduate students at the University of Iowa: in particular, Maura Brady and Bruce McLeod challenged my readings of Bacon and Milton with very different interpretations of their own. If I echo Davenant's preface to *Gondibert* and say that 'I have found Frends as ready as Bookes, to regulate my conceptions,' I do so with a clear sense that whatever faults remain are my own.

The University of Iowa generously provided both a semester of leave in which I could complete the manuscript, and publication support from the office of the Vice-President for Research. Other institutional help came from the Folger Shakespeare Library, where I spent the fall of 1988 as a fellow. Three readers for the University of Toronto Press, one Paul Delany and the others anonymous, offered incisive criticism and valuable suggestions for revision. At the Press, Ron Schoeffel helped in a variety of crucial ways. The late Prudence Tracy, whose service to scholarly publishing in Canada was legendary, contributed invaluable advice and encouragement. I am truly saddened she could not see this book in print.

At a late stage, I had the patient help of Darlene Money, who copyedited the manuscript, and of Dan Collins, who read proofs and assisted with the indexing.

Earlier versions of chapters 3 and 4 appeared in *Prose Studies* and *The Eighteenth Century: Theory and Interpretation.* Material in part 3 first appeared in *PQ* and *The Seventeenth Century.* I have substantially revised an article in *University of Toronto Quarterly* that is now incorporated into part 2. I thank the editors of those journals for their permissions.

A Note on Texts

Parenthetic references to Bacon cite *The Works of Francis Bacon*, ed. James Spedding, Robert Leslie Ellis, and Douglas Denon Heath, 7 vols. (London 1857–9), and the *Letters and Life of Francis Bacon*, also in seven volumes (1861–74). The *Novum Organum* (*NO*) is cited by book and aphorism number. For Milton's poetry I have used the edition by Merritt Y. Hughes, *John Milton: Complete Poems and Major Prose* (New York: Odyssey 1957), and for the prose, the edition by Don M. Wolfe et al. *Complete Prose Works of John Milton*, 8 vols. (New Haven: Yale UP 1953–82). Samuel Butler's *Hudibras* is quoted in John Wilders' edition (Oxford: Clarendon 1967), by part, canto, and line numbers. The miscellaneous prose is available in Samuel Butler, *Prose Observations*, ed. Hugh de Quehen (Oxford: Clarendon 1979), which appears parenthetically as *PO*.

For consistency among the older texts, I have normalized *i*, *j*, *u*, and *v*, expanded abbreviated words, and silently corrected obvious misprints.

ORIGIN AND AUTHORITY IN SEVENTEENTH-
CENTURY ENGLAND: BACON, MILTON, BUTLER

Introduction: Origin, Error, Ideology

The aim of this book is to describe the seventeenth-century discourse of origin, its construction, reproduction, and dissemination over several decades. My basic claim is that a desire to establish the legitimacy of the present through the recovery and representation of origins figured prominently in the writing of both philosophy and epic poetry. Throughout the seventeenth century writers agreed in locating authority in the pristine, original, and uncorrupted. Establishing truth at an absolute beginning that conditioned and controlled the emergent present, they regarded the pursuit of origins as a basic philosophical activity. Grappling with the problem of 'certain knowledge,' philosophers sought to secure themselves against error by methodically arranging beliefs in order of epistemic priority. In order to lay scepticism to rest they turned to the validating authority of metaphysical absolutes identified with a concealed or reclaimed origin.

The desire to recuperate origins had the effect of foregrounding problems of representation and authority. In a wide range of texts, truth appears as an antidote to error, a moment of special clarity associated with a phenomenon's beginning. The enabling fiction of a clearly demarcated genesis encouraged people to think that through the retrieval of an originary source they could overturn the effects of time and reposition themselves in respect to first principles. By asserting a non-biased rationality and divesting knowledge of accumulated falsities, they hoped to loose philosophy from the grip of endless interpretation. Knowledge of nature could then reoccupy the neutral space in which it had first appeared, and reverse the ongoing process of etiolation and decline. Many writers invoke origins as if they uniquely defined the terms of a phenomenon's continued existence. If a 'cause' is simply that which produces an effect, an 'origin' designates something more ambiguous: origins define the contingencies, differences, and unique events that precede or accompany a beginning. Sometimes seen as a hidden reality residing below the surface of things, origins remain implicit in every subsequent manifestation. Despite this ideal of recuperability, writers repeatedly came into confrontation with the difficulty of getting back to an ultimate origin, of retrieving their animating force and transmitting it to succeeding ages. Gradually they lost confidence in the origin as an easily recovered unifying point. Although the positing of origins remained an authoritative strategy, philosophers realized how susceptible to error such procedures were, having disclosed dubious origins in the theories of their predecessors. Poets who hoped to connect modernity to an archaic world of epic also found themselves at a loss where and how to begin.

In this book I describe a particular, historically bound response to the problem of certain knowledge: ways in which origins, points of departure, and moments of inception were produced as a solution to an array of questions endemic to seventeenth-century England. I argue that a desire to mark off a primary instance underlies the strategies of both philosophy and epic. In the course of the seventeenth century, once the discourse of originary knowledge established itself as an alternative to 'error,' origins underwent a decisive transformation. The practice of making the primary manifestation of a given phenomenon purer than subsequent iterations of it collides with a growing awareness of how language and social institutions condition all knowledge. Situating truth in proximity to a primal source continues to motivate various methods for the acquisition of knowledge, but the process of recovery becomes increasingly problematic.

The determining power of the primary instance has long been recognized as a landmark on the map of early modern culture. Several studies have explored the idea of origin in the Renaissance through its role in undergirding the metaphorics of influence, or in informing notions of anterior authority and literary convention. David Quint's study of the classical topoi of origin shows how poets read the Virgilian 'source' as an allegory of poetic origins. Quint discusses how the concept of originality proceeded from the invention of a historical relativism that considered literary works within their cultural matrices rather than as timeless and transcendent. The concept of literary originality, he argues, had its beginnings in humanist rhetoric, philology, and a general movement towards historicizing. John Guillory, taking a similar literary-historical approach to the construction of an autonomous 'imagination,' shows how Spenser and Milton deploy fictions of origin to achieve particular ends, gesturing towards cryptic first-order sources in order to re-form the authority of the present. Guillory describes a process of anxious secularization in which Scripture and literature trade places, and the post-Miltonic imagination becomes a groundless origin pointing towards the restoration of the sacred text.[1] Both of these important studies invoke history, yet conceive it abstractly — in Quint's case, as an interlingual conversation among poets, or in Guillory's, as a contest between the self-begetting imagination and historical consciousness. Both remain wary of origin claims as mystifications of authority, yet advance arguments about the ascendance of originality as a new literary value, and emphasize the aesthetic as the dominant textual function. Both take up history only to abandon it for allegories of authorship, influence, and the imagination.

The seventeenth century's grounding of authority in seminal texts and originary instances extends well beyond problems of influence within the closed circuit of literary filiation. The principle of primary pre-eminence — first in occurrence, first in all — has immediate effects on the social and political life of early modern England, underpinning the practice of primogeniture, theories of ancient right and monarchical legitimacy, and the privileged standing of particular poets in a hierarchy of literary genres. The exposé of erroneous origins — which propelled the demystifications of Reformation theology and the procedures of the new philosophy — occurs at various institutional sites. We can map the effects of this practice across different intellectual and political terrains. The belief that first manifestations retain more of their essential selves than successive iterations had far-reaching consequences. This study seeks to efface the institutional boundaries that demarcate philosophy from literature and politics, high from popular culture — or at least to recuperate something of the problematical relation that existed between them in the seventeenth century. Since the problem of origin engaged writers of all sorts, I include philosophical, political, and theological texts among the variables that constitute its history. Complex interrelations and connections among diverse levels of meaning render a complete account impossible, but the traffic between different sociocultural realms becomes part of the picture I present.

Philosophies of knowledge have long put forward arguments that banish doubt by referring to stabilizing moments of inauguration. Recuperating an origin constitutes a philosophical method, a way of knowing, a technique of analysis. The importance of *archai* (or underlying concepts) to Aristotelianism resided in their providing an indispensable starting-point for deciphering the world and determining scientific knowledge. Origins supplied an index to the interpretation of disparate phenomena. The Aristotelian tradition recognized a paradox that the seventeenth century strove to repress: establishing the sources from which knowledge derives proceeds through an impossible process. If demonstrated truths necessarily follow from true premises, the premises themselves remain indemonstrable, or at least not susceptible to ordinary forms of demonstration.

In the twentieth century, methodological prescriptions that appeal to origins have fallen before theories of knowledge that emphasize the pre-determining powers of inherited perspectives. Post-structuralism has convinced us of the constructedness of every origin. Our awareness of how historical forces condition the acts of experiencing and understanding has undermined confidence in the explanatory power of the primary instance. Edward Said pinpoints the particular moment at which anti-original consciousness made its historical entrance: 'One of the special characteristics of thought ever since the eighteenth century,' he writes, 'is an obsession with beginnings that seem to infect and render exceedingly problematic the location of a beginning.' From Said, I borrow the idea of 'beginnings' – which he distinguishes from 'origins' on the basis of its secular frame of reference – as retrospectively fixed in order to define the present moment in continuity with the past. As Said argues, a desire for self-delineation produces the notion of a temporal threshold, which later generations can view retrospectively.[2] By looking backwards towards an authorizing figure or primary stage in a temporal succession, we mark the present as an intentional break in the production of meaning, and establish authority over the present.

Michel Foucault considers the rejection of an unequivocal beginning as central to the hermeneutics of Nietzsche, Marx, and Freud, who deeply fissure Western thought in the nineteenth century. Foucault sees the rejection of origin as a necessary step in establishing an infinitely regressive model of interpretation, where signs interpret other signs, and so on ad infinitum. In 'Nietzsche, Genealogy, History,' Foucault credits Nietzsche with a critique – one that informs his own method – that exposes the fragmentariness and divisions underlying myths of unitary origin: 'What is found at the historical beginning of things is not the inviolable identity of their origin; it is the dissension of other things. It is disparity.' The metaphysical pursuit of essence, Foucault argues, cannot withstand the discovery that essence itself, like the notion of a perfect origin before the Fall, is a fabrication. Foucault's genealogizing method aims to reveal the fragmentation and randomness residing behind the event-as-unitary-origin, which conventional histories teleologize or ritually celebrate. Foucault refuses the seductions of causal analysis, or the reductionism of correlating developments within a particular discursive domain to a set of socio-economic determinants. His archaeological analysis 'does not claim to efface itself in the ambiguous modesty of a reading that would bring back, in all its purity, the distant, precarious, almost effaced light of the origin.' In Foucault's terms, archaeology rewrites, rather than returns to, 'the innermost secret of the origin.'[3]

To some extent, I emulate Foucault's comparative method of disclosing epistemic parameters and unconscious rules through the juxtaposition of different forms of knowledge and levels of discourse. I also resist the lure of histories written in the shape of teleological narratives, in which one paradigm dominates a period before falling before a competing doctrine. Any study of seventeenth-century notions of origin should take care to avoid participating in the ideological structures it hopes to lay open for scrutiny. The following chapters, however, take a view of agency and the institution of authorship quite different from Foucault's. Foucault's interest lies in how human beings are constituted as subjects within discourse, and in the operations of power on language and practice. His objective, as Edward Said has written, is 'to overwhelm the individual subject or will and replace it instead with minutely responsive rules of discursive formation, rules that no one individual can either alter or circumvent.'[4] The question of 'who speaks?' becomes less significant than the task of determining under what conditions a particular utterance becomes possible. By positing an anonymous discursivity Foucault and his followers neatly solve the intractable problems of intentionality and authorial consciousness. A theory of agentless discourse, however, mystifies the operations of authority and puts us at a loss to understand the production of knowledge or the institution of authorship. It also severely limits the possibilities for historical change and human agency. Imprisoned within the limits of the sayable, human beings can only capitulate to the system or await an irruption from without. Language becomes the vehicle of a power that resides everywhere and nowhere. Few would dispute the claims that discursive systems condition society, that social institutions in their turn sustain and circulate these discourses. Yet this need not entail seeing history as the purely contingent product of discursive discontinuities, or making linguistic structures self-constituting norms. This study takes as its subject the complex but differentiated discourse of origin, its formation and transformation throughout the seventeenth century. Yet I depart from theories that totally decentre cultural authority, that conceive origins as a purely formal structure, a set of unconscious rules, or a nameless law.

In other words, I have not thought to dispense with the categories of 'author' and *oeuvre*. Instead my strategy is to describe correlations across disciplines at a particular moment in time. Because an attempt to render a complete account of this process would soon run aground on a huge range of texts, the project concentrates on three English writers: Francis Bacon, John Milton, and Samuel Butler. My scope is chronologically delimited by the publication of the *Novum Organum* (1620), the second edition of *Paradise Lost* (1674), and the third part of *Hudibras* (1678), although I move to establish continuities in the historical preconditions and 'afterlife' of these texts. These figures are not chosen at random: all invoke myths of a normative primacy and attempt to ground subjectivity in transcendent realities they link to the origin.

The three interlocking parts that constitute this study examine the discursive features and effects of origin in relation to questions of cultural authority. The chapters, taken together, follow a trajectory that begins in Baconianism, revolution, and aphorism, and ends with 'Royal Science,' Restoration, and anti-epic. As an instrument of inquiry, the concept of origin inevitably takes on a circular form as the rightness of the present is shown to depend on events located in a distant past. Epic plays a key role in this process as the literary form inextricably linked to an absolutely remote and mythic past. It embodied the supreme authority of the origin in a particularly concrete and sanctioned form. At a time when heroic values and quasi-historical myths of founding faced challenges from various directions, the discourse of origin became coextensive with the narrative strategies of epic poetry. If epic represented a system of values in some respects antithetical to science and rationality, it still remained worth cultivating for its proximity to an absolute source poets could refigure and reconstitute.

In many recent studies, seventeenth-century England stands as a point of ideological origination, the site and moment of the bourgeois subject's official installation. The term *ideology* dates back to the end of the eighteenth century and to Antoine Destutt de Tracy, whose 'science of ideas' strove to locate the basis of thought in sense perception. Destutt de Tracy considered the *Novum Organum* the beginning of modern philosophy, and included a 'Sommaire raisonée de l'Instauratio Magna' in his four-volume *Elémens d'Idéologie* (1803–15). In historical terms, my argument connects to a debate that first appeared in the wake of Baconian theory. Since parts of the following analysis move in and around the concept of ideology, we might pause to specify its importance to this study as a whole.

Ideology, as I use the term throughout this book, is not a class-determined rationale that claims a universal validity, but an intersubjective system for producing meaning and constituting cognitively meaningful beliefs. I avoid affiliating my argument with any theory that posits a unifying principle behind every social formation, that makes economics or class the determination 'in the last instance.' Another study might emphasize the production of ideology by dominant groups, the economic, legal, and religious institutions that supposedly control meaning from the top down. Still another might stress the historical construction of authorship and the regulatory practices that made some writers authoritative and others subject to prosecution. My own analysis focuses on origins as a means for establishing self-evident truths at a time when authoritative paradigms of knowledge had begun to slip away. The seventeenth century's attempt to ground truth in a non-contingent absolute made the equation of knowledge with the recovery of origin a matter of 'common sense.' The idea of origin, in this respect, is based on a trope that naturalizes a particular theory of knowledge. Although it serves to circumscribe the boundaries of the thinkable, origin serves no single political function: Milton and radical Protestants used it to assail the institution of prelacy, while Butler wielded it to ridicule sectarianism. Although it often serves the interest of establishing a claim in circumstances where competing claims might seem equally plausible, it attaches to no specific set of doctrines. Nor is it doctrinaire in the sense of being removed from positive knowledge or experience. While the ideology of origins could function to legitimize or preserve relations of inequality, it operated over a wide range of discursive sites.

In recent years, a view of ideology as pure illusion, as historical distortion and misrecognition of 'real' social relations, has generally faded from view. Louis Althusser provides an interesting example, at a crucial juncture in the fortunes of Western Marxism, of the theory of ideological analysis at a transitional stage. Althusser revised the concept of ideology away from the view that it designates an erroneous or interested form of consciousness, reshaping it in accordance with psychoanalytic theories of subject-formation and 'scientific' standards of knowledge. Althusser moves well beyond a conception of ideology as false consciousness or camouflaged class interest, recasting it as an indispensable part of the social totality. Ideology plays an indispensable role in the 'interpellation' of individuals as subjects, and guarantees the reproduction of social relations.

For Althusser, 'the author, insofar as he writes the lines of a discourse which claims to be scientific, is completely absent as a "subject" from "his" scientific discourse (for all scientific discourse is by definition a subject-less discourse, there is no "subject of science" except in an ideology of science).' Thus Althusser inadvertently enacts one point of his own critique, that 'one of the effects of ideology is the practical *denegation* of the ideological character of ideology by ideology.' According to Althusser, the subject must be positioned outside ideology ('in scientific knowledge') in order to recognize its presence or to effect a removal. Althusser adopts the position that ideology is a system of representations that structures life in society, and is indispensable in allowing members of a society to contend with the conditions of their existence. Yet Althusser also drives a wedge between the social function ideology serves in fitting subjects to a specific historical project, and the theoretical function of science. There is a familiar joke about ideology, which Althusser retells in the following version: 'the accusation of being in ideology only applies to others, never to oneself.' Nevertheless, Althusser's theory of ideology as representing an 'imaginary relationship of individuals to their real conditions of existence' suggests an antithetical relation between ideology and truth. Althusser brackets 'science and reality' as ideology's antidote, virtually equating science with the non-ideological. Although ideologies remain profoundly necessary and truth and falsity are irrelevant to their concerns, science exercises a unique capacity to achieve absolute standards of truth. Thus, before we can position ourselves in a critical relation to the ideological, we must occupy a position outside ideology 'in scientific knowledge.' As Althusser phrases the problem in his 'Philosophy Course for Scientists,' given at the Ecole Normale Supérieure in 1967, philosophy's 'essential function' is to draw 'a line of demarcation between the scientific and the ideological,' a line obscured by the ideology of interdisciplinarity.'[5] Theory occupies a high ground from which it can adjudicate all claims to knowledge, including its own.

For Althusser's post-structuralist critics, this concept of ideology is thoroughly ideologized because it posits a notion of a scientific discourse reading 'outside' of an ideology that has 'no outside.' Michel Foucault prefers 'discourse' to 'ideology' largely because discourse theory requires no help from scientificity, truth, and materiality. Materialist critics detect the opposite problem. E.P. Thompson, in a lengthy polemic against Althusserian theoreticism, accuses it of mystifying the real and historically contingent, invoking the 'material' merely as a theoretical slogan. Interestingly, Thompson compares Althusser's crypto-idealism to Bacon's crypto-atheism and crypto-scepticism, quoting *The Advancement of Learning* on the mind's resemblance to 'an enchanted glass, full of superstition and imposture, if it be not delivered and reduced.'[6] Since Althusser denies the possibility of theory-neutral observation, he has no basis for implying that we can 'know' whether an object of perception corresponds to our idea of it. At some points he argues the materialist thesis that the internal-external distinction is meaningless, at others, the conventionalist thesis that what counts as 'real' is a function of the paradigm in which it is situated and of internal criteria.

Pierre Macherey develops a theory of ideology on the authority of Althusser, from whom, however, he significantly diverges. Macherey proposes a view of ideology as a force that produces contradictions. We see these disparities of meaning most clearly in the aesthetic realm, where the illusion of unity and reconciliation perpetually threatens to come undone. For Macherey, literature gives shape to ideological experience and thus reveals its ruptures and limitations. Ideology, conceived in such terms, is a web of symptomatic dissonances and contradictions, rendered especially visible in literature.[7] In a chapter addressing the Baconian 'origin' of Restoration science, I return to Macherey's work on ideological contradiction.

The call of recent criticism for an empowering oppositional knowledge that occupies a space simultaneously within and without ideology renews the issue of 'disinterestedness.' If putting up an effective resistance to ideological pressures can occur only within an ideological context, we need to redefine ideology as a system of meaning governing social acts rather than as an illusion or imaginary relation.[8] We must cast the entire problematic in terms that recognize how such systems of value are constituted in the linguistic and social realms. Clifford Geertz provides one such definition of ideology, articulated from the vantage point of the social sciences. Reacting to the sociology of the 1950s, which claimed scientific objectivity for its highly politicized analyses, Geertz makes a case for 'a genuinely nonevaluative conception of ideology.' One person's ideologue, Geertz again reminds us, is another person's scientist. Geertz denies that ideology entails 'distorted' knowledge of reality, and strives to rescue the term from polemic. In place of a ideology–science dichotomy he posits a theory of ideology as symbolic practice, a form of 'symbolic action,' in Kenneth Burke's phrase. According to the textual model Geertz develops, ideological expressions do not 'distort' reality but tropologically transfigure it into a social force. Geertz proposes a non-pejorative (but not neutral) conception of ideology, one that places interpretation before evaluation, semiotic process before linguistic 'distortion.'[9] His theory of culture makes the distinction between science and ideology hinge solely on the different symbolic and stylistic strategies appropriate to each.

In the twentieth century the myth of a unified subjectivity capable of grasping the world and expressing it in transparent language has collapsed under sustained critique. This study concerns itself with aspects of this breakdown as it appeared at an earlier stage. The historicist method of this book makes no pretence of studying the seventeenth century exclusively according to its own codes and vocabularies. Throughout I endeavour to bring early modern and contemporary texts into a dialogue, to establish the past in a meaningful relation to the present. The reconstruction I undertake here locates the discourse of origin in a wide range of seventeenth-century texts, yet avoids invoking history as an autonomous and stable domain upon which to ground literary interpretation.

In the period I cover, epistemology, politics, and language theory worked closely together, their inseparability becoming most explicit in the 1660s as cultural differences and questions of style fused with matters of social value. Interest in the problem of origin appears inscribed outside the parameters of any single field, written across a wide range of texts. Text after text promotes a program of absolute erasure and re-creation *ex nihilo*. In the course of analyzing the congeries of theories, metaphors, and structures that constitute the seventeenth-century discourse of origin, I make reference to multiple forms of writing. The available conventions operate within complex and overlapping fields, and thus become structurally relational. Just as texts can sound 'political' on occasions outwardly removed from politics, they can also communicate theoretical meanings and raise philosophical problems when striving most for polemical effect. Theories and metaphors migrate from philosophy and poetry to take up residence in new domains, inserting new meanings and retrospectively fixing older ones. Political speech, as J.G.A. Pocock remarks, 'consists of a dense texture of undifferentiated intimations,' which 'may be differentiated into a variety of specialized linguistic (and political) activities.' Even so, 'nothing can prevent these from continuing to affect and redound upon one another.' The language of politics moves from one context to another, encompassing activities often relegated by society to the non-political realm. Since political speech prescribes an 'authority-structure,' as well as performing a linguistic function, it serves as 'a multivalent paradigm,' which can perform in different contexts and uphold 'diverse definitions and distributions of authority.'[10] Origins exemplify Pocock's notion of multivalence, expanding over disciplinary boundaries to prescribe and condition various forms of authority.

Origin and Authority in Seventeenth-Century England considers multivalent responses to the challenge of the infinitely receding origin. It studies the desire to recuperate an authentic meaning, an authorizing origin, as a means of gaining special access to reality. The emergence of the ideal of scientific truth, I claim, owes something to a widely shared tendency, also present in epic, to see origins as something true in themselves, as having a validity that guarantees the truth of that which would normally seem doubtful. Locating an origin presented a technique for organizing various domains of knowledge and contributed strategies for affirming or negating methodical doubt. In the construction of modern science, origin-hunting involves arraying knowledge in continuous and unbroken chains, beginning with the simplest entities and moving towards certainty by incremental steps. Scientists could apprehend an origin, they reasoned, because something intrinsic to the origin itself (its simplicity, clarity, singularity, authoritative status, or whatever) placed it beyond doubt. In this progression from simple to complex structures, everything depended on identifying the proper starting point. Yet origins remained slippery, a concept riddled with doubt and contradiction.

More than an idea, origins are an entire system of representation, a myth as much as a theory, with its own characteristic logic and tropes. Bacon, who figures prominently in the seventeenth-century production and regulation of cultural authority, recommended 'for the recovery of a sound and healthy condition' that 'the entire work of the understanding be commenced afresh.' In the three opening chapters on Bacon I show how conflicts of origination cut across the domains of philosophy, language theory, and literature. Chapter 1 explores how Bacon hoped to effect a renewal of all the disciplines of knowledge by rebuilding knowledge from the very foundations. I concentrate on a central contradiction in Bacon's thought: his basing philosophical authority on foundational assumptions even though he remains sceptical about the value of tradition and the mind's capacity to perceive any reality deeper than language itself. I argue in chapter 2 that the problem of linguistic mediation is central to Bacon's thought, and prevents him from naïvely laying claim to any simple method for recapturing an uncontaminated origin. He roots his method in etiologizing error in its multiple forms, and grounds his language theory on the study of 'notions.' I conclude that while the *Novum Organum* dedicates itself to a program of ideological analysis, it remains entangled in an ideology of unmediated perception. Bacon uses aphorisms, which are examined in chapter 3, to connect unmediated thoughts to the realm of language. By breaking down experience into its original components, he thought to dislodge the power of idolatrous thinking.

For those who lived through a period of civil war and revolution, the discourse of origin took on a distinctly conservative cast, and, by the 1660s, had come to rest in the institutional program of the Royal Society. These decades witnessed the emergence of a conception of origin increasingly informed by specific political and religious overtones. Never entirely neutral (certainly not for Bacon), origination becomes the point of reference by which scientists authorize their rewriting of the past. The Restoration's use of Bacon as a token for its own passage into modernity, as both pre-text and agent of legitimation, forms an important part of the history of science. Chapter 4 discusses how, as Bacon's writings attained a canonical status, writers began to adduce his authority for its stabilizing originary associations. Bacon's desire to abolish error through a systematic renovation of authority, I argue, directly contributed to the formation of an ideology of scientific objectivity.

Turning from the validating authority of origins in science to the writing of epic, part 2 discusses how *Paradise Lost* connects a distant and authentic past to the present. Milton, too, concerned himself with systems of thought that make the remote beginnings of human prehistory the sole point of origin and everything thereafter mere duplication. The idea of initial transgression, original sin, transposes the discourse of origin into a theological key. A form especially well suited to explore questions of truth and historicity, epic grants an imaginary access to a world where unmediated understanding persists. Milton associates epic with an originary realm of experience to which he must constantly revert in his attempt to make accessible a moment before history. As in Bacon, where authoritative notions substitute for uncertain errors, Milton constructs a fiction of origination that establishes the present on a secure foundation. More than just a literary form, epic becomes a determinant in Milton's treatment of the problem of knowledge and in its renovation of the past. My first chapter on Milton surveys various theories of epic, William Davenant's and Mikhail Bakhtin's among them, that emphasize epic's status as an originary and authoritative genre. Chapter 6 argues that *Paradise Lost* adopts a narrative strategy of tracing itself backwards to an absolute but still recoverable origin. Milton uses the originary associations of epic to delineate a form of consciousness capable of excavating the layers of accumulated error that obscure the capacities of the mind. The poem represents truth as the reanimation of a suppressed but nevertheless retrievable origin, even while it casts the quest for certain origins and transparent language into doubt.

Chapter 7 explores the mirror as an emblem of the impossible correspondence between origins and representations, of doubling as a paradigm for knowledge. Eve's encounter with her own reflection in book 4 confronts the enigma of consciousness and identity, of a knowledge that is distorted yet somehow true. The mirror Eve gazes into does not provide

Origin, Error, Ideology 15

objective corroboration of an intuition; the uncontaminated origin she seeks remains inaccessible from the beginning. Just as all reflections are interpretations produced by anomalies within a mirror's surface, human knowledge is situated in doubtful contingencies. The mirror image's status as erroneous interpretation masquerading as transparent origin casts doubt on the possibility of attaining a neutral framework in which to conduct inquiry into nature, or of tracing an idea to its first moment of luminous creation. In *Paradise Lost* we see origins represented in terms of the question: How can ideas and perceptions be true of a mind-independent world, given the breach, situated at a remote point of human history, between the understanding and the reality it shadows?

Under the pressure of Baconian philosophy and a progressive estrangement from humanist ideals, appeals to the authoritative source eventually diverge from the originary claims of epic. Samuel Butler confronts the paradox of origins by fashioning a counter-epic mode and establishing his thought within a self-consciously post-humanist framework. The idea of a remote and inaccessible origin informs Butler's politics of genre and philosophy of knowledge. Part 3 follows the problems of origin and authority to Butler's *Hudibras*. If Milton reworks Virgilian epic with high purpose and solemnity, Butler parodies its conventions and delegitimizes its form. In chapter 8 I show how a sense of belatedness induces Butler to circumvent the past, to reach back behind an accretion of literary representations and renew contact with reality. Epic emerges from his work as an obsolete system of ideas no longer able to contend with experience and reality. Unremittingly topical and self-conscious, *Hudibras* treats the epic origin as an absurd idealization, and demonstrates the historically conditioned character of heroic values. Writing epic in post-epic world – a world of origins from which the present is estranged – Butler faces a crisis of authority and of representation.

An authoritative discourse of rationality and truth sustains Butler's polemic against sectarian error. At a time when appeals to orthodoxy had to contend with charges of adulteration through transmission, when assertions of timeless truth had to confront a suspicion that time could corrupt an original, Butler expresses intense nostalgia for a fixed truth associated with origins. He seeks the security of an authorizing origin to stabilize the relation between signs and their meanings. Nevertheless, his attempt to justify specific social arrangements and one form of church governance by reference to an authority situated 'in the beginning' finally founders. Butler's interrogation of the principle of apodictic certainty ultimately subverts his own claims. A second chapter on Butler returns to the problem, explored earlier in relation to Bacon and Milton, of bringing notions into conformity with the world.

If Butler's royalist admirers hoped that his satire would drive nonconformists into silence, depriving them of a language in which to express their disaffection, they overlooked the way in which *Hudibras* recovers and reproduces the scepticism that incites resistance to authority. Chapter 10 unpacks the highly charged phrase 'a *Babylonish* Dialect,' Butler's trope for linguistic fragmentation and the uncertain alignment between words and things. While the other two tropes of origin I examine, wandering error and the mirror, have structured a wide range of poetic and philosophical discourses, Babel-Babylon occurs in a context circumscribed by the early history of English Protestantism. Moving towards the political and historical specificities of the 1650s and 1660s, the last chapter examines casuistry in *Hudibras*. Butler's satire on the science of casuistry projects the philosophical problems of origin, error, and certain knowledge into the world of interregnum politics, where they have predictably disastrous consequences.

This book, then, ranges from the supposed origin of modern science in Bacon to the collapse of epic in Butler, and links the emergence of a discourse of origin to the decline of an antiquated literary tradition. The three sections bring into conjunction writers generally thought to have little in common. Rather than concentrate on uncovering lines of continuity between them, I emphasize assumptions that link their ideas in mutually sustaining networks of belief. For this reason, the model I bring to bear on these questions is broadly intertextual, and works through an ensemble of texts drawn from the domains of poetry, philosophy, and politics. Throughout the book I situate my argument across a variety of intellectual domains where the necessity of regaining the originative point becomes an imperative.

My inclusion of Butler is not intended merely as an act of canon-opening (although he surely deserves a wider audience), but as a way of testing my generalizations about seventeenth-century culture at different levels and through changing sociohistorical registers. In the following analyses I move across various disciplines to reconstruct a pattern of interrelatedness and explore the multiple ties that constitute thinking on the problem of origin and error. The distance between Miltonic strategies for return and circumvention and Butler's retreat to 'commonsense' objectivity is less than at first might appear. For the writers I discuss, we need to consider (without unduly privileging) high culture along with more heterogeneous forms of writing. To ignore texts from either side of the equation would be to overlook the symbiotic relationship that obtains between them. The multilayered textuality and complex signifying practices that constitute a 'culture' remain forever beyond the reach of total reconstruction. Yet we can understand much about historical experience, the social and intellectual logic of particular periods, by crossing the boundaries of traditional periodizations and specializations, by veering from explanatory origins to search out differences and similarities.

Bacon, Milton, and Butler, who all occupy a historical space where literature, philosophy, and politics converge, are ideal for this purpose. A writer whose energies and intellectual commitments helped inaugurate many different projects, Bacon also provides the starting point of the present study.

PART ONE

Francis Bacon: Organon and Origin

1

'Pure and Uncorrupted Natural Knowledge'

Beginning in his own lifetime and continuing into the Restoration, Bacon's writings have surrounded themselves with an aura of 'originality.' Bacon's desire to sweep away the accumulated error of the past and begin the enterprise of learning anew involves recapturing a perceptual purity uncontaminated by time. The rhetoric of regeneration and beginning anew is a feature of his work that readers have fastened on to and pressed into the service of different ideologies. Modern studies continue to accept the fiction that Bacon's work represents a privileged point of origin, a *principium,* either confirming or denying his presence at the 'intellectual origins' of the English revolution or the 'birth' of modern science. These assumptions inform the ongoing debate over whether Bacon's method is truly modern and 'scientific' or residually Aristotelian, rhetorical, and alchemical.

Karl Popper's influential appraisal supports the latter view, and provides an example of how Bacon's status in the history of science is treated as a function of originality. Popper regards Bacon as an apostle of absolute certainty who sought to derive a finite body of infallible rules from the mechanical accumulation of data. Bacon failed to observe two of Popper's cardinal principles: that knowledge of the world need not derive from the world, and that the mind can engage reality without recourse to a particular method. Baconian method becomes incoherent the moment we realize that observational repetition makes sense only in relation to observers equipped with theoretical backgrounds and perceptions conditioned by consistent expectations. Perfect 'repetition' would entail duplicating an event located in some Platonic realm of pure Form. Drawing on a type of Humean scepticism, Popper declares that empirical experience of a particular phenomenon does not permit us to predict other phenomena of supposedly the same type. Scientific or historical predictions based on past experience, he insists, are logically indefensible, therefore evidentially worthless. Popper explains Bacon's disastrous error as a manifestation of 'the strange view that the truth of a statement may be decided upon by inquiring into its sources – that is to say its *origin*.'[1] The originative principle has its psychological roots in ambivalence towards parental authority, in semantic misconception, and in a Christian teleology fixated on original sin. Bacon, with his Platonism, providentialism, and anxieties of filial dependence, would appear guilty on all counts.

On Popper's view, we cannot expect truth forcibly to imprint itself on consciousness once we have barred supposition and hypothesis from scientific activity. What Bacon spurns as premature 'anticipations,' Popper finds 'marvellously imaginative and bold conjectures,' which genuine scientists probe and test in order to put equally premature hypotheses in their place. Science, he argues, does not advance through reclaiming knowledge from a source or through the method of Socratic *maieutic* (cleansing the soul and senses of error). Rather it progresses by means of vigorous competition, political freedom, and unfettered individualism – in short, all the virtues of classic liberalism. Popper imagines an evolutionary growth of knowledge, a Darwinian contest of theories in which the stronger supplants the weaker. Despite admirable 'individualistic tendencies,' Popper's Bacon incorporates into his science a mystifying authoritarianism that threatens individual autonomy. On this view, Bacon aspires to enthrone the authority of observation and the senses where Aristotle and the Bible once ruled. In his desire to eliminate error and establish an authoritative starting place, Bacon thus becomes an embodiment of European absolutism, and Baconian science synonymous with the idol of demonstrated Truth.

Although Bacon's new organon undeniably suffers from erecting truth on the shaky foundation of recovery through correct observation, Popper's critique remains very much open to question. One defence of Bacon virtually stands the Popperian critique on its head by arguing that Popper shares the basic assumptions of Baconian science.[2] Despite Bacon's overemphasis on the role of investigation in the formation of general theories, his account remains consistent with the Anglo-American empiricist tradition.

The twentieth century continues to assimilate Bacon to modern scientific practice because his notions of experimental corroboration seem to anticipate an important paradigm. 'Postempiricist' philosophers of science such as Thomas Kuhn, Paul Feyerabend, and Mary Hesse find Bacon interesting because he put forward an empiricist logic of discovery that continues into our own time. From their perspective, making Bacon an index of 'naïve' positivism merely clears the way for another, more sophisticated, positivism. The Bacon-Popper polarity appears as internecine struggle within a single theory, which has finally collapsed under the scrutiny of historicism and the sociology of knowledge. Giving Bacon a fair hearing enables these philosophers of science to demonstrate the groundlessness of formal scientific method and logico-empiricist theories. In general, Bacon shares with the Anglo-American tradition an underlying set of assumptions about science and reality that Mary Hesse summarizes thus:

The scientist, as both observer and language-user, can capture the external facts of the world in propositions that are true if they correspond to the facts and false if they do not. Science is ideally a linguistic system in which true propositions are in one-to-one relation to facts, including facts that are not directly observed because they involve hidden entities or properties, or past events or far distant events. These hidden events are described in theories, and theories can be inferred from observation, that is, the hidden explanatory mechanism of the world can be discovered from what is open to observation. Man as scientist is regarded as standing apart from the world and able to experiment and theorize about it objectively and dispassionately.[3]

Hesse divides the premises embodied in this world-view into three faulty assumptions: naïve realism, a universal scientific language, and the correspondence theory of truth. Taken together, the categories provide a reasonably accurate portrait of Baconian epistemology. Bacon embraces a brand of metaphysical realism, viewing reality as the totality of mind-independent phenomena and truth as the correspondence of signs to external objects. He offers his copy or correspondence theory as the sole alternative to treating truth as a problem of coherence within a set of self-sustaining beliefs.

At the same time, this theory becomes contraposed to another, almost antithetical view of Bacon's: that languages encode within themselves different mentalities and cultural perspectives. As Paul Feyerabend observes, Bacon looks forward to Benjamin Whorf's conception of language as a shaper, rather than a describer, of events, and the theory that a linguistic system constitutes a determinative force, 'a cosmology, a comprehensive view of the world, of society, of the situation of man which influences thought, behaviour, perception.'[4] According to Bacon, language mediates the external world and bridges the distance between mind and nature in a process that ideally issues in 'truth.' Yet language remains inherently deceptive because of a predisposition to 'distorting' influences, particularly the human yearning for metaphysical perfection and wholeness. Bacon intuits that language tends towards relative autonomy and that linguistic systems embody theoretical presuppositions. Yet he would utterly reject the idea of a 'language-dependent' truth. Nor would he allow social practices a predeterminative role in the constitution of scientific knowledge through sense data.

Bacon regarded the natural world ('things themselves') as a pre-semiotic order of experience that only awaited correct interpretation. He points out how the mind constitutes the world according to social structures and linguistic categories, but clings to the idea of a fixed and immutable, although sometimes inaccessible, truth. An attentive reading of the *Novum Organum* will dispel the oversimplification that he advocated a theory-free accumulation of data, bare facts unmediated by prior determinations. Nor did Bacon grant equal weight to every positive experimental instance in support of a hypothesis. His mistake was subtler than calling for induction by simple enumeration. In shifting the balance away from theory he imagined the existence of a foolproof technique for grounding knowledge in correct observation and reasoning. In epistemological terms, he made the mistake of positing an ontology separate from knowledge. His method absurdly offers to inform us what constitutes 'real' knowledge in advance of our knowing it. Bacon never recognized that failed predictions do not overturn entire theories, that many theories are 'underdetermined' by empirical data, and that science does not proceed automatically by steady and predictable increments. All these shortcomings ensue from positing an untenable distinction between 'observation' and 'theory.' Bacon portrays his movement away from theory as a rebellion against philosophic authoritarianism. Theory seemed to him the preserve of autocrats within the realm of learning. Theoreticians (particularly Aristotle, but also Galen, Cardan, Ramus, Aquinas, and many others) prefer to subdue and colonize other thinkers rather than enlist their cooperation. They cite predecessors mainly to contradict or reprove them, and expend tremendous energy trying to make their own positions unassailable.

Powerful theories, according to Bacon, interfere with technique and impede the further refinement of theory. They remain persuasive only in so far as they stand apart from and perpetually prior to practice. Theory can become a force in the world only if it engenders a new form of consciousness capable of standing in a new historical relation to materiality. As Thomas Kuhn points out, Baconian experimental science was hardly novel in its theoretical insistence on the need for empirical observation. Aristotle and his medieval followers were hardly less emphatic. Unlike their predecessors, however, Baconian scientists rarely performed hypothesis-testing experiments designed only to elaborate or confirm existing theories. Instead they 'vexed' nature or studied it under formerly unobserved or artificially induced circumstances.[5] The innovations associated with Bacon occurred on the level of praxis and in reconceptualizing the idea of theory itself. His failure to understand that observation and theory always intermingle – that observation depends on theoretical assumptions concerning the conditions of reliable observation – proceeds from regarding facticity as a likeness of reality. Bacon intended the eclipse of theory to have profound theoretical implications, yet these necessarily had to be kept in abeyance. He hoped to do away with any trace of retrograde movement in the ascent of knowledge and to avoid periodic relapses by identifying his system with an absolutely primal moment. Intent upon avoiding the perpetuation of error, he strove to bring nature, mind, and language into closer conjunction, redirecting philosophy away from the study of written texts, and bringing 'the inquiry nearer the source than men have done heretofore' (*Great Instauration* [hereafter *GI*] Plan).

Most early modern methodizers promise the advantages of speed and efficiency by consolidating *theoria* into *techne*. They transform into a neatly assimilated product what their predecessors have attained through prolonged application. Bacon, however, describes his system [*ratio*] as 'hard to practise' but 'easy to explain,' and avoids attaching it to any simple objective (*NO* Preface). His inductivism does not offer itself as a convenient substitute for a laborious process but as a system of incalculably greater explanatory power. Rejecting on one hand the arduous collection of data in support of preconceived theories, and on the other the casual use of observations to bolster dubious conclusions, Bacon attempts to establish an alternative technique. He opposes any concept of method that claims comprehensiveness or that would reduce the enterprise of science to the achievements of a single thinker. We can distinguish Bacon's 'way' of knowledge from the Aristotelian 'rule' of knowledge by its avoidance of closure. While he resists the principle of perpetual deferral, deeming technological innovation evidence of scientific progress, he emphasizes corroboration and demonstration as incremental processes. The aggregate of individual discoveries not only increases the sum of the whole but also affects our understanding of the constituent parts.

Bacon's view of method, to borrow Hans-Georg Gadamer's terminology, divides error between two poles: prejudices due to human authority and prejudices due to hastiness. To redress the latter 'internal' problem Bacon counsels patience and a lowering of expectations: we must proceed gradually in the accumulation of knowledge and not 'fly at once' from minute particulars to general axioms (*GI* Plan). The former will disappear with devaluation of the practice of taking beliefs on trust. Bacon does not express the purely hostile view of tradition that Gadamer ascribes to the influence of Cartesianism in the Enlightenment tradition. Although Bacon helps to inculcate 'the prejudice against prejudice itself, which deprives tradition of its power,' he never simply dismisses tradition as authoritarian and incapable of producing truth. Neither would he, however, accept Gadamer's ideal and wholly benign concept of an authority derived from recognition of the superior capacities of others, and willingness to incorporate the 'valuable prejudices' we receive from them.[6] Bacon demanded that authority submit itself to interrogation and constant revision. After dwelling on the susceptibility of human institutions to decay and exhaustion, he scrutinizes his own instauration for signs of conceptual rigidity and advocates a course of ongoing revolution, endless new beginnings. Philosophy could free itself from unreasonable prejudices if cultural authority somehow succeeded in getting back behind itself and observation detached itself from theory. Bacon hoped to move beyond syllogistic logic by reconceptualizing truth as something other than an assemblage of canonical axioms in new configurations.

Bacon claims objectivity for his method, which he portrays as capable of representing 'things as they really are,' and of separating valid sense data from phantasms. Bacon hoped to replace intricate, contentious, and endlessly self-referential disputation based on the scholastic model with measurably productive dialogue and collective endeavour. He set for himself goals that seem to us both modest and ultimately impossible: first, to slow the rush to an overhasty codification of knowledge by establishing 'progressive stages of certainty'; and second, to move scientific theory away from a philosophy that interminably talked but never did.

Whether we choose to regard Bacon as pragmatically indifferent to theory, or regard his program, as Victoria Kahn suggests, as marking a return to theory after humanist resistance to it depends on how we understand the term *theory*. Throughout the period, 'theory' (*via, ratio, modus, dialecticus, methodus*) described disparate intellectual practices.[7] Bacon never calls for the abolition of theory, but represents 'pure contemplation' (another possible translation of *theoria*) as productive of theoretical deformations. Instead of judging theories by their power to compel assent, he asks us to consider their effects on social and material conditions as factors in assessing value. Although Bacon too facilely separates observation from theory, he never embraces a crude utilitarianism that equates truth with utility. Rather Bacon regards any arbitrary cleavage (to quote Paolo Rossi) as an impediment both to 'the construction of "true" theories' and to 'the achievement of "effective" results.' A careful examination of past philosophies, Bacon thought, would show how this fissure first appeared with the Greeks, and became an article of faith among the scholastics.[8]

Paolo Rossi has made this historical critique of past philosophies central to his reading of Bacon. He suggests that Bacon embraces a mild form of historicism in order to demolish spurious knowledge: 'For him the best way to overcome the dogmatism of the various philosophical factions was to prove that Greek philosophy was an historical and not an eternal supratemporal phenomenon.' John Dewey makes much the same point about the importance of social and historical forces to Baconian epistemology: 'To Bacon, error had been produced and perpetuated by social influences, and truth must be discovered by social agencies organized for that purpose.'[9] Bacon's historicizing refutation of Greek learning argues that, regardless of its original worth, the Socratic tradition had long ago played itself out. To restrict learning to ancient boundaries would mean accomplishing no more – probably less – than the Greeks. Europe had long ago lost contact with the cultural and linguistic sources of Greek philosophy, which now paid diminishing returns on a substantial intellectual investment. Bacon attempts to undercut his society's official reverence for Greek and scholastic philosophies by pointing out their ideological functions in their own ages. He links this procedure to one of King James's 'own most wise and princely maxims, that in all usages and precedents, the times be considered wherein they first began; which if they were weak or ignorant, it derogateth from the authority of the usage, and leaveth it for suspect' (3: 326). Bacon understood the importance of social structures and institutional forces in determining thought, even though he rejected the notion of a contingent or time-dependent truth.

Bacon conceives truth as unitary and error as endlessly protean in its transformations. A proliferation of theories, methodologies, and viewpoints does not suggest to him a healthy pluralism or the possibility of attaining knowledge through a variety of disposable paradigms, but a thoroughgoing scepticism that would make knowledge and science impossible. When he reaffirms the principle of the variability of error and the unity of truth – 'Errori varietas, veritati unitas competit' (3: 535) – he banishes any possibility of truth being a 'regime' or historical order. Bacon's enthusiasm for eradicating entrenched opinion and beginning the work of philosophy anew must contend with anxiety over his own belatedness and historicity. As much as James's principle seemed useful in subverting accepted theories, Bacon intuited the difficulty of exempting himself from its reach. If claims to truth are 'true' only in relation to the historical forces conditioning them, the principle might apply to Bacon himself. Bacon's break with tradition might then appear no less self-deluding and refutable than the philosophies he refutes.

Scholars have long smoothed over the complexities of Bacon's position by saying that he faults innovation for innovation's sake equally with blind adherence to past authority, and that, despite momentary lapses, he sides with the moderns in the quarrel between ancients and moderns. In fact, he takes a far more complex view than such analysis would suggest. Although Bacon speaks of innovation encomiastically, he nevertheless aligns himself with a reverential attitude towards tradition. At times he promotes and denounces the pursuit of innovation in practically the same breath. In his essay 'Of Innovations' he recommends that *'Novelty*, though it be not rejected, yet be held for a Suspect,' yet cautions against holding fast to old ways.[10] In the *Advancement* Bacon cites, with apparent approbation, the proverb 'Nil novi super terram' [there is nothing new under the sun] a few pages before commending books for their powers of 'perpetual renovation.' He sees no contradiction in professing himself 'zealous and affectionate' to maintain the authority of antiquity just prior to savaging Aristotle for unfounded pride in his originality. As for the social implications of pursuing novelty, it is no accident that King Solamona of the *New Atlantis* cuts off his people from contact with the outside world, 'doubting novelties, and commixture of manners' (3: 314–18, 352, 144).

Bacon's peculiar combination of a future-oriented perspective with a backwards-looking respect for antiquity has not gone unnoticed. One thinks of the surprisingly conventional classicism of his 1609 letter to Isaac Casaubon, where he claims 'to have my conversation among the ancients more than among these with whom I live' (*Letters* 4: 147). We can attribute some of Bacon's tone here to the rhetorical situation. Intimacy with classical learning, however, seems no less typical of Bacon than his better-known remarks on the darkness of antiquity. Many scholars have rejected the view of Bacon as modernity's first partisan, someone who broke the stranglehold of antiquity by challenging the myths of a Golden Age and the unsurpassability of classical models. They note Bacon's coupling of a radical critique of credulity with credulous acceptance of erroneous traditions. John Dewey's remark that Bacon, like many other prophets, 'suffers from confused intermingling of old and new,' hints at the problem of inscribing a *prisca sapientia* within inherited systems. Bacon recognized the problematic necessity of explaining new contents by reference to old ('ex analogia veterum'), of making himself understood through traditional vocabularies and methodologies (*NO* 1: 34). His use of the epithet *novus*, for example, signals both rupture and continuity.[11]

Bacon still provides a point of reference for those who see themselves as positioned on historical thresholds or precariously balanced between old and new orders. He regarded truth as an assertion of will, a clearing away of the detritus of the past to find an unoccupied space. Yet he could not immunize himself from believing in the value of knowledge accumulated over an extended period because his 'levelling' inductive project hoped to achieve precisely that end. To regard the philosophical tradition as the march of error and correct epistemology as the sole means of delivering humanity required the adoption of a peculiar position. Bacon thought to remove himself from history by placing himself at its beginning, reaching back behind the past to screen out intervening influences. His method for actively pursuing knowledge traces a pattern of circularity back to an originary state. Since genuine knowledge means reinstating a mythic past, we must recede into time in order to reach the future. Bacon subscribes to a method of chronological figuring that effects a paradoxical reversal and makes the 'ancient' new and the 'new' ancient: 'For the old age of the world is to be accounted the true antiquity' (*NO* 1: 84). The principles of 'antiquity the world's youth' and 'truth the daughter of time' [antiquitas seculi iuventus mundi, veritas filia temporis] refute a vision of human history as condemned to endless repetition and irreversible degeneration.[12] By transforming knowledge into a cumulative undertaking Bacon seeks to establish authority on a rational basis and overcome the occlusions of belatedness. Undue reverence for what goes by the name of 'antiquity' – in reality a senescent second childhood – keeps modernity from exercising its right to pass judgment on the inflated claims of classical culture. Once we have resituated the horizon of truth within the reach of human understanding and across time, the work of recuperation can begin in earnest.

Bacon's theory of knowledge takes as its foundation the proposition that in order to make measurable progress we must realistically evaluate the reach of our understanding, not overestimate or demean it. Our inability to free ourselves from the dead hand of the past derives from our reluctance to trust to our judgment. On the one hand, he presents himself as painfully conscious of his own intellectual limitations, ostentatiously refusing to enter an ancients-versus-moderns quarrel. On the other, he trumpets his reverence for classical culture while impugning its worth. In his age Bacon saw authority and truth at loggerheads, ruling out any possibility of genuine advances in learning. Much of the blame for this inertia he laid at the doorstep of the schoolmen, with their habitual bowing to Aristotelian authority. Bacon intends his work to circumvent the shadows of error and opinion that books and faulty institutions interpose. Hoping to do away with traces of retrograde movement in the ascent of knowledge, he identifies his method with an absolutely primal moment and himself with various ancient figures.

As much as Bacon commits himself to the idea of progress, he retains allegiance to an older faith that sees all knowledge as a falling away from an original purity. Highly self-conscious in his assertions of novelty, Bacon repeatedly calls on the authority of origins, of observation at the source. Presenting himself as nature's spokesman and fashioning a style that proclaimed its proximity to an absolute beginning, Bacon perfectly articulates his culture's originary nostalgia. To convince us that God will not lose mystery and majesty under the relentless gaze of science he invokes a symbolic return to mythic origins. He banishes the spectre of self-aggrandizement by imagining his instauration under a variety of figures that depict learning as a form of recovery, and knowledge as a divine restitution of our rightful powers.

In Bacon's imagination, the absolutely novel tends to fuse with the originary or the 'real,' a fusion he predicates on the authority of Scripture and the 'primitive but seeming new' opinions of Reformation theology.[13] Bacon thought that the study of the Bible and ancient authors in the 'languages original' had produced a cross-fertilization between theology and humanist scholarship. Divine providence had overseen a general renovation of philosophic and textual learning at the same time as it precipitated the decline of papal power. Just as reasoning at a remove from reality — from analogy or 'by similitude' – can conduce to scientific discovery, so myth and allegory can bring us closer to the origins they represent. Bacon employs tropes and apologues because they have proved themselves effective in the transmission of knowledge: 'in the infancy of learning, and in rude times,' when unfamiliar concepts abounded, 'the world was full of Parables and Similitudes' (3: 283, 218, 407).[14] Bacon's so-called 'distrust' of language (and of mathematics) proceeds from his positing an unbridgeable gap between the world and symbolic representations of it. Invoking the principle of primal authenticity, he describes the possibility of a more perfect commerce between mind and nature. In this mythic realm, truth presents itself as likeness and proximity to the real.

The myth of fall and regeneration provides Bacon with a trope for expressing his culture's complex relation to the past. By the standard of the privileged origin, historical maturation must figure as a type of restoration. On occasion he speaks of paradisal recovery as a stripping away of false assumptions that enables us to become, in the words of Christ, 'as little children' (Matt. 18: 3). Bacon recommends that we gain access to the truth on the same terms that we seek admittance 'into the kingdom of heaven, whereinto none may enter except as a little child.' Making the analogy between secular and divine absolute, he finds it 'no less true in this human kingdom of knowledge than in God's kingdom of heaven, that no man shall enter into it *except he become first as a little child*' (NO 1: 68; 3: 224). This exercise in self-abnegation will bring us to see 'certainties' as mere prejudices and superstition. Bacon uses metaphors of childhood perception to stress the reader's resistance to constructing a new ground on which to proceed. He draws on rituals of humiliation and rebirth precisely because they provide analogies for a conceptually difficult process: psychic empowerment through the reclaiming of an inaccessible source. His work provides instructions for inducing a state of mind that erases or 'unwrites' experience, rendering us temporarily devoid of personal history: 'as in divine truth man cannot endure to become as a child; so in human, they reputed the attending the Inductions (whereof we speak) as if it were a second infancy or childhood' (3: 387). The advancement of learning proceeds according to a program by which intensified perception constitutes a reliable ground floor. Truth lodges in a place distinct from observation. Yet when we become again as little children, we offset our estrangement from the determining origin. Divesting ourselves of presuppositions and assuming a literally 'impressionable' frame of mind become urgent desiderata in the quest for knowledge. Placing the impress of a fallen understanding on nature inevitably leads to the forfeiture of human autonomy and further alienation from reality. Once we have had our minds 'washed clean from opinions,' we can study the world in 'purity and integrity' and relearn the pre-Babelian tongue as children first acquire language (5: 132–3).

Bacon does not think that we can turn our backs on several millennia of cumulative human error. We can, however, create an intellectual disposition that will, in effect, wipe the slate clean. By studying the primordial text of nature we erase from our minds traces of prejudice and mere opinion. Bacon alludes to Adam's naming of the creatures as evidence of our divinely infused capacity to investigate nature without stumbling in the snares of language. He draws on a long exegetical tradition regarding the passage in Genesis where God brings the creatures 'unto Adam to see what he would call them: and whatsoever Adam called every living creature, that was the name thereof' (Gen. 2: 19). According to most commentators, Adam knew what to call the animals when he named them because he could read their names in their natures, and label each according to its essential properties. The *lingua adamica*'s countertype, the myth of Babel, figured in the history of human error as the original sin of language. Babel represents the moment of disjuncture that irrevocably split mind and world into the duality of subject and object.[15]

For Bacon Adam's imposition of names functions as the archetypal instance of scientific inquiry and taxonomic analysis. His consummate skill as philosopher and naturalist emerges in his command of a language that facilitates, not impedes, philosophical enquiry. Bacon defends scientific investigation against charges of atheism and unbelief by portraying paradisal naming as a pattern for improved understanding. He professes to follow Adam's original, hence irreproachable, example. Ironically, it is the overreaching metaphysician, not the Adam-like scientist, who contravenes the original prohibition: 'For it was not that pure and uncorrupted natural knowledge whereby Adam gave names to the creatures according to their propriety, which gave occasion to the fall. It was the ambitious and proud desire of moral knowledge to judge of good and evil, to the end that man may revolt from God and give laws to himself, which was the form and manner of the temptation' (*GI* Preface; cf. *NO* 2: 52; 3: 264–5, 219, 296). While the tautologies of scholasticism perpetually re-enact original sin, the natural philosophy of the new Adam acts as an instrument for regaining paradise. Our failure to achieve steady and irreversible progress grows out of misunderstanding the implications of the Fall, from conceiving our capacity to learn in either overly modest or absurdly ambitious terms. In constantly referring our knowledge back to an overvalued antiquity, we fail to see that Scripture itself points us towards the perfections of a remoter past and the promise of an apocalyptic future. In this way progress becomes a form of recovery, a paradise regained, rather than a sifting through successive layers of historical error.

Bacon's views met with resistance during his life, especially from those contemporaries who thought the inescapable consequences of the Fall made the quest for recovery unrealizable and absurd.[16] As one might expect, Bacon remained highly sensitive to the charge of originary presumption. He counters such accusations by offering an official credo that posits

God as an irreducible basis and metaphysics as the pinnacle of knowledge. On the first score, he insists that the sin of our first parents originated in thinking 'that Good and Evil had their own principles and beginnings' apart from God, and for pursuing 'the knowledge of those imagined beginnings' (7: 222). On the second, he conspicuously clears a space for metaphysics in his division of knowledge, defining it as both an enquiry into formal and final causes, and 'the investigation of Forms, which are ... eternal and immutable' (3: 352–9; *NO* 2: 9). Metaphysicians seriously err, however, when they refuse to bound their aspirations within the limits of the knowable. In *On Principles and Origins, according to the Fables of Cupid and Cœlum*, Bacon offers an allegory of philosophy's decline in the form of 'seeking after the parents of Cupid.' A philosopher must continually remind himself 'that Cupid has no parents, lest his understanding turn aside to unrealities.' He must avoid moving ever upwards towards transcendental ultimates and 'striving after things still more original' (5: 462–3). The primitive starting-point Bacon envisions is not a higher level of generality but matter itself. The desire to attain to fundamental laws at once drives us back to what is ironically most proximate, the mind itself. The metaphysical impulse, if left unchecked, imprisons us in abstractions and the self-perpetuating generalities 'of those who wish to talk much, and know little' (5: 467–8).

The mirror-mind analogy becomes Bacon's characteristic figure for representing the failings of a speculative hermeneutic that can never begin anew. The tropes of the 'enchanted glass' and 'uneven mirror' symbolize the undeniable importance of innate factors in determining how and what we perceive. Assumptions of identity and simplicity emanate outward from the human mind, which has blinded itself to nature's variability and particularity. The constitution of reality by consciousness makes it difficult, if not impossible, to grasp the objective essence of things in themselves, or to render natural phenomena intelligible to (and interpretable by) the intellect. God, in His wisdom, 'hath framed the mind of man as a mirror or glass capable of the image of the universal world.' Yet the reflective mind projects itself onto an uninflected natural order whenever it forms 'notions.' Human understanding remains unequal to the work of induction without the assistance of methodological discipline and critical self-contemplation: 'For let men please themselves as they will in admiring and almost adoring the human mind, this is certain: that as an uneven mirror distorts the rays of objects according to its own figure and section, so the mind, when it receives impressions of objects through the sense, cannot be trusted to report them truly, but in forming its notions mixes up its own nature with the nature of things.'[17] Bacon diverges from Neoplatonic and traditional uses of mirror imagery by encompassing traditional paradigms themselves in the problem of circularity. The myth of Narcissus, as Bacon describes it in *De Sapientia Veterum,* becomes an allegory of the career of philosophy. After a brief glimmer of insight, those of thoughtful disposition surround themselves with acolytes who echo their every word and thus become enthralled to a single idea. Reproducing countless images of their own subjectivity, they end up 'besotted at last with self-admiration' and subside into stupor and endless repetition (6: 705).

In a recent essay and in an earlier book, Michael McCanles argues (as I have, too) that Bacon's desire to heal the gap between mental and symbolic signifiers centres his philosophy on origins, an ideal of unmediated knowledge of things in themselves. Bacon's use of mirror metaphors manifests this drive towards intuitive knowledge and nostalgia for 'presence.' McCanles finds in Bacon's nominalism and critique of the idols an analogy to Jacques Derrida's deconstruction of logocentrism, with one key difference: 'while Bacon believes it is possible to substitute true mental conceptions for false, Derrida insists that finally all mental conceptions (i.e., all signs, all lexicons) are necessarily false.'[18] Bacon never paused to question his equation of knowledge with avoidance of error, or his tying 'truth' to accurate mental representation. He remained a willing captive of the idea that concepts and what they refer to could be matched on the basis of congruence or similarity. He could hardly foresee the objection that we cannot compare sensations and ideas to anything but other sensations and ideas, nor affirm truth by matching mental and non-mental phenomena. Yet Bacon did understand that reference entails a complex system of signification, not a simple isomorphism. His customary emphasis on *mis*representation provides the germ of a counter-theory that anticipates, if only pre-emptively to defuse, the arguments of his critics.

For Bacon, reconnecting philosophy to the world means immersing theory in experience and devising a well-founded experimental logic. The humanism of the fifteenth and sixteenth centuries had presented itself as the restoration of a normative primal condition. Bacon establishes the complementary goal of providing the groundwork for humanism's eventual supersession by a scientific practice that could reposition knowledge at a historical degree zero. The givenness of humane letters, its exaggerated deference to antiquity, had produced a new form of historical entrapment, a neo-scholasticism. Henceforth, the overwritten and underinterpreted present would serve as a staging place for future enquiry, and Baconian method break open the speculative circle. Bacon saw himself standing at a juncture where a systematic ingathering of certain knowledge would produce an inexhaustible methodology for understanding an infinite, yet none the less determinate, nature.

Bacon's anti-theoretical methodologism, his hope of abolishing error through the renovation of authority, his continually checked drift towards a simple of equation of *res* and *verba* – all these issues occupy prominent places in the debate on language-in-culture as it unfolds throughout the seventeenth century.

2

Writing Error in the *Novum Organum*

Origins, as they appear in Bacon, are not just an idea or concept, but an entire system of representations – a myth, a discourse, an ideology. By an 'ideology,' as I have argued, I do not mean to signify a form of consciousness or belief system that fails to meet the criteria of scientific objectivity. Objectivity itself has a central place in the history of polemic. We need to remind ourselves, as we take up the Baconian origin as a theoretical and historical issue, that ideologies are indispensable to social life. The seventeenth-century discourse of origin provides a perspective, a framework for understanding, one that plays a role in constituting the subjects of philosophy and epic poetry. At one level the determining power of the origin can sometimes seem intuitive, almost self-evident. At another, gaining access to immediate experience becomes problematic, a question disputed and formalized by philosophers. The desire to recuperate a lost purity, to reach backward to a time when things were somehow more themselves, is considered the task of a mind freed from prejudice, not saturated with presuppositions. Origin-seeking is the activity of minds educated in history, theology, literature, and philosophy.

The *Novum Organum* epitomizes Bacon's attempt to achieve a renovation of authority through a discourse of origin. In it error takes on multiple, categorically differentiated, and protean forms. Bacon views his Great Instauration as a therapeutic task, a way of releasing humanity from the grip of obsolete authorities and bringing about the 'true end and termination of infinite error' (*GI* Preface). Below the surface of his writing he mines a vein of images, founded on the substratum of epic and allegory, that figure forth journeys to a hidden source. He bids us to redirect our 'course' to new and more satisfactory goals. This elaborate nexus of linearity and ascent along a methodological path functions in direct opposition to the imagery of error. The noun *error* and various forms of the verb *to err* appear throughout the *Novum Organum* with some regularity.¹ Playing on the sense of the Latin verb *errare* as 'to wander,' Bacon disparages modern experimental scientists for pursuing 'a kind of wandering inquiry' that leads nowhere. Or he applies the Latin adjective *vagum* ('vague' or 'wandering') to the peripatetics, implicitly comparing them to vagrants and vagabonds. Bacon imagines error as circular entrapment or labyrinthine entanglement, as 'a whirling round about, and perpetual agitation, ending where it began,' or as aimless 'wandering round and round as in a labyrinth' (*GI* Proem; *NO* 1: 71, 16, 82). Bacon picks his quarrel with established schools of thought not only for their abstruseness and muddled comprehensiveness, but also for misunderstanding the relation between origin and *telos*.

Constantly returning to allegories of journeying, Bacon portrays himself throughout the 1620 *Instauratio Magna* and *Novum Organum* as a pathfinder whose object is 'to open a new way [*via*] for the understanding.' Bacon's view of deductive logic comes to resemble the allegorical Way of Destruction – easily negotiable at first sight but opening out into 'pathless and precipitous places.' The alternate route he chooses may seem 'arduous and difficult in the beginning,' but eventually brings us out into the open country. Bacon imagines truth as a goal achieved only by relentlessly moving forward along untrodden roads. The slight tautological insistence of the titular phrase 'the proficience (ie progress) and advancement of learning' underscores an idea that become integral to the *Novum Organum*'s entire imagery and rhetoric, with its emphasis on a new logic as the means for freeing us from 'the errors and impediments' we might meet along 'the way' (*GI* Proem, Preface; *NO* Preface).

Nothing better suits Bacon's temperament, his combination of theological and juridical impulses and a methodological commitment to categorization, than branding various intellectual malefactors with their crimes. Everywhere he turns he finds error and deficiency. The cause of truth demands that he evangelize in its service, pointing out that which has escaped notice through a conspiracy of silence and inattention. Bacon could not take his scepticism to the point where our capacity to make sense of the world was in doubt. He identified this position with the worst tendencies in Greek philosophy – Pyrrhonism and *acatalepsia*, 'denial of the capacity of the mind to comprehend truth' (*NO* 1: 126). Bacon's system precludes epistemic relativism, and his scepticism usually serves a mainly strategic purpose. When, for example, he points to the limitations of unreconstructed reason, Bacon defies us to contradict him: 'I cannot be fairly asked to abide by the decision of a tribunal,' he writes, 'which is itself on trial' (*GI* Preface). The rational capacity cannot presume to judge itself at a time when doubt has compelled the capitulation of dogmatically resistant certitude and problematized the whole question of knowledge.

Bacon never pitches his great instauration to the disputatious many who seek dominance in debate but to a select few with a Faustian craving for power over nature itself. From the very outset Bacon's instauration locates its moral centre in exemplary figures who shun reading and pure contemplation to combine intellectual and institutional power. In an epistle Bacon dedicates the *Instauratio Magna* to 'our most gracious and mighty prince and lord' King James. The central figure around whom contemporary questions of authority and the articulation of power revolved, James certainly disqualified himself as likely to understand the work's philosophical import when he compared it to 'the peace of God, that passeth all understanding.' Bacon nevertheless deemed him the fittest audience the work was likely to win, especially in establishing the social organization of Bacon's ideal research program. He approaches James keenly aware of the king's authority and claim to authorship, and suggests an affinity between prince and subject. He identifies James with his own refusal to circumscribe himself within a single disciplinary sphere. In a letter acknowledging receipt of a presentation copy of the book, James acknowledges the congruence of temperament and abilities between himself and the Lord Chancellor: 'I can with comfort assure you, that you could not have made choice of a subject more befitting your place, and your universal and methodick knowledge' (*Letters* 7: 122). James confers his benediction on the *Novum Organum* by finding it suited to the talents of the author, the temperament of the king, and the interests of the state. He reassures Bacon that his 'universal and methodick knowledge' supports the authority of the monarchy.[2]

James's reassurance may have come in response to a tentativeness in Bacon's dedictatory epistle. Bacon begins it by conceding the seemingly outrageous novelty of his ideas: 'Certainly they are quite new,' he writes, 'totally new in their very kind.' Then he goes on: 'yet they are copied from a very ancient model; even the world itself and the nature of things and of the mind.' We must not think of originality as based in an unregulated subjectivity. If James frequently fell back on the prerogatives of kingship to justify his right to interpret, Bacon appeals to an even higher court of judgment: an objective reality that the mind somehow 'copies.' Bacon establishes himself as the faithful transcriber of a perfectly rational and transparent semiotic, whose writings give us access to things in themselves rather than mere interpretations. He promises to separate out the mind-independent elements of experience into individual constituents and make our objectifications of phenomena a rational process. His 'total reconstruction' of human knowledge brings mind and matter into contact with each other and strives to restore the commerce between them 'to its perfect and original condition' (*GI* Proem).

In the *Novum Organum* Bacon goes to considerable lengths to allay the suspicion that his plan to renovate all human knowledge constitutes an ambitious bid for pre-eminence and influence. What may appear as self-aggrandizing on the surface he invites us to see as an act of heroic selflessness. What may strike us as fragmentary and unfinished becomes an integral part of his plan. In order to supplant deeply ingrained habits of mind and constitute authority on a new basis, Bacon formulates an ideal of achieving knowledge through self-doubt, constant vigilance, and the expectation of future revision. Accusations of overreaching ambition could be shrugged off only with some difficulty by a philosopher who persisted in doubt yet knew his own merit. Bacon thus takes a pre-emptive stand against charges of intellectual vanity, justifying his shift of authority from written texts to observation, and claiming to advance human power, not personal ambition. To this end, he depersonalizes and objectifies his accomplishment, describing his attempt to institutionalize the means for acquiring truth as a new intellectual disposition or attitude rather than a formal set of techniques. He separates his 'new logic' from Aristotelian and Ramist methods on the basis of its demonstrable productiveness in rooting out error and disclosing objective truth.

Studies that traverse the space between the seventeenth century and the present often see Bacon as occupying a crucial place in the formation of an ideology of scientific objectivity. In Joyce Appleby's account of the origin of economic thought, Bacon stands as an architect of the myth of scientific neutrality. According to Appleby, the modern model of economic relations, of a natural order untrammelled by social or political structures, emerged out of a Baconian matrix. This desire to eliminate all contingencies from models of economic relations, to theorize according to models purified of human factors, had a profound influence on the subsequent course of economics as a field. Adopting an 'unbiased' mode of analysis, writers on trade borrowed Baconian theories of observation and model-building. In Appleby's account, Bacon bears responsibility for dehumanizing the social subject and mandating an approach to the exchange of goods and commodities that encouraged an ideology of economic impersonality.[3]

Without challenging Appleby's conclusions, I would argue that this analysis overlooks the interrelation of ideology and critique in Bacon's writings. Bacon outlined a theory of 'the idols and false notions which are now in possession of the human understanding, and have taken deep root therein' (*NO* 1: 38). The theory represents a significant moment in the early history of ideological analysis. What constitutes a significant form of ideology in Bacon's writings is not the usefulness of his theory of objectivity in the service of nascent capitalism. Rather it resides in the methodological ideal of recovering notions by penetrating accumulated layers of error to seize a reality that precedes the formation of ideas. Once Bacon had identified the inherent biases of the mind derived from social and linguistic factors, he made the error, subsequently repeated, of thinking to rid humanity of them. The fallacies that enter the mind, Bacon argued, derive from a structural flaw – the mind's tendency to mirror itself and generate false appearances. By projecting mental constructions onto the world and making man *communis mensura* [the measure of all things] the mind fabricates and perpetuates an infinitude of error. Although he attempted to unify practice and theory, Bacon continued to identify truth with the recovery of origin and to take as his first principle the necessity of establishing first principles. When Bacon diagnoses the mind's predisposition to find order and uniformity in whatever it perceives, he hopes to eliminate it.

The vagaries of communication, the idols imposed on the understanding through irregularities of language, exacerbate the process, giving erroneous notions an aura of solidity they otherwise could not obtain. Science provides no simple escape from this bind. Nor can language be transcended. The usual paradigm for interpreting Bacon's place in seventeenth-century theories of the sign looks for a moment of decisive rupture and divides the period into neat halves. According to this model, a commitment to language's divinely instituted origin precluded an understanding of language as a human invention. Murray Cohen's book on linguistic practice from 1640 to 1785, for example, discovers a fault line running through the period. Cohen divides English culture between two models of language: the first, lexically based systems that emphasize the materiality of words and their implication in the order of things, and the second a grammar of syntactic and mental structures. According to Cohen's analytical schema, the two discourses coexist and run parallel throughout the century, yet a fissure always remains visible: 'Seventeenth-century linguists sought to establish an isomorphic relationship between language and nature; in the early eighteenth century, linguists assumed that language reflects the structure of the mind.' This implicit dichotomy finds echoes in an epochal movement Cohen traces from rebellion to Restoration in politics, metaphysical to Augustan in literature, and scholasticism to empiricism in science. While earlier models often erected a barricade of secularization across the century (and put Bacon on its progressive side), Martin Elsky posits a congruence between the old magic and the new science, the hieroglyphic tradition of Du Bartas and Bacon's mentalistic theories. Elsky suggests that Bacon's contribution resides not in his closing the gap between language and reality, but in setting the two orders of experience asunder. Bacon may have 'affirmed the close connection between words and things,' and shared contemporary belief in the restitution of Adamic language. Yet he also made language purely contingent, severing it from analogical structures. Despite his affinities with cabbalistic theories that concretize and visualize the linguistic sign, 'for Bacon, there is no one language that by its very nature properly matches words and things.'[4]

In short, Bacon turns up in some accounts as an exponent of an outmoded analogical world-view, and in others as a prophet of nominalistic desacralization. This paradox partly derives from the uneasy coexistence of contradictory views within his corpus. Bacon sometimes endorses a conception of the sign that places it within the totality of signifiers where it contributes 'resemblance'; and at other times insists that language remains phenomenally distinct from the material world, to which it imperfectly and provisionally makes reference. Beyond this, bifurcating approaches to Bacon's theories of knowledge and signification generally go unchallenged because they satisfy several needs: first, to cordon off the later decades of the century; second, to map the cultural coordinates of the period in a manner that provides holistic explanations of synchronous phenomena; and third, to exalt particular texts and authors to positions of pre-eminence. While many studies recognize the diversity of views available to the period, they often adhere to strictly diachronic schema. Theories of culture 'in crisis' or undergoing 'secularization' tend to elide significant differences by setting up loaded epitomes or neat contrastive models. 'Bacon,' in this sense, provides a fulcrum on which balanced periodizations can pivot.

Behind the schematics of epistemic disjuncture invoked by critics of Bacon stands Michel Foucault's analysis in *The Order of Things*, which posits a radical disjuncture between a sixteenth-century *episteme* – universal similitude within the book of nature – and seventeenth-century representationalism. Recent studies have tended to refute the view of Renaissance theories of signification as monolithically analogical, non-conventional, and encoded within the book of nature.[5] Foucault himself suggests that 'the critique of resemblance' implicit in Bacon's doctrine of the idols hardly amounts to a systematic refutation since Bacon remained committed to its logic: 'Bacon does not dissipate similitudes by means of evidence and its attendant rules. He shows them, shimmering before our eyes, vanishing as one draws near, then re-forming again a moment later, a little further off.' Seeing resemblance places one under the sway of mental fictions, stubborn structures that may dissipate somewhat in the face of continued attentiveness but remain solidly entrenched. Bacon asks us to mistrust resemblance as a form of knowledge, but not to excise it altogether from the processes of thought. Divinity remains of necessity dependent on parables and tropes, along with other forms of knowledge at early stages of development. For Bacon, the adequacy of our concepts to represent an original 'in the world' becomes a problem in the theory of metaphor and predication.[6]

Timothy Reiss's *The Discourse of Modernism* presents an especially subtle and extensive application of Foucauldian ideas to Bacon. Reiss connects Bacon to the category of 'analytico-referential discourse,' a system he associates with experimentation and truth in science, possessive individualism and contract theory in politics, taste and common sense in aesthetics and philosophy. Building on the premiss that reason coincides with the syntactic structure of language, Bacon assumes that 'understanding' entails constructing a description of the discursive relationship between object and the perceiving mind. Errors result from limitations inherent to the discourse (or mind) that forms the description: 'The distinction between reason and language, between reason and things, between language and things, poses an enormous difficulty, particularly because the distinction cannot in any event be absolute: "for men believe that their reason governs words; but it is also true that words react on the understanding"' (see *NO* 1: 59). According to Reiss, Bacon grapples with the problem of separating reason from language by inventing 'a kind of logical atomism *avant la lettre*,' pointing us to the elements (or 'alphabet') of a language that precedes the advent of Babel. Seeing the linguistic sign as a strictly conventional nexus encouraged Bacon to challenge claims of representational accuracy and to analyse particular significations for their referential adequacy.[7]

Bacon's desire for a rationalized or 'philosophic' language, while 'Adamic' or mystical on its face, implicitly abandons the search for the lost ur-language. All such schemes cast their lot instead with the construction of an invented but none the less artificial semiotic system. In a roundabout way, they trumpet their commitment to language as a social institution at the same time they renounce ordinary language, and insist on the force of convention at the precise moment they strive for correspondence. As Ian Hacking observes: 'These enterprises are the practical effect of the thesis that all language is conventional. They also represent the antithesis, that language must in some way correspond to the world.'[8] Throughout Bacon's own work, conventionalist theories of language achieve a kind of equilibrium, or at least an uneasy coexistence, with the mythology of a divine origin. Despite repeated allusions to the language of Adam, Bacon insisted on the conventional nature of language and remained sceptical about the value of Platonic (or 'Cratylic') etymologizing. The inquiry into linguistic origins was founded on the assumption that words 'were not arbitrarily fixed at first, but derived and deduced by reason and according to significance' (4: 441). Bacon, like many of his contemporaries, invokes the *lingua adamica* as a shorthand notation for unrealized human potential, everything we forfeited with the disappearance of a mysteriously perfect primal idiom. Yet he rejects the possibility of a 'natural' or non-conventional language.

From the opening of *De interpretatione* – part of the logical canon that comprises the Aristotelian organon – Bacon borrowed a definition of *onoma* as 'spoken sound significant by convention.' He also took the idea that 'spoken sounds are symbols of affections in the soul, and written marks symbols of spoken sounds.' Bacon quotes this widely influential text in the *Advancement*: 'for Aristotle saith well, Words are the images of cogitations, and letters are the images of words.' It comes up again in *De Augmentis*, just prior to the discussion of Chinese ideograms: 'words are the images of thoughts and letters are the images of words' (3: 399, 4: 439). Bacon apparently concurs with Aristotle's theory that a fixed relation holds between a significantly used word and the extra-linguistic entity designated as the word's meaning.[9] For Aristotle, what words signify (thoughts or 'affections in the soul') are uniform from individual to individual, and the mental modifications or 'likenesses' arising from them likewise uniform. In other words, since inner experience remains uniform from person to person, we all think the same thoughts, even though we might express them differently. Henry King, author of 'The Exequy,' invokes this commonplace in a 1625 sermon: 'When the tongues were dispersed at *Babel*, the *thoughts* were not; and howsoever each Nation be distinguished in his peculiar speech, we all thinke alike; even as anger and laughter have the same wayes of expression in all parts of the world.'[10]

Despite its obvious defects, this theory had a profound effect on Bacon and his followers, providing, for example, a rationale for schemes of a universal character or language.[11] Stephen Greenblatt detects in this theory the implications of a humanist essentialism that denies cultural difference and posits a single human reality. The quest for universal language, Greenblatt writes, arose form the same 'unspoken belief in the isomorphic relationship between language and reality' that encouraged sixteenth-century observers of American Indians to pronounce them either altogether lacking in language, or speaking a tongue essentially no different from their own.[12] Such theories also arose from a notion of deep linguistic structures, or the presence of universal principles operating across languages, despite obvious differences of diction and grammar. From this Aristotelian premiss Bacon and his contemporaries concluded that significations remain constant over time and among different individuals. Yet Bacon also believed that a complete uniformity of impression and thought lay beyond our grasp. As Timothy Reiss maintains, Bacon regards language, thought, and reality as three separate domains, and 'the first can be made a "neutral" mediator between the second and third only with laborious effort.' The distinction is never absolute because reason and language easily become confused with each other, and 'neither words nor thought has any longer a direct relation with things.'[13] For Bacon, 'signs' by definition signify (or *represent* concepts to the mind), a process that generally entails the mind's making contact with an origin distinct from its own operations. Describing the precise nature of this contact remains problematic because of the enormous range of mental events to which we normally attach the terms 'signification,' 'ideas,' and 'concepts.' Bacon also believed that if the impediments blocking congruence between ideas and their origin were critiqued and anatomized, we could make considerable progress towards this ideal. By redirecting our attention to conceptual and semiotic factors in the construction of knowledge, we could glimpse fragments of an antecedent reality.

Bacon assumes (and partially expounds) an ideational theory of perception, according to which ideas 'in the mind' become a link in a cognitive process that joins together *res et verbum*. Following Locke, we usually call mediating signs that represent objects, qualities, or universals to the mind 'ideas.' The English words *idea* and *concept*, however, were rarely used in their modern senses before the seventeenth century, and Bacon usually relies on the term *notion*. As Vivian Salmon has shown, the Latin word *notio* originated in the technical vocabulary of grammar and psychology. It may have first appeared in J.C. Scaliger's *De Causis Linguae Latinae* (1540), which defines *notiones* as 'imagines rerum,' and 'rerum species mente comprehensas' [species of things comprehended by the mind]. The word's relative unfamiliarity to compositors emerges in a misprint recorded in the Errata to the 1605 edition of the *Advancement*: 'motions' had been substituted for 'notions' in the phrase 'Plato's opinion, that all knowledge is but remembrance, and that the mind of man by nature knoweth all things, and hath but her own native and original notions.'[14]

Bacon draws our attention to ideology as a function of language when he speaks of the mind's tendency to generate 'primary notions of things' [notiones rerum primae] that are 'false, confused, and overhastily abstracted from the facts.' Bacon introduces a ternary model of signification, encompassing things, notions, and words. For Bacon, 'notions' are the basic constituents of reality, derived from individual things on a correspondent basis. To regulate the semantic process we need to make mental impressions conform to their originals and words conform to mental impressions.[15] Bacon bases inductive method on 'notions themselves,' which he calls 'the root of the matter.' Notions must not, he reiterates, be 'confused' and 'over-hastily abstracted' from things. He rejects certain notions out of hand, including the metaphysical concepts of substance, quality, essence, and the scientific principles of corruption, matter, and form. Anything other than 'general species' or 'immediate perceptions' he dismisses as 'wanderings' or aberrations (*NO* 1: 14, 16).

Referring words back to primitive notions initiates a process of uncovering the artificiality of what we, as language users, mistakenly regard as 'natural' and universal categories. Since our understanding of primary notions remains deficient, philosophy must direct itself to enquiring into simple rather than 'fantastical and ill defined' conceptions (*NO* 1: 15). What Bacon means by a 'sound notion' rests on a theoretical foundation of corpuscularianism, and suggests an attribute placed among fundamental properties. Yet if our primary notions are indeed unsound, how can we reverse this error through an inductive process that itself depends on the prior possession of such notions? The crux of the problem rests in the difficulty of guaranteeing method by reference to 'notions' when Bacon has already disallowed the antecedent formation of them.

Once Bacon has established the notional basis of thought and language to his satisfaction, he dissects and classifies 'the idols and false notions' that afflict human understanding. Historians of 'ideology' as a term of analysis often mention Bacon's critique of the idols. According to one account, the systematic study of ideology by Marxists, sociologists, and political scientists is a possibility glimpsed ('using different terminology') by Machiavelli and Bacon, long before the more systematic thinkers of the French Enlightenment.[16] As I have suggested, the diagnosis of the idols unites with the Baconian discourse of origin and primary notions. The quarrel over 'first principles and very notions' must resolve itself before Baconian doctrine can enter into the mind. In order to achieve knowledge of reality itself we must cast aside received ideas ('notions' in the mildly pejorative sense) and understand the social forces or *idola* that have alienated us from truth (*NO* 1: 35, 36, 38). Bacon's choice of the word 'idol,' with its manifold layers of association (fictions, illusions, fallacies, heresies), deliberately blurs boundaries. An 'idol' is primarily the product of competing subjectivities and socialized perceptions gone awry, a false image formed under the impress of deceitful sense. It also bears comparison to the *eidolon* (viewer-determined shape) of the atomist, and the *eikon* (or 'likeness') of the Platonist. Bacon uses 'idol' to signify any human error or departure from an authoritative origin that becomes a reproducible ideology. These vary in seriousness. The idols of the Tribe, Cave, and Marketplace are ineradicable, while the illusions of the Theatre (bankrupt methodologies and spurious dogmas, and so on) are presumably more amenable to correction. With the doctrine Bacon again embroils himself in apparent contradiction. One view, implicit in the Idols of the Theatre, suggests that the critique of spurious dogmas and false methodologies liberates us to study truth. The second, implicit in the more 'innate' Idols of the Tribe, Cave, and Marketplace, implies that while we may reject the errors of the past we can never erase them entirely.

The Idols of the Tribe arise from humanist conceptions of man as the measure of all things, and from what we now might call the neurobiology of the species. Saddled with an inescapable tendency to interject human interests into every sphere, the human mind has come to resemble a distorting mirror that commingles its nature with the 'nature of things.' The Idols of the Cave are individual idiosyncrasies or predispositions, which include the biases of education and a disabling veneration of authority. In this respect they shade into the Idols of the Theatre, systematic misconceptions received from canonical writers and 'the various dogmas of philosophies.' The Idols of the Marketplace, which Bacon considers the most pernicious of the four, involve language: 'There are also Idols formed by the intercourse and association of men with each other, which I call Idols of the Market-place, on account of the commerce and consort of men there. For it is by discourse that men associate; and words are imposed according to the apprehension of the vulgar. And therefore the ill and unfit choice of words wonderfully obstructs the understanding.' Bacon rejects the idea of repairing learning simply by giving particular attention to the scientific lexicon. He has no faith in careful definition as a vehicle for reform since definitions themselves consist of words, 'and those words beget others.' To break free from circularity we would have to go back behind words to recapture an original presence. Words take on a life of their own, resisting change, contaminating the understanding, and generating endless controversy and confusion. Drawing on the conventional metaphor of words as a commodity or currency, he explains improper use of language as a product of commerce and human interaction: 'But the *Idols of the Market-place* are the most troublesome of all: idols which have crept into the understanding through the alliances of words and names' (*NO* 1: 43, 59). Bacon conceives language not only as a potential contaminant of intellectual rigour, but also as the paradigmatic example of the tendency for all social institutions to give way to degeneration and constant flux. The further knowledge becomes estranged from its defining moment of origin, the more resistant it becomes to systematic or learned regulation.

Bacon's complaint has numerous classical and humanist precedents: grammarians and rhetoricians long bemoaned the fact that words originated among ordinary people, who dictated usage through custom and prevailing practice. Bacon remained distrustful of the rule of 'custom' and feared 'the false appearances that are imposed upon us by words, which are framed and applied according to the conceit and capacities of the vulgar sort' (3: 396). Learned attempts to impose order on the lexicon seldom meet with success because they misunderstand the source of the problem. The Idols of the Marketplace break down into two categories: 'They are either names of things which do not exist ... or they are names of things which exist, but yet confused and ill-defined, and hastily and irregularly derived from realities.' Non-referential words, words correspondent to nothing in reality, will wither away when scientists explode the theories underlying them; but the second class of error, category mistakes and faulty abstraction, resists easy extirpation (*NO* 1: 60).

In order to make the passage from impression to word simple and correct, Bacon asks us to look continually to our perceptions and flawed understanding. We should not let the rule of discourse blind us to the material world. Although not an ostensible focus of his work, the inadequacy of existing language becomes an insistent motif. Begotten from haphazard and unsystematic notions, faulty words beget further error in their turn. Language is fraught with irregularities, ambiguities, and groundless assumptions that form a barrier to productive enquiry. An ever-widening gap between sign and referent has accompanied the fall from simplicity to complexity, and since language monopolizes cognition, only a radical reformation of language could achieve ideal results. Reproducing 'nature' in the form of accurate mental impressions becomes bound up with the dream of a common language in which word and referent unequivocally mesh. Bacon's call to reform fluctuates between conceding the adequacy of ordinary language and a barely restrained desire for the renovation of our fallen linguistic dispensation. He resolves one of the central questions we associate with logical positivism – whether we can compare sentences with facts or only with other sentences – in favour of the former. Natural philosophy, properly understood, went directly to the heart of conceptual and linguistic problems. Its unique explanatory and descriptive powers made it the discipline against which all the arts of language must finally measure themselves.

Realizing the enormous difficulty of trying to transform language in a world of unlimited change and diversity, Bacon seizes upon whatever hope of mitigation presents itself. He finds reason for optimism in three distinct phenomena that all promise recovery of a lost logographic power and linguistic ideal: the Pentecostal tongues, Chinese ideograms, and Egyptian hieroglyphics. While the Established Church interpreted the miracle of Pentecostal de-Babelization (described in Acts) as a unique occurrence, Bacon ranks it among the *'vehicula scientiae'* granted us by God for our spiritual and material betterment, implying the phenomenon's iterability (3: 296–9). The possibility of somehow re-enacting the miracle of tongues plays an important part in Bacon's utopianism. The inhabitants of Bensalem in the *New Atlantis,* for example, owe their Christian faith to 'a great miracle,' similar to the original Pentecost, which enabled the island's early polyglot inhabitants to 'read' Scripture in whatever language they happened to speak (3: 138–9).

The *Advancement* turns away from Western culture for models of character-writing, basing its hopes for a radical transformation on a naïve view of Chinese ideograms and Egyptian hieroglyphics. As Bacon explains them, Chinese characters resemble the Pentecostal tongues in that they, too, can be 'read off' by speakers in their own language. Widespread dissemination in the East has made a written lexicon generally familiar: 'And we understand further that it is the use of China and the kingdoms of the high Levant to write in Characters Real, which express neither letters nor words in gross, but Things or Notions; insomuch as countries and provinces, which understand not one another's language, can nevertheless read one another's writings, because the characters are accepted more generally than the languages do extend; and therefore they have a vast multitude of characters; as many, I suppose, as radical words' (3: 399–400). Bacon's contemporaries admired Chinese writing for its supposed capacity to bypass the intermediary level of phonological representation and directly identify words with objects and ideas. They viewed ideograms as a form capable of transcending the differences inhering in spoken language. The obvious drawback inherent to all forms of logographic writing, the difficulty of memorizing many symbols, naturally troubled them. The example of Chinese proved that far from clarifying and simplifying writing, persons outside of scribal and literary elites were unlikely to master the process of memorizing a separate grapheme for each individual word.[17] While the character's supposed capacity to imprint itself on the mind added to its value, extraordinary memorization was incommensurate with the goal of directing knowledge of origins away from prolonged language study.

Misgivings about linguistic overcomplexity and artificiality explain Bacon's movement from Chinese characters, which signify on a conventional basis or *'ad placitum,'* to Egyptian hieroglyphics, which reach back to an early semasiographic phase of writing and have 'some similitude or congruity with the notion.' Bacon values hieroglyphics for their extreme antiquity, their priority in the development of writing. He believed that hieroglyphic writing had retained, in a fossilized form, its original pictorial quality, combining permanence with the immediacy of gesture (3: 400). In the *Advancement* Bacon identifies hieroglyphics with the 'parabolical wisdom' of Aesop's fables and 'the brief sentences of the Seven [wise men of Greece]' (3: 344). Hieroglyphs represent the possibility of devising a sign system that systematically connects *res* to *verba*. The symbolic representations Bacon describes are notable for two distinct but related reasons. First, they are 'graphic' in that they legibly and indelibly inscribe themselves on the mind. Second, they reach back through intervening levels of complexity to a primary authenticity.[18] Hieroglyphics, like Chinese ideograms, real characters, and aphorisms, constitute a heightened form of semiosis, an ideal of referentiality that complements the myth of origins.

Bacon suffered no delusions about the feasibility of importing pictographic or ideographic writing to England, subjects he pursued in a spirit of pure semiotic enquiry. He readily concedes the highly theoretical nature of his speculation about non-Western graphic systems, and comments: 'And although it may seem of no great use, considering that words and writings by letters do far excel all the other ways; yet because this part concerneth as it were the mint of knowledge, (for words are the tokens current and accepted for conceits, as moneys are for values, and that it is fit men be not ignorant that moneys may be of another kind than gold and silver,) I thought good to propound it to better enquiry' (3: 400). Bacon acknowledges that language, like currency, bases itself on shifting standards and serves the purpose of social interaction. The analogy between money and linguistic reference goes back to *De interpretatione* and Horace's *Ars Poetica* (lines 57–9). Bacon's use of the trope, however, stresses the absolute contingency of monetary and semiotic value. Currency and words are kinds of fiction, representations that endlessly duplicate themselves. As mediums of exchange, both impose meaning within a community, thereby enabling trade and communication. Bacon locates language at the point where social and economic forces intersect, becoming determinants of human behaviour. In the same way that we fix exchange rates and order commerce according to convention, we also agree to convey 'cogitations' according to standardized discursive practices. Bacon contends that words acquire meaning through their identification with 'conceits,' or mental images, an operation subject to natural fluctuations. While certain symbolic systems may seem especially efficient, we cannot attribute anything 'natural' to them.

Bacon's use of the terminology of *res et verba* proceeds from the view that words can mirror an external reality of material objects through the intermediate stage of 'notions.' Our divinely infused capacity to read the world aright derives from the reception and reproduction of impressions. Our seemingly limitless capacity for error grows out of the gap between a 'Nature' infinitely more complex than the understanding that represents it. Bacon's anxious concern over the rift between sign and referent has interested commentators for its supposed anticipation of and resemblance to modern semantic theories.[19] Philosophy and linguistics have taught us to conceive of meaning as the product of language, not merely the reflection of non-linguistic consciousness through a verbal medium. Language does not 'reflect' reality, it constitutes it; and the mind does not detect order in nature, it projects order onto it. Bacon's confidence that 'all depends on keeping the eye steadily fixed upon the facts of nature and so receiving their images simply as they are' (*GI* Plan), assumes an easy transaction. His commitment to the possibility of developing a direct correlation between thought and language seems symptomatic of an originary nostalgia and linguistic utopianism.

From the perspective of the later seventeenth century, Bacon helped to effect a clarification of issues inherited from (but occluded in) medieval sign theory. Bacon's instrumental role in bringing about a new 'notional' order surfaces in a variety of texts that credit him with an important role in assessing the problem of notional worlds implicit in language. John Webster's *Academiarum Examen* considers notions the ultimate constituents of reality. Webster rejects any logic constructed on mistaken apprehensions and half-understood words for neglecting rules 'by which either notions may be truly abstracted and gathered from things,' or 'due and fit words may be appropriated to notions.' On the key relation of propositions to words, he quotes the *Novum Organum* 1: 14, associating Bacon with the theory that infallible rules must be used to regulate the semantic process and make words conform to mental impressions: 'Therefore if notions themselves (which is the very bottom of the matter) be confused, or rashly abstracted from things, there is nothing of firmitude in those things that are superstructed.' The word *notion,* with all of its shades and nuances, had strong Baconian associations throughout the century. In a poem written in praise of Bacon, George Herbert leads off his list of flattering attributes with the phrase 'Dux Notionum; veritatis Pontifex' [master of enquiry, high priest of truth]. Joseph Glanvill's *Plus Ultra* makes Bacon's critique of 'the *defects* and unprofitableness of the *Notional* way' a major part of his contribution, and describes his proposal to replace the notional way with an inductive technique designed so 'that our Notions may have a *Foundation* upon which a *solid Philosophy* may be built.' Robert Boyle's *A Discourse of Things above Reason* (1681), comparing sight to the understanding, concludes that the 'Intellect is as well a Looking-glass as a Sensory, since it does not only see other things, but it self too': 'Upon which consideration, we may justifie the boldness of our excellent *Verulam*, who, when he sets forth the four sorts of Idols (as he calls them) that mislead the studiers of Philosophy, makes one of them to be *Idola Tribûs*, by which he means those Notions, that tho' radicated in the very nature of mankind, are yet apt to mislead us.'[20] Boyle suggests, on Bacon's authority, that the rational capacity remains capable of judging its own performance, of compensating for its innate flaws or 'original Notions, by which she is wont to judge of other things,' if it approaches the problem systematically. Bacon had transformed the scholastic conception of knowledge as the product of 'common notions' into another tool in the arsenal against error and 'mere' opinion. Disciplined self-reflection on the act of reflection would henceforth contribute to the task of advancing knowledge and dispelling ignorance.

Bacon sought to supplant the fragmentary theories and uncertainties of received philosophy with a system for producing notions more conformable to reality. The first stage of the undertaking seemed clear enough. In place of deduction (and crude theories of enumerative induction), Bacon posited the concept of gradatim ascent through axioms, a process of continual transaction between particular and universal, experiment and theory. Language, when properly aligned with science, would put up less resistance, and no longer present an insurmountable problem. The widespread desire to consign verbalism to oblivion immediately faced a problem not easily masked: the creation and testing of axioms would inescapably plunge philosophers back into the realm of language and ideology. If righting (or correcting) error means ontologically grounding knowledge in reality and healing the rift between subject and object, writing error suggests the inevitable reinscription of the very problem philosophers hoped to redress. It implies a commitment to endlessly rethinking and reiterating the linguistic foundations of thought by tracking ideas and words back to their starting points.

Bacon championed one verbal form, aphorism, as a technique for conquering problems of language from within language itself. Resistant ideologies, empty traditions, and theories entrenched in the structure of language would henceforth be challenged through a particular type of verbal construction. Highly conscious of the problems of representation, aphorists could confront the difficulty of reaching a truth sedimented over by layers of history and ideology. The quest for authenticity required reconnecting writing with an origin dwelling outside of language. Through the systematic use of aphorism, outmoded 'truths' would undergo interrogation, eventually fall, and a newly productive method take their place. Aphorists could understand the extreme difficulty of representing truth in language because they laboured to overcome it with every sentence they wrote. Aphorism would proceed by pursuing the origin on its own terrain.

To further the work of dismantling and reconstruction Bacon developed an aphoristic method that sought to heal the breach between origins and their representation. For Bacon, aphorism functions as a critique of philosophical writing and a simultaneous assertion of truth's accessibility to investigators who realize the importance of origins. Bacon's self-conscious appropriation of this particular form, conditioned by the rhetorician's practice of turning to different modes of communication on different occasions, returns us to the question of intellectual authority. The following chapter shifts the centre of our discussion from Bacon's theory of signs to the signs of self-authorization found within his text.

3

Authorizing Aphorism

To resist the incursions of error and false consciousness, Bacon cultivated the aphorism, which he considered preferable to more highly determined prose forms. Just as induction functions as a heuristic, a procedure, or routine, aphorism provides the means for inducing recognition. Consecutively numbered aphorisms attempt to break up thought into particles of experience in the same way Bacon would have us break down syllogisms into words and words into correspondent notions. They are an approximation of ideographs, hieroglyphs, and tabular taxonomies, and subject to similar principles. If individual words are 'symbols of notions,' then words chained syntactically together can function as potentially verifiable symbolic representations of reality. This emphasis on original impression as the basis of thought finds expression in a prose that aspires to renew writing's prelinguistic sources and inscribe literary conventions with a new form of power.

Studies of Bacon's aphorisms often take note of a gap between Bacon's announced theory of the form and his actual practice. Brevity and self-containment are perhaps the two most obvious characteristics of aphorism, but very few of the *Novum Organum*'s aphorisms are either self-contained or pithy. They tend to grow in length as the book develops, and take their place within interlocking groups. Bacon designed his aphoristic style to direct the reader back to the evidence of sensation and to provide an antidote to the 'idols.' Aphorisms are the preferred vehicle of inquiry because they allow no room for imposing order upon experience prematurely, or making potentially erroneous connections. Bacon's stylistic project involves stripping away anything capable of producing error – illustrations, descriptions, artificial connections, verbiage – through a rigorous process of elimination. He develops the aphorism to serve as a conduit through which raw empirical data can pass, barely touched by the mind's generalizing and methodizing tendencies. Bacon's theory of knowledge reduces all mental experience into discrete, concrete impressions, which first imprint themselves directly and singly on consciousness, and then attach themselves, by convention, to corresponding words. This search for a foundational principle on which to base communication gives rise to an ideal of lexical univocacy and envisions syntax as a means for producing eidetically clear speaking-pictures. Bacon cannot, however, abandon sequence and connectedness in his prose any more than he can cut his work adrift from Aristotelian influence or science from ordinary language. His prose style testifies to the inevitability of discursive method and to the efficacy of metaphor and sustained argument. Aphorism functions in his system as an impossible ideal from which we inevitably must fall.

Any study of aphorism must contend with the term's powerful resistance to definition or historical genealogizing. Lexicographers reflect and embody, rather than clarify, the confusion. Since 'aphorism' serves as a term of approbation, definitions tend to inscribe values prevailing at a given moment in time. Theorists of the aphorism have more success defining their subject negatively or prescriptively, saying what it is not or should be, than formulating a normative description. In general, studies of aphorism fall into two patterns. Either they divide aphorism according to discipline, making authors literary, political, philosophical, psychological, or scientific. Or they devise a taxonomy of type based on syntactical and logical features. The first approach views genre from a perspective that projects autonomous and fully formed disciplines onto the early modern period. The second – which takes a variety of methodological shapes, some more sophisticated than others – reveals all the dangers of an enclosed, self-certifying formalism. We could, along with Roland Barthes and other structuralist critics, reject the notion of aphorism as aspiring to a transcendent truth, and see it as a play of forces, a linguistic game that perpetually calls attention to its own significative nature. Yet we lose something important. Almost invariably, aphorists see their work as embodying positive truth in form, not as a hermeneutic meditation on form or the free play of signifiers.[1]

To analyse the value-laden term *aphorism* on the basis of purely formal considerations means ignoring the genre's historical specificity, its ultimate dependence on social and discursive practices. The practice of joining subject and predicate by means of a copula may adequately explain the Heraclitean fragments ('War is the father of us all and our king'), but contributes little to our understanding of Nietzsche ('Under peaceful conditions a warlike man sets upon himself'). As much as certain aphorists might favour one structural option, it means little without reference to the cultural conditions that produce and authorize their utterances. In an intellectual environment where the meaning of universal propositions and the truthfulness of metaphor are philosophically central, equivalent and dyadic structures will flourish. The grammar of the predicative style encourages one sort of interest (sweeping generalizations about human nature, society, knowledge, and so forth), syntactic parallelism another (startling antitheses and comparisons, the proverbial and oracular modes).[2] In the age succeeding Bacon's, the antithetical aphorism came close to driving all other forms before it. In order to achieve the objective of winning universal assent through concision and minute particularity, it hardened into a set manner, succumbing to the limitations of canonical form and thus losing its capacity to speak with an authority readers could experience as genuine. In our own century, aphorism meshes with the objectives of various modernist projects, including surrealism, montage, and the representation of fragmented consciousness. The disappearance of the human subject and the 'withering away of reason' supply other rationales for aphorism. The cultivation of aphorism, *notizen,* and theses by the Frankfurt school, for example, confronts a suspicion that totalized and transcendent critiques merely replicate an already reified world in miniature.[3]

In the sixteenth century the penetration of genre theory by Aristotelian philosophemes produced a thoroughly prescriptivist and essentialist model of aphorism. Erasmus' introduction to the *Adagia* tries to resolve the problem of classification by defining proverb according to genus, *differentia,* and particular characteristic. The consequent definition, 'a saying in popular use, remarkable for some shrewd and novel turn,' soon founders in the network of resemblance among proverb (*paroemia proverbium, adagium*), aphorism (*sententia, gnome*), and apothegm.[4] Erasmus sets aside the interesting question of proverb's association with oral tradition ('popular use'), and the paradox of its combining novelty and conventionality. Instead he embarks on a quest for generic essence. Modern criticism has not yet abandoned this effort, overlooking aphorism's relation to the configuration of expectations generic codes enjoin, and pursuing instead an elusive form or essential difference.

In fact, aphorisms have no fixed formal determinants apart from brevity – in itself a subjective matter – and a tendency, when taken together, to exert a gravitational pull, hence the need to number or otherwise divide them. Aphorists often speak without reservation or hesitation, but do not always shun modifiers and qualifications. Bacon's aphorisms can take the form of carefully weighed, even tentative, judgments. If aphorism constitutes a separate genre, then it is a genre without a recognized canon. Outside of a general consensus on the merit of La Rochefoucauld, the marquis of Halifax, Georg Christoph Lichtenberg, Marquis Vauvenargues, Nietzsche, and possibly Wittgenstein, there is little agreement about what represents mastery of the form. Aphorism is an anti-canonical form, which locates itself on the margins of the literary system and between the boundaries of science and philosophy.[5]

Bacon's theoretical discussions of aphorism pose a threat to scholars who would isolate and privilege either its 'literary' or 'scientific' functions. His famous negative definition of aphorism in the *Advancement of Learning* subordinates formal description to cognitive instrumentality, and calls for the avoidance of closure, or 'knowledge broken,' to challenge an engrossment of learning by method-wielding codifiers: 'Aphorisms, except they should be ridiculous, cannot be made but of the pith and heart of sciences; for discourse of illustration is cut off; recitals of examples are cut off; discourse of connexion and order is cut off; descriptions of practice are cut off; so there remaineth nothing to fill the Aphorisms but some good quantity of observation: and therefore no man can suffice, nor in reason will attempt, to write Aphorisms, but he that is sound and grounded ... Aphorisms, representing a knowledge broken, do invite men to enquire farther; whereas Methods, carrying the shew of a total, do secure men, as if they were at furthest' (3: 405). His approach remains centred on aphorism's affective dimension, on its value as a means for freeing readers from hidebound procedures and opinions. Bacon deems aphorism's unique combination of particularity of thought and multiplicity of purpose superior to error-prone demonstrations or 'methods,' which 'are more fit to win consent or belief, but less fit to point to action.'

Bacon seems undisturbed by the term's elasticity. He represents himself as drawing on a tradition of aphorism writing that embraces Greek poetry, legal maxims, the observations of Hippocrates, Machiavelli's exposition of historical examples, axiom, parable, fable, and Hebrew wisdom literature. Looking at his actual practice, however, we can draw lines of demarcation between aphorism and related forms. Maxims, *sententiae,* and apothegms deliberately retain tokens of their origin in reading and interpretation while aphorisms are usually composed as part of a unitary authorial design.[6] *Sententiae* are, in a very literal way, written by a reader who interprets and collects them. Compiling them places writers in the roles of editor and preservationist, committing them first to the transmission, rather than the production, of meaning. The distinction between aphorism and *sententia* cannot be made hard and fast since a few of Bacon's texts occupy an intermediate stage between the two. For example *De Interpretatione Naturae Sententiae XII* (3: 785-8) follows the general pattern of aphorism – continuously numbered and independent of any obvious source – yet Bacon labels them 'sententiae' and organizes them under interpretive rubrics.

In Bacon's aphorisms theory and practice continually range themselves in oppositional relations, and systematic procedures bend under the weight of his eclecticism. In the preface to the *Maxims of the Law* Bacon writes that 'whereas I could have digested these rules into a certain method or order,' he has avoided that strategy: 'because this delivering of knowledge in distinct and disjoined aphorisms doth leave the wit of man more free to turn and toss, and to make use of that which is so delivered to more several purposes and applications' (7: 321). To authorize his practice Bacon cites the moral and scientific writings of Solomon, Hippocrates, Theognis, as well as legal models such as Justinian's Digest. Yet the text that follows hardly adheres to the systematic program outlined in the preface. The *Maxims of the Law* presents twenty-five Latin headings or *regulae* that receive extended exposition in conventional pedagogical fashion. Bacon cites cases, establishes a chain of reasoning, draws analogies and connections. In analysing Bacon's theory of aphorism we must pay closer attention to the ways it deviates from his stated intention, the fissure between his conscious theoretical positioning and his improvisational practice. Freedom 'to turn and toss,' to resolve how best to make 'application' of detached principles, remains well within the bounds of a traditional education in law and rhetoric and the conventions of methodical orderliness.

The *Advancement*'s discussion of Solomon's proverbs adopts a similar technique of commentary and textual accretion. Again revealing an uncustomary laxity concerning terminological precision, he speaks of the proverbs as 'profound and excellent cautions, precepts, positions,' and as 'sentences politic' (3: 448-52). After selecting several verses, mainly counsels on prudent public conduct, Bacon proceeds to expound them. The subsequent elaboration of these exegeses in *De Augmentis Scientiarum*, under the heading 'doctrina de Occasionibus sparsis,' [doctrine concerning scattered occasions], discloses a movement towards elucidation and enlargement similar to the technique of the *Adagia* (1: 751-68, 5: 37-56). Once Solomon's dicta have been dismembered and decontextualized, they cease being aphorisms and take on new life as 'sentences,' or text reconstituted for editorial commentary.

In the *Apophthegmes New and Old,* a collection of witticisms integrated into short narrative frames, Bacon effaces any obvious trace of his presence from the work beyond its preface (7: 121–65). Although he has selected and shaped the assembled discourses, he willingly subordinates himself to the heterogeneous materials. The work derives some consistency from the fame of the speakers, but makes no attempt to homogenize the plurality of voices. Aphorists, to borrow Mikhail Bakhtin's term, adopt a monological world-view that attempts to contain multiple perspectives that otherwise might break loose from the control of a single authorial consciousness.[7] As much as they goad readers to further thought, aphorisms resist isolation by seeking the coherence that resides in a name or title. This makes them functionally and affectively distinct from what we find in the pages of the florilegia.

The aphorism, as Bacon employs it in the *Novum Organum,* is a text of a certain length that depends for its effect on a larger sense of authorial presence, derived either externally or implied throughout an entire sequence. Like the apothegm, the aphorism offers itself as the distinctive outgrowth of a particular mind and experience, and serves either to confirm or establish a writer's intellectual or social pre-eminence. Aphorism is conditioned by external forces that confer authority upon writers, and pronounce their utterances worthy of study and transmission. Post-structuralist visions of authorless discourse – which proceed from questioning the autonomy of the human subject and displacing the 'author function' to a realm where meanings can proliferate – leave us at a loss for understanding Baconian authority. Michel Foucault denies seeing any advantage in substituting passive constructions ('it was known that') for the standard formula of intellectual history ('X thought that'). Yet his concept of the subject's existence in language sets aside intention and action, stressing instead the ideological articulations of vast impersonal forces. In a 1968 response to a question about the consequences of this critical move, Foucault has a nameless voice respond: '"What does it matter who is speaking; someone has said: what does it matter who is speaking."'[8] The voice within the sentence, the voice of language itself, articulates its indifference to individual speakers.

Aphorisms are not anonymous products of language but an integral part of the authorial name attached to them. They are tokens of a writer's authority and assimilability. This is not to say that the subject readers secure with the name 'Bacon' or 'Verulam' is a monolithic entity whose 'real' existence we can locate prior or exterior to the text. Yet by his use of aphorism Bacon situates his work within a generic system that entails rank and social standing among its means for encoding utterance.[9] Bacon identified aphorism with 'the first and most ancient seekers after truth' (*NO* 1: 86), and offers himself as a source of axiomatic or regulatory knowledge, a new point of origin. With aphorism Bacon adopts a voice that draws attention to its own subjectivity while speaking from heights of external authority. This forms the motive behind the *Instauratio Magna*'s famous heading, at once magisterial and self-effacing: 'Francis of Verulam reasoned thus with himself, and judged it to be for the interest of the present and future generations that they should be made acquainted with his thoughts.' Bacon's shifting identity, his place in a complex network of social relations and kinship bonds, achieves a transitory stability in the dignities and titles attached to his (rather prosaic) English surname. Lord chancellor and Baron Verulam from 1618, Bacon would be created Viscount St Albans in 1621, the same year scandal drove him from his government post.

Authority, as Edward Said reminds us, means not only the capacity to compel obedience but also the power of an *author*, 'that is, a person who originates or gives existence to something, a begetter, beginner, father, or ancestor, a person also who sets forth written statements.' *Authority* signifies a power that initiates, controls, and continues a particular course of action.[10] To understand the status relations that define aphorism, we must attend to the question of 'who is representing?' along with 'what is represented?' The representation of authority in aphorism embodies an ideology of power and privilege. Aphorism serves as a vehicle for the writer engaged in public life. Social standing justifies a form that lacks marks of a professionalized erudition. Aphorism needs no ostentatious show of rhetorical skill to establish its authority. In his translation of the Italian historian Francesco Guicciardini, Sir Robert Dallington connects 'instances' with history, proofs with philosophy, citations with the scholar, and axiom and aphorism with 'bookes of civill discourse.' F.J. Levy has argued that Bacon valued aphorism as a tool of political persuasion, indispensable to the prudent statesman because of its inherent ambiguity. Finding aphorism ideally suited to the objectives of the 1597 *Essayes*, Levy proceeds on the assumption that an outward affinity with Montaigne masks a deeper allegiance to collections of maxims out of Guicciardini and Machiavelli.[11] The *Novum Organum* appeared later, at the zenith of Bacon's career, and intervenes in a different cultural and political situation. By using it in an ostensibly philosophical work Bacon implies a continuity between his scientific studies and political activities. He locates his book at a juncture where disciplines converge and authorship becomes the site of varied social and rhetorical functions.

The aphorisms of the *Novum Organum* are intended to function as points of origin to which we repeatedly return. In theory they provide a more direct and unmediated access to reality than that normally obtainable from ordinary prose. Consider aphorism 3: 'Human knowledge and human power meet in one; for where the cause is not known the effect cannot be produced. Nature to be commanded must be obeyed; and that which in contemplation is as the cause is in operation as the rule.' Here Bacon carefully constructs a set of balanced antitheses, juxtaposing 'knowledge' and 'power,' 'cause' and 'effect,' 'commanded' and 'obeyed,' 'contemplation' and 'operation.' The opening statement strikes us as axiomatic: since readers have experienced the proposition on various levels, they can consult appropriate examples and make the necessary connections. The clause following the semicolon complicates the matter in a self-consciously logical manner, pointing us to causality as the concept most obviously relevant to the problem at hand. Bacon calls our attention to potential applications of his principles, encouraging us to dream of unlimited possibilities for discovery and control. In saying that nature must be obeyed in order to be commanded he partially retracts the most pragmatic applications of his theory and falls back on a paradox with faintly religious overtones: true dominion lies in obedience. To this thought he adds a clarification roughly analogous in form to the second half of the first sentence, portraying the relation between contemplation and action, theory and practice in terms that make them indivisible. One stands in relation to the other as both preliminary first step and inevitable consequence. Without labouring the point – certainly without exploring its full implications – Bacon situates the problematic relation between knowledge and power at the centre of his project, where it surely belongs.

Aphorism 129 stands as a conclusion to the entire first book, prior to a final transitional section. It marks an attempt to dissolve the central contradiction of aphorism 3 by recapitulating, in expanded form, the proposition 'Nature to be commanded must be obeyed.' The aphorism functions to inspire possible co-workers in Bacon's great foundational project, promising them a share of the glory that will proceed from recovering a divinely granted 'right over nature.' Bacon accordingly treats voyages of discovery, technological innovation, colonialism, and his own relation to posterity as continuous fields.

Again, discoveries are as it were new creations, and imitations of God's works; as well sang the poet [Lucretius]: –

'To man's frail race great Athens long ago
First gave the seed whence waving harvests grow,
And *re-created* all our life below.'

And it appears worthy of remark in Solomon, that though mighty in empire and in gold; in the magnificence of his works, his court, his household, and his fleet; in the lustre of his name and the worship of mankind; yet he took none of these to glory in, but pronounced that 'The glory of God is to conceal a thing; the glory of the king to search it out' ...

Again, it is well to observe the force and virtue and consequences of discoveries; and these are to be seen nowhere more conspicuously than in those three which were unknown to the ancients, and of which the origin, though recent, is obscure and inglorious; namely, printing, gunpowder, and the magnet. For these three have changed the whole face and state of things throughout the world; the first in literature, the second in warfare, the third in navigation; whence have followed innumerable changes; insomuch that no empire, no sect, no star seems to have exerted greater power and influence in human affairs than these mechanical discoveries.

Further, it will not be amiss to distinguish the three kinds and as it were grades of ambition in mankind. The first is of those who desire to extend their own power in their native country; which kind is vulgar and degenerate. The second is of those who labour to extend the power of their country and its dominion among men. This certainly has more dignity, though not less covetousness. But if a man endeavour to establish and extend the power and dominion of the human race itself over the universe, his ambition (if ambition it can be called) is without doubt both a more wholesome thing and a more noble than the other two. Now the empire of man over things depends wholly on the arts and sciences. For we cannot command nature except by obeying her.

Again, if men have thought so much of some one particular discovery as to regard him as more than man who has been able by some benefit to make the whole human race his debtor, how much higher a thing to discover that by means of which all things else shall be discovered with ease! And yet (to speak the whole truth), as the uses of light are infinite, in enabling us to walk, to ply our arts, to read, to recognise one another; and nevertheless the very beholding of the light is itself a more excellent and a fairer thing than all the uses of it; – so assuredly the very contemplation of things, as they are, without superstition or imposture, error or confusion, is in itself more worthy than all the fruit of inventions.

The aphorism elaborately subordinates point after point in a logico-temporal sequence of coordinate conjunctions and adverbs that link together its paragraphs. In order to understand precisely how its tangled web of statement, restatement, and counter-statement develops, we must move to the aphorisms preceding it and the one following. Bacon's Latin prose deftly coordinates para- and hypotactic structures so as to embed detachable sententious elements in the schematics of the entire aphorism. The summary proposition 'For we cannot command nature except by obeying her' enacts the principle of syntactic incorporation through recurrence and grammatical conjunction.[12] Bacon re-establishes the unity of his concerns by his identification with various exemplary figures (Epicurus, Solomon, Columbus) whose excellence emanates from an intellectual labour clearly distinguished from passive contemplation and reading. Having himself broken the artificial barrier between knowledge and power, Bacon can reflect on his relation to his readers, whose assent and admiration he now commands.

Since their inception Bacon's aphorisms on knowledge and power have accumulated a substantial body of commentary. There are of course the responses of those who applaud Bacon for his Promethean revolt against limits, and see in the principle a call for the rational ordering of our environment in order to bring about freedom from scarcity and want. Read in this way, the Baconian conquest of nature anticipates the ideal of moving humanity out of the realm of necessity. To others, however, the principle appears to put rationality at the service of the will to power and to signal the onset of a dualism that objectifies and finally degrades nature. Max Horkheimer and Theodor Adorno's *Dialectic of Enlightenment* finds implicit in Bacon's project the roots of a drive to subjugate nature and humanity through a program of rationalization. Bacon bears the blame for initiating Enlightenment 'disenchantment of the world' and the increasingly authoritarian and bureaucratic tendencies of modern life. Bacon's aphorisms on nature thus become prophetic of twentieth-century instrumentalism, of the complicity between science and political domination: 'The concordance between the mind of man and the nature of things that he had in mind is patriarchal: the human mind, which overcomes superstition, is to hold sway over a disenchanted nature. Knowledge, which is power, knows no obstacles: neither in the enslavement of men nor in compliance with the world's rulers.' Because Bacon appears to welcome the consequences of a scientific assault on nature, the *Novum Organum*'s doctrine of aphoristic propagation is taken at its word, and its author apportioned blame for the future course of science in the West. Similar remarks in Descartes and other seventeenth-century writers excite less disapproval because they appear abstracted from the technological and political implications of their vision.[13]

In equating knowledge with power Bacon does not mean that science will necessarily produce useful technological innovations or that the learned can derive concrete advantages from their hard-won skills. Rather he sees power and knowledge as interrelated and mutually productive forces, and scientific learning as the fruit of specific institutional arrangements. Bacon still finds sympathy for declaring war on outmoded intellectual systems but comes under fire for paving the way for a destructive and oppressive technocracy, and for promoting the subjugation of a feminized nature. Bacon's pursuit of dominion over nature arises from a desire to perform heroic service, to bring humanity out from the labyrinth of language into a community of vastly improved communication and cooperation. The three inventions of 'obscure and inglorious' origin – printing, gunpowder, and the sailor's compass – had all migrated to the West from China between the thirteenth and the fifteenth centuries, and had been grouped together by Cardan and others well before Bacon. This traditional triumvirate symbolizes the benefits of collaborative and cumulative 'mechanical' work, even over national boundaries. The inclusion of gunpowder should alert us to technology's potential destructiveness, its role in territorial and religious disputes.

If the reference to gunpowder suggests some degree of ambivalence, Bacon would not have acknowledged it. In the fragmentary *Valerius Terminus* he defends his project of empowerment by citing I Corinthians on 'the tongues of men and angels.' Bacon identifies himself with St Paul's disavowal of 'both power and knowledge such as is not dedicated to goodness or love,' and argues that knowledge should serve the Utopian goal of recovering linguistic and material conditions lost with Eden (3: 222). He makes a similar case for scientific altruism and innocence in the concluding sentences of aphorism 129: 'Only let the human race recover that right over nature which belongs to it by divine bequest, and let power be given it; the exercise thereof will be governed by sound reason and true religion.' Bacon's (apparently misplaced) confidence in humanity's capacity to manipulate science to its advantage arises from a perspective in which technological autonomy is literally unthinkable. The expansion of knowledge cannot help but serve human interests since knowledge of things 'as they are' puts us beyond the reach of superstition, error, and confusion.

Bacon takes the position that in order to make measurable progress we must replace endlessly self-referential disputation based on the scholastic model with measurably productive doubt. Aphorism's urgent invitation to inquiry agrees perfectly with the methodological program that animates the *Novum Organum*. By displacing the burden of interpretation onto the reader yet retaining a sense of authorial control, aphorisms encourage a continuing quest for knowledge. To borrow Bacon's imagery – or Lucretius' description of the dissemination of Epicureanism, quoted in aphorism 129 – they are seeds implanted in the minds of contemporaries to exfoliate in future generations. Bacon excuses the inconclusiveness and defects of his writing by presenting himself as a pioneering guide, the completion of whose work remains to successors. His aphorisms are not intended as *aperçus* or epiphanic insights but as a call to action.[14] Their generative and interactive powers affirm the perlocutionary force attaching to utterance, or language's capacity to produce discernible effects.

Bacon formulates an ideal of attaining knowledge through self-doubt, constant vigilance, and the expectation of future revision. Since aphorism does not seek an authority outside of its own experience or strain for comprehensiveness, it provides the means for detaching language from unproductive modes of philosophical analysis. Although Bacon regards the replacement of one methodological paradigm by another as an agonistic encounter, he opposes any system that claims totality. Such theories, he believes, remain persuasive only in so far as they stand apart from and perpetually preliminary to practice. To free us from the tyranny of self-enclosed systems he attempts the impossible: devising a theory that shuns the theoretical, a method that reluctantly methodizes, a rhetoric that throws off the shackles of convention, and a form that transcends the constraints of form. Aphorism affirms the authority of the unified subject by expanding the traditional limits of rationality, permeating the boundaries between different discourses, and demonstrating the unity of the particularistic and universal, the private and the public.

Many eighteenth- and nineteenth-century critiques of Bacon operate on the assumption that he failed in his chosen endeavour because he squandered intellectual energy pursuing politicized goals. Involvement in public life, his critics assume, dissipates the single-minded concentration necessary to a philosophical career. Those who consider philosophy an autonomous domain have trouble comprehending Bacon's desire to institutionalize the production of knowledge and reform of institutions. In so far as Bacon involved himself in the mobilization of political and material resources for the benefit of learning, they saw his project as hopelessly compromised from the outset. David Hume appraises Bacon as someone who comes off better when considered 'as a public speaker, a man of business, a wit, a courtier, a companion, an author, a philosopher,' than 'merely as an author and philosopher.' Ludwig Feuerbach, in his *History of Modern Philosophy from Bacon to Spinoza* (1833), depicts Bacon as too much enmired in public life and lacking the 'unity of spirit' that could have moved his thought beyond eclectic amateurism. Lord Macaulay's famous essay on Bacon takes the argument one step further and divulges an apparent fissure in Bacon's psyche to explain his riven career and writings. While Macaulay considers the enormous range of Bacon's achievements grounds for admiration, he regrets to see such talents and intellect 'unworthily employed.' The moral of his biographical sketch comes down to this: if Bacon had turned his back on ambition and self-advancement he would not have descended to posterity as a seller of justice.[15] We can say rather that if Bacon had curtailed his ambition and given himself over entirely to a single pursuit, it would have placed restrictions on his ability to forge conceptual links and understand the place of language in culture, and of method in the human sciences.

While later readers repeatedly try to divorce Bacon the philosopher from Bacon the public official, his contemporaries and immediate successors dissolved such disjunctures of authorship in the overarching idea of authority that unified his career. An early editor, Thomas Tenison, implies that an absence of specialized training encouraged Bacon's capacity to penetrate 'the mists of Authority,' and enabled an order of accomplishment far greater than that accorded those devoted exclusively to science. Tenison marvels 'that in such a Life as his, so thickly set with Business of such Height, it is a Miracle that all Seeds of Philosophy were not daily overdropped, and in a short time, quite choaked; and that any one of them sprung up to Maturity. And yet his prosper'd beyond those of the Philosophers before-mentioned [Copernicus, Galileo, Harvey, Gilbert], though they were not pressed on with such a crowd of secular Business.' Rhetorical, forensic, and literary abilities coalesce with rank to make the polymathic lord chancellor a commanding, if somewhat chilling, figure. Looking back towards Bacon and his age, Henry Oldenburg expresses the amazement of a society beginning to undergo the professionalization of letters:

It cannot be doubted, but that *England* had then better knowledge of the abstrusities, many troubles and burthens of our Municipal Laws, and Chancery, which lay long and much upon his shoulders; And that he bore the stress of State affairs in almost all King *James's* days, and in Queen *Elizabeth's* later days; That he adorned the solemn Addresses, and was the Extra-Ordinary Pen-man for most

Apologies, Deliberations, and gravest Adviso's in Parliaments, and otherwise: Here they saw also, how he excelled in the best Theology of that Age, and in the Politest of Civil and Moral Essays: And therefore here they might justly wonder, how a person so publickly immersed in all Civil Interests should find leisure to do any thing at all in *Philosophy*.[16]

Oldenburg magnifies Bacon's cultural and literary authority ('here they might justly wonder') in the same breath as he devalues Bacon's work in natural philosophy ('a person so publickly immersed in all Civil Interests'). Tenison and Oldenburg consider Bacon perfectly suited to the role of elite spokesmanship. Bacon's capacity to operate across disciplinary fields imparts unusual force to his analysis. His intellectual scope not only compensates for his blind spots as a philosopher but becomes productive of his entire angle of vision. He brings to philosophy a perspective rendered especially valuable by a refusal to insulate theory from wider cultural and political trends, and a self-groundedness that confers authority in various fields.

In this chapter I have resisted treating Bacon as a culturally determined embodiment of structure, as a historical placeholder who is spoken by discourses. I have retained the model of an author who actively forged meanings out of the heterogeneous materials available to him, whose productive power his contemporaries acknowledged, celebrated, or belittled. This study has chosen Bacon as one possible beginning among many, and the choice is not entirely arbitrary. Behind the clichéd picture of Bacon as 'first philosopher of the modern age' is a writer whose work indeed prefigures subsequent developments and encourages refutation and multiple re-engagements. This is a view promulgated by Bacon himself and by his seventeenth-century admirers, who found in his work a blank page on which to inscribe their own rebellions against dominant paradigms and worn-out beliefs.

The presence of 'Bacon' as a self-constituting author located at a decisive and heroic beginning has implications for Baconianism as both style and scientific praxis. The discursive system that produced Baconianism (and that Baconianism produced) had need of an indisputable source to ensure its future reproduction. Stylistic reform and acknowledgment of Bacon's role as the scientific movement's primary theorist would form part of the institutionalized discourse of the Royal Society.

4

Legitimation and the Origin of Restoration Science

As we have seen from twentieth-century responses to the aphorisms discussed in chapter 3, Bacon's writings retain a surprising capacity to polarize opinion. Readers either sing Bacon's praises as a hero of progress and rational enquiry or make him personally responsible for the ills besetting humanity. In our time outright hostility has ceded ground to indifference and neglect: the absence of any twentieth-century complete edition of his writings testifies to his low status among philosophers and literary critics. William Harvey's famous remark to John Aubrey that Bacon 'writes philosophy like a Lord Chancellor' anticipates the modern dismissal of Bacon as rhetorically adept but scientifically negligible, a thinker whose Olympian detachment hinders his pursuit of 'real' science.

Paolo Rossi notes that 'glorifications and denigrations continuously alternate in the history of Baconism and of Bacon's fortunes.'[1] What Bacon's glorifiers (and many of his denigrators) share in common is an assumption about his originative role in the epochal shift to modernity. Although Bacon sometimes represents his ideas as 'the offspring of time' and himself as the public figure through whom the age spoke itself, he also describes his work as a new beginning from a historical degree zero. Later generations have taken up this latter claim, seeing him as a 'founder' (or 'father' or 'prophet' or 'forerunner') of various movements, including scientific positivism (G.H. Lewes), utilitarianism (Macaulay), Enlightenment atheism (de Maistre), and the 'pragmatic conception of knowledge' (Dewey). When Bacon still wins praise, as he still occasionally does, it is usually for bringing conflicting views of language to productive *aporiai*, or for initiating a radical new beginning that marks the 'birth' of the modern.[2] The search for legitimating genealogies continues to lead back to Bacon in part because Bacon offered himself as a cultural prototype, an Adam reinvented, or symbolic progenitor of futurity.

By the Restoration, Bacon's admirers had secured for him a prominent niche in the British intellectual pantheon. To fulfil their own ambitions for science they had to mythologize his accomplishments and make the issue of his cultural authority ever more explicit, even as they found themselves increasingly unwilling or unable to defer to it. Rather than situate the origin of their praxis in a shared, trans-European culture, they assigned to Bacon an originary function that his writings could hardly bear. Bacon had excused the inconclusiveness of his work by presenting himself as a pioneering guide, the completion of whose 'instauration' remains to later generations. The myth of Bacon borrows his rhetoric of primordial recovery, and endorses his fantasy of carting away the rubbish of tradition to install a method of absolute objectivity. Bacon had portrayed himself as the forerunner of a widely diffused scientific practice, *buccinator* or herald of the new philosophy, the layer of a philosophical 'foundation,' a sower of seeds 'for future ages,' and spiritual father to the 'true sons of knowledge' (1: 579; *NO* 1: 38, 116, preface). After 1660, when his impact on English culture reaches a peak, the myth of Bacon comes to underwrite a Restoration myth of Charles's return as a providential reimposition of order and justice.[3] Bacon's representation of his work as both cornerstone and embryonic beginning paves the way for his later canonization as the only begetter of English science.

The process whereby Bacon, the iconoclastic demolisher of false idols, becomes an idolized progenitor of Restoration science, took several decades to set in. By about 1667 we find an almost universal acceptance of his originary role in the rise of science, often expressed through his own metaphors of engendering and birth. Writers claimed that Bacon had done for philosophy in general what he desired for himself: liberated knowledge from the past and reconstituted the mind as a *tabula abrasa,* 'a fair sheet of paper with no writing on it' (*GI* Plan). My aim in this chapter, in charting the process of Bacon's apotheosis and installation as a motivating force in English culture, is not to amplify the range of Baconian intertextuality or demonstrate the tremendous prestige his name carried throughout Europe.[4] Instead I hope further to situate my reading of the *Novum Organum* within historical parameters, and show that 'Baconianism' is not so much a philosophy, personality cult, or methodology as it is a dialectical process of production and reception between author and readers.

The early dissemination of Baconian ideals was a deliberate program that left indelible marks on our own understanding of his work. Since

'Bacon' remained susceptible to radical revision, his conservative defenders hastened to offer assurances that Baconianism would not depose the cultural authority of established institutions. Within the culture of late seventeenth-century England, Bacon stood as a 'seminal' thinker whose writings propagated a new methodology and whose 'originality' remained incontestable. Bacon's vision of Salomon's house stands as the imaginary prototype of the Royal Society, the foundation of a new collaborative order. As work on the beginnings of the Royal Society has shown, Baconianism contributed importantly to the legitimation of early English science, projecting an image of neutrality and enabling the Society 'to establish its work against rivals and opponents as true and useful and, equally important, free from ideological bias.'[5] Part of this process involves the transformation of Bacon's imagery of disowning the past and generational succession into a less contestatory model of collaboration, progress, and renewal.

Bacon's contribution to early-modern science seems written around a recurrent plot, an origin tale of dazzling genesis. The counterplot of his false claim to priority has its roots in the same network of assumptions. Our understanding of Bacon continues to operate within parameters established by Restoration scientists who, anxious to legitimize their work, cast recent history in the form of a narrative tracing back to a privileged beginning. Although multiple interpretations of Bacon have obtained, a palimpsestic quality clings to Bacon scholarship, a tendency to reinscribe variant readings within a single template. The continuing history of Baconianism reveals how one line of interpretation can endure even after its primary social function has become obsolete. We can revise our institutionalized understanding of Bacon only if we bring this reading to the threshold of critical self-consciousness and make ourselves aware of earlier phases in the production of meaning.

Literary critics who focus on actual readers (as opposed to ideal, implied, or encoded readers) attempt to register the gap between past and present modes of understanding and to shift the emphasis to texts as critical constructions. They perceive a difficulty, however, in outlining a method capable of rendering the past visible without projecting subsequent cultural inscriptions onto it. Hans Robert Jauss speaks of literature as an event mediated in a 'horizon of expectations,' and of historically constituted readerships that bring complex but identifiable sets of conventions to interpretation. In seeking to move beyond a materialist view of literature as production, Jauss posits a dialogical model of interaction and reappropriation, one that moves us across history and through a succession of interpretive acts. Jauss's approach to historical understanding requires that we study texts through a series of highly complex mediations, beginning at their inception; it also reminds us that although textual traces of historical meaning remain recoverable, we cannot experience a text as its original readers did.[6] Although Jauss finally cannot explain why we should accept the authority of tradition-bound 'preunderstandings,' or how we can transcend our historicity to avoid reconfiguring the past in our own image, he does demonstrate the importance of studying a work's historical reception. Bacon provides an example of how the reinterpretation of canonical texts and their authors also can serve the interest of self-authorization.

With some justification, Jauss critiques Marxist and other sociological methodologies for operating within a 'closed circle' of production and representation, for either ignoring the reader altogether or embracing a reflection theory that neglects literature's socially formative function – its capacity to modify conditions present at its first creation. In Pierre Macherey's account of the forces surrounding literary production, however, we find an argument for regarding textual production, transmission, and consumption as mutually sustaining facets of a single complex structure. Although Macherey posits a continuity between conditions determining a book's production and its communication, he also argues against substituting a single field of determinations – the work itself, an autonomous creator, the conventions of reading, and so on – for circulations among text, ideology, and history. For Macherey, the representation of ideology in literature embeds a text in contradictions and disruptions that must be brought to the surface.[7] Ideological reflexes played a key role in the intellectual and social processes that constituted the Restoration interpretation of Bacon. We can best disclose their operations by examining the interests of those who invoked his name while asserting their own legitimacy.

We need not look very far to see how ideas of genesis, reproduction, and paternal authority shaped Bacon's career. As early as the *Temporis Partus Masculus* (1602–3?), he had assumed the stance of a loving father addressing an attentive 'son,' adopting the rhetorical strategy he calls 'magistral' in order to propagate knowledge among the already indoctrinated (4: 449). Assuming an almost priestly tone, Bacon leads an assault on philosophic tradition as a great debaucher of youth while offering himself as the incarnation of the father's will. Feminist criticism of Bacon has exposed an ideological strain in the Baconian struggle to realize paternity and achieve mastery over nature. Critics have argued that the scientific ideal first takes shape in a climate of sexual assault and as part of a program of patriarchal exploitation. Bacon's favoured metaphors for describing science's relation to Nature seem to depict a seduction-rape. The scientist must 'hound,' 'lead,' 'drive,' 'conquer,' and 'subdue' the recalcitrant object. Susan Bordo finds in Bacon's 'flight from the feminine' a psychocultural explanation for the insistence on 'objectivity' and 'masculinity' that characterizes both Cartesian rationalism and Baconian empiricism. Londa Schiebinger sees in 'the masculine allegory' of Bacon and his Royal Society followers an attack on the continental iconology of a feminine Scientia, and remnants of Aristotle's gendered polarities of active spirit (*pneuma*) and sluggish feminine matter (*hyle*).[8]

Along with this imagery of ravishment and penetration we find the language of marriage, insemination, and reproduction. Monogamous generativity and plodding conjugality are typically Baconian expressions of the scientist's relation to nature. In the *Instauratio Magna* Bacon claims to 'have established for ever a true and lawful marriage between the empirical and the rational faculty, the unkind and ill-starred divorce and separation of which has thrown into confusion all the affairs of the human family.' He considers his program 'as the strewing and decoration of the bridal chamber of the Mind and the Universe, the Divine Goodness assisting; out of which marriage let us hope (and be this the prayer of the bridal song) there may spring helps to man, and a line and race of inventions that may in some degree subdue and overcome the necessities and miseries of humanity.' Bacon proposes to unite our minds 'with *things themselves* in a chaste, holy, and legal wedlock,' a union from which will spring 'a blessed race of Heroes or Supermen' capable of ameliorating the human condition. In stressing the necessity of interrogating and reconstructing tradition, Bacon expresses his belief that 'there is no hope except in a new birth of science; that is, in raising it regularly up from experience and building it afresh; which no one (I think) will say has yet been done or thought of.' The language of parturition figures prominently in the two works addressed to the 'sons' of science, in which Bacon suggests a contrast between the new and fruitful Scientia, a dutiful wife, and the old Metaphysica, a courtesan possessed of meretricious charm: 'Possess Lais but do not let her possess you,' he counsels, alluding to a remark of Aristippus about his affair with a courtesan, reported by Diogenes Laertius. Bacon's ideal of promulgating a masculine philosophy suggests a distinction between socially (re)productive activities and the 'merely' pleasurable. We aspire to truth because it instils an incomparable sense of mastery. Yet a purely speculative hermeneutic, or 'barren knowledge,' can never satisfy this longing: 'knowledge that tendeth but to satisfaction is but as a courtesan, which is for pleasure and not for fruit or generation.'[9] In this network of gendered imagery, male domination becomes intertwined with the symbolic reproduction of science's institutional apparatus of discovery.

In the earlier seventeenth century, the engendering of Baconian science proceeded without recourse to violent or coercive imagery. In a 1620 poem commending the *Novum Organum*, George Herbert revises the familiar image of truth as Time's daughter and applies it to Bacon the 'grandson of time / From Mother Truth.' Herbert's depiction of Bacon in terms of filial dependence, rather than paternal authority, takes a turn after Bacon's death. Thomas Randolph's elegy on Bacon eulogizes him for possessing a generative power greater than the ancients: 'Infantes illi Musas, hic gignit adultas; / Mortales illi, gignit at iste Deas' [They engendered infant Muses, he adult; they, mortal, but he brought forth goddesses]. In this version, Bacon combines the rejuvenative powers of Aeson, who regained his youth in old age, with the perpetual renewal of the resurrected phoenix. Randolph depicts Bacon as a self-generating figure who gives birth to the instauration through a kind of parthenogenesis. Then, perhaps remembering that Bacon in the dedication to *De Sapientia Veterum* had addressed Cambridge as his 'nursing-mother,' Randolph transforms him (in a Virgilian phrase) into a child suckling at the breast of his Alma Mater: 'Sed cum Granta labris admoverit ubera tantis, / Jus habet in laudes (maxime Alumne) tuas' [But since Granta gave suck to someone so eminent, she has a right, distinguished offspring, to your praise].[10] The elegy combines the language of patriarchal generativity with images of birth and infancy.

Although the imagery of childlike receptivity and restored innocence never drops entirely out of sight, in the years between his death and the Restoration Bacon appears more often as a figure of authority, an autonomous and self-creating architect of modernity. Bacon brought to England a cultural prestige that challenged Greek primacy in philosophy and Roman domination of eloquence. In *Timber: or, Discoveries* – a title that obliquely alludes to Bacon's *Sylva Sylvarum* – Ben Jonson commends Bacon's oratory and praises his performance in prose as worthy to rival 'insolent *Greece*, or haughty *Rome*.' By naturalizing philosophy, by teaching it to speak English, Bacon inaugurates England's coming-of-age as a great intellectual power. He assumes the role of 'our' noble and learned Lord Verulam. As Charles Webster reminds us, religious reformers found Bacon's emphasis on 'the ideological obstacles' that impeded the transformation of society especially useful. Yet the trope of Baconian mastery takes an authoritarian turn by the 1660s. Henry Power, an early member of the Royal Society, buttresses a point by quoting 'that Patriark of Experimental Philosophy, the learned Lord *Bacon*.' Emphasis falls increasingly on Bacon's originative position. He becomes a prototype or pattern of the scientist. After the Restoration Bacon's royalism and orthodoxy are brought to the fore in order to serve the ideological needs of writers anxious to lay to rest anxiety over the taint of atheism and radical scepticism. When in 1661 Thomas Forde compares Bacon favourably to Cicero and Seneca, he completes the process of canonization by half-jocularly pronouncing Bacon 'that great *Dictator* of Learning.' Bacon begins to look more and more like the authoritarian figures he had hoped to displace, and thus susceptible to his own critique of blind obedience to authority.[11]

If Bacon's disgrace and fall from power tarnished his reputation towards the end of his life, the less creditable biographical episodes soon became subordinated to his writings. Yet not until the Restoration did Bacon become an effigy, the remote pantheonic figure he remained until well into the nineteenth century. If some of the allusions to Bacon in the 1640s and 1650s adopt a mildly critical tone, most appear intimately familiar with his writings. Lord Brooke quarrels with the Utopian speculation in the *Republic* and *New Atlantis*, but bows to Baconian authority even when he cites *De Augmentis Scientiarum* against its author: 'All this while I doe not reject an industrious search after wisedom ... I doe only, with Sir *Francis Bacon*, condemne *doctrinam phantasticam, litigiosam, fucatam, & mollem*; a nice, unnecessary, prying into those things which profit not.' Bacon figures as a source of fertile speculation and elegant Latinity who was read deferentially, but with little trace of adulation. Sir Thomas Browne's *Pseudodoxia Epidemica* (1646) echoes the *Advancement* and borrows its general structure. Bacon's amanuensis, William Rawley, accurately summarizes the state of Bacon's reputation in the 1650s as more firmly established on the Continent than at home, but 'great in his own nation also, especially amongst those that are of a more acute and sharper judgment.'[12] His philosophy did not lie fallow over these decades.

The only sustained anti-Baconianism before 1670 arises from defenders of the Aristotelian-scholastic tradition, who find it bitterly ironic that Bacon's admirers paid tribute to him (in John Wilkins' phrase) as 'our English *Aristotle*,' or (in George Herbert's) as 'champion over / The herculean Stagirite.' (Indeed, by referring in the title of the *Novum Organum* to the Aristotelian canon of logical treatises, 'the organon,' Bacon had already conferred the honour upon himself.) Alexander Ross's criticism of the new philosophy records dismay over the dethronement of classical antiquity and installation of Bacon in its place. Ross's *The New Planet No Planet* (1646) responds to Wilkins' *A Discourse Concerning a New World* (1640) by directly confronting the post-Baconian imagery of paternity and redemptive innovation. Where Wilkins blandly reiterated the Baconian doctrines that in non-theological learning "tis we are the Fathers, and of more Authority than former Ages ... and Truth (wee say) is the Daughter of Time,' Ross retorts by invoking the antithetical Baconian principle of time as a river: 'but indeed you are not the fathers of learning, you are onely fathers of your new discoveries and fresh experiments; that is, of new, fond, and savourlesse phansies: and why you must be of more authority then former ages, I see no reason ... You say, *Truth is the daughter of time*; so say I, but errors, heresies, falsehoods, are times daughters too. We see how fruitfull this later age of the world is of new and frivolous opinions.'

Ross's basic strategy in crusading against the new philosophy is to find in the substrate of figuration on which Bacon erected his instauration evidence of a degradation of authority conducing to the subversion of order. Bacon's dismissal of Aristotelian tradition as mostly sophistry and delusion produced precisely the right formula to gall Ross, who thought he saw the real revolution Baconianism portended. In his *Arcana Microcosmi* Ross denounces Bacon, Browne, and others for perverse anti-Aristotelianism, an infatuation with originality, and a relentless pursuit of novelty that masks a reversion to ignorance. In the dedicatory epistle Ross claims that 'modern Innovators' create straw men out of ancient theories by deliberately misinterpreting them. Ross would have us maintain a position of childish subordination and deference in respect to their authority: 'we are but children in understanding, and ought to be directed by those Fathers of Knowledge.' Later Ross berates the proponents of 'our new Philosophy, or rather old pseudosophy' for their difficulty and obscurantism and for attempting to revive 'old obsolete and rejected errors, raked out again from under their ashes, where they have lain buried many years.' He refutes Bacon by troping on Baconian metaphors, portraying, for example, the 'new way for the understanding' as a cul de sac and the *Sylva Sylvarum* an enchanted forest where 'a young Scholar may quickly lose himselfe, and shal encounter with many bryers and brambles.'[13]

The practice of turning to Bacon's writing for a resonant phrase or dignified precedent gained steady momentum throughout the middle decades of the century, a period that produced highly favourable conditions for the dissemination of Bacon's texts. Bacon and his admirers (*pace* Ross) hardly formed a unified front, especially in matters of religion. Both royalists and radicals portrayed their encounter with Bacon as a type of liberation, yet took from him only those ideas they were predisposed to receive, ideas that were already theirs. Baconianism only became an official ideology after its orthodoxy and harmlessness had been demonstrated by followers with unimpeachable credentials. This nomination of Bacon as official precursor owes as much to sociopolitical factors as to a sense of indebtedness.

The turn towards scientific objectivism after 1660 formed part of a coordinated strategy to regulate involvement in public affairs and to defuse the threat of a resurgent radicalism. Since little could diminish Bacon's prestige or tarnish his reputation, the early supporters of the Royal Society moved to define Bacon according to their own program, transforming him into the prophetic father of royally sanctioned science. In a letter to John Evelyn, John Beale pointed out Bacon's potential use as part of a coordinated promotional strategy: 'our way to support our owne Enterprise is to devise all wayes to revive Lord Bacons lustre.' Robert Boyle similarly used Bacon to legitimate the Society's foundational project, arguing that systematic reflection on the idols would permanently contribute to the task of dispelling ignorance. In his *Discourse of Things above Reason*, Boyle suggests, as we have seen, that the rational capacity remains capable of objectively evaluating its own performance and of permanently demystifying mental processes. When Boyle and other latitudinarian opponents of radical republicanism attributed this kind of objectivism to Bacon, they well understood its value in reproducing a unified social formation.[14]

Thomas Sprat's *History of the Royal Society* (1667) constitutes itself as the very voice and presence of this new order, a carefully calibrated collection of position papers written with an eye towards favourably influencing public opinion. Since Bacon's writings easily accommodated radical revision, post-revolutionary defenders such as Sprat hasten to assure us that Baconianism would not depose the cultural authority of established institutions. While older studies took at face value Sprat's portrayal of Bacon as the 'one great Man, who had the true Imagination of the whole extent of this Enterprize, as it is now set on foot,' recent work has underscored the apologetic functions such official Baconianism served, how it helped to stifle criticism and smooth over heterogeneous interests among a diverse membership. P.B. Wood has provided perhaps the most detailed account of Sprat's work as a systematic apologia for established interests. Wood argues that the political climate of the Restoration settlement provoked widespread disaffection and renewed concern about the atheistic and materialist implications of the new science. Institutional support was slow to materialize in part because the Society's activities were viewed with hostility or derision by commercial interests and segments of the church. Sprat depicts the Royal Society as a natural ally of the Established Church, a force dedicated to preserving social stability and enlarging national prosperity. By portraying Baconianism as immediately relevant to the political and ecclesiastical problems England faced in the early 1660s, Sprat's stylistically polished book offset the subversive implications of experimental science.[15] Empiricism served as a bulwark against radicalism and political instability, and energized an ideology that sought to integrate religion, science, and politics into a unified cultural field.

Sprat kidnaps Bacon to lend credibility to the Society's insistence on remaining innocent of large generalities and experimental 'anticipations,' depicting him – in implicit contrast to Descartes, Gassendi, and Hobbes – as anti-theoretical. Throughout the 1660s, as Steven Shapin and Simon Schaffer show in their *Leviathan and the Air-Pump*, English promoters of new science found it imperative to dissociate their work from 'dogmatic' Hobbesianism.[16] Their program for institutionalizing science involved mobilizing assent through appeals to 'matters of fact' and a rhetorical practice designed to simulate the consensual nature of experimental knowledge. While disagreement over non-foundational knowledge remained tolerable, they hoped to maintain a high level of social solidarity within the experimental community. To this end they rigorously policed the boundaries of dissent by ruling out disputes over 'facts' or the method by which facts were obtained. Boyle and his associates addressed the problem – made increasingly pressing by the repressive conditions of the Restoration settlement – of securing voluntary assent without relying on more blatant forms of coercion or disturbing the public peace.

Perhaps the most overt expression of the institutional role of Baconianism in relation to the early Royal Society is Abraham Cowley's commendatory poem prefixed to the *History*. Cowley's ode 'To the Royal Society' portrays Bacon as a type of epic forefather whose heroism resides in his willingness to demythologize scholasticism and assume a prophetic role. Since Cowley appears to have conceived the poem as a supplement to and commentary on his friend Sprat's work, we must read the two in conjunction. In a letter dated 13 May 1667, Cowley told John Evelyn that he had seen 'some part' of Sprat's effort and thought Evelyn would be 'very well satisfied with it.'[17] Cowley's prefatory verses reinforce Sprat's attribution of Baconian influence, presenting the lord chancellor as the *fons et origo* of everything expected to proceed from the institution. To forestall controversy about science as a breeding ground for heresy, Cowley gives extended treatment to Bacon's dependence upon tradition. He portrays Bacon's exegesis of the book of nature as entirely compatible with piety, and makes his decisive break and renewal consonant with the protestant rebellion against papal domination. In the poem, submission to authority becomes a form of subjugation likened to the dependencies of childhood. Bacon heroically liberates himself and his successors from their influence without usurping their authoritarian role.

Cowley's ode invokes the nascent ideology of Baconianism to resolve the contradictions that shaped the early Royal Society and aspects of his own career. Cowley's loyalty, as Sprat acknowledges in his 'Life' of Cowley, had fallen under suspicion because of remarks included in the preface to his 1656 *Poems*. There Cowley rationalized his suppression of an epic poem celebrating the civil war, and offered a revealing justification for writing it in the first place: 'in all *Civil Dissentions*, when they break into open hostilities, the *War* of the *Pen* is allowed to accompany that of the *Sword*, and every one is in a manner obliged with his *Tongue*, as well as *Hand*, to serve and assist the side which he engages in.'[18] Cowley's poem invests the Society with the dignity of a politically reliable precursor, to whom, however, the future owes a limited debt. Although Bacon initially appears as a virile supplanter of the old order, eventually he is relegated to the place of a venerated elder whose mantle must pass to the present generation. Cowley finally rebels against the notion of the one great man who commands all learning, and redistributes the project in the hands of the Society. His show of deference becomes an act of self-credentializing, a necessary preliminary to portraying the Royal Society as undeserving of the opprobrium heaped upon it, the sole legitimate heir to Bacon's patrimony, and the only scientific 'body' capable of surpassing his accomplishments.

The first two stanzas of the poem allegorize the figure of philosophy as an aging eldest son kept from his inheritance by unscrupulous tutors. Either through negligence or ambition they refuse to relinquish their guardianship, 'Or his own Natural Powers to let him see, / Lest that should put an end to their Autoritie.' The language of primogeniture and property transaction fuses with the familiar catchwords and concerns of Baconian science. Cowley moves quickly to vindicate the pretensions of the new philosophy by clearing it of the old charge of satanic aspiration, making it the legitimate heir of 'all that Human Knowledge which has bin / Unforfeited by Mans rebellious Sin.' Cowley understands that his allegory contradicts the authority of traditional iconography and parenthetically counters possible objections about his re-gendered *sophia*: '(Philosophy, I say, and call it, He, / For whatsoe're the Painters Fancy be, / It a Male Virtu seems to me.)'

The verses provide compelling evidence for the view that the Society sought to effect a masculinization of science as part of a general program to mobilize support. Yet factors other than gender, including class and the ideologies of revisionist history, come into play here. From the very outset of the poem, Cowley establishes a binary framework for his dialectic: verbalism versus solid knowledge, age versus youth, male virtue versus feminine seduction. Philosophy's undutiful guardians keep the boy under control by plying him with the delights of rhetoric in place of knowledge, leading him, 'into the pleasant Labyr[i]nths of ever-fresh Discours.' Philosophy becomes 'captiv'd' in habitual indolence and reliance on external authority. Cowley envisages the 'femininity' of colonized philosophy as a usurpation of male privilege, and the advent of the Society as a liberation: 'But 'twas Rebellion call'd to fight / For such a long oppressed Right.' He offsets any tendency to consider the interregnum reformers as precursors of the Baconian revolution that he heralds by transforming Philosophy's guardians into 'usurpers,' and Bacon's instauration into a prophetic Restoration. Cowley portrays philosophy as passive or 'effeminized' because he hopes to commend intellectual rebellion without making a correlative case for political disobedience. He deliberately engenders his imagery in order to divert attention away from troubling political issues, trying to recast social polarization in terms of sexuality and individual freedom. By intertwining science with the interests of the rising mercantile class, he rationalizes the Society's value in promoting economic expansion in the New World.[19]

Wenceslaus Hollar's frontispiece to the *History* offers a reassuring image of Bacon as guardian of monarchical power. Hollar joins Bacon's portrait ('artium instaurator') with one of the president of the Royal Society in 1662 (William, second viscount Brouncker), and a bust of Charles II ('author & patronus'). Hyperbolic veneration of Bacon as the Society's co-begetter offsets French and other foreign influences. As Antonio Pérez-Ramos comments, 'nationalist rhetoric and the urgent need for an ideology of science as a *locus neutrus* of gentlemanly pursuit played a non-negligible part in the Baconian clothing of natural philosophy in Newton's age.'[20] Patronage, patriotism, and paternal authority all revolve around the figure of 'Bacon,' who demonstrates the Englishness of science and its harmony with monarchical government.

In Cowley's condensed version of the history of philosophy, a vigorously male Bacon, a patriarchal embodiment of the Law, at long last arises to drive away the phantoms of error and overthrow a monstrous phallic god:

Bacon at last, a mighty Man, arose,
   Whom a wise King and Nature chose
   Lord Chancellour of both their Laws,
And boldly undertook the injur'd Pupils caus.

Autority, which did a Body boast,
Though 'twas but Air condens'd, and stalk'd about,
Like some old Giants more Gigantic Ghost,
   To terrifie the Learned Rout
With the plain Magique of tru Reasons Light,
   He chac'd out of our sight,
Nor suffer'd Living Men to be misled
   By the vain shadows of the Dead:
To Graves, from whence it rose, the conquer'd Phantome fled;
   He broke that Monstrous God which stood
In midst of th' Orchard, and the whole did claim,
   Which with a useless Sith of Wood,
   And something else not worth a name,
   (Both vast for shew, yet neither fit
   Or to Defend, or to Beget;
   Ridiculous and senceless Terrors!) made
Children and superstitious Men afraid.
   The Orchards open now, and free;
Bacon has broke that Scar-crow Deitie;
   Come, enter, all that will,
Behold the rip'ned Fruit, come gather now your Fill.

Bacon has the role of nature's interpreter thrust upon him by both king and Nature herself, at whose behest he intervenes in Philosophy's 'case.' The equation of natural with civic law hinges on Bacon's dual authority, his capacity to function in the political and philosophical realms according to a unified code of impartiality and even-handedness. As iconoclastic as his actions may seem, his smashing of images becomes an act of piety, a casting out of alien gods. Before Bacon, a disincarnate 'Autority' stalked learning and commanded unthinking obedience. Bacon's demystification of ancient learning has made any attempt to resacralize the natural world impossible and absurd. The old gods have simply vanished and Baconian science, apotheosized, has taken their place. Cowley lays to rest the familiar charges of hubris by renewing Bacon's insistence that presuming to understand truth and falsehood, good and evil, without reference to nature, constitutes the ultimate pride. The study of nature practiced by Adam in the Garden remains separate from the immodest ambitions of Eve: 'Yet still, methinks, we fain would be / Catching at the Forbidden Tree.' The scientist, if he is to function effectively, must recognize, not resist, the limitations inherent to the human condition.

Sprat's apology appeals to the argument, almost synonymous with Bacon, that Adam's naming of the creatures constituted an act of reverence, not ambition. Had he contented himself with such knowledge, 'men had continued innocent in *Paradise*, and had not wanted a *Redemption*' (350). Such modest and value-free natural inquiry would furnish the state with valuable servants. Religion had nothing to fear from science and 'the subversion of old Opinions about *Nature*' going on everywhere around it, because science remained consonant with the goals of the reformation. The church and the Royal Society 'both have taken a like cours to bring this about; each of them passing by the *corrupt Copies*, and referring themselves to the *perfect Originals* for their instruction; the one to the *Scripture*, the other to the large Volume of the *Creatures.*' Renewing Bacon's language and reasoning, Sprat considers the accusation 'of having forsaken the *Ancient Traditions*, and ventur'd on *Novelties*' unjust to institutions that have revived the perfect orthodoxy of the earliest instance (370–1). Baconian method in the hands of Sprat and Cowley becomes an ideology of self-conscious disengagement from volatile political and social issues. In his *Proposition for the Advancement of Experimental Philosophy* (1661), Cowley had rushed to allay the fears of those who might oppose the foundation of a philosophical college in a passage that takes on something of the *History*'s apologetic tenor. The proposed college, he argues, does nothing to 'enterfere with any parties in State or Religion, but is indifferently to be embraced by all Differences in opinion, and can hardly be conceived capable (as many good Institutions have done) even of Degeneration into any thing harmful.'[21] Cowley represents the Baconian goal of advancement as value-neutral and incapable of the institutional 'degeneration' suffered by the universities and church in the recent past. Novelty becomes a guarantor of disinterestedness, a universal good that nevertheless conduces to the advantage of the established religion. With Bacon impedestalled as its patron saint, science appears as a regenerative, non-threatening, and stabilizing force.

The legacy Bacon bequeaths to his successors is a view of knowledge that constantly refers the pursuit of knowledge to a recuperative process that seeks to bridge the gap between reality and its graphic or symbolic representations: 'From Words, which are but Pictures of the Thought, /

(Though we our Thoughts from them perversely drew) / To Things, the Minds right Object, he it brought.' These lines provided an earlier generation of scholars with evidence for the supposed transformation of prose style that occurred during the Restoration. Sprat probably remains best known to literary critics for promulgating the development of a programmatic 'plain style,' a new 'utilitarian' ethos after the vertiginous flights of Andrewes, Browne, and other Ciceronians. Sprat considers tropes and figures initially valuable in bringing '*Knowledg* back again to our very senses, from whence it was at first deriv'd to our understandings'; yet they had undergone steady degeneration into 'the easie vanity of *fine speaking*' and the excrescence of empty metaphor. The Society has endeavoured to remedy such excesses, Sprat writes, by turning 'back to the primitive purity, and shortness, when men deliver'd so many *things,* almost in an equal number of *words*' (112–13). Those who aspire to represent the external world accurately, Cowley writes, 'must not from others Work a Copy take,' but draw on firsthand experience of originals: 'Th'Idæas and the Images' lodged in their memories will invariably betray them. Henceforth philosophers must hew closely to neutral observation, which would confer on their work a new level of groundedness.²²

Once Cowley has achieved a Baconian apotheosis he at once undercuts it, troping on metaphors of wandering and error closely associated with Bacon:

From these and all long Errors of the way,
In which our wandring Prædecessors went,
And like th' old *Hebrews* many years did stray
   In Desarts but of small extent,
Bacon, like *Moses*, led us forth at last.

In the ode's network of colonizing metaphors, Bacon becomes less a new Aristotle than a type of failed Alexander: 'But Life did never to one Man allow / Time to Discover Worlds, and Conquer too.' A balanced evaluation of Bacon's work must take into account its shortcomings as well as its genius, and recognize the limited influence even a 'great man' can have after the explosion and consequent specialization of knowledge: 'The work he did we ought t' admire, / And were unjust if we should more require / From his few years.' From here Cowley passes to the Society's future victories in subduing nature, predicting great success in subduing the 'large and wealthy Regions' that lie about. Bacon has served the immediate purpose and now recedes from view. Cowley echoes the appraisal offered by

Sprat, which anticipates the modern view of Bacon as blind to the value of hypothesis (the *Sylva Sylvarum* 'seems rather to take all that comes, then to choose; and to heap, rather, then to register'), and then displaces him as an object of hero-worship: 'But I hope this accusation of mine can be no great injury to his Memory; seeing, at the same time, that I say he had not the strength of a thousand men; I do also allow him to have had as much as twenty' (36).

By 1670 English scientific culture had become officially Baconian. The climate in which Baconianism thrived, however, grew politically charged in ways Bacon could not have anticipated. Whereas Ross's early critique reveals a muted polemical dimension, the anti-Baconianism of Henry Stubbe becomes overtly political. Between 1670 and 1671 Stubbe engaged in a series of heated exchanges with Joseph Glanvill, probably the century's most sustained effort to undermine Bacon's reputation and influence. *The Plus Ultra Reduced to a Non Plus*, nominally an attack on Glanvill's *Plus Ultra*, becomes a wide-ranging assault on all '*Neoterick* Endeavors.' Using a battery of arguments and displaying considerable expertise in both medicine and classical learning, he challenges the new philosophy for labouring to supplant antiquity. At this stage, he seems to share the general respect for Bacon, employing the technique of casting Bacon's writings in the teeth of epigones like Glanvill and Sprat. On a title page he ironically juxtaposes three epigraphs, one from Horace's *Epistles* on the trivialization of Greek culture after the great wars; a remark from Sprat's *History* that 'it is but reasonable, that the original *Invention* should be ascribed to the true *Author*, rather than the *Finishers*' (317); and a sentence from Bacon's dedication to Cambridge of *De Sapientia Veterum*, 'Yet it is fit that all should be attributed to you and be counted to your honour, since all increase is due in great part to the beginning.'[23] The false appropriation of origin, Stubbe implies, subverts social order and alienates us from reality. To prefer innovation over scholastic metaphysics, the Royal Society over Cambridge, Bacon over Aristotle, is tantamount to apostasy, sedition, and rebellion. Using the tested technique of tarring one's political opponents with the brush of movements they must repudiate, Stubbe refuses to recognize any distinction between radical and 'Establishment' Baconians. A former Independent and parliamentary apologist, he has not forgotten the Society's suppressed Gresham College and parliamentarian affiliations. The usurpation of antiquity strikes Stubbe as having provoked an unprecedented crisis of political and cultural authority, and the episcopal Establishment's adoption of Bacon as a tutelary deity does nothing to set his mind at ease.[24]

Glanvill's second response to Stubbe's repeated assaults on experimental philosophy was to confront him with the authority of Bacon. As 'the *Founder* and one of the Chiefest Men of *that Way*,' Bacon's reputation presumably redeems the activities of his followers. Ironically, the same Bacon who had made experience the final arbiter of truth had become a guarantor of orthodoxy and could now be produced to defuse attacks with an *ipse dixit*.[25] Adamant in his stand, Stubbe replied to the challenge with *The Lord Bacons Relation of the Sweating-Sickness Examined,* which in some copies has the alternate title *A Bacon-face No Beauty* (1671). He begins by assailing Glanvill for foisting 'upon us a *thousand Falsities* out of the *Philosophical* Writings of that Lord, and Lawyer; yet doth it seem requisite that I should say something more in reference to his Authority, lest, what imported little *in the Age when he lived,* should be *prejudicial,* and *destructive* to that which *succeeds.* I will not deny that he was a man of *good Literature,* and *great Eloquence,* accompanied with a *popular,* and *florid way of Expressing himself:* By Profession, he was a Lawyer, and the principal part of *his Studies* were bent that way; and although therein he were surpassed by *others,* yet 'tis there that his *Credit* must seem most *Authentick,* or no where: We acknowledg no Chancellours of Philosophy, Philology, Medicine, &c.' Stubbe, finally bored with treading lightly over Bacon's reputation, bridles at the idea of Bacon's disciples setting him up as infallible in scientific as well as juridical matters. In conscious opposition to the originary imagery associated with Bacon, Stubbe flatly denies him any measure of originality, even charging him with plagiarizing the *Novum Organum* from Aristotle. Stubbe imagined a distinctly sinister process at work here. First, Bacon demythologizes Aristotle as little better than a refiner and codifier of received notions. Then, he has conferred upon him titles rightly belonging to the usurped elder. Stubbe considers Bacon the architect of revolution, not science. He accuses him of demolishing venerable institutions and creating 'in the Breasts of the *English* such a desire of *Novelty,* as rose up to a Contempt of the Ancient Ecclesiastical and *Civil Jurisdiction,* and the *Old Government,* as well as *Governours* of the Realm.' By a dazzlingly improbable *non sequitur* he pronounces Bacon singlehandedly responsible for the interregnum and its aftermath: 'And the *Root* of all our *present Distractions* was planted by His Hand.'[26] Bacon, who had described himself as a 'trumpeter, not a combatant' in the wars of truth, now steps forward as a general in the English logomachy. Bacon, who had set his face against 'contentious' learning as an enemy of light, now becomes embroiled in fierce controversies. The surrogate of King James and eloquent 'pen-man' for monarchical absolutism fades before the overreaching projector, Prometheus, corrupt magistrate, littérateur, and sower of rebellion. In 1652, 'Agricola Carpenter' alluded to the allegory on the title-page of the *Instauratio Magna,* a ship sailing beyond the pillars of Hercules, to confirm the possibility of effecting 'a Reverse to the first perfection,' whereby people can experience 'a sensible improvement in their Cognition' and reinvent Adam.[27]

A decade after the Restoration, Bacon's writings were enlisted, with some success, in the service of securing social harmony and managing dissent. The Baconian imagery of recovery, reversal, and rebirth exercised a powerful appeal on those who aspired to liberate humanity from the disabling effects of fallen nature and the myth of modern inferiority. Based on the evidence we have sampled, I would suggest that we revise current views of Bacon's place in the cultural formation of the Restoration in two important respects. First, the increasingly accepted conclusion that the fathers of modern science built their endeavour on a foundation of Baconian-patriarchal imagery might be modified to consider the political and intellectual climate in which this process occurred.[28] The Royal Society's nomination of Bacon as official precursor owes as much to polemical and religious factors as to sexual politics. Second, we can better understand these tropes of masculine domination and scientific propagation by reading them against the originary metaphors that inform them. Bacon regarded himself as both initiator and renewer of a vast collaborative enterprise that extended endlessly into the future. His self-appointed successors publicly identified themselves with this goal, adopting the strategy of representing Bacon as a forerunner whose prescience enabled future accomplishments. Their identifying Bacon with the authority of origins helped secure his modern reputation as a progenitor of science. They annexed Bacon's generative imagery and paternal mystique in order to position themselves at the beginning of a 'revolution,' a revolution founded on an ideology of scientific objectivity.

Bacon's theory of knowledge posited a more complex relation to social practice. He had depicted philosophy as a multitiered system, a source with branches and tributaries, or a body with veins and capillaries: 'And generally let this be a rule, that all partitions of knowledges be accepted rather for lines and veins, than for sections and separations; and that the continuance and entireness of knowledge be preserved.' The opposite assumption, he thinks, had made 'particular sciences to become barren, shallow, and erroneous; while they have not been nourished and maintained from the common fountain.' Knowledge ultimately derives from one of two sources, one consisting of 'the notions of the mind and the reports of the senses,' and the other of knowledge absorbed through tradition, the 'cumulative and not original' residue of written texts. Together they form 'a water' fed by two tributaries, which offer 'two differing illuminations or originals' (3: 366–7, 346).

When Bacon argued the necessity of retaining traditions conducing to social stability, he had to contend with a suspicion that his instauration might create an environment where all traditions would have to justify themselves. According to Timothy Reiss, Bacon's 'new discourse of analysis and reference is an utterly new space making use of an inhabitual set of axioms.'[29] Other critics detect in his writings a symptomatically modern (or post-modern) commingling of old and new. Whatever the case, Bacon's quest for novelty and for origins sustains a contradiction that the *Novum Organum* does little to resolve. Language is the irreducible medium of the 'new' theory even though it remains beset by erroneous ideas. Emerging out of a social matrix, out of the existing world of signs and meanings, language carries within itself the burden of ideology. Bacon's recognition of how language structures experience and the difficulty of rising above representation to seize a transparent origin deters him from adopting a crude positivism. He understood the verbal character of our claims about the world. Nevertheless, he persisted in wanting to free humanity from errors of reflexivity. Verbal and mental representations, he thought, obscured the truth embodied in the origin. Making observation theory-independent and free from preconceptions remained his basic goal. Origins provided the core of certainty upon which scientific knowledge could rest.

Although Bacon does not advocate an absolute, top-down control of the institutions of learning, neither does he concede equal authority to every position and every discursive site. Locating an origin forms part of a process of establishing boundaries, of defining the limits of legitimate inquiry. In the essay 'Of Great Place' Bacon advises: 'Reduce things, to the first Institution, and observe, wherein, and how, they have degenerate.' Adding the question of historicity to the originary principle, he remarks: 'but yet aske Counsell of both Times; Of the Ancient Time, what is best; and of the Latter Time, what is fittest' (*Essayes* 35). Prudential counsel unites with method, public life with philosophical investigation, scholarship with courtiership. The advancement of learning proceeds by systematically seeking out an ever-receding origin. Looking towards antiquity, those in positions 'of great place,' holders of high office, can unearth the truth in its clearest manifestation, take note of its decline over time, and then adapt their thinking and actions to the present.

Armed with the concept of logical method, Bacon divides up problems to obtain starting-points, from which he attempts synthetic reconstructions. By proceeding according to ascending levels of complexity, he hopes to disentangle complex structures and render them intelligible. This goal of rebuilding knowledge from the very foundations, of stripping away prejudice and preconception, links the Baconian enterprise to other developments in seventeenth-century philosophy. Although we tend to draw a line between Cartesian ratiocinative method and Bacon's experimental logic, both systems attempted to isolate the simple natures or elemental components that furnished the building blocks of more complex phenomena. Most projects for formulating an authoritative method involve securing first principles capable of transcending historical conditions and avoiding erroneous judgment. The *Novum Organum* manifests the quest for origins as a corrective to error and uncertainty. Bacon's desire to recuperate the moment of primal nomination, the ultimate origin of language, motivates his interest in Genesis and the naming of the creatures, a move that brings him to the same originary narratives and metaphors that inform *Paradise Lost*.

In section 1 I have examined Bacon's critique of language and the idols in relation to his use of aphorism, closing with a sketch of his role as the originator of Baconianism. Turning to *Paradise Lost*, I want to consider the ideal of epic unity as a function of recovering an absolute historical starting-point. The difficulty of writing an epic poem in the seventeenth century, even a Christian religious epic with a new type of hero, was compounded by the difficulty of situating experience in an utterly past world. I argue that epic has associations not only with the generic models provided by Homer and Virgil, the 'first' of poets, but also with the philosophical problem of retrieving an origin. *Paradise Lost* succeeds in establishing itself in a complex relation to tradition, emphasizing, rather than suppressing, the historic specificity of classical epic. The generic superiority of epic was thought to reside both in its historical primacy and in its power to represent 'worthy' images to the mind. Milton's quest for origins, I argue in 'Seeing Double in *Paradise Lost*,' takes up (as Bacon took up) the metaphor of mirroring as knowledge and treats knowledge as a process of representation and reduplication. The poem authenticates particular forms of knowing, and, at the same time, exposes the difficulty of making experience of the world a reliable standard of truth. In it we see Milton represent the mind's encounter with the external world through the structure of epic, the discourse of origin, and the figure of the mirror.

PART TWO

Seeing Double in *Paradise Lost*

5

Beginning Late

Like most of his contemporaries, Milton admired Bacon, sharing his antischolasticism and immersion in history and politics. As a student at Christ's College, Cambridge, Milton found himself drawn towards the new philosophy and the scientific ideology of the Great Instauration. To most readers, the youthful author of the *Prolusions* (1628–32) sounds unmistakably Baconian. *The Advancement of Learning* left an imprint on Milton's Third and Seventh Prolusions, and the influence of the *Novum Organum* also seems probable. Prolusion 7, 'Beatiores reddit Homines Ars quam Ignorantia' [Learning brings more Blessings to Men than Ignorance], culminates in a vision of scientific knowledge that expands to occupy the universe. In some glorious future, the natural philosopher will gain mastery and appear as 'one whose rule and dominion the stars obey, to whose command earth and sea hearken, and whom winds and tempests serve.' Revealing the full extent of his Baconian affinities, Milton pictures the triumphant scientist as someone to whom 'Mother Nature [Parens Natura] herself has surrendered, as if indeed some god had abdicated the throne of the world and entrusted its rights, laws, and administration to him as governor.' Much like the historian who imaginatively ranges through time and space, becoming 'as it were coeval with time itself,' the natural philosopher establishes authority over the phenomenal world. If historical knowledge extends 'our lives backward before our birth,' giving consciousness the power to antedate itself, scientific knowledge aspires to perfect control over the present (*Complete Prose* 1: 295–7).

Milton later comes to understand something of the unstable relation between the polymathic Baconian ideal and a scientistic curiosity that leaves no belief unexamined. Before the Restoration, however, philosophers rarely valorized the term 'science' by contrasting it favourably with disciplines that address something other than 'nature.' The Latin word *scientia*, which Bacon uses more frequently than its English derivative, refers to the systematic character of multiple forms of knowledge, not to a specific branch of study. Despite occasional moments of grandiosity, Bacon never aspires to colonize every discipline by planting the flag of 'science' on adjacent territories, and despite his tendency to divide knowledge into constituent disciplines arranged according to implicit hierarchies, Bacon maintains the unity of knowledge. Different disciplines may address themselves to various questions and derive their subjects from different starting-points. Together, however, they contribute to the advancement of learning.

In part 2 I explore the structural homology between Bacon's techniques for the acquisition of knowledge and the epic quest to uncover historical and spiritual origins. Milton's habit of turning to legend, genealogy, classical epic, and archaic tradition in general to understand the present represents a 'scientific' process in so far as it attempts to articulate the difference between demonstrated truth and other domains of knowledge. Edward Said locates the loss of 'the authority of a privileged Origin that commands, guarantees, and perpetuates meaning' at a historical moment arriving as early as *Paradise Lost*.[1] Where Said connects beginnings to a historical transformation of ideas about language – anticipated by Milton and Vico and fully realized by structuralism – I argue that Milton's epic is informed by the contradiction of origins, the problematic relation between a copy and its original. In this one respect a good Baconian, Milton locates truth at the site of a suppressed origin, which can be recovered by following canonical procedures for the reconstruction and revision of knowledge. Milton strives to preserve the integrity of origins as transcendental absolutes, even though he understands the difficulty of locating an absolute truth outside of language. Baconian reassurances to the contrary, scrutinizing origins can engender error as well as authenticate self-awareness or knowledge of the creation. In three chapters on *Paradise Lost* I explore Milton's fascination with epic origins, the origination of human consciousness, and mirroring as a metaphor for the authentication of the self in another. I argue that questions of doubt and certainty in the poem relate to Milton's originary epistemology of belief and self-discovery.

In Aristotelian tradition, *scientia* is knowledge of why things are necessarily so, understood by reference to 'causes.' The doctrine of the four causes (material, formal, efficient, final) posits a hierarchy, according to which investigators strive towards knowledge of first and universal causes.

By the seventeenth century, philosophers had come to find the shifting distinctions entailed by this complex logic incapable of producing 'science' in any productive sense. The word *cause* undergoes so much slippage in Aristotle it can mean anything from constitutive matter, to external source, to governing principle, to final *telos*. Some thinkers rejected a model of causation that seemed confusingly bound up with related Aristotelian theories of form, nature, and essence. Even so, many others continued to embrace a form of methodical reductionism that organized knowledge atomically, beginning with irreducible particularities and moving upward towards complex entities.

Milton establishes his position in implicit opposition to materialist epistemology and science in a narrow sense. He places the word 'science,' its sole occurrence in *Paradise Lost*, in the mouth of Satan as part of his oration on the necessity of exceeding the narrow bounds of an arbitrary authority. Satan apostrophizes the forbidden fruit with the words: 'O Sacred, Wise, and Wisdom-giving Plant, / Mother of Science.' The inherent 'Power' of the fruit not only includes the capacity 'to discern / Things in thir Causes,' but also to 'trace the ways' of superior and mysterious beings. Adam's initial inquiry of himself and the creation – 'what cause?' – has its counterpart in Satan's rationalizing temptation by producing 'these, these and many more / Causes' (9.679–83, 731–2). The will to knowledge, specifically knowledge of causes, propels the events that lead to the Fall.

The problem of origin in *Paradise Lost* emerges in the Latin verses S.B. (Samuel Barrow) contributed to the second edition. Barrow's poem accompanies the other prefatory materials written by Andrew Marvell and the author himself. Like Marvell, whose verses on the poem commend its 'vast Design' for comprehending multiple worlds, Barrow lavishes praise on Milton for gathering in 'Res cunctas, & cunctarum primordia rerum, / Et fata, & fines' [everything and the origin of things / Their destiny and purpose]. The word *finis*, which means 'end,' 'limit,' and 'beginning,' moves in opposite directions. Milton's poem, Barrow suggests, inscribes the beginning and end of time, telescoping universal history into the space of twelve books. Barrow ranks Milton with the Greeks and Romans, to whose works his own invites comparison. Yet in the closing lines he complicates the flattering comparison by alluding to the Homeric mock-epic *Batrachomyomachia* [Battle of the Frogs and Mice], and the Virgilian pastiche *Culex*, which Spenser translated as *Virgils Gnat:* 'Hæc quicunque leget tantum cecinisse putabit / *Mæonidem* ranas, *Virgilium* culices' [Whoever will read these things will think that Homer wrote only about frogs and Virgil only the *Culex*].² The lines dislodge readers from an uncritical adulation of epic by recalling ironic inversions even within classical models. With these lines, Barrow draws attention to the fate of poems bearing a derivative relation to epic, and so exposes the difficulty of Milton's historical position. Imitation and homage border dangerously on parody; and epic, precisely because it embraces 'all,' can collapse into repetition and parodic allusion at the very moment of its creation. The parasitic, comic, and even bathetic aspects of epic seem integral to the tradition itself, not later excrescences that Milton could safely set aside.

As King Charles's Physician in Ordinary, Barrow would seem an unlikely admirer of the republican poet and polemicist. Yet other royalists, including Dryden, put aside political difference in order to clear a place for the English epic (or attempted to assimilate Milton to an ethos he would instantly repudiate). Like others of his generation, including Butler, Milton deferred his epic ambitions throughout the 1640s and 1650s. Also like Butler, Milton emerged from the civil war somehow galvanized by the experience and determined to attain the recognition that attached to the successful performance of a long poetic narrative. Milton, however, accomplished what Butler, Cowley, Davenant, and others could not: he produced a poem regarded not merely as a gloss on classical epic, but something capable of rivalling earlier attempts in the form.

What Milton's seventeenth-century admirers – including Marvell and Barrow – found most impressive about the poem was its success in positioning itself in relation to a tradition that exhausted itself with every new beginning. Milton's self-conscious situating of the poem occurs in the context of a climate made hospitable to epic aspirations and to theoretical statements about the genre. His political and religious affiliations presented an obstacle to some admirers. Nathaniel Lee praised Dryden's *Absalom and Achitophel* by picturing its triumphant transcendence of partisanship in opposition to Milton, 'As if a Milton from the dead arose, / Fil'd off the Rust, and the right Party chose.' In a poem on Dryden's *State of Innocence* (1677), Lee again attempts to install Dryden in Milton's place, portraying the latter as a unpolished precursor of Dryden's absolute monarchy over verse. The strain of the compliment, however, immediately shows.³ As Lee well understood, a tremendous amount of cultural prestige attached to epic. The poet who achieved genuine distinction in epic might shape for posterity the image of seventeenth-century England and of its struggle to found a new political order. If Milton had to occupy this niche, his views needs must undergo correction, or at least refraction through the prism of Drydenian orthodoxy.

When Milton came to write *Paradise Lost* the civil war had not provided the momentous literary-historical occasion that Davenant, Cowley, and others anticipated. On the contrary, it had compounded the general sense of epic's extreme difficulty and the possible barrier of their modernity. Although the experience of defeat never drove Milton from a belief in reform, his lifelong emphasis on social change underwent transformation with the failure of the revolution.[4] If epic had not vanished altogether into antiquity, it had certainly receded from view. Poets who ignored the imperatives of their historical situation and chose to write as if they inhabited imperial Rome, or even the England of Spenser's epic-cum-dynastic romance, risked appearing ludicrous. Although the times might have seemed unpropitious for writing epic, the market for it showed no signs of diminishing. Both Davenant and Cowley could view their forays into epic as a means of consolidating their literary reputations. Yet they found little to encourage them. The stigma of spectacular failure, which attached to inept performances, would give any poet pause before investing large quantities of time and intellectual capital in such risky ventures.

Directly tapping into an epic source remained problematic for poets conscious of the difficulty of determining specific inaugural points, and of modernity's distance from subjects suitable for epic treatment. Davenant – using a figure with strong Baconian associations – regarded Homer's status as an 'eminent Sea-marke' better suited to poets 'whose satisfy'd witt will not venture beyond the track of others, then to them, who affect a new and remote way of thinking; who esteem it a deficiency and meanesse of minde, to stay and depend upon the authority of example.'[5] Narratives that elucidated the present from the vantage point of the distant past had to contend with the complexity and variability of the relationship. Since all recorded history would emanate from a single moment, poets first needed to identify a suitable starting-point before performing multiple acts of inclusion and exclusion. Cowley's *Davideis* describes the Creation itself as closely akin to the poetic process, and attributes to epic poets a godlike talent for contending with multeity:

As first a various unform'd *Hint* we find
Rise in some god-like *Poets* fertile *Mind*,
Till all the parts and words their places take,
And with just marches *verse* and *musick* make;
Such was *Gods Poem*, this *Worlds* new *Essay*;
So wild and rude in its first *draught* it lay;
Th'ungovern'd parts no *Correspondence* knew,

An artless *war* from thwarting *Motions* grew;
Till they to *Number* and fixt Rules were brought
By the *æternal minds Poetick Thought.*[6]

Epic poets, in relation to the jumbled notions inhabiting their brains, become 'makers,' lords of syntax, inventors of history, arbiters of culture. Cast in a quasi-military role, they distinguish among converging ideas and establish order by creating elaborate networks of rules and 'Correspondence.' They exert control over the present by erecting verbal structures, establishing a contingent order (or 'essay') that resolves complexity and discord by imposing 'rules' upon it. Ficticity in this sense becomes an instrument of order, the tool of a divine disposer who must arrange materials as a shapely narrative. Poetic thought becomes an act of creation, a means of establishing a particular dispensation, of averting 'artless' war by placing undifferentiated elements in due order and subordination. The creative act requires 'invention' of the poet, who must devise or fabricate a beginning.

The gesture towards marking a clear beginning remains indispensable to writers who wish to retain a sense of their historical position at the opposite end of a provisionally fixed sequence. The historian who addresses us from a position of summarizing, even as events unfold, inscribes closure and thus requires a beginning. Milton's projected *Arthuriad*, a long poem chronicling the Trojans in Britain and adopting Arthur as its hero, proposed a simple solution to the problem of finding a beginning. Milton thought he would transform the matter of Troy into a patriotic narrative of national establishment. Although the choice of Arthur as a subject would have permitted Milton to represent a 'pure' pre-Norman Britain, it also would have blurred the boundary between epic and romance and embroiled him in a doubtful origin. If epic were to continue in its privileged position, it would have to suppress the taint of the fabulous beginning. In *The History of Britain* Milton rejects Arthur as historically too shadowy for his purposes: 'But who *Arthur* was, and whether ever any such reign'd in *Britain*, hath bin doubted heertofore, and may again with good reason.' Arthur's unsuitability proceeds from the impossibility of establishing his originative claim. The difficulty – but, equally, the necessity – of pinpointing certain points of origin, especially when dealing with the history of remote times, appears throughout the *History*: 'the beginnings of Nations,' Milton writes in the opening sentences, with the exception of those recorded in Scripture, have faded into obscurity or been 'blemisht with Fables.' Time and successive layers of narrative invention have covered over the primal moment. This would seem an inauspicious note on which to commence a work advertising itself as starting 'from the first Traditional Beginning' of British history (*CP* 5: 164). Yet the double modifier 'first Traditional' hedges, and presents its chosen beginning as a convenient point of departure, a heuristic. The humanist technique of amassing evidence and working a subject up from earliest times necessitates this methodology and structural framework. Milton demands the presence of a beginning as an organizing principle, not as an absolute and irrefutable revelation of fact. The legend of Britain's Trojan descent and of Brute's peregrinations enjoyed wide currency even as late as the seventeenth century. Milton, like others before him, had serious doubts about the veracity of the Brutus legend but nevertheless conceded the appeal of making 'the *Britan* of one Original with the *Roman*.' Although he shied away from asserting 'too strict an incredulity' that would dismiss the legend altogether, he stressed the doubtfulness of all such legends, even in classical epic: 'But to examin these things with diligence, were but to confute the Fables of *Britan* with the Fables of *Greece* or *Italy*; for of this Age, what we have to say, as well concerning most other Countries, as this Iland, is equally under Question' (*CP* 5: 8–11). Speculating on historical origins as remote as these plunged the writer into a welter of assertions and counter-assertions, most of them equally probable. What was true of historiographical controversy went doubly for poetic representations of the deeds of fabled knights in battles feigned.

With the substitution of Genesis for Geoffrey of Monmouth and Jewish for British history, Milton paradoxically made historical verisimilitude a function of extreme distance in space and time. His reconceptualization of epic beginnings pushes the poem to the furthest originative limit, and, at the same time, drives it back onto the most authoritative materials. Harold Bloom views Milton's displacement of epic onto sacred history as a master-stroke, the means for outflanking his rivals and contending with the problem of belatedness.[7] In general, criticism of *Paradise Lost* as 'Christian epic' has generally aligned itself between two coordinates: studies that see *Paradise Lost* as supplanting classical epic, and those that regard it as a Christianizing revision of the genre. Milton's famous statement, in 1642, that what the Greeks, Hebrews, and Romans accomplished for their own nations, 'I in my proportion with this over and above of being a Christian, might doe for mine,' steers somewhere between the two positions (*CP* 1: 812). Most studies of Milton's relation to classical epic (beginning with the poem's early editors) evolve out of the assumption, often couched in architectonic metaphors, that 'Milton built his epic out of those of Homer and Virgil, like a cathedral erected out of the ruins of pagan temples whose remains can still be seen.' A few critics shift the emphasis onto the major poems' counter-tendency to move towards palinode or 'anti-epic.' *Paradise Lost*, according to the first formulation, embraces the epic tradition while subjecting it to 'revision,' 'revaluation,' 'transformation,' or critique. Studies committed to the second, anti-epic formulation take note, particularly in *Paradise Regained*, of an increasingly strong Miltonic tendency to interrogate a reverential humanism and to hold many forms of classicizing at arm's length.[8]

The wide range of effect within the category of epic – its ambition to incorporate within itself 'everything and the origin of things,' in Samuel Barrow's phrase – has a tendency to render critical discussions of the genre opaque. Epic, in this sense, provides an open text (*epos* as 'narration' or 'discourse') into which we can pour vast numbers of pre-texts. Miltonists have dropped, as theoretically untenable, the practice of distinguishing between two epic traditions on the basis of an orality–literacy dichotomy that made the *Iliad* 'primary' and the *Aeneid* 'secondary' or 'artificial.' The recent trend has been towards enlarging the definitional boundaries of epic while maintaining its continuity across various historical thresholds. In the classroom, however, many teachers, still proceed according to a plan of discussing stylistic and structural resemblances between *Paradise Lost* and a monolithic and imposing 'epic tradition' as a prelude to juxtaposing parallel passages. 'Epic' in this sense consists of a body of poems, or a list of attributes dispersed among them. Although we can hardly read epic without reference to the network of generic expectations readers bring to it, enumerating 'norms' adds little to our understanding of Miltonic intertextuality. In the absence of a cogent theory of epic, source study and an increasingly restless search for generic analogy has come to dominate interpretations of the poem. It is hardly an overstatement, at this point in the history of Milton criticism, to say that very few classical texts of importance have not been claimed as Miltonic antecedents.

In much of the recent scholarship, epic inclusiveness has become a strategy for coordinating the tensions that fissure the poem while still maintaining the ideal of Milton's authorial unity and artistic success. The correlative tendency, to locate the source of Milton's poetics, style, and thematics in the Bible, functions in a similar manner. Where an older generation of scholars argued that Milton's 'rigorous adherence to the epic form does not preclude contact with other traditions' – specifically theodicy and Protestant theology – recent criticism has assimilated the Bible itself to literary tradition. By grounding Milton's epic practice in a generically amorphous ensemble of texts, a repository of genres written in different languages (literally *biblia*), critics can establish Milton's coherence and unity in relation to an infinitely variable 'form.'

Mary Ann Radzinowicz invokes the concept of 'epic encyclopedism' to describe the relation of poetic to scriptural models, an approach that expands the scope of Miltonic borrowings while privileging a particular biblical genre (Psalms) as the master-key to his work.[9] Taking a broadly inclusionist approach towards epic, now redefined as the total aggregate of biblical form and effect, such analyses divest the genre of a specific repertoire of conventions. 'Epic' in this sense functions as an honorific, a term detached from classical texts, and bestowed upon Milton and the Bible as the twin pillars of a single hermeneutic. Where Northrop Frye described the Renaissance ideal as 'a poem that derived its structure from the epic tradition of Homer and Virgil and still had the quality of universal knowledge which belonged to the encyclopedic poem and included the extra dimension of reality that was afforded by Christianity,' the newer model telescopes all into the Bible-as-literature. Frye, with his keen eye for large structures, developed a working definition of epic that enables an important insight: that the beginning *in media res* propels a 'total action' that takes a cyclical shape in Homer, but in Virgil and Milton 'begins and ends, not at precisely the same point, but at the same point renewed and transformed by the heroic action itself.'[10] For Frye, problematic beginnings that enfold into ends constitute a determinant feature of epic.

When Renaissance humanism attached the epic label to Scripture, it engaged a double strategy of self-defence and self-promotion. The claim allowed poets to justify writing on biblical subjects by reading aesthetic values into Scripture and discounting the obvious tension entailed by their 'Christian humanism.'[11] The biblical epics of the sixteenth and seventeenth centuries subsumed their hybridizing impulses under the dignified rubric of epic universality. Epic remained a historically constrained form, despite its official aesthetic of inclusiveness and timelessness. As one critic points out, in basing his epic on the story of the Fall, Milton moved in a conspicuously retrograde direction. By the 1660s the traditions of Du Bartas and the divine epic would have seemed distinctly old-fashioned and out of step. In other ways, however, 'the poem that he [Milton] wrote ran with the time: in structure, in Virgilian tone, and particularly in depth of pious and learned allusion.'[12]

In reading Milton, we should not neglect the political and historical associations with which epic came burdened, and the ways in which his contemporaries associated specific modes of thinking with epic models.

According to Christopher Kendrick, epic descended to Milton from Virgil 'with a pre-given political determination' attached to its narrative structure, one that mandated a type of primitive nationalism. Kendrick argues that the Virgilian idea of national destiny derives from Rome's dependence on the use of slave labour, which made imperial conquest necessary. In *Paradise Lost*, according to Kendrick, we find nationalism displaced by an Independent ideology antipathetic to absolutism, mercantilism, and presbyterianism. Thus, the poem's content becomes radicalized by its distance from the conventions it inherits.[13] Kendrick proposes a reading of *Paradise Lost* that points out patterns of resistance in Milton's absorption of epic conceived in historically determinate terms. Virgilian epic incorporates much that Milton would necessarily view with circumspection if not outright disapprobation. Virgil charts the fate of a nation whose ascendance animates the heroic vocation of 'civilizing' under the leadership of kings and other autocrats. The 'high walls of Rome' symbolize military conquest, the concentration of power in an urban elite, and the displacement of indigenous cultures by Roman colonization. Empire building, the *Aeneid*'s 'empire without end' (1.279), seen as a process of national aggrandizement and restless expansion, had fixed associations with Babylon and Rome. Tasso's relation to Virgil, which Davenant considered one of absolute dependency, was unavailable to any English poet who wished to maintain a safe distance from romance and Romanism.[14] We are not surprised to see epic delusions of endless empire get swept away in the final books of *Paradise Lost*, nor to find among Christ's mounting refusals in *Paradise Regained* a refusal to become the agent of imperial power.

Milton criticism has, of course, considered the difficulty of Milton's epic intention, which it often construes as a principle of structural duality that pits one *Paradise Lost* against its antitype: one true, the other false; one epic, the other parodic; one Christic, the other Satanic; one scriptural, the other classical; one conservative, the other revolutionary.[15] This ongoing dialogue between contending forces, which critics often contain by affixing to it the label 'Christian humanism,' faces powerful contradictions on either side of the equation. We can stretch the model of genre we bring to *Paradise Lost* to encompass many of the contrary impulses we find in it; but conceiving epic as a compendious or infinitely assimilative generic catch-all undercuts the sense in which epic, as practiced and theorized in the Renaissance, committed a poet to a highly determined mode of writing. Although the definition of 'epic' favoured by more recent Milton criticism has become less prescriptive than formerly, it still remains the mechanism by which critics achieve their objective of unifying a poem that perpetually threatens to become unravelled.

Barbara Lewalski considers Milton's comments in *The Reason of Church-Government* typical of Renaissance theories in using 'epic' to denote 'the specific genre for which the poems of Homer and Virgil were normative,' and 'heroic poetry' interchangeably with it. According to Lewalski, Milton cobbles *Paradise Lost* together, 'in accordance with normative Renaissance models and critical precepts,' from a huge range of generic scraps: Hesiodic gigantomachy, romance, biblical prophecy, pastoral, Boethian dialogue, Golden Age georgic, formal debate, Homeric hymn, among many others. The critical model she adopts for reading Milton's compendious and multiform poem is one of literary assimilation and displacement. No sense of tension or anxiety attends this process, nor does literary formation come under external influence. Lewalski raises, only to dismiss, the relation of *Paradise Lost*'s *genera mixta* to Mikhail Bakhtin's theory of 'novelization,' the idea that the emergent novel incorporates multiple genres and a diversity of perspectives. Where Bakhtin finds the novel characterized by the dialogic interaction of multiple voices, which incorporate and supplant the official monoglossia of the epic, Lewalski locates Milton within the parameters of a carefully moderated literary humanism. 'Multiple genres give Milton's modern epic great complexity, but not the indeterminacy and inconclusiveness Bakhtin identifies as the product of generic multiplicity in the modern novel.'[16] Milton, according to Lewalski, employs literary genre to evaluate and impart order to complex forms of life and expression. Encyclopaedic yet orderly, hierarchical yet dynamic, the poem gets situated in a generic universe that contains an enormous range of verse forms. Lewalski includes in this totality a broad spectrum of verse forms existing prior to Milton's poem, but excludes almost everything contemporaneous with it, including prose fiction. Milton's humanism thus takes on a formalistic and apolitical character. Every classical text he comes into contact with becomes grist for his poeticizing mill, and gets instantly divested of its historical and ideological effects.

The alternative literary history Lewalski mentions, Bakhtin's evolutionary model of the novel, outlines a scheme in which congeries of social forces result in a form that supplants the hegemony of epic. Bakhtin views the epic as assiduously avoiding the present by burying itself in a distant, prehistorical, and moribund past. Epic assumes a retrospective posture, moving episodically and in line with a sense of history that emphasizes transcendence (*forsan et haec olim meminisse iuvabit*). Fixation on bloodlines and first causes (whether in the form of *causus belli* or the root of all our woe) comes down to a repudiation of modernity in favour of a distant and idealized past. Epic's emphasis on normative behaviour and communal values, *mos,* produces an ossification of perception:

> The world of the epic is the national heroic past: it is a world of 'beginnings' and 'peak times' in the national history, a world of fathers and of founders of families, a world of 'firsts' and 'bests' ... The epic was never a poem about the present, about its own time (one that became a poem about the past only for those who came later). The epic, as the specific genre known to us today, has been from the beginning a poem about the past, and the authorial position immanent in the epic and constitutive for it (that is, the position of the one who utters the epic word) is the environment of a man speaking about a past that is to him inaccessible, the reverent point of view of a descendent.

Bakhtin's argument points up a feature of epic that most studies overlook: its establishment of historical and aesthetic authority through identification of and in the moment that initiated the present.[17] Where traditional genre criticism contents itself with merely observing Milton's intertextual valorization of a multiplicity of texts within *Paradise Lost,* Bakhtin's conception suggests an explanation of epic's boundedness by particular modes of representation. Where genre criticism ultimately neutralizes uncertainty and inconclusiveness in a capacious conception of epic, Bakhtin speaks of an epic world that admits no place 'for any openendedness, indecision, indeterminacy.' Epic strives to authorize itself by reference to an authority derived from withdrawing from contemporaneity, and to reconstruct a world coextensive with the past. The critical impetus to glance backwards in every encounter with Milton's text would then appear a function of a conscious strategy to deflect the present onto the past, to establish a zone around which Milton can hold intrusive reality at bay.

Bakhtin's approach to epic remains problematic in so far as it merely inverts the model of generic hierarchies it claims to overturn. Novel replaces epic as the genre whose features circumscribe all literary forms contemporaneous with it. Despite his emphasis on the collective and sociohistorical aspects of genre, he retains an evolutionary model of the 'major' genres, according to which every subsequent development can trace its being back to a latency present at its beginnings. 'Epic' and 'novel' function simultaneously as historically bounded descriptors and the vaguest of modal definitions. In the final analysis, Bakhtin's generic reshuffling makes over the novel into the mirror image of epic, the master form towards which all other forms conduce. Even so, Bakhtin helps to explain the givenness and self-containment of epic, its lending form to a separate reality (life *in illo tempore*), which nevertheless continues to maintain control over the present. Epic in this sense has a sociohistorical dimension. It also suggests why the epic's habitation of a distant and impenetrable past became a problematic constraint on modern poets who adopted the form. The gradual, although never complete, dissolution of the epic impulse into novel becomes a process of generic exchange, with representations of contemporaneity and the subjective self on one side, and antiquity and the national destiny on the other.

We can further modify and augment Bakhtin's definition by turning to Georg Lukács, whose viewpoint Bakhtin knew and to whom he implicitly responds. Lukács' *The Theory of the Novel* (1914) juxtaposes epic and its representation of 'the extensive totality of life' with the novel's coming into consciousness. Where Bakhtin emphasizes the opposition between novel and pre- or non-novel, Lukács divides literary history into four phases: Homeric epic; 'a historico-philosophical transition from the pure epic to the novel' typified by Dante; the novel, which Lukács, like Bakhtin, divides into subgenres; and the novel's death and transfiguration foreshadowed in Dostoyevsky. The narrative form of the *Iliad* 'has no beginning and no end,' and encompasses all life. In epic, as in the drama 'the past either does not exist or is completely present. Because these forms know nothing of the passage of time, they allow of no qualitative difference between the experiencing of past and present; time has no power of transformation, it neither intensifies nor diminishes the meaning of anything.' Epic achieves a suspension of temporality by ignoring the forces of change and historicity. As an embodiment of an integrated and non-individualistic world, the epic narrator narrowly restricts the role of subjectivity, isolating fragments of a separate reality, and bringing them to rest within the passive, reflective subjectivity of the hero. The novel continues in the epic habit of moving towards totality, but at a time when psychic wholeness and belief have broken down. In a famous formulation, Lukács describes the novel as 'the epic of a world that has been abandoned by God.'[18]

If we position *Paradise Lost* along the historical axis traced out by Lukács, it would fall somewhere in the interstitial space between epic and novel. Harold Toliver places Milton's epic in a direct line 'from feudal to bourgeois narrative,' and treats *Paradise Lost* as an epic of everyday domestic life: 'The novel picks up daily life as one of its subjects, but on a different scale and in a totally different tone.' If we follow Toliver in seeing the novel as generically committed to the representation of familial relations, Milton occupies a transitional place in the history of narrative. His interest in techniques of psychological individuation, combined with his manipulation of narrative and verse technique to highlight the conditions and qualities of subjectivity, suggests a powerful affinity between epic and the novel.[19]

We should not allow a historical teleology focused on the novel to obscure the close relationship that obtained between epic and the newer forms of prose narrative that eventually supplanted it. Epic, especially Virgilian epic, continued to occupy a central place in the curriculum, its preeminence consolidated by frequent citation and close study. Despite growing enthusiasm for novel and romance throughout the seventeenth century, the *Aeneid*'s authority and prestige extended epic's control over newer forms of narrative. In a preface published in England in the same year as the second edition of *Paradise Lost*, Georges de Scudéry (or perhaps Madeleine de Scudéry, or both in collaboration) answered charges of anachronism by invoking the masterwork: 'great *Virgil* shall be my Warrant, who in his Divine *Æneids* hath made *Dido* appear four Ages after her own.' The romance writer acquainted with Virgil had no fear of 'erring, as long as I followed so good a guide.'[20] This continuing dependency of newer forms of narrative on the theory and imitation of epic suggests the instability of generic interactions throughout the period. If Milton (and Butler) write epic (and anti-epic) moving towards the novel, romancers such as the de Scudérys located themselves in a cultural space defined by Virgilian standards. Even as late as the mid-eighteenth century, the novelty of the novel and the historical boundedness of *epos* remained questions of considerable interest and immediacy.

Critics often point out the *Aeneid*'s profound influence throughout seventeenth-century England, and its particular influence on *Paradise Lost*.[21] We might also remember the difficulties posed by the Virgilian model: it arrived in seventeenth-century England with a long history of poetic and critical mediations behind it, which had retroactively fixed certain meanings to the text. Virgil played an important role in defining notions of originary perception and firstness as specific functions of epic. His official status as the 'first of poets' and exemplar of the epic ideal coalesced in the *Aeneid*'s embodiment of the origin-idea as a representation of the critical moment of founding, analogous to birth.

The *Aeneid* takes as its subject 'pater Aeneas, Romanae stirpis origo' [father Aeneas, source of the Roman stock], the founding of Rome and the empire growing from it (12.166). The word *primus* recurs frequently throughout the poem, most significantly in the context of a capsulized history or genealogy connected to the rise of a particular civilization. Aeneas, we learn from the opening lines, is the man who first came to Italy from Troy, 'Troiae qui primus ab oris / Italiam.' When Aeneas seeks to establish his legitimacy and secure the cooperation of King Evander, he reminds him of their common ancestry and describes the mythical founder of Troy, Dardanus, as 'Iliacae primus pater urbis et auctor' [first father and creator of the city of Ilium] (8.134). Virgil's interest in the category of firstness extends far beyond the narrative structure of the epic and his use of interlocking verbal patterns. What to modern criticism may seem a straightforward question of imitation and influence, must have appeared to Virgil as the fundamental issue of what could be called origins. Gian Biagio Conte relates the problem of origin to the interchange between text and tradition, genre and cultural foundation: 'The problem of origins faced Virgil when he turned in another direction, too. His task was to write a new cultural text for the Roman community. In it the poet would have to go back to Rome's earliest foundation, to uncover a set of national deeds, customs, and ways of behaving (making up a "value system") that, despite digressions and pauses, backslidings and denials, would account for the essential elements of the present.'[22] As Conte goes on to suggest, primacy constitutes more than a chronological category in Virgil. It provides a means for the members of a community to consolidate and articulate their collective experiences. For later readers of Virgil, the matter of Troy takes on a special status, providing an explanation of the West's cultural identity. The Troy legend and the *translatio imperii et studii* (the westward movement of Roman culture) function to explain the entire network of cultural practices that define Europe as a separate historical entity. The myth of continuous Trojan ancestry provided an explanation of occidental generation; it permitted Europe to trace its civilization to a single source located in a geographical and temporal space outside of the terrain where it continued to flourish. As Richard Waswo argues, to focus on Troy and on a narrative of migration and cultural transmission, 'was to impose an origin that was always already destroyed, and hence required a narrative of displacement, exile, and reconstruction.'[23] Virgil provided later poets with a code for structuring and sometimes allegorizing the problem of origin.

It should not surprise us, then, to learn that the qualities considered essential to epic by the Renaissance were precisely those singled out in the *Aeneid*. Having defined epic in terms of a subset of Virgilian characteristics, they designated Virgil epic's principal exponent. Renaissance poetics maintain not only the pre-eminence of epic as the most difficult of genres, but also its authority as a universal standard by which to judge other genres. In this sense epic serves as the 'original' or archetype of all poetry and Virgil as the art's supreme exemplar. J.C. Scaliger outlines a system, based on the principle of conformity to a primary pattern, in which epic stands as a generic point of reference: 'for objects of every kind there exists one perfect original to which all the rest can be referred as their norm and standard. In epic poetry, which describes the descent, life, and deeds of heroes, all other kinds of poetry have such a norm, so that to it they turn for their regulative principles.'[24] The nomothetic, law-giving function of epic immediately renders problematic the question of succeeding attempts to revise or work through the tradition. The ideal of epic as supreme and absolute, combined with Virgil's pedagogical elevation as poetic *princeps,* meant that every alteration acquired the aura of deviation.

The problem of epic exhaustion, the widely shared conviction that direct appropriation merely produces anachronism and strengthens a sense of epic's inapproachability, derives from the form itself. Epic comes equipped with built-in obsolescence. For the Renaissance poet who hopes to reconnect with epic by transmuting its materials, his likelihood of success must confront a long history of similarly motivated failures. The mere fact of completion, apart from realizing any standard of quality, confers upon the epic poet a version of the heroic status that attaches to epic characters. By the close of the Renaissance, with numerous post-Homeric failures behind, it seemed obvious that a gift for writing epic 'flow'd but in few, and even those streames descended but from one Grecian Spring: And tis with Originall Poems as with the Originall Peeces of Painters, whose Coppies abate the excessive price of the first Hand.' This typical originary image appears in the preface to *Gondibert,* and arises from Davenant's finding himself in the 'Baconian' situation of having to defend a half-realized and unrealizable project. Davenant's historical survey of 'Heroick' poetry includes Homer, Virgil, Lucan, Statius, Tasso ('the first of the Modernes'), and Spenser. Attending to the strengths and limitations of each one in his historical situation, Davenant vindicates Virgil against the aspersions of 'some (who perhaps are affected Antiquaries, and make priority of time the measure of excellence).'[25] The weight of the entire tradition comes to rest on the problem of maintaining continuity with predecessors in a genre that requires each poet to begin at the beginning.

The status of epic as a single, unapproachable source encouraged Renaissance theorists to view the genre in agonistic terms, as a contest in which Homer and Virgil vie for primacy. Establishing Virgil's superiority, whose language they knew better and whose writings they preferred, required some dexterity in light of the primacy principle. In grappling with the question of Virgil's 'secondary' status, some Roman authorities resolved the issue of priority by shifting the argument from chronological precedence to evaluation. There was a well-established tradition, initiated by the Romans themselves, of comparing Homer to Virgil. The learned woman of Juvenal's sixth satire compares the two, and '*Virgil* layes / In one Scale, in the other *Homer* waighes.' Many of these comparatist exercises concluded, after lengthy analysis, in favor of the Roman poet. Quintilian quotes the comment of Domitus Afer, '"Virgil comes second, but is nearer first than third,"' and then continues: 'And in truth, although we must needs bow before the immortal and superhuman genius of Homer, there is greater diligence and exactness in the work of Virgil just because his task was harder.'[26] The principle of priority undergoes revision to support Roman claims of epic foundation. Virgil's position had to be rethought in order to transform belatedness, inherently a deficiency, into a difficulty compensated for by a superiority of art and refinement.

The debate revived in the sixteenth century, at a time when the problem of valuation had a crucial bearing on the production of epic and the practice of imitation. Marco Girolamo Vida helped to establish the Virgilian model as a cultural foundation, and made adulation of the *Aeneid* a function of nationalism. Vida views Virgil, in direct opposition to the primitive and long-winded Homer, as prince of poets, a writer whose renovation of rough antiquity has transmitted Roman imperial and cultural power to the present. *De Arte Poetica* shores up the theoretical basis for the enthronement of Virgil by trumpeting the supremacy of epic. Of all the various genres none compares to epic. In this generic and cultural economy, Virgil occupies a paramount position that entitles him to veneration and respectful imitation. Italian poets in particular should regard him as superior to all others, and dedicate themselves to following in his path. J.C. Scaliger, who had no national interest vested in asserting the supremacy of an Italian poet, claimed that his preference lay in the model of conduct he found implicit in Virgil. Compared to the barbarism of Homeric Greece, Virgil's heroes provide better standards of aristocratic conduct. Scaliger thought Virgil had perfectly assimilated Homeric influence, producing a cumulative improvement or modernization of epic.[27]

René Rapin, in a 1664 treatise, undertook a comparison of Homer and Virgil, and concluded that Homer's inventiveness and seniority cannot outweigh Virgil's superior 'art.' From the perspective of furnishing a model for modern poets, Virgil deserves a pride of place: 'si j'aymerois mieux avoir esté Homere que Virgile, j'aymerois aussi beaucoup mieux avoir fait l'Eneïde que l'Iliade & L'Odyssée' [If I would rather have been Homer than Virgil, I would much rather have written the *Aeneid* than the *Iliad* and *Odyssey*]. At a late phase in the seventeenth-century history of this critical argument, Hobbes steps into the fray, with the preface to his *Iliads and Odysses of Homer*. Hobbes's discourse on the relative virtues of Homer and Virgil and Lucan swims against the modern tide to side with the judgment of antiquity: 'It is no wonder therefore if all the ancient learned men both of Greece and Rome have given the first place in poetry to Homer.' He concludes his remarks on the importance of 'discretion' or decorum to epic by undercutting claims for Virgil's superiority: 'It is rather strange that two or three, and of late time, and but learners of the Greek tongue, should dare to contradict so many competent judges both of language and discretion.' Hobbes appeals to the authority of antiquity in two senses: first, to the cumulative weight of its evaluation, according to the humanistic standards most relevant to the matter; and second, to the chronological priority (and hence deeper linguistic and literary knowledge) of the critics who supposedly preferred Homer. This invented rivalry, while uninteresting in itself, exposes the problem inherent in transforming epic into an aesthetic manifestation of the originary ideal. Epic depended on the normative status of a unitary model. Its theorists attempted to restrict the implicit latitude of a bi-cultural standard, one that encompassed a wide range of positions between two quite dissimilar texts, to a single text. In this sense, epic had become incapable of renovation. Poets who 'found it marble' could either leave it marble or leave it altogether alone.[28]

In 1635, the industrious and deeply read George Hakewill surveyed the Homer–Virgil debate in order to contest the thesis of continual degeneration, specifically in relation to literary production. Hakewill makes his own Virgilian preference clear, citing verses by his friend John Downe on the challenge Scaliger mounted to Homer's position as 'primus, / Rerumque origo ... unde cæteri vates, / Suumque suxit ipse Publius nectar' [the first and the origin of things from whence came other poets, and Virgil himself drew nectar]. This, however, is subordinate to his main purpose. On the authority of Pliny, Lucretius, Cyprian, among others, writers of the earlier-seventeenth century suggested that the world had grown degenerate and was winding down through a process of entropy. Taking the contrary position, Hakewill argued that heavenly bodies are not subject to impairment, that only individuals suffer natural decay and dissolution, that the Creation remains no less varied and vigorous now than at the time of the flood. Hakewill's governing conception revolves around the idea that the genius and spirit of each age varies, and offers a cyclical and regenerative view of history in place of the degenerative principle. The Reformation itself provides evidence of periodic renewal and improvement since even the conversion of the Jews seems within the range of possibility. A substantial body of traditional scholarship has pitted the 'medieval' doctrine of nature's universal decay against utopianism and the 'idea of progress,' supposedly embraced by Milton. Although the doctrine of progressive degeneration faced mounting challenges from the sixteenth century onwards, its underlying logic provided an integral part of the period's epistemic set. Even an outspoken opponent of theories of progressive decay, such as Hakewill, never thought to deny that the universal narrative would conclude apocalyptically. Nor did he refute the general principle underlying it, that 'every thing the farther it departs from its originall, the more it loses of its perfection.' Rather he challenges the principle's applicability to the downward movement of creation as a whole. It goes almost without saying 'that the Creature the nearer it approaches to the first mould, the more perfect it is, and according to the degrees of its removeall and distance from thence, it incurres the more imperfection and weaknesse, as streames of a fountaine, the farther they runne thorow uncleane passages, the more they contract corruption.'[29] The figure of the fountain, of the source, neatly encapsulates Hakewell's sense of a 'circular' progress. Put in larger perspective, every apparent moment of decline actually participates in an oblique and paradoxically cyclical pattern of ascent.

Beginning early in his career, Milton delved into the question of whether the universe declines or simply undergoes perpetual change until the end of time. In Prolusion 7 he condescendingly dismisses the view 'that whereas a long succession and course of years has bestowed glory on the illustrious men of old, we live under the shadow of the world's old age and decreptitude, and of the impending dissolution of all things' (*CP* 1: 302). In the immediate context of the prolusion, however, Milton does not depreciate degenerative cosmologies in order to champion the protestant ideology of progress, or to refute Donne's *Anniversaries*. Rather he speaks against the theory's negative implications for learning. At no point, however, does he dismiss the importance of those 'uncertainties and perplexities' that induce professions of ignorance or the suspension of judgment. Milton again considers the problem in a work that probably bears the direct imprint of Hakewill's 1627 edition: 'Naturam non Pati Senium' [that

Nature does not suffer from old age], a set of Latin verses apparently composed as an academic exercise. Milton agrees that nature is not subject to senescence and decay, but rather retains the primal energy of its earliest days. The poem begins: 'Heu quam perpetuis erroribus acta fatiscit / Avia mens hominum, tenebrisque immersa profundis / Oedipodioniam volvit sub pectore noctem!' [Alas! how persistent are the errors by which the wandering mind of man is pursued and overwearied, and how profound is the darkness of the Oedipean night in his breast!] Milton proceeds in this school exercise in conventional form by piecing together an ensemble of classical and neo-Latin tags. The editors of the Variorum commentary connect the first line to several sources, most significantly for our purposes, to book 6 of the *Aeneid*, where the shade of Deiphobus queries Aeneas about his adventures: 'pelagine venis erroribus actus / an monitu Diuum?' ('what storms by seas or land have hether dryvn yow? / or hath some god soch hard commawndment gevn yow?')[30] The condition of doubt that the poem describes falls somewhere between the epic quest for foundation and Sophoclean tragedy of obscure birth and hidden origins. Human understanding wanders through self-constructed mazes of doubt and perplexity, always conflating the inward and the outward. Plunged into Oedipean darkness, the mind proceeds to 'make its own acts the measure of those of the gods and compares its own laws to those that are written upon eternal adamant' (ll. 2–6). Despite this condition of epistemic anxiety, we can rest assured that the object of our understanding, the world itself, remains immutable, unchanged from 'earliest time' (60–1). We must not overstep preordained bounds and prematurely reach for closure before the fullness of time. Milton concludes the poem (in a phrase oddly anticipative of Samuel Barrow 'Res cunctas, & cunctarum primordia rerum') by reaffirming his faith in a universal narrative of predetermined consummation: 'in aevum / Ibit cunctarum series iustissima rerum, / Donec flamma orbem populabitur ultima' [the righteous sequence of all things shall go on perpetually, until the final fire shall destroy the world]. Existing outside of our wayward institutions lies an unalterable structure, which manifests itself through history and in time and provides a fixed point in a universe of constant flux.

In *Paradise Lost* Milton seems unwilling to discount the possibility of being 'an age too late' for undertaking epic (9.44). He raises the question of the determinant role of history (and climate) on the formation of the poetic temperament only to let it drop. The very act of writing drains his statement of any real conviction, especially coming so late in the poem. Why, we might ask, should epic remain especially susceptible to generational pressures? As William Kerrigan points out, the doctrine of the world's decay appears nowhere else in the poem and apparently had not caused Milton much anxiety since the 1640s. Kerrigan follows other commentators on these lines by connecting them with Milton's remarks on 'Epick form' in *The Reason of Church-Government*, specifically the passage following his description of Tasso's putting the choice of his epic subject in the hands of Duke Alfonso II of Ferrara: 'if to the instinct of nature and the imboldning of art ought may be trusted, and that there be nothing advers in our climat, or the fate of this age, it haply would be no rashnesse from an equal diligence and inclination to present the like offer in our own ancient stories' (*CP* 1: 814.) Kerrigan and others suggest that we should understand 'the fate of this age' as 'a comment, poignant but unsentimental, about the effect of the Civil War on an attempt to write a Christian, English, and inspired poem.'[31] The political disturbances and military struggles looming ahead were precisely the stuff out of which epic might be made. Milton would indeed require prophetic power to see the 1640s as a time unpropitious for poetic composition. If he were contemplating a career as a playwright we might understand his hesitation: the movement for suppressing the playhouses gained ground in early 1642 and the 'distracted' state of the nation furnished an excuse for closing the theatres in September. Milton, however, generally thought that the period's revolutionary excitement reinvigorated intellectual life, and in *Areopagitica* sees such ferment as a sign that 'betokens us not degenerated, nor drooping to a fatal decay.' The collocation of texts suggests a continuity of circumstances between the 1640s and 1660s that contradicts Milton's own acute sense of his historical position. The subtext of his argument is the cultural distance he finds himself from an admired Tasso, and even from English Spenser. If Milton had entertained serious doubts about the impact of impending revolution on his poetic production, why would he repeat the objection in a post-revolutionary situation that left him on the defensive but with an abundance of time for writing? If something remains constant from one decade to the other, we cannot identify it as Milton's attitude towards the 'distraction' of contemporary politics.

Another answer may lie in the immediate context and occasion of *The Reason of Church-Government*. Milton has been set to thinking about historical belatedness by the work to which he responds: *Certain Briefe Treatises ... Concerning the Ancient and Moderne Government of the Church. Wherein ... the Primitive Institution of Episcopacie is Maintained* (Oxford 1641). To this work Lancelot Andrewes contributed 'A Summary view of the Government both of the Old and New Testament,' which bristles with citations and roots episcopal authority in biblical history. Andrewes argues that bishops stand in direct lineal descent from the apostles, whose powers of commanding, correcting, ordaining, and disposing ecclesiastical affairs were necessary for establishing the primitive church. If episcopal authority remained unshakable at a time when the 'graces' of healing, speaking in tongues, and other divinely infused gifts regularly evinced themselves, 'much more in the ages ensuing, when all those graces ceased, and no means but it to keep things in order' (33). In Milton's view, the defenders of prelacy support their positions through dubious appeals to antiquity; if their positions had any merit, they would not 'run questing up as high as *Adam* to fetch their originall.' Milton, however, satirically grants them their precedent: 'they are so insatiable of antiquity, I should have gladly assented, and confest them yet more ancient. For *Lucifer* before *Adam* was the first prelat Angel, and both ... for aspiring above their orders, were miserably degraded' (*CP* 1: 762).

In describing his 'long choosing' of a subject and 'beginning late' (9.26), Milton suggests another reason for postponing the project until the onset of middle age. These slightly defensive phrases provide him with a pattern of self-justification built around the long preparation necessary for undertaking epic and the poet's conformity to the threefold creative sequence associated with Virgil's movement from pastoral to georgic to epic (*pascua, rura, duces*). The traditional beginning of the *Aeneid*, dubiously attributed to Virgil but included in Renaissance editions of the poem, made the progression from pastoral through georgic to epic a schematic division of all human life: 'Ille ego qui quondam gracili modulatus avena / Carmen ... at nunc horrentia Martis' [I who once piped a song on a slender reed ... now sing the dread weapons of Mars]. Known in the Middle Ages as the *rota Virgilii*, it divided style into low, middle, and high, social rank into the professions of shepherd, farmer, and soldier.[32] Milton echoes Virgil's lines quite closely in the opening of *Paradise Regained*, and more distantly in *Paradise Lost*, where they form part of a rationale that reveals the difficulty of beginning epic. Epic comes only as the result of a long preparatory process, making its seizure of an origin both difficult and paradoxical. The invocation to book 9 marks the transition from Eden to a world of labour and yet another beginning: thereafter Adam will eat bread in the sweat of his brow. As Milton shifts the poem from 'Rural repast' to events 'more Heroic' than romance or the wrath of Achilles, he marks the onset of a mode both tragic and epic. At this generically divided but important narrative juncture, Milton commences the poem afresh by making explicit reference to its epic genesis:

> Sad task, yet argument
> Not less but more Heroic than the wrath
> Of stern *Achilles* on his Foe pursu'd
> Thrice Fugitive about *Troy* Wall; or rage
> Of *Turnus* for *Lavinia* disespous'd,
> Or *Neptune's* ire or *Juno's*, that so long
> Perplex'd the *Greek* and *Cytherea's* Son.   (9.13–20)

'Of *Turnus* for *Lavinia* disespous'd, / Or *Neptune's* ire or *Juno's*' comically displaces epic's martial impulse on domestic relations in a manner not dissimilar from Butler's. 'Disespous'd' suggests a correlation between civil war and marriage, between sexuality and violence, between poetic and amorous rivalries. Aeneas' destined wife, Lavinia, becomes a type of Helen, a source of discord. In the immediate context of this passage, Milton presents himself as over-going Virgil's model of successive stages of poetic accomplishment. By advertising the difficulty of settling on a subject suitable for epic treatment, Milton reminds us of his immediate predecessors and their failed strategies for circumventing them.

'Beginning late,' as Milton presents it in book 9, stresses the artistic maturity of his effort, but also suggests the poem's adherence to the convention of *in medias res*. Although fixed on absolute beginnings, epic makes a point of avoiding strict patterns of chronological development. The prescription for beginning epic *in medias res* derives principally from Horace's *Ars Poetica*:

> nor *Troyes* sad Warre begins
> From the *two Egges*, that did disclose the twins.
> He ever hastens to the end, and so
> (As if he knew it) rapps his hearer to
> The middle of his matter.   (146–9)

According to Horace (here quoted in Jonson's translation), the epic poet thrusts the reader into the events of a narrative rather than beginning, for example, the story of Troy with Leda and the birth of Helen. Poets forestall achieving the goal of epic, the elemental founding of some existing institution, until a later moment. Through a deliberate strategy of deferment and delay, recapitulation and digression, they implicate auditors into the process of discovery. As in most epic formulas of this type, Horatian lawgiving derived only partial authority from classical precedent. The *Odyssey* and *Aeneid* conform to the rule, while Lucan's *Pharsalia* and the *Thebaid* of Statius do not. We find a similarly varied practice among the moderns: Vida's *Christiad* begins with a later episode in the life of Jesus, but *Gondibert* progresses in chronological order. As Edward Tayler, among others, has argued, the simultaneous movement of *Paradise Lost* backward and forward in time, and its detour to a new beginning halfway through (in conscious allusion to the *Aeneid*), encourage the reader to adopt a perspective in which past, present, and future appear as coordinates of a single timeless moment. Milton uses the *in medias res* beginning to order temporality according to a scheme in which all history dissolves into the present, a present that contains within it every past and subsequent moment.[33] Implicit from the poem's beginning, the final effect of this reduplicative technique is to obscure the origin it seeks to recover and deliberately to complicate the whole process of recovery.

As we have seen, epical origin serves to define the past as a normative totality. It helps epic to achieve a radical defamiliarization of the present by contemplating lived experience in relation to a mythical past, and it reconstructs national beginnings in order to position history in a confirmatory relation to its own time of writing. Writing epic becomes a process of disappearing beneath a distant, prehistorical, and absolute past in order to create a fixed point upon which to superimpose the present. The account of beginnings marks the textual incipience of the collective writing to which Milton contributes. In his note on the verse, Milton pronounces unfavourably on rhyme in epic as 'the Invention of a barbarous Age,' dismissing it as a 'trivial' supplement to the genre. He offers his poem as 'an example set, the first in *English*,' a performance designed to release successors from the burden of their historicity and the 'modern bondage' of subsequent traditions.

Genesis remains unusual among creation myths in that it maintains a strict separation between the origin of the world and the origin of evil, the distance between them conceived as an absolute distinction between goodness and its negation. Milton's determination to develop a rational theodicy and fully to explain the enigma of evil drives him progressively farther back in time, to increasingly distant and uncertain acts of begetting. The structural and narrative complexity of *Paradise Lost* is such that we can never determine a single point at which the epic action unquestionably gets under way: the Creation (book 7), the creation of Eve and Adam (books 4 and 8), and the elevation of the Son (book 5) all have reasonable claims on a position of pre-eminence. The two scenes that deal directly with the travails of knowing describe the earliest impressions and recollections of Adam and Eve. As critics often note, the scenes representing their initial awakenings together constitute an important instance of 'structural parallelism' in the poem, a Miltonic device that provides the means for drawing subtle distinctions through contrastive recurrence.[34] In these two scenes of inauguration and the birth of consciousness, we find a pattern of epic origin beset by uncertainty and error.

6

Who Himself Beginning Knew?

In *Paradise Lost* the knowledge of origins is beleaguered by doubt. The opening lines of book 1 assert the principle of absolute primacy at first emphatically, but then more tentatively: 'Of Man's First Disobedience,' '*Eden*,' 'first taught the chosen Seed, / In the Beginning,' 'Things unattempted yet,' 'Thou from the first / Wast present.' Milton suspends the crucial phrase 'in the beginning' until the ninth line, which has the effect of underlining his own text's revisionary relation to Genesis. Milton's realignment of this sacred beginning signals the existence of a temporal and creative space between his epic and its scriptural source: it asserts the poem's separate identity in relation to what it recalls and transfigures. By first presenting the idea of beginning as a syntactic–temporal puzzle, Milton sets us on a path where ultimate destinations get relocated farther and farther back in time. He accomplishes this by deferring the occurrence of the expected phrase, by holding it in reverse until after the culmination of universal history ('till one greater Man / Restore us'), and by attaching it to Moses (who antedates Christ in history but here follows him syntactically).

Milton's attempt to narrate a universal history obliquely confronts the difficulties involved in staging a narrative *ab initio mundi*. The *in principio* of Genesis 1:1 diverts our attention from the question of what preceded the beginning (and the difficult doctrine of *creatio ex nihilo*) by occupying the initial position. Jewish commentators regarded the formula 'in the beginning' [*Bereshit*], which gives Genesis its Hebrew title, as an allegory of knowledge. Sir Walter Ralegh's *History of the World* discusses the phrase at length, noting the obscurity of 'this word *beginning*,' and referring the reader to a Targumic translation, where *bereshit* 'is converted by the word *Sapientia*.' Other English poets who fictionalized the birth of consciousness narrated in Genesis found the notion of divine inauguration equally mysterious. Thomas Heywood's *The Hierarchie of the Blessed Angells* (1635) describes an ultimate being who 'is without beginning, and yet gives / A First,' but declines to import into his poem '*Philosophers* to brall / And quarrell 'bout the Worlds orginall.'[1] Milton chose a more oblique strategy to coordinate the tensions surrounding his commitment to the recovery of lost origins. He displaces the postlapsarian inutterability of the primordial creation onto the syntax of the invocation itself, making its postponement a function of our temporal distance from Edenic consciousness.

Book 1 of *Paradise Lost* repeatedly promises an extensive etiology of sin and error along with full disclosure of 'who first seduc'd them to that foul revolt.' Yet as Milton 'hastes into the midst of things,' he defers explanation to depict an episode of no obvious immediate importance: the fall of Satan and his demonic cohorts into hell. With this episode the poem plunges us into confoundedness and utter darkness, where the first question to break the silence is 'If thou beest hee' (1.84). Even before this, readers meet with uncertainty and multifarious beginnings where they might expect an isolated moment at which the action commences. When the poet invokes the Holy Spirit, he professes himself in need of instruction on precisely the point at issue: 'Instruct me, for thou know'st; Thou from the first / Wast present.'[2] Although invocations dedicate themselves to re-inaugurating a pattern of beginning, the difficulty of this process of cyclical recreation comes into view in the invocation itself. The potential multiplicity of beginnings first achieves visibility with Milton's iteration of his injunction to capture the originary point: 'Say first ... say first what cause.' Nothing remains hidden from the Holy Spirit, who compensates for the poet's confessed limitations. Because of the Spirit's contemporaneity with the events narrated, it alone can provide answers to the questions of 'what cause?' and 'who first seduc'd them?' This inaugural question, as William Kerrigan points out, carries a 'threat of infinite regress,' and defers dealing with the problem of evil through a relentless logic of substitution and symbolic interchange.[3]

Milton's concern with the problematic and potentially erroneous beginning has not escaped critical attention. According to David Quint, Milton's assertion of antiquity's secondariness clears away 'a tradition of error from his sacred source,' and empties 'the field of potential rivals in order to make room for his own voice.' In Quint's version of the Bloomian scenario of rivalry and influence, Milton effects a reversal of his relationship to antecedents, and achieves literary authority by placing *Paradise Lost* in a position of absolute priority. Having reduced his predecessors to authoring fictions that imperfectly imitate his own archetypal narrative, Milton transforms biblical authority into the desacralized value of literary originality. Making a related claim for Milton's historical 'originality,' Marshall Grossman situates psychoanalysis 'within a historical formation of the self of which Milton's narrative is exemplary,' and makes *Paradise Lost* 'the epic of the origin of Freudian man, discovering the form and subject of psychoanalytic inquiry.' Grossman argues that Milton's epic deploys the resources of form, typology, and narrative to construct a historical subject capable of authoring its own self-defining history. As 'authors to themselves,' Adam and Eve inscribe their life histories unimpeded by the superscription of divine providence or typological intervention.[4]

Northrop Frye, evidently with Milton in mind, has argued that the myth of a fall from original perfection benefits from an internal mechanism that defuses critique and closes inquiry. If we cannot understand the creation myth on its own terms, no matter how carefully we analyse and reanalyse the Genesis account, we simply blame the limitations of fallen consciousness. The myth of an absolute beginning, superior to everything that follows but recuperable through repeated renewal, has also attracted Regina Schwartz's attention. Combining biblical hermeneutics with Derridean notions of origin-as-iteration, Schwartz explores Milton's preoccupation with repeated beginnings. The Milton who emerges from her study appears unsure of the accessibility of beginnings, his accounts of creation invariably mediated by other (mainly biblical) accounts, and every beginning asserted and re-asserted against the constant threat of encroaching chaos. Schwartz relates Milton's binary 'counterplot' to a series of oppositions: forbidden versus licit knowledge; domination versus revelation; and 'pathological' or compulsive repetition versus ritual commemoration. Milton, she concludes, embraces a moral logic in which the denial of origin (for example, Satan's thinking himself self-begot) issues in evil, while the ritual repetition of an origin confirms the inevitability and rightness of the present.[5]

A general understanding that *Paradise Lost* is a type of origin tale, a poem about an empire at its founding moment, has not been seen in relation to its rendering of Adam's primary consciousness. In book 8, the explanatory power of origins, their status as a condition of existence, becomes the object of the instruction Adam undergoes at the hands of his divine tutors. As soon as Adam experiences his first glimmerings of consciousness, he apprehends the createdness, along with the creativity, of creation. As Gordon Teskey observes, what Milton has Adam perceive, 'almost immediately upon waking, as being the deepest truth of the world,' is 'that it is a thing made.'[6] Shortly after, Adam begins naming the creatures, a process intended to impose a taxonomic grid on the natural world and assert his mastery over it. The artificiality of paradise alerts him to the possibility of straying from the origin, even in the Edenic state. Inescapably, the institution of 'Adamic' language interposes another reality between the knower and the known, the product and its unitary source.

Considering the importance to Milton of the concepts surrounding them, 'origin' and 'original' do not figure prominently in his poetic lexicon. The words retained a slightly Latinate tinge in the seventeenth century, perhaps carried over from their use in philosophy. Aristotle placed the term *arche* in the basic philosophical lexicon provided in book 5 of the *Metaphysics*, defining it roughly as 'the first point from which a thing is or comes to be known,' and 'that part of a thing from which something first arises.' The difference between the two is the difference between a 'starting-point' (something distinct from 'cause') and an 'authority' or 'rule.' Since Aristotle associates continuity with political authority, the two concepts blur into one: we apply the word *arche* to those who possess social authority, 'just as the origins in cities, and dynasties and kingships and tyrannies, are called origins.' Throughout the sixteenth century the Latin word *origo* often described or justified the systematic establishment of authority. Used in association with terms such as *auctor, parens,* and *fons,* it continued to play a part in the legitimation of specific forms of political and social organization. Claude-Gilbert Dubois describes the genealogizing and archaeologizing impulses surrounding the word as contributing to an aristocratic notion of the origin, a vehicle useful for legitimizing a name, title, or legal right.[7]

Late in *Paradise Lost,* Milton uses the word *original* three times, in each case in the context of 'original' sin (11.424, 12.83, 9.1004–5). Books 1 and 2 contain the schematically coupled 'Original brightness' and 'original darkness,' the first in reference to the fallen Satan's lost lustre and the second to his hoped-for resumption of chaos and ancient night (1.592, 2.984). The double valence of 'original,' which, as the OED 2 points out, refers both to the origination of persons and to an originator, emerges in a textual variant between the 1667 and 1674 editions.[8] Neither reading has superior authority, and each conveys a quite different meaning: 'when his darlings Sons / Hurl'd headlong to partake with us, shall curse / Thir frail Original, and faded bliss, / Faded so soon' (2.373–6). In the first edition the penultimate line pluralizes the first noun: 'Thir frail Originals, and faded bliss.' The speaker is Beëlzebub, whose contempt for submitting to 'the popular vote' and building 'a growing Empire' in Hell evolves into a scheme for plotting revenge on humanity. The politics of resentment he practices feeds on the thought that God 'still first and last will Reign,' despite the boldness of their undertakings. His plan, concocted with Satan, to seduce humanity 'to our Party,' or in some other way engineer its downfall, hinges on the idea that God, as a parent, will feel his offsprings' misfortunes more keenly than his own. The prospect of winning over humanity to share the fallen angels' hatred, to generalize the rebellion against arbitrary rule and so demonstrate its unbearableness, makes this revenge especially appealing. Beëlzebub's appeal mixes a particularly spiteful version of *Schadenfreude*, pleasure in the misfortune of others, with the assurance of minimal effort. He images the double satisfaction they will derive from a second fall as both humanity and Heaven feel the force of the unbounded malice set loose in the world.

Since Beëlzebub expects the animus of posterity to fall upon the source from which it has proceeded, he must refer either to the fallen angels' supreme foe, or to our first parents. 'Originals' suggests parentage in an inclusive sense: Adam and Eve. In this reading, the male children of God ('sons') will revile the authors of their woe, and perhaps even provide surrogates for the fallen angels. In the singular, 'original' suggests that future generations will curse God, much like the Hebrews whom Isaiah imagines living under conditions of Assyrian oppression and despair: 'they shall fret themselves, and curse their King, and their God, and looke upward' (Isa. 8: 21). The Fall thus establishes, at least in the minds of subsequent generations, the 'frailty' of an all-powerful God. Beëlzebub thus undermines the godhead by raising the question, the implicit counter-argument to Milton's optimistic theodicy, of God's ultimate culpability, given the authorial or originative claims advanced on his behalf.

A substantial body of critical commentary has accumulated around the word *error* (and related words *err*, *errands*, *erroneous*) in *Paradise Lost*. The best known occurrence comes in book 1, following the description of Vulcan's day-long fall, suddenly punctuated with the disclaimer: 'thus they relate, / Erring' (1.747). By first suggesting the epic simile and then retracting it, Milton implies a negative evaluation of the tradition from which it is drawn. Useful as a heuristic, the trope's adequacy as a vehicle of transcendent truth immediately comes into question. Earl Miner cites the phrase as an example of the figure he calls 'dissimile' and comments: 'Butler had published the first part of his *Hudibras* with many such dissimiles before *Paradise Lost* appeared.'[9] Milton has a tendency to complicate and compound the negative valence of 'error' by joining it to other negatives. The verb *to err* appears four times compounded with a negative, 'err not,' as if to alert us to error's multitudinous possibilities and the difficulty of ascertaining the truth. To the assembled fallen angels Beëlzebub speaks of Eden's rumoured existence 'if ancient and prophetic fame in Heav'n / Err not.' By informing the council of the existence of another inhabited world, Beëlzebub opens up the possibility of faulty transmission, rumour, uncertainty. We soon hear Satan employ the phrase more emphatically in warning Michael that threats alone cannot vanquish him: 'err not that so shall end / The strife which thou call'st evil' (2.346–7, 6.288–9). Here the phrase 'err not' means 'make no mistake,' or 'don't delude yourself into believing.'

Although Satan has an obvious claim on our attention as the dominant vehicle of erring in its many manifestations, we cannot attach the word to any single character. At times we see God's emissaries winging about 'on errands of supernal Grace,' yet we repeatedly hear of Satan's sallying forth on his 'bad Errand.' Later, Death takes on this errant role, saying to Sin: 'I shall not lag behind, nor err / The way' (7.573; 4.795; 10.41, 266). At the close of book 9, as Adam and Eve fall to acrimonious discussion, Adam considers himself to have 'err'd in overmuch admiring / What seem'd in thee so perfet.' He has come to repent 'that error now, which is become my crime.' His initial blunder of mistaking weakness for perfection produces his moral failure. Eve refers back to this accusation when she speaks of her inability to console Adam, her words having been 'found so erroneous' and their outcome 'found so unfortunate' (10.969–70). Throughout the poem the words vacillate between ethical and epistemological registers, as the two domains periodically interfuse. More susceptible to error after the Fall, Adam's decodings of the natural signs and omens around him continue to reveal his acuity. When Michael approaches him to convey Heaven's latest instructions, Adam moves from vague discernment to confirmation. As the narrator interjects a resounding 'He err'd not,' the poem begins its upward ascent to the revelation of history contained in the final books (11.208).[10]

Some critics associate Milton's language of error and wandering with allegory and the strategies of romance, where readers typically find themselves entangled in wayward narrative structures and the uncertainties of language. Other critics contrast Milton's apparently binarized distinction between error (sin) and origin (Truth) with the turns and counterturns of a romance plot. Thus Gordon Teskey finds Milton's conception of error reductive, and makes a distinction between Spenserian (diegetical) allegory and Miltonic (dialectic) didacticism. Milton's reversion to a prelapsarian origin, Teskey contends, rules out the possibility of perpetual wandering. Rather than finding error an inescapable condition of language and narrative, Milton places a cordon around it and attempts to regulate it.[11]

Viewing Milton's conception of error as the bipolar opposite of a monolithic truth, however, flattens out the process by which he imagines humanity attaining to knowledge. His association of truth with an immutable origin does not eliminate the difficulties we encounter in achieving it, or obviate the need for negotiating the labyrinth of experience. In a recent essay, Stanley Fish argues that the lesson of the *Areopagitica* is that 'knowledge and truth are not measurable or containable entities, properties of this or that object, characteristics of this or that state, but *modes of being*, inward dispositions, conditions of a heart that is always yearning for new revelations.'[12] Avoiding error entails a process of endless deferment and self-revision. When, in *Areopagitica*, Milton follows Scripture (and Bacon) and compares truth to a fountain, he suggests the necessity of having fresh infusions of experience to renovate knowledge: 'Truth is compar'd in Scripture to a streaming fountain; if her waters flow not in a perpetuall progression, they sick'n into a muddy pool of conformity and tradition' (*CP* 2: 543). Knowledge, the image suggests, involves humanity in an ongoing process of construction and reconstruction.

It is Satan, however, who adopts a position of strict constructivism, if only for polemical purposes. On several occasions, the rebellious angels invoke hard evidentiary standards and challenge received doctrine. Typically, they seek experiential proof of God's invincibility, of the existence of Eden, and challenge points open to dispute by referring questions back to basic postulates. Satan challenges Abdiel's contention to know the nature of God 'by experience taught,' and scoffs at the catechistic truth he articulates. The esoteric doctrines of creation by the logos and Christ's agency as the divine word elicit a response from Satan that parodies post-Baconian experimentalism and scepticism: 'Doctrine which we would know whence learnt: who saw / When this creation was?' Satan has just outlined an argument, loosely based on natural-law theory, that God cannot 'introduce / Law and Edict on us, who without law / Err not' (5.856–7, 797–9). Satan believes that God has established right and wrong by fiat, or according to arbitrary definition; by denying God's power, he expects to escape the binarizing consequences of sin and thus avoid its consequences. Abdiel exposes the impossibility of Satan's strategy and depicts him as literally incapable of refraining from error: 'Apostate, still thou err'st, nor end wilt find / Of erring, from the path of truth remote.' Satan's temperamental and theological antithesis, Abdiel nevertheless describes his resistance to Satanic exhortations to rebellion as appearing alone 'in thy World erroneous to dissent / From all,' and singlehandedly maintaining the truth 'when thousands err' (6.172–3, 146–8). When Adam first comes into existence, he cannot adopt either of these stances, but must negotiate a position that encourages his innate appetite for knowledge without thrusting him into heresies.

In *Paradise Lost,* Adam's original perfection in no way prevents his experiencing doubt and uncertainty, or undergoing a process of intellectual growth. Adam's principal employments before the Fall are labour in the garden and conversation, the latter conceived as both recreative and self-improving. From the first moment of his creation, he exhibits signs of a rationality that operates under some constraint. Within the text of Genesis itself, scholars detect a gap between the Adam of the Priestly document, where he figures as a perfect being, and the portrait of the more 'primitive' Yahwist, who attributes a childlike innocence to Adam. Edward Reynolds suggests the outlines of a contemporary debate on Adam's capabilities when he argues that 'wee may not think that God, who made Man in a perfect stature of Body, did give him but an Infant stature of Mind.' Without the possession of perfect knowledge, Reynolds continues, Adam 'could not have given fit Names, and suteable to the Natures of all the Creatures which for that purpose were brought unto him.'[13] The knowledge he instantly acquires is ordinarily attainable through the processes of cognition and experience, through engaging the world and testing its possibilities.

Milton's location of scenes of cognitive initiation in a symbolic state of infancy, in which the human subject makes trial of experience, has a largely unrecognized precedent in the Virgilian tradition. In the complex critical afterlife Virgil assumed in medieval commentaries, the idea of psychic development as an allegorical *primus* played an important role. Around the sixth century, Fabius Planciades Fulgentius developed a *Bildungsroman* reading of the *Aeneid* as an allegory of the 'ages of man,' which influenced Dante's reading and the commentary on Virgil ascribed to Bernardus Silvestris. According to the scheme presented in his *Expositio Virgilianae Continentiae Secundum Philosophos Moralis,* the first five books of the *Aeneid* chart human life from birth through adolescence to young manhood to *virilis aetas* [man's estate]. The pivotal sixth book represents initiation in the mysteries of wisdom, and the last six the soul's battle against vice. Fulgentius treats book 1 as an allegory of infancy, the Trojan shipwreck, for example, signifying childbirth under the power of Juno, goddess of birth. The details of this *expositio* allegorize Virgil in a remarkably ingenious, if slightly mechanical way. Shaping a line of interpretation determined by the requirements of moral allegory and a programmatic Neoplatonism, Fulgentius outlines the 'threefold progression in human life: first, to possess; then to control what you possess; and third, to ornament what you control. Think of these three stages as arranged in my one verse line, as "arms," "man," and "the first." "Arms," that is, manliness, belongs to the corporeal substance; "man," that is, wisdom, belongs to the intellectual substance; and "the first," that is, a ruler (*princeps*), belongs to the power of judgment; whence this order, to possess, to control, to ornament.'[14] The translation of *primum* as 'ruler' – a word Fulgentius takes to refer to an inner wisdom, or self-knowledge – signifies the culmination of a progressive sequence in the dominant faculty of 'judgment.' As Everyman, Aeneas undergoes the stages of a developmental process, moving up a Platonic ladder to reach the apex of wisdom.

The *Aeneid*, with its episodes of confusion, doubt, and mistaken identity, became understood as immersed in the theory of knowledge. The medieval tendency to equate philosophy with poetry and other branches of learning transformed Virgil into a polymathic authority with a special interest in science and the theory of knowledge. Neoplatonism provided an interpretive frame against which readers could allegorize the poem as a systematic treatment of human maturation and growth into wisdom. In episodes such as the one in which Venus cloaks Aeneas and his companion in a cloud, readers detected an allegory of the trials of knowing. Cristoforo Landino, in the *Camaldulensian Dialogues* (1480), devised an approach to Virgil that read the epic as a narrative of psychic drama and spiritual growth. In Landino's version, the attainment of philosophic wisdom proceeded through stages that brought Aeneas from childhood sensuality (Troy) to a life of contemplation. Aeneas' ascent proceeds along a path leading through accumulated experience and repeated errors. Aeneas' wanderings, particularly the episodes where 'inremeabilis error' and 'inextricabilis error' confuse his course (5.591, 6.27), symbolize a process of learning through successive stages of repudiated error.[15]

Adam shows a keen interest in narratives that describe various acts of creation. We might briefly review the circumstances leading up to the scene in book 8 where he shares his recollections with Raphael. Raphael's initial response to Adam's question about the difference between an earthly and a heavenly diet is the oblique comment: 'O *Adam*, one Almighty is, from whom / All things proceed, and up to him return' (5.469–70). The logic of this seemingly unmotivated comment becomes apparent in the subsequent books. Raphael proceeds in his explanations by isolating a series of primal moments: as he explains, God has made Adam perfect and good but time works changes on all created things. Since immutability and atemporality remain God's exclusive prerogatives, Adam cannot expect to understand phenomena without exploring their history and temporal genesis. This poses a unique problem since such histories have disappeared below the surface of phomena, and Adam must penetrate to a realm beyond the visible. The subtext of Raphael's systematic instruction throughout books 5 and 6 entails a method of exploring phenomena by excavating their beginnings. Adam consequently finds himself filled 'with desire to know / What nearer might concern him,' how the heaven and earth began. The 'nearer' here sounds half-ironic since Raphael has depicted the distance between Eden and the upper regions as illimitable. Yet the method of establishing chronology and determining a 'cause' have immediate implications for Adam's own condition. A quick study, Adam takes the initiative in this process of origin-hunting, asking 'How first began this Heav'n?' 'When, and whereof created for what cause?' (7.61–4, 86). Mixing a 'natural' inquisitiveness with caution, he speculates that the story of creation may hold a mystery capable of elucidating other mysteries he has already heard. His use of the tripartite sequence 'when,' 'whereof,' and 'what cause' would seem to support his familiarity with several basic metaphysical concepts. Raphael has already thoroughly established the doctrine of creation *ex deo* (5.469–74), and the notions of creation-in-time and causality have provided the basic parameters of their discourse. Subtract them and the entire exchange would lose coherence. Adam pursues the details of an origin, the mere fact of which he takes for granted. He does so because within this primary explanation might lie an axiom on which to base subsequent interpretations. Even the sun, as he imagines it, stands transfixed in the sky, eager to hear a tale of 'His Generation, and the rising Birth / Of Nature from the unapparent Deep.' The sun itself remains frozen until it has heard a satisfactory account of its origin, after which, presumably, it will continue on its diurnal course. To his question Adam receives a detailed, if finally unsatisfactory, answer. Before answering, Raphael issues a mild warning, which first points out the obstacles to understanding such narratives encounter: 'What words or tongue of Seraph can suffice, / Or heart of man suffice to comprehend?' Raphael advises Adam that God has charged him with the commission of satisfying his 'desire / Of knowledge within bounds,' and he fully intends to police those bounds. God himself, however, has already enforced the limits by occluding the highest mysteries. Beyond licit knowledge lie human 'inventions,' fictions and conjectures, or forms of knowledge devised by humanity on its own terms (7.102–3, 113–14, 119–21). Inevitably, this would include language.

The question at which the 'Divine Interpreter' balks involves why God's hierarchical logic dictates the existence of supernumerary stars and planets, and could 'on thir Orbs impose / Such restless revolution day by day / Repeated' (8.25–32). Adam's cosmological model, of a stationary earth against a backdrop of perpetual planetary rotation, soon dissolves in Raphael's eclectic survey of theories of heliocentricity and geocentricity. Note that while Raphael neither affirms nor denies particular hypotheses, he unequivocally states that God situates himself and the Heavens beyond 'human sense' so that human intelligence, 'if it presume, might err in things too high' (8.119–21). Raphael's description of the birth of the universe does little to put Adam out of doubt, but no amount of further discussion could resolve the question.

Adam, whose quest for meaning encourages him to pursue stories of origin, senses the difficulty of his position. Not only has God, himself invisible and unknowable, placed limits on how much his curiosity may comprehend, he has also implanted a psychic mechanism that makes over 'too much' knowledge as ignorance. To preserve his omniscience and inviolable supremacy, God carefully circumscribes Adam's *curiositas,* allowing knowledge of origins as it pertains to the self, but interdicting knowledge of the ultimate origin. The 'high' knowledge forbidden to Adam and Eve is the knowledge of causes, or of metaphysical 'first principles' in the Aristotelian sense of that phrase.[16] Part of what makes such arcana unknowable is God's attribute of timeless priority. As alpha and omega, beginning and end, God embodies a paradox of a non-linear temporality: 'Him first, him last, him midst, and without end.' Already 'unspeakable' as 'parent of Good,' God's relation to the process of time, which defines the creation, makes him doubly mysterious (5.153–65). Milton attempts to elucidate the notion of an eternal present by depicting God as a comprehensive causality: 'anyone who asks what God did before the creation of the world,' he writes, 'is a fool.' God creates the world at a time earlier than our 'time,' which comes into being only with the first creation of substance.[17] Milton thus postulates a time before time, the consequence of a single creation, and the existence of an ineffable deity for whom every moment is immediately present. Accommodated to consciousness through a series of abstract manifestations, God is 'Omnipotent, / Immutable, Immortal, Infinite, / Eternal King.' The Almighty represents himself as peerless in both temporal and qualitative senses:

'alone / From all Eternity, for none I know / Second to mee or like, equal much less.' Above all else, God is a creator, 'Author of all being' (3.372–4, 8.405–7). When Satan says that 'we know no time when we were not as now,' he not only manifests the heresy of thinking himself 'self-begot, self-rais'd,' he also demonstrates the difficulty consciousness encounters in imagining existence prior to its existence (5.859–60).

Avoiding the intricacies of this question, Raphael redirects their conversation to a narrative detailing another beginning: 'Think only what concerns thee and thy being,' he says, bringing their colloquy around from astronomy to psychology and natural history. After receiving Raphael's counsel to 'be lowly wise,' and to fix this thoughts on the paradise about him, Adam obligingly expresses his own distaste for 'wand'ring thoughts, and notions vain.' The word *notion* – which, as we have seen, has both psychologistic and doctrinal associations – here joins with the motif of errancy. Milton describes this response as spoken by an Adam now 'clear'd of doubt,' a phrase that suggests 'rendered incurious' as much as 'duly informed.' The 'prime Wisdom' of self-knowledge puts us at a distance from errors, 'intricacies,' and 'perplexing thoughts' (8.173–97). The process of clarification that their conversation exemplifies occurs in the realm of discursive reason:

> Thee I have heard relating what was done
> Ere my remembrance: now hear mee relate
> My Story, which perhaps thou has not heard;
> And Day is yet not spent; till then thou seest
> How subtly to detain thee I devise,
> Inviting thee to hear while I relate.   (8.203–8)

The triple concatenation of 'hear' and 'heard' with 'relate,' combined with Adam's noting the passage of time, emphasizes the temporal dimension in which human discourse takes place. By contrast, God's performance of inauguration takes place through the articulation of the Word: his acts, however, 'cannot without process of speech be told' (7.178). Adam dwells within the limits of narration and Edenic language. In the prelapsarian state, speech, the activity that most clearly defines the social relation, has the capacity to beguile (and implicitly mislead) even the most discerning auditor.

Adam, who has learned the lesson of the irrecoverable origin with alacrity, prefaces his own narrative of beginnings with a disclaimer: 'For Man to tell how human Life began / Is hard; for who himself beginning knew?'

Adam obliges Raphael with an account of his creation, but not before almost retracting his offer. As children, the tales we most like to hear involve our own brief histories, stories we cannot tell well ourselves. Adam shares this fascination with autobiographical narrative. Yet he hesitates slightly before setting out the details of his birth, perhaps because his first sensations occur in a state of consciousness that hovers between sleeping and waking. When he relapses into this hypnagogic condition just before receiving the first heavenly visitation, he thinks himself capable of returning to his 'former state / Insensible, and forthwith to dissolve' (8.250–1, 286–91). A regression from infancy to non-being is not possible, and subsequent history traces a progressive accumulation of knowledge, a steady ascent before the Fall. As Adam drifts upward to consciousness, evaporation steams from his body, becoming absorbed into the sun. The succession of verbs moves from the liminal state 'wak't,' to the supine 'laid,' followed by an interchange or transference whereby the sun performs the actions of drying and feeding. Physically and psychically, then, Adam moves in a direction opposite to the autochtonous. Even before he speaks, he immediately seeks knowledge of the creation, and searches the sky for signs of an invisible presence whose existence he intuits:

> Straight toward Heav'n my wond'ring Eyes I turn'd,
> And gaz'd a while the ample Sky, till rais'd
> By quick instinctive motion up I sprung,
> As thitherward endeavoring, and upright
> Stood on my feet; about me round I saw
> Hill, Dale, and shady Woods, and sunny Plains,
> And liquid Lapse of murmuring Streams.   (8.257–63)

Adam's 'wond'ring eyes' recall the moment of self-reproach, some seventy lines earlier, when he dissociated himself from 'wand'ring thoughts, and notions vain.' The subtle distinction between intellectual curiosity (wondering) and the restless motions of the mind (wandering) will provide matter for subsequent instruction. At this point, however, he can give vent to such impulses unchecked. Significantly, only after he examines the natural world about and above him does he turn to investigate himself, seeking reassurance of his bodily integrity in a manner that recalls a soldier's coming to consciousness after battle: 'Myself I then perus'd, and Limb by Limb / Survey'd.' The evidence of his senses, literally the testimony of the body, affords him little knowledge of the metaphysical questions that most intrigue him: 'But who I was, or where, or from what cause, / Knew not' (8.267–8, 270–1). Milton carefully divides this three-part sequence to suggest a progressive movement from self, to locale, to first causes. The mounting series of interrogations – 'who?' 'where?' 'from what cause?' – performs a sequence similar to Fulgentius' threefold progression: corporeality, intellect, rational judgment.

As the question of human origination enters his consciousness, Adam impulsively finds himself moved to articulate his condition. His first linguistic act is to attach names to natural phenomena. Although he will later advance from simple nomination to inquiry and petition (his request for a companion to share his solitude), his initial imposing of names establishes his place at the pinnacle of creation. Adam relates:

> to speak I tri'd, and forthwith spake,
> My Tongue obey'd and readily could name
> Whate'er I saw. Thou Sun, said I, fair Light,
> And thou enlight'n'd Earth, so fresh and gay,
> Ye Hills and Dales, ye Rivers, Woods, and Plains
> And ye that live and move, fair Creatures, tell,
> Tell, if ye saw, how came I thus, how here?
> Not of myself; by some great Maker then,
> In goodness and in power preëminent;
> Tell me, how may I know him, how adore,
> From whom I have that thus I move and live,
> And feel that I am happier than I know.   (8.271–82)

Milton's position on the Adamic language, in this passage and elsewhere, is often contrasted with the Lockean doctrine of linguistic conventionalism, which posits no natural correlation between names and their referents. Critics thus associate Milton with the *Cratylus* and literalist readings of Genesis 2: 19 ('and whatsoever Adam called every living creature, that was the name thereof').[18] At this point, however, Milton says virtually nothing about the accuracy or rightness of the names with which Adam apostrophizes nature. The emphasis falls strictly on the impulse that provokes Adam to talk, the intentionality that motivates his utterance. The brief interval between 'to speak I tri'd' and 'forthwith spake' condenses the laborious process of language acquisition into a single conjunction.

Expressing himself for the first time, Adam exhorts the mute, but richly significative world to impart some knowledge of his origin ('tell, / Tell … tell me'). In asserting his power, Adam assumes the existence of a greater 'power' from whom he derives being. Despite his twice reiterated claim to 'know,' the difficulty of knowing is precisely the issue at point: Adam goes from verbally registering 'whate'er I saw' to entreating the creatures to disclose what remains hidden from him, 'if ye saw.' Right from the beginning, he feels the presence of limitations placed on the understanding. He queries a silent nature according to an ascending sequence, which begins with 'how came I thus?' but soon moves on to 'how here?' and 'how may I know him, how adore?' First, he addresses the circumstances of his creation, but then, the presence that animates all creation.

The best evidence for a 'Cratylic' reading of Adam's imposition of names occurs after God has pronounced his interdiction and continues in a more encouraging tone:

> Not only these fair bounds, but all the Earth
> To thee and to thy Race I give; as Lords
> Possess it, and all things that therein live,
> Or live in Sea, or Air, Beast, Fish, and Fowl.
> In sign whereof each Bird and Beast behold
> After thir kinds; I bring them to receive
> From thee thir Names, and pay thee fealty
> With low subjection;
> ...
> I nam'd them, as they pass'd, and understood
> Thir Nature, with such knowledge God endu'd
> My sudden apprehension. (8.338–54)

On the basis of this passage, however, we have little reason to think that the Edenic language corresponds perfectly and uniquely to truth, signifying things in their essences. What God infuses into Adam is not names themselves but the 'knowledge' whereby Adam can transform his ideas into appropriate appellations. The Adamic language, even at its earliest moment, is a fabrication, a 'man-made' entity, although brought into being with divine assistance. In *Christian Doctrine* Milton cites Genesis 2: 20 as evidence of Adam's 'natural wisdom,' but advances no claim about the perfection of the primal tongue. Adam, he comments, 'could not have given names to the animals in that extempore way, without very great intelligence' (*CP* 6: 324). In book 7 of *Paradise Lost*, the earliest description of Adam's naming, Raphael implies that knowledge precedes nomination, that word follows thought: 'And thou thir Natures know'st, and gav'st them Names' (7.493). According to some critics, Adam's ability to name the creatures according to their properties represents a unique occasion. Ordinarily, knowledge in paradise is imparted through a mediating voice or vision, not directly. Even here, however, Milton posits a process of mediation. Adam invents language by systematically, although effortlessly, choosing nouns to match the animals brought before him. Adam accomplishes, in his own limited sphere, an act of creation analogous to God's, providing a sign of his rational domination that determines subsequent hierarchies.

If the knowledge Adam obtains through sudden apprehension guides him in the study of natural history, it remains incomplete in certain vital respects. Adam still feels an absence that his imposition of names does nothing to remedy: 'but in these / I found not what methought I wanted still' (8.354-5). As a living being who has speech as a defining characteristic, Adam desires the company of someone with whom he can 'converse,' not as with an 'inferior' being, but in 'fellowship' and 'rational delight' at the prospect of 'social communication' (8.389, 391, 429).

Part of what we inherit from Adam's naming of the creatures, along with the lexical apparatus for obtaining natural knowledge, is the ideology of the sex–gender system. God brings the animals before Adam not only divided into species, 'each with thir kind,' but also 'fitly' combined in pairs, 'Lion with Lioness,' and so on (8.393-4). Adam sees himself as the sole exception to the universal principle of heterosexual union. As the animals parade by in couples, each joined up with an appropriate signifier and mate, he longs to see himself similarly paired.

Despite Adam's vague feelings of unease with his condition of God-like supremacy, his naming of Eve in book 4 places her in a subordinate position. (As we shall see, just prior to Adam's speaking Eve's name for the first time, the invisible voice hails her using the same form of address adopted in line 276: 'fair Creature.') When, in the divorce tracts, Milton comments that Adam, 'who had the wisdom giv'n him to know all creatures, and to name them according to their properties, no doubt but had the gift to discern perfectly, that which concern'd him much more,' he means that Adam understood Eve's fitness to become his helpmeet better than he understood nature because the former affected him more immediately (*CP* 2: 602). The two events merge in Milton's imagination because both involve the acquisition of knowledge necessary for establishing the interest of rationality.

The primal language Adam speaks has no innate capacity to bridge the gap between sign and referent by some miracle of semiological transparency. Rather it is unique for the spontaneous manner in which Adam acquires it, and for its role in validating his dominion over the creatures.

Bacon, we will recall, invokes the myth of Adam as consummate natural philosopher to justify the practice of scientific inquiry, its use in achieving a divinely ordained right of domination over nature. Adam's absolute possession of Eden is symbolically sealed in the feudal homage he receives from the creatures, who pay him 'fealty / With low subjection.' Imposing a name represents the achievement of power and understanding, which is why Adam seeks to extend nomination to its furthest limits. God, however, remains the great unnamable, whose very namelessness (or unpronounceable 'real' name) betokens unknowability: 'O by what Name, for thou above all these, / Above mankind, or aught than mankind higher, / Surpassest far my naming' (8.357-9). The act of naming confers power on whoever performs it, and a degree of subordination on whoever is designated. Milton considers it evidence of God's incontestable priority that the Son derives his name from the Father: 'the giving of a name is always acknowledged to be the function of a superior, whether father or lord' (*CP* 6: 261). Naming operates as a temporal limit, an act of consciousness that summons the later and adventitious into being and places it in a hierarchical order.

In writing *Paradise Lost* Milton faced a situation quite different from that of English Protestant divines who speculated on the nature of the *lingua adamica*, and its dissemination before Babel. Theoretical speculation concerning Adamic speech and privileged modes of consciousness contributed little to solving the problem of representing characters engaged in the processes of reasoning, soliloquizing, and conversing. Itself a linguistic construct, the poem could not transcend language to depict an origin prior to language. Milton's representation of Edenic origins had to operate within the confines of generic structures and semiological codes. Despite Adam's capacity for rational domination, God gives him good reason to sense his inherent limitations. When he contrasts his own capacities to those of the Almighty, he uses the words 'deficience,' and 'defects,' 'imperfection,' and 'defective.' All of these contain the Latin root *facere* [to make], and imply the existence of a natural correlation between createdness ('creation from') and secondariness. Adam's superior intellect apprises him of his alienation from the origin, and hence imperfection, yet offers no linguistic or other mechanism for avoiding error. He finds himself in a situation that differs from ours in degree, not kind. In Loredano's *Life of Adam*, the example of humanity's 'first originall' functions to remind us of our own greater susceptibility to sin: 'Consider, that the greatest errors proceed from the greatest wits, in that the wisest man in the world fell; and that so much the more inexcusably, inasmuch as it was easier not to have sinned.'[19] In Milton, Adam's superior intellectual capacity manifests itself in an effortlessly acquired conventional sign-system. The possession of a perfectly 'adequate' language provides no insurance against error. Adam's self-defining 'creation,' language, imposes a particular logic upon the book of nature, but it cannot penetrate the impenetrable or render humanity impervious to error. Its scientific instrumentality does nothing to dispel the moments of doubt and uncertainty that define the experience of consciousness.

Arnold Stein contends that 'language, to a Milton nurtured in the Renaissance, is God-given, and still capable of revealing authentic relationship with its origin.' According to Edward Said, *Paradise Lost* strives to recapture 'a primeval Origin' that antedates language, but which, 'like Paradise, is lost forever.' Stein suggests that vestiges of the primary code, which necessarily obey the universal principles governing all language, remain accessible. Said regards the language of Miltonic epic as always already fallen, inevitably estranged from the world it represents. Human discourse, Said writes, '*begins* after the Fall,' and retains only the fading memory of its origin 'in the unity and unspoken Word of God's Being.'[20] In Eden discursive reason joins with angelic intuition: Raphael explains the difference between the two as a question of 'degree' (5: 486–90). Humanity inhabits a discursive world where the possibility of unmediated knowledge becomes increasingly remote as words endlessly multiply into other words.

The Renaissance had no single view of Adamic language and its relation to human understanding. As the doctrine of origin came under new scrutiny, Milton grappled with the problem of Adam's primary consciousness and divinely instituted language in a climate of growing uncertainty. For Milton's contemporaries, the circumstances and temporal logic of Adam's creation remained profoundly perplexing. Despite its importance to the religious and philosophical discourses of the seventeenth century, humanity's Adamic origination was far from a self-evident or universally accepted postulate. As exploration and colonization enlarged European ethnographic consciousness, speculation about the feasibility of a single ancestral source increased commensurately. Squaring biblical monogenesis with expanding anthropological knowledge presented a problem for those who would maintain Adam's status as the first and sole source of succeeding generations. The doctrine of 'pre-Adamitism,' while heretical and guaranteed to generate storms of controversy, won some prominent adherents. It gained credit, for example, with Giordano Bruno, who developed the polygenetic theory that Africans and Indians 'cannot be traced to the same descent, nor are they sprung from the generative force of a singe progenitor.' Sir Walter Ralegh, Thomas Harriot, the mathematician and travel writer, and Christopher Marlowe all faced accusations of harbouring versions to this irreligious view. Throughout the 1650s English practitioners of a historical Bible criticism (often pressed into the service of radical politics) questioned the literal truth of Adam's priority, and speculated on the continued existence of peoples descended from sources other than Adam.

In 1655 Isaac La Peyrère's *Prae-Adamitae* appeared, and, in the following year, an anonymous translator produced an English version titled *Men before Adam*. La Peyrère undertook to make biblical exegesis more consonant with pagan historiography and chronologies, an effort that drew fire from many quarters. With great energy, if somewhat limited learning, he argues that Adam deserves to be called the 'first' man in precisely the same say that Christ is the 'second': 'For relatively and Typically, *Christ* and *Adam* are called the first and second *Adam*,' the former having redeemed us of the latter's sin. Adam, by this standard, is 'the first and father of all men' only in so far as he represents the first to lapse into sin and define humanity as we now know it. The consequences of La Peyrère's views are deeply heretical. For example, he enumerates the erroneous beliefs that 'all men should have their original from *Adam,* that all men should be held to have sinn'd in *Adam;* or that the sin of *Adam* should be imputed to them.'[21] Adam, according to this reading, is no literal progenitor but an allegory of the process of mystical diffusion whereby a single act of transgression becomes spread throughout the world. La Peyrère sets himself against an Adamicism that put subsequent generations in the shadow of an unsurpassable but remote progenitor whose misdeeds control every aspect of present existence.

The debate continued into the decades following the Restoration. Establishing the defectiveness of non- or anti-scriptural accounts of the creation occupied Edward Stillingfleet. In his *Origines Sacrae* (1662), Stillingfleet battles the atheistic and heterodox currents then sweeping Europe. Against Epicureanism, Cartesianism, atomism, pre-adamite theories, the new cosmology, and the new biblical criticism, he musters the rearguard action of a defensive orthodoxy. Theories of the world's eternity or of the necessity of its existence or of God's removal from it after the creation undermine the foundations of religion and so require energetic refutation. Since any hint of doubt on these matters triggers an avalanche of atheism and disbelief, he asserts Adam's historical priority and the derivation of all subsequent generations from him as beyond contestation: 'For as it is hard to conceive how the effects of mans fall should extend to all mankinde, unless all mankind were propagated from *Adam*; so it is unconceivable how the account of things given in *Scripture* should be true, if there were persons existent in the world long before *Adam* was.' A great impediment to certainty lies in the *'near resemblance'* of truth to error, but Scripture still provides a reliable guide. Stillingfleet regards knowledge as reunification, an assembling of 'scattered fragments' into an Adamic wholeness. He revives the Platonic idea of knowledge as remembrance and recovery 'of those *notions* and *conceptions* of things which the *mind* of man once had in its pure and primitive *state,* wherein the *understanding* was the truest *Microcosm,* in which all the beings of the *inferiour* world were faithfully represented according to their *true, native,* and *genuine perfections.'*[22] Stillingfleet offers a clear formulation of the view critics attribute to Milton: that Adam spoke a perfect non-conventional language in which word and referent corresponded, that he knew their essential natures and names issued forth of their own accord, that preternaturally appropriate designations virtually assigned themselves.

For Pascal, too, obtaining epistemological guarantees depended on our understanding the circumstances of our creation. Arguing that Cartesian method and the suspension of certainty did nothing to resolve basic problems of knowledge, he enlisted Descartes' hypothesis of a *mauvais génie,* in the first Meditation, to reverse the encroachments of the *nouveau pyrrhonisme.* Since truth remains undemonstrable, we must take refuge in faith or face the possiblity of continuous and irremediable error. Belief in the existence of a good God provides the means for overcoming doubt about the reliability of human reason. The principle of an elusive human origin produces the phenomenon of undecidability, the impossibility of knowing 'if these Principles are given us either true or false, or incertain, according to our Original.'[23] Once we have secured an origin, an entire hierarchical system of belief falls into place.

The reflexivity of language and the consequent disappearance of truth are often viewed as defining features of the post-modern condition. Nietzsche was the first in a line of nineteenth- and twentieth-century philosophers who regarded thought as inseparable from language, and developed that position to undercut every claim of absolute truth. When Nietzsche pronounced language constitutive of reality he removed any possibility of freeing ourselves from its constraints. For post-Nietzschean philosophy, locked in the dilemma of reflexivity, there can be no absolute truth, no ultimate origin, no escape.

Milton, as one would expect, approaches the conundrum of reflexivity from a very different outlook, an outlook that combines Platonic realism with a conventionalist understanding of language. *Paradise Lost* depicts an origin deemed inaccessible from a fallen perspective, but towards which humanity can steadily strive. The unstable and constantly changing condition of language defines postlapsarian experience of reality. Through speech and writing we articulate our presence in the world; yet speech and writing articulate us as social beings. Like Bacon, Milton adopts a version of representationalism that sees language giving shape to a prior reality. Yet language does not 'simply' reflect a pre-existent origin in *Paradise Lost*. For Milton, reflection is never a simple process. We can only gain access to a world of unspoiled perception – Eden in the fullest sense – through structures of language and representation. As words and images bring us into contact with originary truth, they saturate our consciousness and produce the habits of thought that shape our lives and perceptions.

In the following chapter, we see that Milton's construction of Eve's identity attributes to her a form of consciousness, much like Adam's, bounded by the phenomenon of error. When Eve attempts to get back behind appearances to seize an origin, she finds an empty mirror that, paradoxically, fills with her own 'fair' image. Eve's 'error,' in the Baconian sense, resides in her being 'imposed upon' by an idol of the mind, a false appearance in the 'enchanted glass.' Initially, she becomes engulfed in an illusion that dissolves the distinction between self and other. As Eve discovers the alterity of mental representation – the mind's dependence on structures of differentiation in making experience intelligible – she suppresses the instinct to see herself in everything around her. By the close of the scene, and under the influence of Adam's interpretation, her gazing into the mirror comes to embody a mode of cognition closely associated with the phenomenon of reflection.

7

The Figure in the Mirror

Paradise Lost, as critics often point out, is organized around various moments of birth and origin, including the creation in the Logos, the birth of Christ, and the rebirth of the soul. Milton's emphasis on origination practically mandates an engagement with questions of sexuality in the context of his domestic epic. As Edward Said notes, Milton 'unashamedly weaves in the sexual drama, which more than any other image conveys the novelty, as well as the nexus of intention, circumstance, and force, that always characterizes the beginning.'[1] Yet the presence of a debate on gender relations in *Paradise Lost* invites obvious questions about the nature of Milton's sexual politics. How subversive of established hierarchies is a poem that endorses mutuality between the sexes, yet makes mutuality a function of subordination, that identifies itself with human liberty, yet dreads the prospect of female autonomy?

In a recent essay Regina Schwartz calls for critics to move the debate on Milton and women to an area of inquiry more productive than 'the tired question of Milton's old-fashioned patriarchalism.' John Guillory also argues for a new approach to understanding the problem of sexual subjection in *Paradise Lost.* Where feminist readers of Milton read gender 'into' *Paradise* – that is, as a fully formed discourse conditioned by biology and the psychology of sexual difference – Guillory wants to consider gender difference in relation to the nascent discourses of economics and science.[2] Yet the extensive literature on Milton and feminism illustrates a striking phenomenon in the history of *Paradise Lost*'s reception: the same poet who figures for some as the personification of a patriarchalist ethos (as he did for Virginia Woolf), provides others with cues for 'feminist' appropriations – and has apparently done so, according to Joseph Wittreich, since the seventeenth century. Catherine Belsey suggests that since *Para-*

dise Lost regularly exceeds its announced program and self-conscious intentions, we can read it, if not as a 'feminist' text, at least as a text reclaimable on behalf of feminism. Although Milton may labour to objectify difference as sexual difference, his narrative 'uncovers what it cannot explicitly acknowledge, the precariousness which is an inevitable effect of power.' James Turner has provided an account of Milton's gender polarities that stresses inconsistencies in the discourses on sexuality within the Genesis tradition. Turner argues, by reference to the conflicting doctrines and attitudes towards sexuality available to Milton, that Milton 'incorporates both the egalitarian and the hierarchical model into his vision of Paradisal sexuality, with no attempt to reconcile them.' Contradiction becomes a function of Milton's attempting to engage one notion of male supremacy, elaborately legitimized by reference to Genesis, and a contrary view that takes a comparatively egalitarian view of marriage and sexual relations.3 Milton intervenes in this controversy precisely as it reaches a moment of historical crisis.

Within this debate on gender identity in *Paradise Lost* lies the narrower question of the intention and significance of the so-called 'Narcissus scene' of book 4, regarded by many critics as crucial to our sense of the entire poem. In a reworking of the Narcissus myth, Eve falls in love with the figure in the lake, pining for her watery double. Eve, however, avoids Narcissus' fate of hopeless longing and eventual extinction through the intervention of an admonitory voice, which convinces her to abandon her self-fixation and seek fulfilment in conjugal union. Led by this invisible presence, Eve is brought to Adam, and, after an initial moment of hesitation, surrenders herself to Adam's society and to future motherhood. Eve's narration of the engendering of her own consciousness marks off the beginning of history as a process of error and correction:

> That day I oft remember, when from sleep
> I first awak't, and found myself repos'd
> Under a shade on flow'rs, much wond'ring where
> And what I was, whence thither brought, and how.
> Not distant far from thence a murmuring sound
> Of waters issu'd from a Cave and spread
> Into a liquid Plain, then stood unmov'd
> Pure as th' expanse of Heav'n; I thither went
> With unexperienc't thought, and laid me down
> On the green bank, to look into the clear
> Smooth Lake, that to me seem'd another Sky.

> As I bent down to look, just opposite,
> A Shape within the wat'ry gleam appear'd
> Bending to look on me, I started back,
> It started back, but pleas'd I soon return'd,
> Pleas'd it return'd as soon with answering looks
> Of sympathy and love; there I had fixt
> Mine eyes till now, and pin'd with vain desire,
> Had not a voice thus warn'd me, What thou seest,
> What there thou seest fair Creature is thyself,
> With thee it came and goes; but follow me,
> And I will bring thee where no shadow stays
> Thy coming, and thy soft imbraces, hee
> Whose image thou art, him thou shalt enjoy
> Inseparably thine, to him shalt bear
> Multitudes like thyself, and thence be call'd
> Mother of human Race: what could I do,
> But follow straight, invisibly thus led?
> Till I espi'd thee, fair indeed and tall,
> Under a Platan, yet methought less fair,
> Less winning soft, less amiably mild,
> Than that smooth wat'ry image; back I turn'd,
> Thou following cri'd'st aloud, Return fair *Eve*,
> Whom fli'st thou? whom thou fli'st, of him thou art,
> His flesh, his bone; to give thee being I lent
> Out of my side to thee, nearest my heart
> Substantial Life, to have thee by my side
> Henceforth an individual solace dear;
> Part of my Soul I seek thee, and thee claim
> My other half. (4.449–88)

The warning voice that diverts Eve from her image represents, for recent criticism, an embodiment of a mystifying patriarchy. Christine Froula sees Eve's conversion to the authority of Adam and Milton's God as a type of indoctrination. Eve, Froula contends, absorbs the values of God and Adam to the point of becoming their legitimizing spokeswoman. Her co-optation by her mentors is complete when she appears before us as the voice through which patriarchal authority ventriloquially speaks. This self-subordination entails the renunciation of her own experience and her final acceptance of her secondary status. The terms of her conversion, Froula argues, 'require that she abandon not merely her image in the pool but her very self,' which the voice equates with her insubstantial image. By acceding to this mystifying and prohibitive voice of an invisible authority, Eve consigns herself to a secondariness and otherness that persist into our own time. Mary Nyquist also sees an ideological motivation behind Milton's depiction of Eve's first experiences. She regards Eve's speech justifying her subordination as an important moment in the history of gendered subjectivity, a crux, 'historically and culturally, in the construction of the kind of female subjectivity required by a new economy's progressive sentimentalization of the private sphere.'[4]

In this chapter I depart from recent criticism by emphasizing the double movement between self and other in this scene as a function of the problem of origin. Eve's discovery of the phenomenon of alterity, her first encounter with the principle of difference, throws into doubt the authority of the senses and the stability of the self. The epistemological conundrum suggested by the figure of the mirror (and the figure in the mirror) situates the problem of self-reflexivity at the beginning of human consciousness. Bacon used the mirror metaphor to describe the uncertain status of the fleeting images that comprise our knowledge of the material world. His method committed philosophers to a program for differentiating false from accurate impressions, the mind from everything external to it. In book 4 of *Paradise Lost* mirroring functions as a complex sign of the thinking process and of self-consciousness at its Edenic site of origin.

Adam will describe the mirror episode again in book 8, but discrepancies between the two accounts imply a vast distance in perspective. Where Eve never makes a positive identification of the invisible voice, Adam confidently identifies it as the voice of God: 'On she came, / Led by her Heav'nly Maker, though unseen, / And guided by his voice.' In place of the obscurity and doubt of Eve's narration, Adam stresses Eve's apparent knowingness: she is neither 'uninform'd / Of nuptial Sanctity and marriage Rites,' nor unconscious of 'her worth.' From Eve's account it is unclear that Adam engages a rhetoric of seduction, or that Eve's momentary hesitation has the effect of further inflaming him. Eve turns aside from Adam, which, in his eyes, makes her all 'the more desirable.' Adam prefaces a brief explanation of his sexualized response with the comment, 'or to say all,' but continues in the same oblique and decorous vein. His wooing seems playful and self-assured, rather than urgent, as he describes it. The outcome of his colloquy with Eve is assured from the beginning. His eloquence seems superfluous all along when we remember that Eve already has had the options of celibacy and autoeroticism foreclosed. Adam can hardly anticipate resistance from Eve since he has already blurred the distinction between self and other, describing her as 'my Self / Before me,' (8.484–507). Adam follows the 'Yahwistic' creation account of Genesis, chapter 2, describing Eve's creation from his rib, rather than the less stridently masculinist 'Priestly' account: 'male and female created hee them' (Gen. 1: 27). In a trancelike condition, itself analogous to Eve's visionary state, he perceives God's removing his rib, which grows into 'a Creature' under his shaping hands. Adam's emphasis on Eve's secondary creation makes the point, common enough in both Jewish and Christian theology, that Eve's inequality correlates directly with her later succumbing to sin. Reflecting less of the Creator and mediated by Adam's prior creation, Eve's belatedness signifies an inherent flaw to Adam.

Adam treats Eve's surrender after a short dalliance as the triumph of 'reason,' the result of her instruction at the hands of God and his own persuasive power: 'she what was Honor knew, / And with obsequious Majesty approv'd / My pleaded reason' (8.508–10). Milton here echoes St Paul's epistle to the Hebrews (13: 4), 'Marriage is honorable to all, and the bed undefiled,' a text that figured prominently in early Christian defences of marriage. Paul, however, also articulated a number of male-supremacist positions based on Adam's priority: 'Let the woman learne in silence with all subjection: But I suffer not a woman to teach, nor to usurpe authoritie over the man, but to be in silence. For Adam was first formed, then Eve' (1 Tim. 2: 11–13). Eve's belatedness provides a rationale for the silencing of women. The pseudonymous pamphleteer 'Ester Sowernam' argued the homocentric logic of Genesis to the contrary conclusion: 'It appeareth by that Soveraignty which God gave to *Adam* over all the Creatures of Sea and Land, that man was the end of Gods creation, whereupon it doth necessarily, without exception follow, that *Adam*, being the last worke, is therefore the most excellent worke of creation.' Since God fashioned Eve last, she should assume the position of Adam's superior. Sowernam indirectly challenges Aristotelian essentialism, which made female nature passive, secondary, and impaired, and male nature an active first principle. For most commentators, however, Eve's secondariness at her nativity related her to an inferior position thereafter, and explained the visible signs of sexual difference.[5] Patristic writers such as Tertullian and Augustine had argued that woman *qua* woman was not created in the divine image. Although some theologians extended a principle of spiritual equality to religious beliefs and practices, they generally upheld the inferiority of women within the social structures of marriage and motherhood.

In 1 Corinthians Paul equates the institution of marriage with prostitution, and bends the text of Genesis to an implicit attack on conjugal union: 'What, know ye not that he which is joyned to an harlot, is one body: for two (saith he) shalbe one flesh' (6: 16). Milton's use of Paul to authorize paradisal sex within marriage dramatizes Adam's own wavering between opposed views of women and sexuality. As James Turner points out, the same Paul who insists on female subordination uses the phrase 'one flesh' to describe the union of Christ and his church (Eph. 5: 31–2). Taken together, the conflicting statements attributed to Paul reveal an attitude that 'varies between grudging contempt and fervent praise,' between 'erotic mutuality' and 'marriage as a sordid "burning."'[6] Adam, too, in groping towards a view on proper relations between the sexes, seems to steer between the poles of mutuality and rigid hierarchy, between spiritual communion and patriarchal oppression. Adam's oxymoronic phrase 'obsequious Majesty,' sums up his vacillation between deference to a feminine ideal and stiff-necked insistence on Eve's subordinate place in a rigidly hierarchical scheme. Adam's retelling emphasizes the fact of Eve's difference ('Manlike, but different sex, so lovely fair'), and makes this difference problematic right from the beginning. We are not surprised when he speculates that God has bestowed on Eve too much outward ornament, and made her 'of inward less exact.' Adam suspects that Eve's imperfect resemblance to their divine original may testify to her unfitness for exercising the 'Dominion giv'n / O'er other Creatures' (8.471, 538–9, 544–6). Eve, by contrast, tells the story of her birth in a way that suggests her perfect sympathy with the world around her, a complete identification with it.

Much of the scholarship on the 'Narcissus' scene has emphasized Milton's moralizing transformation of Ovidian myth. While such analyses pay careful attention to the specific features of Milton's intertextuality and strategies for revision, they leave open a number of questions. Why, for example, does Milton change the sex of the protagonist? What connection exists between this supposed instance of Miltonic didactic allegory and eroticized representations of female beauty mediated by reflection? Why would Milton think to invoke a passage that retains a residue of auto- and homoerotic overtones? James Holstun's discussion of the episode provides one answer by juxtaposing Milton's scene with poems such as Donne's 'Sappho to Philaenis,' an experiment in the manner of Ovid's *Heroides* (which *Hudibras* parodies in its two 'Heroical Epistles'). Holstun sees Milton as constructing 'a normative model of feminine identity,' one made all the more striking by Milton's inclusion of 'a scene of lesbian desire.'[7] Eve's initial act of transgression, her momentary lapse into error, occurs immediately prior to her being reinstated in an order that makes binary difference its primary operative principle.

To understand the centrality critics attach to the scene, we must understand the larger debate on Milton between liberal feminism and poststructuralist feminism. According to Milton's apologists, *Paradise Lost* articulates a progressive doctrine, a version of the familial arrangement that Lawrence Stone calls 'the companionate marriage.' Where others see the institution of a hierarchical model of human relations based on sexual difference, Milton's defenders question the nature of an 'autonomy' that would allow us to speak of Eve's surrender of an autonomous self. Their Milton is the laureate of individualism and of spiritual equality between men and women within marriage, if not political life. They point to Eve's unconstrained volition, her multiple acts of election, interpretation, and creation, to make a case for her full participation within a community of shared interests.[8] Taking a more ideologically conscious view of subjectivity and individualism, Froula, Nyquist, and Grossman regard Milton as playing a significant role in the construction of female subjectivity. From their point of view, the institution of heterosexual marriage enforces its regime through the illusion of 'mutual' desire and assent. Their analyses are intended to reveal subjectivity (i.e., the ideological as the production of a unified and autonomous self), as a form of subjection, and the polarities of heterosexual hierarchy as providing the basis for structures of domination and repression.

One could say that the voice's invisibility serves to emphasize the essential function of the auditory mode of perception, allied to abstract reason, and that the whole episode makes a point about submitting sense impressions to verification at some higher level of consciousness. Yet readers should take care, in universalizing and intellectualizing such myths of representative womanhood, not to ignore the long history of stereotypes associated with them. Within this context of gender ideology, we are not surprised to see Adam construe the scene to his own advantage, offering himself as God's surrogate and a reliable mediator. To dispel the tension between Eve's experience of the episode and his understanding of it, Adam expounds an unambiguous reading. He convinces Eve, again on God's presumed authority, to see the mirror phenomenon as evidence for the naturalness of female subordination. What begins as an allegory of perception and of the difficulty distinguishing erroneous from distinct ideas, soon appears in a new light. Error undergoes an ideological rewriting that makes it gender-specific (like the allegory of Sin), and transforms Eve's experience of consciousness into an argument for female subordination.

Milton stages Eve's scene of recognition with the help of mirrors, an emblem of the double perspective of seeing and being seen, of desiring and being desired.⁹ The seventeenth century possessed an elaborate symbology of mirrors, a complex repertoire of meanings and associations. Underlying the figure of the water-mirror lies the whole range of philosophical speculation proceeding from Plato's analogy of the line and allegory of the cave in books 6 and 7 of the *Republic*. Critics have detected an overlay of Neoplatonism in the Narcissus scene, particularly the comparison of the 'liquid Plain' to a reflected heaven. Invoking Neoplatonism's symbolic use of mirrors, they see Eve's neonatal state as symbolic of the soul's symbiotic relationship with nature.¹⁰ From this perspective, becoming engulfed in an ecstatic form of consciousness exemplifies the dangers of losing oneself to enraptured self-contemplation. Yet other, no less deeply embedded meanings surround the phenomena of reflection and self-reflexivity.

Well before it became a common household object, the mirror served as a conventionalized metaphor for the conscience and the interiority of the spiritual life; for the practice of meditation and the soul's pursuit of self-knowledge; and for the operations of the intellect in relation to nature. The mirror's iconic function had always depended on context. It could represent conscience and carnality, mimetic truth and gross distortion, all-inclusive plenitude and the yawning abyss, mystical union and fleshly incarnation. In late medieval iconography the unstained mirror symbolized Mary's purity. At the same time *vanitas* and lust retained close associations with mirrors. The mirror emerges as both an emblem of wisdom and a vehicle of edifying meditations on vanity. The symbolic significance of reflection typically divides between two poles: veridicality and illusion. The experience of gazing into mirrored surfaces can reveal something hitherto unrecognized or unseen; but it can also engender deceptions. A tension between distortion and virtual reflection informs the long history of mirror imagery in relation to the philosophy of mind. Mirrored images are demonstrably 'different' from their source. Even from the vantage point of a single viewer, manifestations of an object appear inconsistent from one surface to another and from one perspective to another. As Umberto Eco has noted, the common belief that plane mirrors reverse right and left is incorrect: they reflect right and left positions exactly where they are. A relation of absolute congruence obtains between object and specular image. It is the observer facing a mirror who effects the reversal by imagining herself from the perspective of the figure in the mirror. Since her image is unobscured yet at the same time strangely altered, she initially interprets her reflection as somehow the product of an inexplicable transformation.¹¹

Changing material conditions throughout Europe decisively altered the function and symbolic value of mirror imagery. The introduction of tin- and lead-backed planar looking glasses in the thirteenth century marked a significant technological advance over convex mirrors and flat polished metal mirrors. As the glass industry migrated from sixteenth-century Venice to Germany, France, and eventually England, mirrors became fashionable items of decor and dress (worn at the side). Bacon describes a sumptuously decorated room in his day as 'Glased with *Crystalline* [ie, clear] *Glasse*' (*Essayes* 138). By the Restoration (when the Worshipful Company of Looking-glass makers first incorporated itself and began to compete with Continental glass-makers), mirror-panelled walls came into vogue among the fashionable and wealthy. The duchess of Portsmouth and Nell Gwynne faced the walls of their closets with mirrors. Even though mirror-making remained a rudimentary art – with most mirrors still convex, expensive, and small – glass technology acquired important applications in the fields of navigation, surveying, microscopy. These varied uses encouraged the English to think of mirrors as instructional devices no less than instruments of vanity.

Long before this, beginning in the twelfth century the Latin word *speculum* contributed a common component to book titles. English writers naturalized the *speculum* and perpetuated its use in titles well into the seventeenth century. Books bearing the word *mirror* on their title pages might present themselves as encyclopaedic indices to reality, exemplary treatises on conduct, prognostic views of futurity, or images of an inner world existing only in imagination. Mirrors represented transcendental realities, an immanent realm below the surface of visibility, and natural phenomena.[12] The structural relationship joining all of these uses together is the mirror as metaphor for the process by which the self realizes itself through something other than the self. The iconography of wisdom and truth traditionally visualizes the problem of origin in terms of reflection, and often places a mirror in the hands of Sapientia and Veritas. In seventeenth-century emblematics, Truth appears as a naked woman who gazes at herself in a mirror, but so does Vanity, a doubleness that mandates careful attention to environing contexts. (Prudentia, who, like Wisdom, often is accompanied by a serpent, carries the symbolic accoutrement of a mirror but usually appears robed.) In many of these iconographic representations, the image reflected back to the beholder seems to engage, even entrap, the spectator at whom we gaze. We see a face genetically connected to the 'original' but emphatically different from it. On one level, this doubleness simply emphasizes perspectival shifts. On another, it injects an element of self-questioning as the woman in the mirror registers the gap between self and its visual representation.

One frequently reproduced image of this type appears on the title-page to Pierre Charron's *Of Wisdom*, where a naked Wisdom contemplates her likeness in a mirror held by a hand emerging from a cloud. The 1670 English edition androgynizes the figure and adds some telling commentary in a poem facing the frontispiece. Wisdom, we learn, '*contemplates* her self in *Self* alone; / Like *It*, (for from that Sacred source she flows,) / In her *Reflected Self* she all things knows.'[13] The verses describe the difficulty of knowing anything, including the self, in terms of the 'thing itself.' Acquiring knowledge without the aid of mediating structures, without the presuppositions of the knowing mind, is impossible. The knower must also contend with the problem that all mediations are distortions, some more 'accurate' than others. Thus mirrors become an emblem of the mind's susceptibility to error and the vagaries of perceptual awareness. One popular collection of natural lore notes the phenomenon of our quickly forgetting 'our proper images, after wee have seene them in the Glasse,' and gives the following explanation: 'It is because that wee see the image representing us in the Mirrour, only by reflection, and not by imprint or graving in solid matter, and as it is so lightly represented, it is also as lightly imprinted in the imagination or fantasie, and by consequent lesse profoundly graved in the memory.'[14] Observers noted, again and again, the peculiar properties of mirror images, and puzzled over their relation to a unitary truth.

By the seventeenth century, the mirror had established itself as a plurisignificant and densely layered symbol. The cognitive associations attached to it stem from its double nature as reflector and distorter. The perspectival variability typical of mirrors is also the general condition of consciousness. The mind is mirrorlike in its capacity for infinite modification, for apparently taking on changes without undergoing alteration itself. Mirrors, which had traditionally symbolized the tangled relation between original and replica, come to play a conspicuous role in the philosophy of mind. Philosophers sometimes posed the problem of how internal structures of consciousness condition thinking in metaphorical terms. Does the mind reflect the sensible world accurately and immediately like a mirror or does it interpose a veil of erroneous ideas? With the 'epistemological turn' that philosophy takes after Descartes, mirrors function as a trope to describe knowledge as process of reflection or inner representation.

Richard Rorty's *Philosophy and the Mirror of Nature* locates a moment in the seventeenth century when philosophers began equating knowledge with avoidance of error, and tying truth to accurate mental representation. Rorty argues that the pervasive and misleading metaphor of inspecting and polishing the mirror informs the philosophical project of epistemological foundationalism.[15] Bacon, I have argued, does at times suggest that knowledge is a mirror image of nature, and uses the mirror analogy to express his conception of a correctly 'impressionable' philosophical disposition. When he describes the understanding as an untinctured and faithful glass, however, Bacon means a relative standard of freedom from 'bias,' not an ideal of absolute transparency. In *De Sapientia Veterum* he recasts the Narcissus myth to disparage philosophers who avoid challenges to their self-complacency, and who insulate themselves from the material world. John Locke uses the imagery of reflection to describe the psychological dynamic of perception in a way that reveals the conundrum at the centre of the image. In book 2 of the *Essay,* Locke describes 'ideas' derived through sensation and through 'reflection' as 'the original of all knowledge': 'reflection' in this sense describes the secondary operations of the mind upon sense data. Locke, however, goes on to argue that 'simple ideas,' can no more be altered by the understanding 'than a mirror can refuse, alter, or obliterate the images or *ideas* which the objects set before it do therein produce.' For Locke, receptivity to external stimuli is a form of imprinting, a process in which ideas forcibly stamp themselves on the mind. In this sense, the mind acts as a reflector of the objects of sense that come within its purview. Through the imagery of mirroring Locke does not imply that all cognitive contents ('ideas,' 'notions') are immediately present to the understanding. On the contrary, some forms of cognition occur at a distance from sense experience. But by explicitly applying the word *reflection* both to the mind's conscious recognition of its own internal operations and to 'primary' sense experience, Locke introduces sufficient ambiguity to fuel a continuing controversy over his intentions.[16]

Reflections, then, stand in a double relation to their originals. The familiar associations of brittleness and impermanence with mirrors derive from the blank impressionability of reflective surfaces. The ontological dependence of image upon object seems genuine enough, given the absence constituted by an empty mirror. Yet we can also employ the image to describe the mind's interaction with the world and the process of reshaping it according to its own interior structures. The senses convey knowledge to the understanding by way of notions, which include states of mind, alterations wrought upon the organs of sense, mental pictures, recollections, and other forms of mediation. Philosophical discourses added another dimension to the theological commonplace that the human mind is an imperfect reflector of God, a *speculum dei.* In the *Areopagitica,* Milton writes of 'the mortall glasse wherein we contemplate,' which he contrasts to the certainties of *'beatific* vision,' as a means for attaining wisdom (*CP* 2: 549). Knowledge derived from this source comes 'farre short of Truth' and retains a generally provisional character. The verse in 1 Corinthians 13: 12, 'For now we see through a glasse, darkely: but then face to face,' suggests the problem of encountering the sensible world through distorting mediations. Theologians often compared meditation on the deity to a process of self-contemplation. Raphael's advice to Adam, that he should channel his curiosity about arcana into the quest for self-knowledge, redirects him to the realm of immediate experience. Raphael does not flatly forbid him abstruse learning, but paradoxically enjoins self-study as the most direct path to revelation. The principle remains doubly in force for postlapsarian humanity. When, in *An Apology against a Pamphlet,* Milton refutes Hall's self-attribution of 'equally temper'd' affections, he challenges the very possibility of seeing 'not as through the dim glasse of his affections which in this frail mansion of flesh are every unequally temper'd, pushing forward to error, and keeping back from truth oft times the best of men' (*CP* 1: 909). Milton makes explicit the trope underlying the idea of equal temperament: interior composure resembles the manufacture of substances such as steel and glass, which compound various elements in exact proportions. Those who put their faith in the reliability of their own fallible capacities ('unlesse he only were exempted out of the corrupt masse of *Adam*') unwittingly expose the weakness of their judgment.

When Eve prefaces her account of her creation by saying 'That day I oft remember,' it implies a ritualized remembrance, a meditation on the hidden meaning of an inherently mysterious event. The very frequency of her act suggests the presence of something puzzling within this primal scene, and the necessity of reverting to it in pursuit of clarification. Although she narrates her experience from the standpoint of someone who now grasps its meaning, it remains unclear what or whose lesson she has learned. The shadowiness of the episode emerges in the difficulty of ascertaining, at least in the immediate context, whether she describes the day of her creation or some later moment. The events, however, constitute her earliest memories, and in the sequence of successive retellings (including Raphael's brief allusion in book 7, and Adam's fuller account in book 8), Eve's narrative occupies a strategic primary position. The tribute she pays to Adam, before proceeding in her recollections, describes her relation to him as both instrumental and derivative: 'O thou for whom / And from whom I was form'd.' The phonic interplay among 'for,' 'from,' 'form'd,' combined with the double use of 'whom' and the synecdoche 'flesh of thy flesh,' itself suggests a dynamic of exchange and mingled identity (440–1). The very act of repetition provides a motif and structural principle that binds the scene together and connects it to other moments in the poem. Within the passage, Milton captures an echoic and asymmetrical quality: 'I started back, / It started back, but pleas'd I soon return'd, / Pleas'd it return'd as soon'; 'What thou seest, / What there thou seest ...'; 'Whom fli'st thou? whom thou fli'st, of him thou art.' Michael McCanles describes the scene as participating in an ongoing 'dialectic of mirroring,' in which Milton propounds a distinction between loving one's image in another as a projection of oneself, and loving another as oneself. The two alternatives operate dialectically in a poem that constitutes meaning through patterns of repetition, and that 'acts out on the structural level of poetic discourse the potential idolatry of which this discourse is itself a vehicle.'[17] Throughout *Paradise Lost*, seeing oneself in others and others in oneself, either as simulacrum or replica, becomes constitutive of a process of self-definition. Yet resemblance remains a shifting and fluid category. For Adam, the creation of resemblance through the act of naming marks a moment of epiphany, whereas Eve's seeing double signals her entanglement in error. In this connection, we should take note of the elaborate network of formal and verbal parallels that link Adam's creation and Eve's together.

Although Eve's birth represents the counterpart and structural forerunner of Adam's in book 8, the relation between scenes avoids rigid schematism. Alike yet not alike, the two moments themselves become emblematic of a mirror relation. At times the imagery and diction seem distributed along strict gender lines. The divine interlocutor of book 4 describes Eve to herself, by way of defining her future role, as 'Mother of human race'; 'First Man, of Men innumerable ordain'd / First Father' is how the divine presence addresses Adam (8.297–8). 'So spake our general Mother' is the transitional phrase after her speech; 'thus our Sire' is the narrator's final phrase introducing Adam's speech. Other verbal echoes tie the two scenes together. Eve says, 'I ... laid me down / On the green bank.' Adam says, 'On a green shady Bank profuse of Flow'rs / Pensive I sat me down' (8.286–7). Note, however, that while Eve assumes a recumbent position (in a situation suited to the pastoral-erotic mode), Adam composes himself in a sitting posture that befits meditation and study. The reader begins by observing a systematic congruence, which, on closer examination, discloses subtle and significant patterns of divergence.

Adam's initial impulse is towards worship, and he falls in adoration at the feet of God, who raises him to a more dignified posture. Raphael will later warn him of the dangers of overvaluing his beloved, and turning sexual pleasure into a form of idolatry: 'For what admir'st thou, what transports thee so, / An outside?' (8.567–8). The impulse manifests itself differently in Eve since she worships an idol nearer to hand: 'there I had fixt / Mine eyes till now, and pin'd with vain desire.'

Adam appears from the very beginning as outer-directed, intensely curious about and engaged in the material world. Eve, as critics note, seems more at home within the affective and domestic sphere. Whereas Adam, upon awakening, directs his attention upwards to the archetypally male heaven ('Straight toward Heav'n my wond'ring Eyes I turn'd, / And gaz'd a while the ample Sky'), Eve directs her sight towards the archetypally female water and earth (8.257–8). Eve, however, blurs this neat bipolar distinction when she interprets the water image as an analogy of its conventional opposite: 'Pure as th' expanse of Heav'n'; 'the clear / Smooth Lake, that to me seem'd another Sky.' Myth criticism points to the watery element in which Milton immerses Eve as symbolic of birth and maternity. Yet Adam, too, wakes to consciousness in a haze of steaming evaporation, a deliberate and somewhat bizarre image on which Geoffrey Hartman has written at length: 'In Balmy Sweat, with which his Beams the Sun / Soon dri'd, and on the reeking moisture fed' (8.254–5). Adam's upward movement to the sun/son, which immediately after projects him into the orbit of a traditionally masculine power, the solar Logos that engenders all life.[18]

While Adam becomes fully cognizant only after performing his primal act of naming, identifying the creatures according to their natures and establishing dominion over them, Eve constitutes a sense of herself as a subject within a heterosexual community. Eve's recognition of her identity in relational terms entails establishing a perspective at a deliberate distance from nature, and also from Adam. The parallels disclose numerous contradictions between her point of view and that of her male instructors. God informs Eve that the image she sees in the pond is 'herself.' Adam, who has been promised the appearance of 'Thy likeness, thy fit help, thy other self' (8.450), tells her that what she sees under the platan tree is himself and her 'other half.' Eve, by contrast, believes that what she sees is another like herself – in other words, herself and not herself, an insubstantial image of herself (repeatedly an 'it') that is nonetheless real. Of the three descriptions hers seems most accurate. She soon acquiesces, however, to the position that without her 'Guide / And Head,' she cannot locate her beginning, and consequently is 'to no end.' Their one flesh establishes Adam in a dominant position, duplicating Christ's relation to the *corpus mysticum* of the church.

In Adam's dream, his 'inward apparition' of being taken by the hand, levitated, and placed in Eden, God also arrives on the scene to deliver a lecture. Here, too, a heavenly intercessor interprets what someone has seen. Both Adam and Eve receive instruction through the ear: a disembodied explaining voice appears to Eve; Adam first hears a voice in a dream and then from the mouth of an undescribed 'Presence Divine.' The burden of the divine message is on both occasions the same: distrust the potentially erroneous testimony of your senses, and bow instead to the superior wisdom of abstraction and speech. Yet while Adam learns this lesson at first hand, God authorizes Adam to play the role of interpreter and intermediary to his spouse. When, in book 5, Adam analyses Eve's dream in terms of the theory of faculty psychology, he first recalls Eve's reflective relation to himself ('Best Image of myself and dearer half'), and then feminizes the principle of replication in the figure of Fancy:

> But know that in the Soul
> Are many lesser Faculties that serve
> Reason as chief; among these Fancy next
> Her office holds; of all external things,
> Which the five watchful Senses represent,
> She forms Imaginations, Aery Shapes,
> Which Reason joining or disjoining, frames
> All what we affirm or what deny, and call
> Our knowledge or opinion; then retires
> Into her private Cell when Nature rests.
> Oft in her absence mimic Fancy wakes
> To imitate her; but misjoining shapes,
> Wild work produces oft, and most in dreams,
> Ill matching words and deeds long past or late.   (5.100–13)

Milton entertains a tripartite model of the psyche that divides cognition into sense-data (or representations to the senses), the shaping imagination, and the faculty of reason, which establishes relations and forms knowledge or opinion. Syntactically, it remains uncertain whether 'mimic Fancy' performs in the absence of Fancy, or Fancy (in its capacity as mime) supplants Reason, who retires into 'her' cell.[19] Fancy represents that part of the sensitive soul given to playful duplication, imitation, and the misjoining of images and ideas. In drawing this ambiguously gendered distinction between reason and fancy, Milton departs from Spenser's famous allegory of the house of Alma (*Faerie Queene* 2.9.47–58), which divides wisdom among three wise men: 'The first of them could things to come foresee: / The next could of things present best aduize; / The third things past could keepe in memoree.' Milton may also have in mind Bacon's similar division of the faculties into imagination, reason, and memory. Generally *Paradise Lost* associates reason with the Law and image of the Father, and follows tradition in making Wisdom female. Thus, Eternal Wisdom is 'Sister' to Urania, and Raphael counsels Adam 'Of Wisdom, she deserts thee not, if thou / Dismiss not her.'[20] In book 5 Milton neutralizes the gender distinction first implied in the personification of 'Reason as chief' through the reiterated use of the pronouns 'her' and 'she.' Conceptualized as both female and non-gendered, the mirror becomes a sign of human fallibility.

The final effect, however, of such instances of recapitulation and resemblance is to trace an originary pattern of gender difference. The idea of the female as an inversion of the male (sometimes an imperfect image or reflection) presents a conventional trope in the early-modern repertoire of images associated with sex differentiation. Mary Nyquist argues that Eve's desire for her own image, suggesting both female autoeroticism and the mother-daughter dyad, 'is clearly and unambiguously constituted by illusion, both in the sense of specular illusion and in the sense of error.'[21] I would argue instead that Eve's experience, although finally repudiated and referred to a higher power for reinterpretation, manifests a consistent logic. Her equation of lake and heaven stresses the singularity of her subject position: 'that to me seem'd another Sky.' If Eve appears more prone to error than Adam – in the sense of having less regard for the objective 'truth' of her experience – her perceptions proceed from the uncertainties of self-definition. Both Adam and Eve experience their first moments of consciousness as they emerge from liminal half-waking states, a version of the twilight moments that figure importantly in the *Aeneid*. 'When from sleep / I first awak't' is how Eve sets the scene to describe the circumstances of her birth. While Adam emphasizes his newness, and thus the limitations of his perspective ('As new wak't from soundest sleep'), Eve focuses on the order of events. Her account moves sequentially as her autobiographical narrative unfolds in a series of discrete moments.

Eve's divine tutorial awakens her to the deceptiveness of appearances, the limitations of even unfallen reason. Though she is 'Created pure,' God has not made her infallible. Catherine Belsey emphasizes the sexual connotations of 'knowing,' suggesting that in retelling the mirror episode, Eve draws attention 'to her own ingenuousness in a piece of innocent sexual teasing which places her as simultaneously knowing and naive.'[22] Eve is knowing in other senses, too. Outwardly she appears deferential to

Adam's superior wisdom, which she associates with the analytical discourse of the poem's male characters: 'what thou hast said is just and right' (4.443). If, however, she ascribes to herself a heightened receptivity to male instruction and the erotic possibilities of marriage, her actions and gestures speak a different meaning:

> I yielded, and from that time see
> How beauty is excell'd by manly grace
> And wisdom, which alone is truly fair.
>   So spake our general Mother, and with eyes
> Of conjugal attraction unreprov'd,
> And meek surrender, half imbracing lean'd
> On our first Father, half her swelling Breast
> Naked met his under the flowing Gold
> Of her loose tresses hid: hee in delight
> Both of her Beauty and submissive Charms
> Smil'd with superior Love, as *Jupiter*
> On *Juno* smiles, when he impregns the Clouds
> That shed *May* Flowers; and press'd her Matron lip
> With kisses pure.   (4.489-502)

A close examination of this passage would lead us to question whether Milton intended to portray the satisfactions of erotic mutuality within marriage. Not only does Eve adopt a wholly passive role; her appeal to Adam appears to derive mainly from her show of submission. Adam, whose ardour seems the direct consequence of Eve's display of meekness, appears to force his attentions on Eve, whose 'Matron lip' he presses. If, as William Kerrigan and Gordon Braden suggest,[23] Eve's matronhood validates the scene's sexuality and distinguishes its object from that of libertine literature, why must Milton remind us of Adam's purity? Their interaction inspires Adam with the satisfactions of a condescendingly 'superior Love,' not mutual pleasure. Eve's 'surrender' and her 'half' embracing Adam strongly suggest a vestigial resistance, a continuation of the moment when his 'gentle hand' seized hers. 'What could I do?' she asks rhetorically and helplessly. When she stresses the contrast between herself and Adam, she invokes a negative difference, which brings out the unbridgeable distance between their two perspectives: 'yet methought less fair, / Less winning soft, less amiably mild.' Even after receiving divine guidance, Eve continues to hesitate, a holding back that Milton directs us to interpret as 'sweet reluctant amorous delay' (4.311).

Adam's attempt to appropriate Eve's desire and redirect it towards himself remains only half-successful. 'Unreprov'd,' in the passage quoted above, contains a strong hint of the bitter recriminations and mutual accusations to come. One wonders if the perspectival gap is not still in effect. With the image of Jupiter inseminating the clouds, Milton plunges Eve back into the oceanic formlessness, from which she emerges in the creation scene, to connect her with cycles of birth and generation. What begins, in the water-mirror, as a metaphor of self-contained reflexivity becomes the symbolic manifestation of her capacity for reproduction and her relation to posterity.

As first born and father of humanity, Adam acquires the status of a predeterminative origin. Eve's love song in book 4 emphasizes the power of Adam's conversation to remake her perceptions of an overwhelmingly beautiful natural world:

My Author and Disposer, what thou bidd'st
Unargu'd I obey; so God ordains,
God is thy Law, thou mine: to know no more
Is woman's happiest knowledge and her praise.
With thee conversing I forget all time,
All seasons and thir change, all please alike.
Sweet is the breath of morn, her rising sweet,
With charm of earliest Birds; pleasant the Sun
When first on this delightful Land he spreads
His orient Beams, on herb, tree, fruit, and flow'r,
Glist'ring with dew; fragrant the fertile earth
After soft showers; and sweet the coming on
Of grateful Ev'ning mild, then silent Night
With this her solemn Bird and this fair Moon,
And these the Gems of Heav'n, her starry train:
But neither breath of Morn when she ascends
With charm of earliest Birds, nor rising Sun
On this delightful land, nor herb, fruit, flow'r,
Glist'ring with dew, nor fragrance after showers,
Nor grateful Ev'ning mild, nor silent Night
With this her solemn Bird, nor walk by Moon,
Or glittering Star-light without thee is sweet.
But wherefore all night long shine these, for whom
This glorious sight, when sleep hath shut all eyes? (4.635–58)

Just as Adam's divine instructor in book 8 presents himself as 'Author of all this thou seest,' Adam has claimed the authorial role for himself and the right to inscribe his will upon the *tabula rasa* of Eve's consciousness. Eve slides almost unnoticeably from intimate confession to generalizing her situation to 'woman.' The speech, revealingly, veers between the poles of mutuality ('with thee conversing') and of complete submission to an absolute power ('Unargu'd I obey'). Eve then moves from the affective sphere, to which she willingly consigns herself, to consider the structure of diurnal experience, the 'seasons' of the day. The passage gathers rhetorical force through the artful use of parallel and cyclical syntactic structures. The architectonic effect of formal accumulation, the periodic roll of the clauses, suddenly collapses in the final two lines. The tenacity of Eve's confidence in the rightness of her impressions emerges in her abrupt and *faux-naïf* question: Why do stars shine when there is nobody there to view them? This represents a blunter formulation of the question Adam poses in book 8. Coming from Eve it reminds us that she begins life by having to submit her sense impressions to correction and revision at some deeper level of consciousness. Her first lesson entails learning the superiority of the auditory mode of perception, allied to abstract reason, which revises raw perceptions of the physical world. As critics often remark, a transition from vision to voice is enacted throughout *Paradise Lost*, most notably in book 12 when Michael shifts from instructing Adam through quickened sight to simple narration. As Adam submits to higher authority at his creation and receives the instruction of a tutelary voice, the burden of the divine message is, again: Distrust the erroneous testimony of your senses, and bow instead to the wisdom of discursive reason. The principle of observational validity, the status of 'things known but not seen,' apparently perplexes Eve. She cannot dislodge it from her thoughts, and reverts to it right in the midst of professing her unquestioning devotion.

While the multiplication of Eve's image in book 4 looks forward to her role as 'general Mother,' it also anticipates the continual expansion of sin from generation to generation, the whole chronicle of human error that constitutes history. The burden of obedience and subjection, explicitly imposed on Eve after the Fall, will move from a position of latency to realize its historically defining effects. Eve's error has ramifications that extend to later political life and subsequent domestic arrangements:

> Thy sorrow I will greatly multiply
> By thy Conception; Children thou shalt bring

In sorrow forth, and to thy Husband's will
Thine shall submit, hee over thee shall rule. (10.193–6)

The doctrine of the Fall, as it was expounded in the seventeenth century, could underwrite both Utopian and anti-egalitarian political programs. Emphasizing the Fall's irreversibility sometimes meant defending private property, social hierarchies, and the oppression of women. Other interpreters reached the opposite conclusion, linking Genesis to the Utopian aspirations of Baconian science, the goal of human equality, and the Protestant ideal of returning to a purer state of worship.[24]

In such passages Milton legitimizes hierarchies of difference on the basis of contemporary notions of origin and representation. The period's leading patriarchalist political philosopher, Sir Robert Filmer, also invoked God's injunction in Genesis 3: 16: 'I will greatly multiply thy sorrowe and thy conception.' Filmer advanced an argument, later contested by Locke, that Adam enjoyed monarchical dominion over Eve and other 'subjects' from the time of his creation, a prerogative that has descended unaltered through the patriarchs to modern kings. Filmer's origins-based theory of political authority located monarchical power and fatherly rule 'in the beginning,' and so strove to naturalize and justify it to the present. Milton, of course, does not draw a divine-right theory from Genesis. He takes the opposite position on contract-theories of government, preferring voluntary obedience and the principle of mutual consent. Yet his reading of Genesis lands on the same authoritarian text ('hee over thee shall rule'), which makes the preservation of the human race and the reproduction of its social institutions contingent upon the obedience of women. The explicit analogy between Eve's transgressive behaviour and postlapsarian social structures transforms the Edenic myth into a justification of paternal authority. Milton rationalizes a particular mode of social reproduction by reference to the authority of the origin. As Jonathan Goldberg writes: 'The family/state analogy was embedded in the Renaissance habit of mind to think analogically and to explain events by understanding their origins; indeed, the analogy serves as an image of that ideational process. There is a family structure in thought, and to seek out the causes of things is to find their genealogical principles.'[25] The logic of origins and of reflexivity conditioned Milton's thinking on problems of gender roles and sexual difference. Origins antedate civilization: they represent a latent state in which things become themselves. Pushing history back to a definitive point, to the precise moment of inauguration that defines the present, demands the choice of values that order later experience. Origins are not so much de-

The Figure in the Mirror 159

fined by the particular time or place they occupy, but by the abstract principles they embody. Edward Said contends that 'solemn-dedicated' epics such as *Paradise Lost* and *The Prelude* fasten on beginnings as a way 'of delimiting, defining, and circumscribing human freedom.' From the very outset, Adam and Eve find themselves not absolutely free, but constrained by the conditions of their existence.[26] In books 4 and 8 Milton shows us how God inserts Adam and Eve into a relational matrix where complete autonomy is impossible, where all experience opens to multiple interpretations, where all thinking (even thinking about origins) takes place within the symbolic order of language.

Despite their participation in the project of naturalizing familiar structures, the lines from book 10 quoted above are not bounded by any one meaning. An unexpected ambiguity clings to the words of this sober injunction. The subtle play on 'Conception' in line 195 hints at the correlation between consciousness and sexual difference. Eve's primal experience of conceptualization, of notions that multiply and reproduce themselves, connects to gestation in the womb. The ideas that form in her brain are analogous to biological offspring: they bear a familial resemblance to their 'original,' yet remain independent of them. The biological difference manifested in childbearing informs the parallel difference in woman's 'Conception,' legitimizing the husband's rule over his wife.

Considered in relation to the poem as a whole, Milton's representation of Eve in book 4 wavers between two poles. On the one hand, the poolside scene assigns Eve to a subordinate position and confirms the perpetuation of traditional gender roles. The aura of luxuriousness and sensuality associated with mirrors makes the scene emblematic of the necessity of containing and regulating female sexuality. Milton constitutes Eve as an imperfect duplicate who must learn to submit to the authority of the paternal origin. Although God creates Adam 'in our image ... in our similitude,' and 'in the Image of God / Express' (7.519–20, 527–8), the divine presence infuses itself no less into Eve. Eve, however, remains demonstrably different from the male figures who inhabit the poem, a difference that Adam, almost immediately, interprets as a sign of inferiority. The poem offers no attempt to resolve Adam's perplexity that 'Authority and Reason' defer to Eve as if she were 'intended first, not after made / Occasionally' (8.554–6). The specularity that initially defines her existence becomes a sign of her 'natural' secondariness. Milton's epic validates sexual hierarchy by positioning it at the very beginning of human experience.

At the same time, Eve's primary act of self-objectification asserts her wish for autonomy: she remains 'absolute' and irreversibly 'in herself complete' (8.547–8). The mirror suggests corroboration and authentication of this desire. The self-image Eve catches in the water-mirror is profoundly 'true' in the sense of being reproducible. Despite its status as an authoritative and objective witness, a closer inspection of the figure in the mirror reveals an unequal relation between sensory input and epistemic output. What Eve sees in the mirror involves a delicate transaction between knower and known, between the mirror's inherent structure and what appears 'in' it. The distorting and shadowy mirror suggests the inevitable gap between things in themselves and the world of appearances.

A similar set of transactions, epical, sexual, and epistemological, finds its way into the work of Samuel Butler, but aligns itself along a different cultural axis. My argument to this point has focused on moments of slippage between literary foundations and philosophical foundations, the way in which the epic quest for a founding myth is projected onto philosophy. Origins were supposed to guard truth against the limitations of thought and language, and both Bacon and Milton establish the importance of recovering origins as a way of connecting ideas to the world. In Butler we see another attempt to found reason in experience. Butler hopes to lessen the distance between words and things by demonstrating the reader's alienation from the reified and inaccessible world of epic. In the same way that Bacon and Milton employ the discourse of origin to foster critical self-consciousness about language, Butler exploits the resources of epic to heighten awareness of language in its particular historical and cultural situations.

PART THREE

Butler's *Hudibras*: The Post-Epic Condition

8

'As *Aeneas* Bore His Sire'

If, for most twentieth-century readers, Butler and Milton lie poles apart, from the vantage point of the Restoration they were 'contemporaries' in every sense of the word. Born within a few years of each other, they breathed the same air of revolution and dissent, even though they reacted in obviously different ways. Their writings in prose and verse present alternative political and aesthetic responses to the same problematic: the establishment of a normative literary, religious, and political order after the collapse of an established system of values. Both poets opened new possibilities in the writing of epic. Both sought to achieve modernity by self-consciously situating themselves at a new beginning, accessing a distant point that might serve as a standard of truth. Much like *Paradise Lost*, *Hudibras* is Janus-faced, standing at the threshold of an emergent literary culture. In part, a continuation of Renaissance satire on learning, it also conspicuously immerses itself in the historical particularities of mid-seventeenth-century England.

Learned, even by Milton's standards, Butler remained highly self-conscious about his relation to contemporaries and predecessors. Although *Hudibras*, like Milton's two post-epic poems, establishes itself in conscious opposition to existing canonical orders, everything about it undermines a comparison. Butler's naming his eponymous hero out of *The Faerie Queene* suggests a casual disregard for the native tradition in epic. Yet *Hudibras*, no less than *Paradise Lost*, insists on its originality and superiority to predecessors in the field. If *Paradise Lost* provides an example of epic undergoing the process of novelization, then *Hudibras* occupies a similarly liminal space between the end of epic and the rise of the novel, marking a transitional phase in the history of narrative.

Throughout the seventeenth century the boundaries between epic and mock-epic blur. Among Milton and Butler's immediate precursors are poems such as Samuel Pordage's ponderous *Mundorum Explicatio* (1661), a Behmenist epic in which Christopher Hill finds anticipations of *Paradise Lost*. For most readers, however, Pordage's couplets have closer affinities to hudibrastic: 'Adam invited thus receives the fruit, / And without long delay falls rashly to 't.' By the closing decades of the seventeenth century, contemporaries began juxtaposing Butler's instantly recognizable stylistic tics with equally distinctive Miltonisms. They could not read one epic without filtering its style through the mannerisms of the other. In a free translation of Boileau's *Le Lutrin*, for example, the Butlerian phrase 'To fall together by the ears' appears in close proximity to 'my Advent'rous Verse.'[1] Butler's Miltonic affinities have captured the attention of twentieth-century critics interested in the close interweaving of politics and epic in the later seventeenth century. Michael Wilding explores the Milton-Butler analogy at length, finding in both epics a reconstitution of the heroic ideal, a retreat from politics, and a powerful critique of martial valour. Wilding yokes the two poets together in their replacement of epic values by the concerns of 'private, nonpolitical, domestic life' – the domesticity of Adam and Eve on one hand, and a careful rendering of popular culture and the textures of everyday life on the other. Wilding's reluctance to see 'politics' as an inclusive circumstance of life obscures the ways in which Butler's treatment of marriage and his satire on male supremacy remain 'political' in any adequately theorized sense of the word.[2]

As the poets of Horatian retirement soon discovered, retreat into a private, pre-political realm was an illusion that could not long be maintained in the face of revolutionary conditions. A close and deadly-serious correlation appeared between the epic theme of war and the psychodrama of domestic strife. Michael Seidel connects the 'internecine' conflicts of the civil wars and 'schismatic' conditions of a revolutionary society to *Hudibras*' digression on marriage and its anti-romance plot. The domestic and the political, he suggests, both undergo a general collapse of value. A comment Seidel makes about satire as a genre – that it 'creates a frenzy around points of terminus, penetrates to elaborate moments of regression where origins are ends and where ... all efforts to continue come to nothing' – seems particularly relevant to *Hudibras*.[3] Butler's poem confronts the impossibility of reaching back to lost precedents by inaugurating a counter-epic, counter-romance tradition.

Butler's overtly politicized stance, combined with his affinities with popular culture and systematic avoidance of high seriousness, have long militated against his reputation. Some part of Butler's low contemporary reputation derives from the sort of thinking, common until quite recently, that equates genuine poetry with the private and personal. Although we have learned to question the apolitical aestheticism that rejects as 'impure' any poetry engaged in carrying out a political program, we still seem oblivious to complexities in positions we might not share. By extending the range of Butler's satire we must take care not to drain out its particularity or transform it into a transcendent meditation on the human condition. Equally, we should remember that overt political commitments do not necessarily preclude doubt, complexity, or contradiction. To say that *Hudibras* is affected by historical circumstance or that Butler bears the traces of political engagement seems beside the point when Butler practically spells out his affiliations. Readers familiar with the poem as mediated by Zachary Grey's copiously annotated 1744 edition never doubted that Butler intended it as an exposé of dissent and nonconformity. The past twenty years have witnessed a revaluation of Butler that has qualified his royalism, made the poem's politics subordinate to other concerns, and opened up the epistemological range of his attack on 'puritan hypocrisy.' Critics have insisted upon enlarging the scope of Butler's animus, noting satire's transferential relation to its objects of abuse and Butler's tendency to implicate himself in the very extremism and implacability he assails.[4]

Butler's poetry is no more 'merely' topical than Milton's is transcendently apolitical. Like other contemporaries who at times flirt with ideologically extreme positions, Butler avails himself of the language of moderation while raging with red-faced intensity. At the same time, he leaves very little exempt from the scope of his invective. Butler paraphrases the Horatian maxim 'Dum vitant stulti vitia, in contraria currunt' – 'Men, who one Extravagance would shun, / Into the contrary Extreme have run' – a principle that implicitly extends to the belief that dogmatic certainty virtually guarantees erroneous outcomes.[5] Butler's poem foregrounds its royalist politics, yet does so in such a way that suggests a level of disaffection far greater than that of many oppositional poets. Contestatory gestures inhere in the very language of his poetry, and his seeming accommodation of dominant forms of political and cultural authority lies all on the surface. This in part accounts for the extremity of Butler's style, his hostility to narrative teleologies and to traditional modes of expression and canons of taste.

Butler rejects the ideal of epic as an imaginative rendering of a pristine world according to a unifying aesthetic order. This approach amounted to a new genre, subsidiary to epic, that retrospectively altered epic traditions as the seventeenth century perceived them. If modern criticism tends to see Butler as proto-Augustan, the generations succeeding him viewed him as anomalous, even something of a freak.[6] Hudibrastic found many imitators because its possibilities at first seemed unlimited. Robert Wolseley, in a preface to Rochester's *Valentinian, a Tragedy* (London, 1685), praised Butler as an 'admirable Original,' but went on to contrast him with 'his little Apers,' whose artless imitations bear no resemblance to their model, 'that 'twere impossible to guess after what Hands they drew, if their Vanity did not take care to inform us in the Title-Page.' Stylistically idiosyncratic and difficult to emulate in his range of learning, Butler came to represent an inimitable standard. His epic had traversed a poetic space whose emptiness and newness had consigned him to 'singularity,' in a distinctly ambiguous sense.

As Hudibrastic petered out into lame imitations and parodies, its energies were channelled into other, equally heterogeneous forms. Together with Scarron's *Le Virgile Travesty* (1648–9) and Boileau's *Le Lutrin* (1673–83), *Hudibras* provided the eighteenth century with a literary genealogy for 'mock-epic.' These poems provide a new antitype (and prototype) for anyone hostile to the pretensions of epic. Boileau wrote *Le Lutrin* as a critique of epic and to illustrate the theory, also advanced in *L'Art Poétique*, that the heroic poem must be 'filled with a limited number of incidents' [chargé de peu de matière], a phrase he deliberately misconstrued to mean 'filled with unimportant things.' Determined to write an epic based on the parodic principle of programmatic triviality, Boileau produced a poem about a squabble between two provincial church officials over the disposition of a lectern.[7] Butler's work grows out of a similar quarrel with generic hierarchies, yet retains the traditional epic 'matter' of war, however much deformed and transvalued by the pressures of modernity. His manipulation of epic materials permits him to deflate heroic pretensions without losing sight of the grimmer realities of the 1640s and 1650s. He emphasizes the ideology of post-Virgilian epic, particularly the difficulty of distinguishing it from romance, and its pretensions as a kind of national cultural monument. To this end, Butler invents a protagonist who vacillates between bold interventions in the present, and badly tarnished chivalric and amatory ideals. By having his character brush up against popular culture and thus renew contact with a deflatingly prosaic social norm, he imparts to the poem the means for circumventing tradition and reaching back through an accretion of literary representations. Butler manages to lampoon literary high-mindedness at the same time that he cultivates a formidably dense layer of allusiveness. He equally finds fault with allegorizing lived experience and idealizing the past. Sir Hudibras' metrical-romance name and inflated ambitions establish him as the legitimate heir of the overreachers and violent sociopaths who populate epic.

Butler's response to the decay of epic and general disaffection with the social function of imaginative writing struck a chord among contemporaries. *Hudibras'* immense popularity and extraordinary contemporary reception are perhaps its best-known features. Butler is twice quoted by an anonymous polemicist, probably Richard Leigh, and placed in favourable contrast to the 'Romancer' Marvell and would-be epic poet Milton. Leigh assaults Marvell's *Rehearsal Transpros'd* as an assemblage of '*Romantick* Tales' and allegories of '*Knight-Errantry*,' and mocks the author for shaping armies and battles in his imagination: 'Thus having rais'd and rang'd in order his Martial *Phantômes,* he sets them a fighting through all the Tropes and Figures of Rhetorick. He knew this way of resolving controversie into *Ecclesiastical Combat,* and deeds of Chivalry, would delight, a muse, and all that: Besides he had a politick fetch or two in it, for these Warlike *Notions,* and arm'd *Ideas* being terrible to him, he conceived they would be no less to others, and that no answerer would have the courage to engage such a *Rhetorical Souldier,* unless he were able to give him battell in all the Metaphors of War.' The author locates the same fanciful mixture of metaphor and militarism in 'the *blind* Author of *Paradise lost* (the odds betwixt a *Transproser* and a *Blank Verse Poet,* is not great),' and quotes the opening of book 3, with its temporal paradoxes and 'Eternal Coeternal,' as evidence of the poet's religious enthusiasm. *Paradise Lost,* he suggests, is no different in kind or in quality from 'Bishop *Dav'nants Gondibert,*' which, he implies, inspired Milton in the first place: 'yet I think this *Schismatick* in *Poetry,* though *nonconformable* in point of Rhyme, as authentick ev'ry jot, as any *Bishop Laureat* of them all.' Leigh assimilates Milton to an intellectual climate in which romances have replaced philosophy and Homer and Virgil go unread. While Marvell and Milton delude themselves into thinking they stand in the forefront of revolutionary action, Butler and Cowley confront the inherent absurdity of the post-epic situation, and reveal, perhaps for the first time, the genuine nature of the aggressive impulses exhibited on the battlefield and through the printing press.[8]

The combination of epic and revolutionary impulses in Milton's career presented a puzzle to his royalist contemporaries. The 'fit' between popular political sentiment and literary ambition struck them as egregiously ill matched. Butler plays on this perceived gulf between levels of culture, destabilizing conventional generic and class hierarchies. In the process, the intrinsic merit and cultural value of epic become open questions. The borderline between translation and parodic epic grew increasingly hazy during the second half of the century. Before Dryden temporarily stabilized the translation and 'imitation' of Virgil, parody seemed a reasonable response to the forced feeding many had endured in their youths. Under the combined influences of Scarron, Cotton, Butler, and perhaps his uncle, the poet John Milton, John Phillips produced *Maronides* (London 1672, 1673), a two-part parody of the *Aeneid*, books 5 and 6. Phillips' biographer, Godwin, thought the work written against Milton by his rebellious ward, who had reacted violently against the poet's tutelage, politics, and stylistic innovations. Phillips' career as a controversialist, compiler of a drollery modeled closely on the 1655 anthology of Mennes and Smith, author of a satire against presbyterian 'hypocrisy' (which the eighteenth century improbably attributed to Milton), and translator of French romances and a mock-epic by Scarron, places him on the borderline between epic and anti-epic, Milton and Butler. *Hudibras* had the effect of making the reading and cultural assimilation of epic, already problematic, even more difficult. Most of the epic parodies that followed on its heels bore a strong Butlerian imprint. James Scudamore's *Homer a la Mode* (Oxford, 1664), for example, explicitly acknowledges the debt in its epigraph, as well as its diction and prosody. Butler had become the universally acknowledged inventor and master of a genre, whose possibilities he had practically exhausted in a single poem.

Some years before Butler, a systematic deformation of Virgilian epic took place in Jean Baptiste Lalli's little known *Eneide travestita* (1634) and Scarron's *Le Virgile Travesty*. Scarron's aggressive rewriting undermines the solemnity of Renaissance mythography and the patriarchal proprieties of epic. In England, the word *travesty* took the form of a noun partly as a consequence of its use by Scarron. With its suggestions of cross-dressing, role reversal, and *bal masquerade*, 'travesty' suggests the inversion of gender roles and demystification of sexuality. Scarron's English influence extended equally to prose fiction. His *Roman Comique* (1651, 1657) left an imprint on Congreve's *Incognita* and other English novels. All of Scarron's writings freely intermingle 'romantic' elevation with social commentary, an extreme self-consciousness of literary forebears with a metafictional manipulation of narrative conventions.

Butler's engagement of popular culture (and his apparent alienation from the hegemonic court culture that read and celebrated, though finally neglected him) contributes to our sense of him as an unlikely spokesman for the royalist cause. Butler devised a vehicle for harnessing encyclopaedic learning to the smart topicality of the jest book. An emphatic 'lowness' offsets his bookishness and has important implications for Butler as a critic of society and of its cultural inheritance. For George Wasserman the tripartite structure of carnival informs the poem's immersion in popular culture and provides a scheme for the tripartite structures of bear-baiting (part 1), skimmington (part 2), and masquerade and rump-burnings (part 3).⁹ According to his Bakhtinian model of generic subversion, the body, parody, and polyglossia finally overwhelm the 'official' literariness of epic. *Hudibras* thus challenges the normative status of epic and reshapes the generic order by adding innovation to its petrified categories. Butler's widely assimilative popular eclecticism serves as a supplement to epic encyclopaedism.

My description of *Hudibras* as 'post-epic,' an allusion to the title of Jean-François Lyotard's *The Postmodern Condition,* situates the poem at a moment of historical crisis analogous to our own. Lyotard's influential study defines post-modernism in terms of a progressive loss of confidence in what he calls 'metanarratives.' In Lyotard's view, the grand master-narratives of emancipation and progress (for example, the teleologies of Christianity, Marxism, and liberalism) have lost their persuasive power. Our growing incredulity towards them corresponds to the end of metaphysics, the crisis of late capitalism, and the transformation of scientific knowledge into discursive forms not dependent upon metanarrative apparatuses. When scientists, Lyotard argues, hope to legitimate their research, we see 'the return of the narrative in the non-narrative.' Scientists appear before the public and 'recount an epic of knowledge that is in fact wholly unepic,' adhering to the rules of a 'narrative game' in which they supposedly have no faith. Lyotard urges the complete abandonment of such legitimizing narrative rationales.¹⁰

Butler's contemporaries, I am suggesting, also felt ambivalent towards epic narratives, viewing them with equal measures of adulation, indifference, and condescension. A vogue for epic parody and pastiche grew out of a sense of cultural exhaustion following in the wake of what, from its perspective, represented a period of 'high modernism' (our 'the Renaissance'), and the experience of revolution throughout Europe. Fredric Jameson has identified 'pastiche' as the definitive feature of post-modern culture, one that we can oppose to the 'stable' comic ironies of the eighteenth century. According to Jameson, the blankness and neutrality of pastiche, its inability to invoke a common culture or normative standards, distances us from the ambivalent homage-critique of earlier satire.¹¹ It seems true, however, that even at an earlier stage of modernity many poets and philosophers had developed a comparable sense of imprisonment in history. The idea of antiquity's unsurpassable artistic accomplishment becomes distilled in the valorization of Homer and Virgil.

Criticism of *Hudibras* has long burdened itself with a need to make structural and generic sense of the poem, to find some sort of unifying basis on which to speak of its varied materials. Among the factors that conspire to make *Hudibras* resistant to simple generic analyses is its open hostility to the conventional hierarchies of form and style that such studies invoke. We can best subsume its contradictory impulses by regarding it as anti-generic and post-epic, insofar as epic provided a normative standard against which to measure all genres. Butler assimilated the heroic and chivalric traditions while retaining a powerful sense of their aesthetic and ethical distance from the post-epic condition.

On the basis of its handling of convention, *Hudibras* belongs in the European tradition of anti-romance and anti-novel. Like Rabelais, Cervantes, the *Roman Comique,* or Diderot's *Jacques le Fataliste,* Butler combines elements of picaresque, philosophical speculation, an earthy comedy of the body, social satire, epic action, and unwavering self-consciousness about the processes of narrative. The heterogeneous nature of Butler's poem correlates with the historical development of the novel as a widely assimilative convergence of narrative forms. By turns, *Hudibras* resembles epic, romance, and novel, or various permutations of the three. In so far as Butler locates the poem in the present and recent past, which he positions in self-consciously modern opposition to a distant past, it resembles the novel and romance. In so far as he sets the poem in his own country it resembles the novel and epic, but not romance, which favours exotic locations. In so far as Butler concentrates on a social spectrum that ranges from the 'middling sort' to the lower end it resembles the novel, but not epic and romance. Finally, in so far as Butler aspires to a *vraisemblance* that undercuts the illusions he associates with the idealizing fictionality of epic and romance, *Hudibras* has affinities with the novel. In *Hudibras* we see traces of the larger historical process that Michael McKeon describes: the poem grows out of the same collision between romance idealism and scientific rationalism (or 'naive empiricism') that gave rise to the English novel. Butler's particular admixture of meandering narrative, social critique, and philosophical debunking strikes out in a direction parallel to but independent of prose fiction.[12] In the poem's particular mix of generic ingredients, however, the epic strain occupies a place much closer to the foreground. By insistently calling attention to itself as poetry *Hudibras* makes poetic technique itself absolutely integral to its meaning, a factor that distinguishes it from the novel and romance.

By the close of the seventeenth century, we see the problem of distant derivation result in the wholesale production of post-epic parody and pastiche. A poem written in mock-commendation of James Smith's 'The Innovation of Ulysses and Penelope,' a short anti-epic included in the 1658 collection *Wit Restor'd*, considers the modern writer's case a hard one: 'For if the ancient Poets don't belie us / Nihil jam dictum quod non dictum prius' [Nothing is said today that wasn't said before]. Genial parody and unabashed incompetence are preferred to slavish imitation or failed sublimity. Writers can no longer sustain the pretence of cultivating a moribund form. In another commendatory poem appended to Smith's poem, Philip Massinger pronounces the pseudo-Virgilian *Culex*, a micro-epic on the death of a gnat, superior to epic: 'It shewd more art in *Virgil* to relate, / And make it worth th' heareing, his Gnats fate; / Then to conceive what those great mindes must be / That sought and found out fruitfull Italie.'[13] Historical conditions militate against the production of major poetry, and make the whole notion of a single privileged genre suspect. In the relatively unconstrained space of the post-epic poem, parody rises up to overwhelm art and enact the revenge of materiality on 'civilization.' Epic becomes the very negation of modernity and rational critique, an engine for perpetuating illusions about the human condition. In this respect, Butler makes absolutely explicit what many of his contemporaries intuited: the absurdity of sustaining impossible fictions by general consent.

We find the impulses of post-epic embodiment and parodic revenge at large in many poems contemporaneous with *Hudibras* and *Wit Restor'd*. The response of Davenant's 'friends' to *Gondibert* was to scatologize and debase his work by associating it with a tainted sexuality. They agree in treating his epic pretensions as laughable, especially given the poet's worldliness and nose-lessness. One contribution, 'To Sir W. Davenant,' provides a travesty-summary of the plot, which contains its share of coarse innuendo, and makes a point of characterizing Gondibert as 'Grave in Debate, in Fight audacious; / But in his Ale most pervicatious.' The tribute continues in the same proto-Hudibrastic vein: 'And this was cause of his sad Fate, / For in a Drunken-street-Debate / One Night, he got a broken Pate.'[14] In the eyes of his contemporaries, Davenant's characteristic absurdity resides in his incapacity to read his own age through his chivalric fantasies, to make obvious connections between historical and literary experience. The satire proceeds from the assumption that anyone immersed in the world of mundane affairs, as Davenant certainly was, could not possibly fail to make connections between the representation of epic valour and the world of political and amorous intrigue surrounding him. His contemporaries tax him with having buried the past under ridiculously remote and abstract ideals, not simply with presumption in aligning himself with Virgil and Ovid.

Gondibert's enthusiastic embrace of Baconian ideals and the eagerness with which it incorporated ideas associated with the new science did nothing to push Davenant towards rejecting feudal ideals of love and warfare as outmoded or in need of renovation. For Scarron and his English admirers, translators, and imitators, the process of rewriting epic according to modern standards revealed the contructedness of its codes and ritualized gestures. Their unmasking discloses the transformation of a martial ethos into something unmistakably bourgeois and mercantile. Phillips's translation of Scarron's *Typhon* moves in this direction, depicting, for example, a battle of Jove and Hercules against a rabble of giants so as to confront his audience with a social reality crying out for depiction:

> Did you ne'er see on Lord Mayors day
> The Green-men, how they clear the way
> With firy Clubs; or in a Ring,
> At Cudgel-sport, or Wrastelling,
> A sturdy Butcher, Stick in hand,
> On back Red Wastcoat, ne'er a Band,
> Hat before eyes, and Bandying Shins,
> Smiting by th' way Spectators Chins,
> Till he has made a Circle, great
> Enough for Blades to do the feat:
> Or at Bear-garden, how *Black Will*
> (The Bull, I mean) doth shew his skill
> In tossing Butchers, when got loose,
> With as much ease as Fox doth Goose?
> Just so doth Thunder-thumping *Jove*
> Sometimes beneath, sometimes above,
> On right, on left, behinde, before,
> Till compassed by Wounds and Gore,
> And at his feet lay Gyants dead
> Some score or two, which he had sped.[15]

Scarron's mildly condescending but undisguised enthusiasm for low life suggests layer upon layer of animosity: to violence and physical contests as a sort of diversion; to contemporaries who consciously divorce themselves from the fact of their modernity; to the cultivation of a bookish neoclassicism; to the idealizations of romance writers such as La Calprenède and the de Scudérys; and finally to unthinking acceptance of epic standards at a time when such conventions seemed ripe for parody.

As Milton and Butler both understood, the apparent exhaustion of epic tradition became clear with the unsuccessful efforts of highly successful poets in the 1650s – Cowley and Davenant among others – to revive it. Although Butler never moved in society with the skill and unvarnished ambition of Davenant, his involvement in mid-century culture at various levels suggests an attempt to achieve successful integration, which goes some way explaining his enormous contemporary success. Butler entered an avenue that presented itself to anyone familiar with classical epic and eager to retain a sense of modernity's unbridgeable distance from antiquity. Before Butler, we find a comparable relation to classical models and conventional values in Charles Cotton's *Scarronides*. Cotton borrows, without the benefit of anything strictly analogous in Scarron, a simple phrase from the *Aeneid* ('multa quoque et bello passus ...') and embroiders it to score a point about the changing face of battle: 'Much suffer'd he likewise in War, / Many dry blows, and many a scar: / Many a Rap, and much ado / At quarter-staffe, and Cudgells too ...'[16] The joke here again lies in the disparity between a high-sounding and abstract phrase and the tangible human reality and comedy of the body underpinning it. Like most effective parodies this one functions in two directions simultaneously: it establishes an unabashedly parasitical stance alongside of a genial contempt; it assumes a high level of familiarity with the poem while robbing it of canonical status. Such rewritings of a sacred text serve as complex rites of exorcism and demystification. They present themselves as substitutes for poems no longer accessible or credible, even to readers familiar with the model under 'correction.'

Scarron's success in England reveals the frustration Butler's contemporaries experienced in their attempts to translate the *Aeneid* into a satisfactory English version, one that could do for the poem in the seventeenth century what 'Phaer's *Aeneid*' did the sixteenth. Butler cites the first six books of the *Aeneid* more than any other classical work, in which respect he remains fairly typical of the period. Between 1600 and 1668 many attempts were made at parts of the *Aeneid*, especially books 2, 4, and 6. Only John Ogilby and John Vicars, however, published complete translations of the poem between the Phaer-Twyne version and Dryden. Given Virgil's prestige and the tremendous industry expended on studying the

Aeneid, the absence of an adequate translation would have seemed puzzling. One Restoration translator confessed that his modest ambition in translating book 6 was that 'some glimpse, some lines and features will discover the *Original*.'[17] Virgilianism became a valuable commodity that eluded most of the writers who desperately strove to cultivate it. Butler ironically justifies the awkwardly disjunctive beginning of *Hudibras*' second part as conforming strictly to the prescribed model, 'written of purpose, in imitation of *Virgil*, who begins the IV Book of his *Æneides* in the very same manner.' Butler aims another footnote jest at the translations of Vicars and Harrington; it points to the tendency of translation projects to fall into unconscious parody: 'He [Vicars] Translated *Virgils Æneides* into as horrible Travesty in earnest, as the French *Scaroon* did in Burlesque, and was only out-done ... by the Politique Author of *Oceana*' (notes to 2.1.1 and 1.1.639–40). While Butler barely troubles to conceal the subtext of his gibe against Harrington as a political theorist, Vicars' work does in fact recall Scarron, with its maladroit syntax, brisk descriptions, and forced double rhymes. Butler's comment, as the glance at Harrington underlines, attempts to detach Virgil from politically hostile appropriations on the grounds of aesthetic standards. Even so, his attitude towards these standards remains distinctly ambivalent.

Butler makes no mention of John Ogilby's at best serviceable (and at times inept) translation of Virgil. Yet his slur of Vicars and Harrington, that they incompetently translate 'out of Languages in which / They understand no part of speech,' could apply equally to Ogilby. Ogilby had come to Latin late and Greek even later. His *Works* of Virgil nevertheless found a ready-made market when it first appeared in 1649. In 1654 Ogilby brought out a revised folio edition, with copious annotations, a prefatory Life, and elaborate illustrations by Wenceslaus Hollar, William Faithorne, and other artists. Although Ogilby sometimes suggests parallels between the effects of war of Rome and revolutionary violence in his own time, his prudential royalism generally remains circumspect, evident only to the closest of close readers. In his *Aeneid* – and in the later translations of Homer, which appeared in editions ornamented by engravings and subscribers' coats of arms – Ogilby succeeds in making an ecstatic and baroque royalism part of the experience of reading epic.[18] Annabel Patterson provides a detailed analysis of the historicized nature of Ogilby's Virgil, its political innuendoes, circumspect celebration of heroism, and timely counsel of fortitude and resignation: 'As the choice of Virgil spoke specifically to the educated mind and to the literary imagination, which during the revolution were assumed for the purposes of propaganda to be the property of the royalists, so the address to an economic and cultural elite was expressed in the cost of the volume and the individual dedications, which made the volume visibly the property of the beleaguered upper class.'[19] Given the *Aeneid*'s emphasis on loss, self-denial, and steadfastness in exile, heavy-handed topical applications would seem superfluous. Patient resolve and heroic virtue in the face of adversity were precisely the qualities royalists liked to attribute to themselves after Naseby. Many adopted the belief that fate had conspired to put their fortitude to the test, and that by simply waiting out the crisis they would eventually triumph.[20]

Part of the appeal of Roman epic to the later seventeenth century resided in its suitability to a nation undergoing internal strife and aspiring to a global empire. Cowley's commendatory poem prefaced to *Gondibert* draws attention to the political contests looming just below the work's horizon and to Davenant's struggle to appropriate the cultural prestige of Rome:

By fatall hands whilst present Empires fall,
Thine from the grave past Monarchies recall.
So much more thanks from human kinde does merit
The Poets Fury, then the Zelots Spirit
...
With shame me thinks great *Italy* must see
Her Conqu'rors call'd to life again by thee;
Call'd by such powerfull Arts, that ancient *Rome*
May blush no less to see her Wit o'rcome.
                    'To Sir William Davenant,' *Gondibert* 270-1

Several of Virgil's seventeenth-century English translators (Fanshawe, Harrington, Vicars, Denham, Waller) actively involved themselves in public life. Given their backgrounds and interests, they needed little encouragement to read recent history against Virgilian models, or to regard English history as a saga of national establishment. Le Bossu's treatise on epic (1675; English translation 1695) became influential in England because it codified an emergent conjunction of neo-Aristotelian formalism, historical didacticism, and emphasis on imperial enlargement. The history of Rome, Le Bossu theorized, provided Virgil with a narrative that ensured 'the glory of a primary invention,' and enabled him to instruct '*Augustus* as the Founder of a great Empire.' Le Bossu constructs a prescriptive definition of epic that turns Virgil into the natural fulfilment of the genre's formal and political imperatives: 'In the Scheme we have drawn of the

Fable and Action of this Poem, we have observed, that *Æneas* ought of necessity to be a King newly elected, and the Founder of an Empire rais'd upon the Ruins of a decay'd State.'[21] In this and other constructions, Virgil provided the basis for a naturalization of monarchy and glorification of empire.

In the decades prior to Le Bossu, the nationalistic and imperialist politics of Virgilian epic figured significantly in the reading and interpretation of the poem. The second half of the *Aeneid* deals with internecine conflict, described as *tristia bella* and *miseros … civis* (7.325, 11.360). With Juno's unleashing of the Fury Allecto in book 7, Virgil paints the Trojan-Latin conflict as insanely murderous [*scelerata insania belli*]. Still, the war eventually produces an enduring peace through cultural assimilation. As one recent commentator notes, Virgil took these broils as a 'clear analogue' of the civil wars of Rome, which ended with Octavian's victory over Antony at Actium and the establishment of a *pax Augusta*.[22] Critics who stress Virgil's 'pacifist' strain, his dolorously intoned passages on the woes of war, tend to obscure how this position serves a tendency to regard war as regrettable but sometimes necessary. Even when Virgilian epic recoils from violence, its narrative hinges on the resolution of *discordia* through forcibly imposed peace (see, for example, 6.851–3). The *Aeneid* bolstered the belief – which the seventeenth century also derived from other sources, including Machiavelli – that the arts of ruling included careful administration of an economy of violence, doling out strong measures to achieve optimal results without alienating the people over whom one must rule in the future. The rationalization of violence as productive of future good constitutes an important part of the ideology of epic origins. This attitude finds a place in the campaigns of the 1650s, which achieved levels of violence that appalled some participants.

The application of massive military force could be excused with the rationale that present violence reduces future bloodshed by curbing an 'irrational' and unruly enemy. Thus Cromwell remarks on the capture of Drogheda during the Irish revolt, and his putting the garrison to the sword: 'I am persuaded that this is a righteous judgment of God upon these barbarous wretches who have imbrued their hands in so much innocent blood, and that it will tend to prevent the effusion of blood for the future, which are the satisfactory grounds to such actions, which otherwise cannot but work remorse and regret.' By confronting and subduing a demonic enemy (either foreign or the popish 'foreigner' within), the army serves the imperatives of rationality. Traces of guilt vanish before the conviction that such exercises tame the excesses of an antithetic and erring enemy. When Marvell celebrates Cromwell's triumph in Ireland, urging him to

> keep thy Sword erect:
> Besides the force it has to fright
> The Spirits of the shady Night,
>   The same *Arts* that did *gain*
> A *Pow'r* must it *maintain*,

he deliberately recalls Aeneas' heroic descent into the underworld in book 6 of the *Aeneid*. As the Sibyl and Aeneas negotiate the entrance of the infernal cave, she directs him to hold the howling spirits at bay by unsheathing his sword (6.260). The irrational and chaotic enemy upon which Cromwell unleashes his 'Arts' – the 'party-colour'd' Scots and variable Irish – become one in their many-minded resistance.[23] A type of Aeneas and of Caesar, Cromwell dissolves, rather than energizes, faction and civil strife by realizing a heroic destiny and imposing order.

While political conditions encouraged such topical applications of Virgil's epic to the present, translators also tried to maintain respect for the irremediable otherness of antiquity and avoid any hint of anachronistic incongruity. Hobbes, for example, considered 'discretion' an important part of epic composition. 'Indiscretion' resided, above all else, in the use of 'vulgar' and 'foreign' words and of 'words of art' employed by the schools. 'The character of words that become a hero,' Hobbes writes in his preface to *The Iliads and Odysses of Homer,* 'are property and significancy, but without both the malice and lasciviousness of a satyr.'[24] Vicars' translation of Virgil, by contrast, deliberately closes the gap between imperial Rome and seventeenth-century England. He imparts to Virgil an energetic informality that occasionally tumbles into inadvertent mock-heroic. The sort of translation the age demanded could not ignore Roman historicity or virtually overwrite Virgil's text by placing it in a wholly English register. An element of defamiliarization had to obtain in order fully to respect the cultural gap between text and reader. The otherness of distant history and the remote origin defined heroic poetry; without this aesthetic foundation it descended into incongruity, bathos, and burlesque violence.

Butler associates the conflation of epic and modern cultures, in which he himself participates, with the spiritous inspirations of a barmaid Muse: 'Thou that with Ale, or viler Liquors, / Didst inspire *Withers, Pryn*, and *Vickars*' (1.1.639–40). Urania has indeed descended – into satirists, pamphleteers, and a modern translator of Virgil. The political and social fact of modernity necessitates surrendering the obfuscations of epic. Occasionally, Butler will loosely translate a passage from Virgil, just to maintain contact with the epic model:

> at Venus Ascanio placidam per membra quietem
> inrigat, et fotum gremio dea tollit in altos
> Idaliae lucos, ubi mollis amaracus illum
> floribus et dulci adspirans complectitur umbra.   (1.691–4)

>   and led
> The Warrior to a grassy Bed,
> As Authors write, in a cool shade,
> Which Eglentine and Roses made,
> Close by a softly-murm'ring stream
> Where lovers us'd to loll and dream.   (1.3.157–62)

The key phrase in Butler's passage, 'As Authors write,' widens the ironic distance already established by insisting on the literariness of the pastoralism exhibited in such writing. His choice of the word 'Authors' instead of (say) 'Maro' deepens our sense of the passage as having a 'generic,' in the sense of 'thoroughly conventionalized,' function. Typically, Butler generalizes this intertextual moment, emphasizing his own alienation from such poetic practices rather than singling out a specific text. Butler's satiric object is not so much Virgil's text *per se* as uncritical appropriations of the Virgilian ethos. By encouraging readers to provide their own analogues and examples, he reduces Virgilianism to an undifferentiated mass of texts and classicizing 'Authors.'

Throughout the 1640s and 1650s, Virgil was the beneficiary, in many circles, of widespread adulation and imitation. In 'The Motto,' Cowley chooses Virgil to symbolize the whole poetic craft, and celebrates his bringing 'green Poesie to her perfect age.' Cowley commenced writing his own, subsequently suppressed epic, *The Civil War*, in the summer of 1643, but abandoned the project when the struggle seemed to turn against the king. The poem's modern editor concludes that whereas some English poets, including Marvell, borrowed from Lucan's *Pharsalia* to portray English strife, 'none of the classical poets left more easily discernible marks of influence upon *The Civil War* than Virgil.' The Virgilian model, which Cowley also brought to the *Davideis*, proved inappropriate to a writer who chronicles events as they unfold. Cowley, contrary to Hobbes's prescription quoted above, combines epic elevation with a ferocious satire, producing 'a poem that deplores the evil of civil war and at the same time expresses a fiercely partisan viewpoint.'²⁵ In some respects, *The Civil War* attempts to combine Lucan's portrayal of *bella plus quam civilia* [war worse than civil] with the disengagement and poise associated with Virgil. Cowley could not manage this pose of Olympian detachment when he had a heavy investment in the still-uncertain outcome of the struggle he narrated. The process of writing events in the midst of their unfolding interfered with the ideal of epic as a privileged, historically 'finished' product. Unlike Milton, who generally keeps the satirical impulses of *Paradise Lost* in check, Cowley's unpublished epic oscillates between epic and satiric modes before foundering and finally trailing off in an unworkable mixture of genres. A satisfactory reinvention of epic would have to respect the English poet's historical situatedness without losing touch with the idea of epic origin.

Although critics have faulted Butler for his admixture of non-epic into a hybridized and wildly unstable parody (Cervantic, Rabelaisian, chivalric), one wonders why epic encyclopaedism, commended in Milton, should constitute a fault in Butler. *Hudibras* implies the same critique of epic that *Paradise Lost* states overtly when it disparages writers who chronicle war, and 'With long and tedious havoc fabl'd Knights / In Battles feign'd' (9.30–1). Butler shares something of Milton's official Spenserianism, and draws the name of his dubious hero from *The Faerie Queene*. The name *Hudibras* (and the patriotism associated with it) also derives from the legendary history of Britain: '*Rudhuddibras*, or *Hudibras*,' Milton remarks, summarizing his unreliable sources on pre-Roman history, 'appeasing the commotions which his Father could not,' founded Canterbury, Winchester, and other towns, 'but this by others is contradicted' (*CP* 5: 21). Epic, like the institution of monarchy itself, attempts to distil a national culture in the form of a narrative centred on past deeds and continuity with the first generation.

In *Hudibras* this ideal of recovering a national patrimony, continuous with the Western movement of Troy, comes to rest in the misshapen and grotesque body of the hero:

For as *Æneas* bore his Sire
Upon his shoulders through the fire:
Our Knight did bear no less a Pack
Of his own Buttocks on his back.   (1.1.287–90)

When Aeneas symbolically shoulders the burden of Roman history and destiny represented by his father, he subordinates himself to serve an impersonal power with which he eventually comes to identify. A hero of repression and self-denial, Aeneas attains to immortality by shunning desire. The world-domination Rome achieves comes at the expense of his abandoning Troy, Dido, and other competing sources of desire and attachment. Sir Hudibras, by contrast, bears the weight of tradition – scholastic learning, Protestant religion, vestigial feudal hierarchies – as an intolerable and disfiguring 'Burthen.' Buckling under the weight of historical accumulation, he has undergone a grotesque transformation. Easy conversation or dialogue with antiquity, a humanist ideal occasionally glimpsed in Butler's miscellaneous prose writings, has become impossible. Instead a situation has evolved where the past has gained the 'upper- / Hand' over the present and become an impediment. While Aeneas carries the responsibility of spreading the paternal culture to distant colonies, Hudibras embodies a crippling adherence to and veneration of the past. His very body has become a sign of inversion and disproportion.

Butler recognized the problem of historical disjuncture that plagued his contemporaries, and decided to channel it into post-epic. *Hudibras* deliberately exposes the artificiality of epic convention, including the myth of establishing a lasting political foundation through heroic conquest. Butler directs his energies to playing out, rather than covering over, the fissuring of decorum that occurs when writers refract their experience as a mythologized past. Attempts to naturalize epic by transposing its archaic circumstances into a modern key had produced a jarring sense of disproportion and collapse. Butler's conception of epic demystification revolves around the idea of rupture: between literary encodings and diffuse particularities of lived experience; between philosophical method and the chaos of sensation; between artfully fabricated political fictions and the interests that constantly undermine them; between metaphysical idealizations and the undeniable fact of materiality.

The epic origin, as I have described it, functions as something archaic, a standard still employed but marked by conspicuous difference from modern norms. The origin also has an ideological function best described as 'residual,' a function that implicates it in modern ways of thinking. This distinction between archaic and residual I borrow from Raymond Williams, who describes cultural systems in terms of an internal dynamic that includes the dominant, residual, and emergent as key categories. Williams differentiates between 'residual' and 'archaic' as follows: 'I would call the "archaic" that which is wholly recognized as an element of the past, to be observed, to be examined, or even on occasion to be consciously "revived", in a deliberately specializing way.' The residual, by contrast, 'has been effectively formed in the past, but it is still active in the cultural process, not only and often not at all as an element of the past, but as an effective element of the present.'[26] Thus, the origin defines an experience that, strictly speaking, exists outside of the present, tracing back to some absolutely past moment. In the post-epic poetry of the later seventeenth century, however, the line between these categories grows hazy. Ancient literature and modern philosophy form parts of the same cultural process.

As part of epic literature, origins inhabit a space bounded by a classical tradition, a self-defining selection of approved texts and authors. In the realm of language theory, the origin operates less visibly, but no less powerfully, to shape ideas and integrate them into a reliable framework. This is the subject of the next chapter.

9

Metaphysick Wit

Butler's views on the necessity of bringing notions into conformity with the world and thus making language subordinate to them postulates the existence of an external, stabilizing point of reference: an origin. We find this origin behind his metaphysic of 'Reason' and objective truth, which provides him with a transcendent standard capable of validating the social institutions he values. Truth's ideal correspondence to something residing in nature merges with his anxieties over religious and political cohesion. Butler adumbrates a theory of truth that rests on a dualistic distinction between two orders of mental experience: the testimony of the senses, and the analytical or interpretive operations of the mind, which together constitute 'Reason.' Since we can know the original of a particular phenomenon by its mental representations, we need only to avoid erroneous judgments and false resemblances to align ourselves with truth. Data derived from sensation, although potentially erroneous, derives a privileged status from its putative proximity to the real. Butler thought that concepts and what concepts refer to could be matched on the basis of their congruity. The sole alternative was a corrosive 'equivocation' that ruled out the possibility of verifiable knowledge and invited the disastrous social consequences he depicts in *Hudibras*. According to this view, 'notions' provide the mind with pictures of inaccessible originals. Although things can never be united with the mind, they can be made present to it through the intervening power of concepts. Notions, then, inhabit the mind, and when correctly determined, provide a royal road to the truth.

Underwriting *Hudibras* we find yet another version of the correspondence theory explored by Bacon early in the century, and repudiated (or, by some accounts, qualified) by Locke towards the end.[1] *Hudibras* satirizes the supposed consequences of conflating originals with copies. Like

Paradise Lost, it explores how fissures between 'original' phenomena and derivative language conduce to error, but goes further in attempting to lay bare the social consequences of this problem, charting error's effects into the realm of the micro-political.

In his notebooks Butler repeatedly asserts that error and contradiction pervade every intellectual endeavour, becoming the omnipresent conditions of all human undertaking. The propensity of things to merge into their opposites and produce irreconcilable 'contradictions' underpins his entire conception of wit. This interest in revealing hitherto unnoticed similarities among ostensibly disparate phenomena has the unintended effect of destabilizing much of his theorizing on language. His quickness to point out antithetical resemblances, to harp on inconsistencies, to denounce established institutions as encouraging departures from truth, infuses a highly unstable quality into his work. John Wilders, among other commentators, considers Butler's sceptical critique of error 'Baconian,' especially its contrasting an unproductive scholasticism with the rigorous ideal of empirical demonstration.[2] Butler, however, pronounced 'Baconian' philosophy overly credulous, and greeted its claims of new knowledge with a derisive riposte: 'The Lord Bacon was not so much a Naturall Philosopher as a Naturall Historian: who of all others is the most fabulous, especially if hee takes up what hee writes upon Tick' (*PO* 280). As Wilders notes, Butler interweaves his theory of knowledge with a powerful negative critique that dismisses the possibility of attaining to any real degree of certainty. In the minds of 'the Rabble,' the 'Millions of Errors and falsities' at loose in the world easily prevail over an inaccessible and singular truth (*PO* 78). The infinite variety of error, compounded with its inherent appeal to the self-deluding mind, makes false conjecture an almost universal condition.

Philosophic empiricism, John Dewey maintains, is 'disintegrative' in intent. From the seventeenth century onwards, empiricists laboured 'to show that some current belief or institution that claimed the sanction of innate ideas or necessary conceptions, or an origin in an authoritative revelation of reason, had in fact proceeded from a lowly origin in experience, and had been confirmed by accident, class interest or by biased authority.'[3] Butler wants to regard sensation as a criterion of truth, but fears demystifying appeals to experience as a rationale for subversion and social reform. He never advocates following in the path of classical scepticism and suspending judgment when faced with difficult questions. Rather he casts in doubt the whole question of real knowledge in matters beyond empirical observation. 'Among so many Millions of Errors, and Mistakes,' he writes, 'as are to be found among Authors, I do not remember any one that is grounded upon the Deceit or Misreport of Sense.' The fallible intellect must submit itself to the superior authority of sense, beyond which it cannot venture. Always subject to the discipline of verification, the mind must continually refer itself back to a primary evidence of sensation: 'for there is nothing in the Intellect that it did not either receive immediatly from the Sense or by Tradition and at second hand as by collection and Consequence' (*PO* 127, 82). Butler believes that the truth of this second class of propositions, derived from 'Tradition,' must be measured through the senses, which function as a conduit between the mind and nature. Using an image we have already examined at length, he writes: 'For the Minde and understanding of Man is but a Mirror, that receive's, and Represents, the Images of those Objects that Nature set's before it at a just Distance, as far as it is able to receive them, and therefore the more remote things are, the more uncapable it is to enterteine them; and if it ever hap to be in the Right, it is like a lucky cast at Dice, but by mere chance, and Hap-hazzard' (*PO* 80). This process of verifying ideas by reference to an external 'nature' remains beset with all the dangers of human fallibility. Mirroring the external world faithfully requires both mental susceptibility and physical proximity on the part of the knower. Butler does not explain how we know we have accurately matched internal representations with external objects of knowledge, but he clearly senses the difficulty of this standard. Like Locke some years after, Butler draws on the language of 'probability' to describe degrees of uncertainty. Although probability tries, methodically, to 'look severall ways at once' it offers the only acceptable alternative to 'mere Opinion.' What Butler means by 'probability' is an evidentiary standard supported by the authority of sense, which is itself subject to some undescribed formal principle of demonstration (*PO* 8–9).

As we have seen, theories that make meaningfulness contingent upon verification go hand in hand with Restoration science. Hudibras personifies everything repugnant to the Baconian temper: Aristotelian dogmatism, scholastic metaphysics, and a fondness for heated controversy. Yet Butler's particular brand of 'verificationism' remains non-committal and anti-scientific. He asserts that we can never be absolutely certain how well our conceptions signify phenomena since no method exists for bringing the two into demonstrable conjunction: 'No Man can possibly be a Competent Judge of his own Conceptions, unless he coud have more Reason than he has' (*PO* 6). Nevertheless, the belief that we can in some way test assertions against our observations of the external world resurfaces; it provides

Butler with a fixed point against which he navigates the dangerous waters of phenomenal subjectivity.

In Butler's view, avoidance of error, in so far as it lies within our grasp, depends on bringing ideas into line with simple elements of an immensely complex nature. Knowledge, therefore, 'is nothing but a right observation of Nature; He who suppose's he can understand any other way, is in an Error.' Butler continues, in this passage, to invoke the familiar Baconian vein, and speak of Adam as a type of proto-naturalist who exceeded his original divine mandate when he entered into the study of abstruse subjects. He retreats from the unwelcome implications of his position by appealing to a divine source as 'the Original of Reason' and template of an orderly, well-disposed 'Nature' (*PO* 19, 66). Such conventional efforts to shore up a 'limited' scepticism with theological supports do little to resolve the contradictions entailed by positing error as a normative state. Like many of his English contemporaries, once he has expounded about the unreliability of the senses and their capacity for error, he then must execute an acrobatic leap of faith to land back within the boundaries of theism.

As Butler saw it, school philosophy merely systematized and consolidated a natural propensity towards error, teaching us 'from false Grounds solidly t' infer / And how Judiciously to erre.' Truth continually recedes from our view, becoming locked in an unequal struggle with power and interest. Contestants in the wars of truth advance improbable opinions to extend the reach of their authority, or claim a transcendent foundation for immediate political goals. 'The False are Numerous,' Butler says, while vanishing truth remains the property of beleaguered (and rhetorically ineffectual) minority. Among the implacable enemies of truth is metaphysics, which Butler dismisses as 'the Notion of a Notion, / The Copy of a Copy,' and which 'turns truth to falshood, Falshood into Truth / By vertu of the Babilonians Tooth' (*Satires* 157, 179, 160).

Nicolas Malebranche recorded a similar sense of error as a viscous medium through which philosophy wades, although from a Cartesian rather than post-Baconian point of view. His *Recherche de la verité*, later translated into English, begins with a vast enumeration of errors of the senses, errors of the imagination, errors of the pure understanding, errors of the passions. Before moving on to outline a method for securing ourselves from deception by building on clear and distinct ideas and avoiding mere probabilities, he re-emphasizes 'how subject to Error the Mind of Man is,' and offers this recommendation: 'We ought never to give our entire Assent, except to such Propositions as appear so evidently true, that we cannot refuse it them, without feeling some inward Pain, and secret Reproaches of our Reason.' The standard of 'clearness' and the supposed irresistibility of 'self-evident' propositions become articles of faith in the seventeenth-century philosophy of mind.[4]

Hudibras' tendency to pursue ideas as entities in their own right, rather than as the vehicle of empirical knowledge, is nowhere better seen than in the following description of his standing among philosophers:

> Knew more then forty of them do,
> As far as words and termes could goe.
> All which he understood by Rote,
> And as occasion serv'd, would quote;
> No matter whether right or wrong:
> They might be either said or sung.
> His Notions fitted things so well,
> That which was which he could not tell;
> But oftentimes mistook the one
> For th'other, as Great Clerks have done.
> He could reduce all things to Acts
> And knew their Natures by Abstracts,
> Where Entity and Quiddity,
> The Ghosts of defunct Bodies, flie;
> Where Truth in Person does appear,
> Like words congeal'd in Northern Air.
> He knew *what's what*, and that's as high
> As *Metaphysick* wit can flie. (1.1.133–50)

Here, in a passage rife with the terminology of Aristotelian metaphysics, we are shown the philosophical source of Hudibras' strange inability to connect with the world by using words with an empirically verifiable referential function.

To begin with, the extent of Hudibras' knowledge is circumscribed by the phrase 'words and termes.' Butler uses the phrase to suggest 'terms of art,' the technical vocabularies of the professions and trades that 'are generally Nonsense that signify nothing, or very improperly what they are Meant to do, and are more Difficult to be learn'd then the things they are designd to teach' (*PO* 179). The word also carries a hint of its specialized use by Ockham and the 'Terminist' school of the late Middle Ages, for whom a 'term' was a sign that represents an object to the mind. The extent of Hudibras' understanding of the world is circumscribed by mental representations of it. The learning of the universities has encouraged him to erect a barrier of verbal representations between his perceptions and other phenomena. His fondness for quoting authority is a function of a deep-dyed scholasticism that utterly disregards the primacy of perception and the particularities of individual experience. Typically, Hudibras responds to a philosophical problem by sifting through an abundant stock of arguments. The appropriateness or applicability of these is of no importance to him. They are a form of verbal ritual and could as easily be intoned or 'sung' as spoken. His supposed understanding of 'acts,' 'Entity,' and 'Quiddity' argues an exclusive familiarity with concepts having no correspondent existence in nature and only a confused and shadowy existence in the mind.[5]

According to Butler, the idea-centred outlook of traditional metaphysics gives philosophers little reason to suspect that notional constructs should correspond to an objective reality. They remain convinced that speakers must make the natural world conform to verbal anomalies rather than the contrary. For Butler, as for most of his contemporaries, 'words' (or 'terms' or 'names') carried with it an implicit opposition to 'things' (or 'matter'). On numerous occasions in his prose writings, he places the two in conjunction. Butler does not deride the use of 'hard words' just because they are unfamiliar, or ostentatious, or conducive to violent confrontation.[6] He also depreciates them because they fail to meet the criterion of 'significance,' or correspondence to a distinct notion in the minds of those who use them. Early in the poem we learn that Hudibras has trouble separating images of the external word – and, by implication, words derived from those images – from material reality *per se*. As a consequence, he commits the error of projecting 'insubstantial' words and thoughts onto the phenomenal world, continually making the world over in the image of his conceptions rather than deriving them from an antecedent knowledge of the world. The understanding, Butler thought, should not 'make' truth in its complex relations but simply find or observe it in experience. For Butler, the consequences of such misrecognitions are largely sociopolitical. Thus Butler pours derision on Neoplatonist realism in a telling comparison: democracy, he writes, is 'like the intelligible World, where the Models and Ideas of all Things are, but no Things' (*Characters* 59). The joke here revolves around the Platonic tendency to hypostatize abstractions, which paradoxically denies the external world's materiality. Although the Forms were supposedly immaterial, the possibility of correspondence between our experience of particulars and the apprehension of universal 'ideas' implicitly placed them upon the same logical footing. The political message is that democratic ideals, absorbed largely through classical texts, have produced a series of frightening dystopias throughout modern Europe.

In such attempts to drag into prominence half-hidden subtexts and histories that lie below the surface of individual words we can hardly tell where poetry begins and politics leaves off. Butler systematically merges the vocabularies of philosophy and politics, caricaturing, for example, scholasticism and the republican theories of James Harrington simultaneously: 'A Republican Is a civil Fanatic, an *Utopian* Senator; and as all Fanatics cheat themselves with Words, mistaking them for Things; so does he with the false Sense of Liberty ... He is a great lover of his own Imaginations, which he calls his Country; and is very much for Obedience to his own Sense, but not further. He is a nominal Politician, a faithful and loyal Subject to notional Governments, but an obstinate Rebel to the real.'[7] Butler playfully sides with 'the real' in its everyday sense of 'straightforward,' or 'having an existence in fact.' Monarchical rule and episcopacy become embodiments of objective reality and antidotes to the excesses of radical subjectivism, especially religious independency and social utopianism. Butler connects failures of the representational process in language to the rise of representation in politics. Another Character speculates on how the 'Politician' systematically builds his theory from misconceptions, particularly the error of deriving 'the Pedigree of Government from its first Original ... from whom all that are at present in the World are lineally descended' (*Characters* 61).

The binary model of *res et verba* that Butler invokes, as I have argued, coexisted with a model that provided a place for 'notions' as the intermediary stage between signifier and significant. The word *notion* appears in various contexts throughout the middle decades of the century. A holdover from humanist logic, it remained a crucial technical term in the philosophy of mind. In the specialized discourses of seventeenth-century epistemology and metaphysics, a 'notion' entails knowledge *of* something, that is to say, specific knowledge in opposition to knowledge in general. The historian of philosophy Thomas Stanley, for example, attempts to clarify the terminology of 'notions' in his discussion of Stoic logic. Drawing on Cicero and other authorities, Stanley speculates how our souls from the time of birth, 'like unto clean paper,' have notions inscribed upon them 'by the Senses.' Strictly speaking, notions are states of mind implanted through experience, 'which right reason conformeth in us, being long examined, are true, and suitable to the natures of things.'[8] It remains uncertain, however, how notions derive only (either directly or by 'similitude') from the outside world before they come to function as instruments of the discerning mind.

Throughout the seventeenth century, philosophers re-engaged this question of how ideas mediate between the knowing mind and the ultimate object named in the cognitive process. Sir Kenelm Digby was among the first after Bacon to consider the question at length. Butler served the countess of Kent for several years, and very likely met Digby at her house at Wrest Park in Bedfordshire. We know for certain that Butler had read the first of Digby's *Two Treatises* because he cites it once by title in a note, and on another occasion mockingly alludes to it (2.1.725–8; 2.3.1115–23). Although Butler had no great opinion of Digby's attempted reconciliation of Aristotle with modern science, he appears to have been affected by his use of the technical term *notion*. Digby was an exponent of what was called 'the notional way,' an epistemological argument at the set up the notion, in contradistinction to the idea, as the pivotal component in the cognitive process from object to subject. For Digby 'notions' were not something doubtful, insubstantial, or merely imaginary, but stood, as John W. Yolton explains, 'as intermediary between the real natures (what Locke later called the real essences) and the knowing mind.'[9] Digby treats notions as the sense impressions into which an object is broken down by the mind. Several such impressions are required to frame a single entity correctly. Notions must be distinct in the minds of those who would understand phenomena, but on no account should they identify notions with the phenomena themselves: 'It is true, wordes serve to express things: but if you observe the matter well; you will perceive they doe so, onely according to the pictures we make of them in our owne thoughts, and not according as the thinges are in theire proper natures. Which is very reasonable it should be so; since the soule, that giveth the names, hath nothing of things in her but these notions ... and therefore can not give other names but such as must signify the thinges by mediation of these notions.'[10] Every conception may appear to have a distinct thing as its object, but this is merely a deception of the mind. Digby's theory begins with the rebuttal of the Cartesian 'ideist' doctrine that science should concern itself with material substances. If this were true, Digby argued, there could be no real knowledge or useful science since it is impossible to compare our ideas with the substances of which they were supposed to be likenesses. Substance for Digby was not just a collection of observable instances, but an 'innate notion' that could not be derived from sense experience. Ideas are given to the mind, whereas notions are constructed by the mind and contain elements not obtainable from sense experience. The first principles of Digby's philosophy are that all knowledge is notional, and that sensible qualities are distinct from realities external to the mind and thus cannot correspond to things.[11]

Digby dismisses the impossible doctrines of the metaphysicians as straightforward mistakes in the framing of notions, producing confusion between mental contents and 'thinges as they are in themselves.' For Digby, the philosophical doctrine that grants universals a real status, existing in and apart from things, is untenable. He adopts instead a nominalism that makes every existent particular, and words simply 'common names' of notions. The chief importance of Digby's position lies in his avoidance of a realist theory of names, according to which words are considered to arise from objects and embody their real natures or essences. He offered, a decade before Hobbes, a kind of therapeutic nominalism and a remedial approach to errors of discourse.

Digby's notional way gained adherents and his doctrines underwent development in the years preceding and following the Restoration. Questions about the epistemic content of notions – how they are 'framed' by the operations of the mind, and whether they depend at all on the mind for their construction – enter into the main current of philosophy. In the work of the Catholic theologian, metaphysician, and controversialist John Sergeant there appears an astute historical analysis of the doctrine of notions and its evolution throughout the seventeenth century. Sergeant, who engaged in polemical exchanges with Jeremy Taylor, Stillingfleet, and John Tillotson, among others, found time, late in life, to critique the way of ideas. Sergeant embraces a philosophy of direct realism and rejects contemporary theories of ideas as semblances of reality lodged in the mind. Building on a scholastic doctrine derived from Aristotle but still extant in 'moderns' such as Pierre Gassendi, Sergeant theorized that the organs of sense receive the form of an object without its matter, that objects throw off images from their surface which produce perceptions (*eidolon, species*). One of his earliest publications, *To Sir Kenelme Digby upon His Two Incomparable Treatises of Philosophy*, commended Digby for showing us the mind's 'double errour, / In the smooth steady Glass of Reason's mirrour,' and teaching words 'their origin, true sense, and why.'[12]

On logical and theological grounds, Sergeant remains committed, in a way Digby avoids, to direct realism, whose restoration he urges to remedy various dualisms. His *Solid Philosophy Asserted against the Fancies of the Ideists* begins with a survey of an entrenched and erroneous way of ideas, an impasse he blames largely on Descartes and Locke. The activity of the past few decades, he argues, has deprived philosophy of its 'Immovable

Grounds,' and resulted in an '*Unmethodiz'd Disputation*' that leaves nothing decisively concluded. The procedures of ideist philosophers have not only divorced knowledge from truth, they have virtually brought about the end of philosophy through breeding radical scepticism, endless contradiction, and covert atheism. They have presumed to ground truth on a basis of mere resemblance ('fancies,' 'similitudes'), and as a result have 'introduced a kind of Fanaticism into Philosophy.' Sergeant claims to have found philosophy languishing under an epidemic of '*Distempers,*' making it necessary to uproot error and 'to break in pieces the brittle Glassy Essences of those Fantastick Apparitions' before re-establishing 'solid' knowledge.[13]

Sergeant anticipates a well-known argument against representationalism: that we cannot either assert or deny 'resemblance' when we possess no grounds for establishing it. If ideas are copies or resemblances, we cannot gauge their clarity or accuracy in comparison to an unknowable original. A 'notion,' in Sergeant's system, is the thing itself existing in the understanding. In ideational terms that is how notions 'exist.' In so far as existence is an intellectual property, notions are things, and we should not presume to identify a resemblance between notion and thing. In short, notions are the very nature of the thing, not an idea or similitude, and having a notion in mind is to understand the thing. Sergeant solves the riddle of the ontological status of 'ideas in the mind' by collapsing any hard-and-fast distinction between object and mind, saying instead that the sole difference between notions and objects resides in their mode of being. Whereas ideas or phantasms mediate between world and mind, notions are derived from them and are reliable objects of cognition. We would better understand the distinction between notions and objects as logical rather than real since speakers think of themselves as signifying meanings and things, not ideas. The materiality or immateriality of notions is irrelevant. Sergeant thus can explain the ontological status of notions without recourse to the principle of mental mediation, appealing instead to a theory of meaning and intention.

I summarize Sergeant's and Digby's positions for two reasons: first, to show that the better-known efforts of Hobbes and Locke were hardly unique in attempting to explicate an epistemology of ideas. A variety of obscure English theorists carried the debate some distance without fully understanding the contributions of Malebranche, Arnauld, and Leibnitz. Second, the gap between Digby and Sergeant shows how the question of notional ontology took on a sense of social urgency as the century wore on. Where Digby coordinates a familiar critique of Platonism and scholasticism, systems safely embalmed in the museum of dead theories, the seasoned polemicist Sergeant tackles the work of contemporaries, whom he makes responsible for the growth of error, 'fanaticism,' and irreligion. Given the importance accorded to unravelling this theoretical problem, contemporaries responded with a sense of metaphysical unease when confronted with theoretical options that had equally unwelcome (but logically necessary) consequences. One could not deny that ideas matched or resembled their object without, on one hand, unleashing a corrosive scepticism, or, on the other, falling back on intuition and appeals to faith. Nor could one, along with Sergeant, argue that ideas were 'of' their objects or 'in' the mind without implying a perplexing continuity between a perceiver and an object perceived.

What Digby objects to above all else is the realist's separation of qualities (or sensible properties) from substance, and the consequent reification of mental contents. In a striking convergence of phrasing, Digby ridicules 'these great Clerkes,' supposed followers of Aristotle, who solemnly invoke the terminology of 'entity,' 'quality,' or 'mood' to answer all questions involving substance or sensible quality. Hudibras' 'notions,' which Butler ironically praises for their indistinguishability from material 'things,' are first cousin to those described by Digby. Notion was for Butler, as for Digby, a technical term: 'Notions are but Pictures of things in the Imagination of Man, and if they agree with their originals in Nature, they are true, and if not False. And yet some Men are so unwary in their Thoughts, as to confound them and mistake the one for the other, as if the Picture of a Man, were really the Person for whom it was drawn.'[14] Digby's 'notions' are, similarly, 'pictures' of things 'in our owne thoughts,' and he warns us not to confuse notions with things 'in theire proper natures.' We might think it unlikely that someone could actually confound ideas with external reality. Yet, according to Butler, certain philosophers and 'Great Clerks' who promulgated a realist theory of universals did something very close to it. Above all, Butler faults philosophers for confusing their sensible impressions of things with 'the things themselves,' and duly according these phantasms names. The reduction of things into 'acts' (the Aristotelian-Thomistic term for the essences that underlie accidents) is both an example of a meaningless word, and an explanation of how such words arise.

Hudibras 'abstracts' the essential natures of things from their properties, confers material existence upon them, and finally ransacks scholastic terminology for an 'appropriate' name. In a footnote to 1.1.143 Butler impugns the procedures of scholastic metaphysics: 'The old Philosophers thought to extract Notions out of Natural things, as Chymists do Spirits and Essences, and when they had refin'd them into the nicest subtleties, gave them as insignificant Names, as those Operators do their Extractions: But (as *Seneca* says) the subtler things are render'd, they are but the nearer to Nothing. So are all their definitions of things by Acts, the nearer to Nonsense.' Butler seems to have in mind the Thomistic distinction between act and potentiality, by which a thing's actuality (its being one thing or another) is set against its capability to change (take on new accidents). He alludes to this theory in order to make a point about notions, which are, he implies, intangible, sensorily derived impressions. When abstracting or 'extracting' properties from things, we must take care not to attach names to notions that are not distinct in our minds. The more refined a thought, the less likely it has a foundation in the observable world: 'the subtler all Things are, / They're but to *nothing* the more near.'[15]

Lines 143 to 145 have an immediate relevance to the problems of metaphysics. Two of the terms Butler parodically echoes, 'Entity' and 'Quiddity,' are used in the Thomistic tradition to distinguish between being, as it is considered apart from attribute, and the universal essence abstracted from sense experience. When Hudibras separates entity from quiddity, he grants existence or 'thingness' to mental images. Butler's note to line 147 sheds some light on this problem: 'Some Authors have mistaken Truth for a Real thing, when it is nothing but a right Method of putting those Notions, or Images of things (in the understanding of Man) into the same state and order, that their Originals hold in Nature.' He then casts Aristotle in the teeth of the schoolmen, quoting from the *Metaphysics* on the correct derivation of causes: 'and therefore *Aristotle* says, *unum quodque sicut se habet secundum esse ita se habet secundum veritatem.*' Butler slants his reading of Aristotle's statement, 'as each thing is in respect of being, so is it in respect of truth,' in a very interesting way. The *Metaphysics* argues that just as general laws in nature must be universally valid in order for things to exist as they do on all levels of creation, so the philosopher must begin correctly in order to generate correct theories about the world (1038b–9b). Butler understands Aristotle to mean that knowledge can only be attained when our impressions of things conform to the order of things, but that truth and falsity are conferred on statements by properties intrinsic to cognition itself. 'Truth,' then, is not an essence but a value function of the correct ordering of notions. 'Reason,' Butler writes under that heading in his notebook, 'is a Faculty of the Minde, whereby she put's the Notions, and Images of things (with their operations, effects, and circumstances) that are confusd in the understanding, into the same order and condition, in which they are really disposd by Nature, or event: The Right Performance of this is cald Truth' (*PO* 65). Butler describes truth in relational terms, as a multidimensional system of ideas whose correctness we should methodically determine in the relation to one another rather than directly to 'nature.' 'Truth,' Butler thinks, 'is no Original, but Lines / Drawn Perfectly from Natures own Designes.' This context-related or structural model of reason offers a significant modification of a naïve correspondence theory, and we see many writers of the later seventeenth century moving towards one or another version of it. Butler imagines the acquisition of truth as a laborious process in which the mind imperfectly copies out an unattainable original. For Butler the goal of learning is nevertheless to pursue a hidden truth, and 'To Copy out th' Originals of Nature / As Far as Human wit can Imitate her.' Sovereign truth rules 'supreme and absolute,' and cannot allow inferior powers 'to try / The dictates of its high Authority' (*Satires* 185).

Butler's exposition might lead us to conclude that notions are the images of things, and truth a wordless ordering of notions reflected in the mind. Lines 147 and 148, however, seem to parody crude correspondence theories. Here Butler likens the insubstantiality of truth to the illusory substantiality of words spoken out-of-doors in a cold climate. Butler alludes to the 'paroles gelées' episode in Rabelais, where Pantagruel and Panurge reach the edge of the Frozen Sea and hear thawing words descend on them, transforming it into the error of lending substance to immaterial concepts.[16] Congealed words not only possess water's capacity to undergo changes in form while retaining its original composition, but also the attributes of personhood. 'Truth,' a conventional personification, appears to the naïve realist as a living and breathing entity. To know, as Hudibras supposedly 'knows,' the literal location of 'Truth' implies the existence of abstractions on a physical plane.

Although Butler implies that satisfiability in the world is the sole criterion of meaningfulness, he criticizes Hudibras for reifying or giving material being to insubstantial 'notions.' He doubts if a word can be meaningful, within or without a sentential context, when its referent seems confused or indeterminate. Butler accepts a notional theory of meaning, according to which words copy notions and notions copy sensory experience. He also adopts the position of regarding all human sign systems as intractable and inadequate because of the gulf between notations and their notional counterparts.

For Hudibras the erring metaphysician, words, notions, and things dwell in a mysterious third dimension contiguous to the mind. By fixating upon his own mental operations, he replicates what, according to Butler, was the great error of Aristotle himself: 'Aristotle thought to reduce Nature to his own Notions, rather then to suite them agreable to her; and studied her more in the metaphysiques of his own Braine, then her own certaine operations' (*PO* 132). Butler reasons that if words are to have any general meaning, the notions 'behind' them should be 'discovered,' not made. The mistake of treating truth, or *to kalon*, or 'the Good' as noncorporeal entities, as if every grammatical subject somehow had its real subsistence on another plane, is the characteristic blunder of metaphysics. Metaphysicians, Hobbes thought, fail to understand the words about which they argue when they dispute the question of what names signify.

Hudibras, as Butler describes him, 'knew *what's what*, and that's as high / As *Metaphysick* wit can flie.' The tautology 'what's what' usually suggests a commonplace, self-evident knowledge; in colloquial speech, the person who knows 'what's what' is a pragmatist in possession of the necessary facts. In Hudibras' case, knowing what's what means apprehending formal causes, essences, quidditas, in other words, knowing no-thing. Significantly, his intellectual development has come under the hobbling influence of training in scholasticism:

> In *School-Divinity* as able
> As he that high *Irrefragable;*
> Profound in all the Nominal
> And real ways beyond them all,
> And with as delicate a Hand
> Could twist as tough a Rope of Sand.   (1.1.151–6)

Butler removed from later editions lines that had a particular relevance to metaphysics: lines 153 and 154 originally read 'A second *Thomas,* or, at once / To name them all, another *Dunce.*' The reference to Alexander of Hales – whose sobriquet, Doctor Irrefragabilis, becomes a joke about Hudibras' invincibility in argument – and suppressed allusion to Duns Scotus reveal more than an unthinking anti-scholasticism. Both natives of Britain, Alexander and Duns exemplify the metaphysical tradition Hudibras has inherited. The 'barbarism' and dialectical ferocity of British scholasticism provided a conventional smear for Continental humanists, and Bacon incorporates some of their contempt into his comments on 'contentious' learning. Those who endured instruction in metaphysics often retained a distaste for such speculation well into later life. Controversies among the schools of Aquinas, Scotus, and Ockham constituted a large part of a university education in the seventeenth century. When Milton voiced a preference for Spenser as 'a better teacher' than Scotus or Aquinas (*CP* 2: 516), he spoke as an orthodox humanist with a distaste for metaphysical problems. By the Restoration, however, blanket dismissals of medieval philosophy become unfashionable, and Ockham and Scotus in particular regain some of their former prestige.[17]

Butler places a strong emphasis on ideas as the mediating point between sense data and the word, and parodies the metaphysical realism that treats universals as having a material existence. Where a contemporary philosopher might argue that all knowledge is knowledge of meanings and that we can have no experience of reality beyond our representations of it, Butler considered the truth of semiological codes dependent on a notional order beyond the codes themselves. When we peer into nature we gain glimpses of something other than ourselves and our preconceptions, reflected back. Nature is not structured like consciousness but possesses a hidden order penetrable through language. Butler regards wiping one's mind clean of presuppositions as unimaginably difficult, mired, as we are, in habits of thinking and deeply ingrained expectations. We must instead try to study nature without lapsing back into a scholasticism that perpetually rereads nature as an single transcendent meaning produced by one original cause. This does not involve repressing the problems of correspondence and referentiality, or stripping the mind of every prior concept and belief. Rather we must carefully attend to mediating structures, models of understanding, modes of perception, philosophical and mythological constructions. To arbitrate problems of meaning and interpretation Butler refers us to a pretextual, originary realm where error exerts less force, a logical extension of Bacon's program for extricating ourselves from epistemological entanglements.

Butler's playful version of 'metaphysical' wit begins by self-consciously embodying the human proneness to error within his poetic style. While poets have no monopoly on error, their faults of naming and predication appear particularly egregious. His characteristic practice of literalizing, etymologizing, and otherwise demystifying figures of speech constitutes itself as both a critique and an instantiation of verbal indeterminacy. Having established the theoretical parameters of a program for avoiding error, he observes his poem inevitably falling back into error and polysemy. Butler suspects metaphor because it unleashes the shaping, de-formative powers of wit and imagination. Along with the other verbal resources, metaphor has the potential to wrest 'things from their right meaning to a Sense that was never intended.' As untruths in the service of a higher truth, poetic fictions and figurative language have an incontestable value. For Butler, as for Bacon and Hobbes, 'apt Metaphor' and 'similitude' are inescapable. Butler sees them not only as the indispensable currency of the professional writer, but of Christ himself, 'who cald himself life' (*PO* 65, 46). Christ did so, however, at his peril, for 'the Jewes put him to Death for using but a Metaphor, and only borrowing the Name of their Temple, to express the Condition of this Body by.' Figuration, allegory, and other powers of unreason almost invariably prevail. Idolatry itself, Butler observes in his notebook, began when 'The Ignorant vulgar' mistook hieroglyphical characters 'for the things themselves' (*PO* 46). Butler considers primitive, pre-rational humanity incapable of making elementary distinctions between symbols and the objects in the external world. The doctrine of transubstantiation provides further proof that readers of Scripture cannot safely determine when to take Christ's words 'either in a Plaine or Metaphoricall Sense.' Although he sometimes appropriates scriptural authority to battle against metaphysical mystifications, Butler finds little evidence for a unified consciousness existing at the beginning of the world in the language of the Bible. Rational theology repeatedly founders in its attempts to square revelation with Cartesian standards of doubt and clarity.

While many of his contemporaries thought biblical providentialism could serve to justify the status quo, Butler appears more alive to the subversive aspects of religion, especially to apocalyptic narratives and symbols. His appropriation of 'cant' expressions for the purpose of self-refutation recalls the techniques of Thomas Edwards' anti-tolerationist pamphlet *Gangræna*. Edwards makes his case by recording 'the opinions and errours *in terminis,* and in their own words and phrases syllabically, as neer as possible can be, or I can remember them; and that as themselves have expressed them in books, manuscripts, Sermons, conferences.' Drawing attention to the supposed uniformity of truth, Edwards explains why some of the opinions he reproduces might seem contradictory and inconsistent: 'many of these errours fight among themselves; this indeed is one great difference between truth and errour, that truth though it be contrary to errour, yet one truth is never contrary to another, truth is one and uniforme; but many errours are not only contrary to truth, but to errours also.'[18] Edwards considers the mere fact of sectarian multiplicity (Brownists, Chiliasts, or Antinomians, Anabaptists, Arminians, familiasts, seekers, waiters, socinians, Arians, etc) proof enough of their proneness to error and estrangement from a uniform truth. In contrast, the slippage of *Hudibras* into a unintended radicalism results from Butler's scepticism, and also his recovery of wildly subversive metaphors that resist all efforts at containment.

Butler remained less than sanguine about using a unified religion as a prop for shoring up hierarchical conceptions of society. In *Hudibras* Butler transforms error into a religious and political category and explores the social implications of *humanum est errare*. He represents the beliefs of the two main characters as both motivating and justifying their respective delusions: Hudibras is a presbyterian knight and justice of the peace, concerned with administering public order and securing theological conformity; Ralph an Anabaptist with strong mystical and millenarian inclinations who views presbyterian hegemony with barely disguised contempt. While Hudibras aligns himself with a quasi-official presbyterianism, Ralph tilts towards a heterodox mystical Neoplatonism. As Butler portrays them, however, they reveal a common inability to understand the crucial relation between words and mental representations. The following chapters study two extended examples in the poem of semantic misalignment and social misunderstanding.

10

A Babylonish Dialect

I began this book with Bacon's confident prediction that correct method and scientific collaboration could lead humanity back to determinate origins. In Bacon's specular epistemology, language should and can connect to the world but at present does not. For Milton retrieving origins from a distant Edenic site presents an immensely difficult task. His renewal of epic form and recreation of paradisal language testify to the uncertainty of recapturing origins. For all his misgivings about science, Milton sounds thoroughly Baconian on the subject of referentiality in *Of Education*: 'though a linguist should pride himselfe to have all the tongues that *Babel* cleft the world into,' but has 'not studied the solid things in them as well as the words and lexicons,' he will understand no more than a tradesman or yeoman who speaks a single tongue (*CP* 2: 369–70). Milton does not, however, prescribe a technique for repossessing the point prior to 'words and lexicons' when we must use words to reach that origin. The central paradox remains: if truth resides in a prelinguistic realm of 'solid things,' how can we approach this originary domain without the assistance of language?

With Butler, the possibility of retrieving an originary truth becomes more remote. Claims to recover an authoritative original truth are vitiated by the problems of error and language. To a greater extent than Milton, Butler criticized his contemporaries for overinvesting in the study of language. Although he encouraged them to search out the origins of their experience, he scoffs at the practice of looking for the roots of language in the tongues of the Far or Middle East. He knew, of course, that some radical sectarians, believing in the continual operation of the Holy Spirit on earth, claimed to speak 'Hebrew' and other tongues they had not naturally acquired. Others insisted that they could speak a Pentecostal tongue intelligible to all, which they associated with Eden. In this chapter I return to the relation between language and ideology. I describe how, in a specific political and religious context, Butler attacks sectarians for steeping themselves in error. Butler's customary trope for the process of false recovery and argumentative disintegration is Babel-Babylon. A general desire to repair 'the Curse of Babilon' and renovate language, Butler says in different contexts, had paradoxically worsened the confusion and permeated English speech and writing with false conceptions (*Satires* 69). Butler's satire on the problem of linguistic origins in *Hudibras* represents a type of demystification, an early attempt at ideological critique from within ideology.

Butler rejected the 'truth' embodied in the shared meanings of a linguistic community, even though his experience of language convinced him of its power. He believed, as Bacon believed, that speakers cannot easily divorce themselves from the communal and cultural aspects of their speech. All language users trade in an inherited sign system, a shared code. Since they inhabit a system that antedates them and whose structures are borrowed, unintended meanings creep into what they say, even as they generate new meanings. Butler considers linguistic difference, diversity of dialect, inflectional irregularities, and syntactic ambiguities to be barriers to comprehension. For him, the proliferation of dialects offers further evidence, if any were needed, of the fragmentary and intractable nature of human consciousness (*Satires* 158). The enormous diachronic and synchronic variation that lies within even a single tongue undermines any hope for future standardization and finally subverts the fiction of a unitary 'rationality' tied to clear and distinct ideas.

Hudibras, as I have suggested, confronts the boundless frustration of trying to make our descriptions and analyses of the world align with their notional origins. Incontrovertible evidence of this semiotic and epistemological rift resides in the particulars of social life and in language itself. Butler looks to a supposed decline in the culture at large, evident in a pervasive uncertainty that challenges all the old hegemonies. Religious and political controversy presents the worst arena imaginable in which to work out theories of knowledge, the field in which reason must confront its limitations or find itself implicated in an endless round of assertion and counter-assertion.

Through the trope of Babel-Babylon Butler makes explicit his rejection of the ecclesiastical, political, and linguistic questions that so exercised his contemporaries. In *Hudibras* Butler fuses Babel, the symbol of ideological imprisonment in the bonds of language, with Babylon, the symbol of political imprisonment under a monolithic state religion. We hear an especially bitter note of irony in his use of the topos, for with it the poem strives to turn tables on the groups that most often laid claim to it as a shorthand term of moral condemnation.

In Revelation, Babylon is a prototype of Rome, and its fall foretells the destruction of the Roman Empire. Familiar in England from sermons, polemic, and emblem books, the typology and iconography of Babel-Babylon had its native sources in the campaign, coordinated by sixteenth-century anti-papal writers such as John Bale and John Foxe, to diabolize the papacy. Their extensive application of Revelations' prophecies concerning the Great Beast established a national myth of England as a stalwart defender of European Protestantism. The figure resurfaces in later debates on social order and the form of church governance. Throughout the civil war the metaphor belonged mainly to radical Protestantism, which read it in close conjunction with the story of the Babylonian captivity. Through a process of associative expansion they laid the groundwork for the politicization of clarity of discourse as a religious and social issue. To emphasize the historical outcome of verbal misunderstanding, Babel-Babylon was fused into a single symbolic entity, with its use divided along ideological lines. Both radical and royalist agreed, at least for polemical purposes, in regarding English and biblical history as potentially homologous. Assimilating biblical narratives of exile and persecution to English experience, both groups convinced themselves of the transience of forced religious observance and the future defeat of a seemingly invincible power.

In the 1640s radical Protestants began to depict the official representatives of the church as Antichrist's agents, the writhing tentacles of a hydra-headed monster whose grip would loosen only with decapitation. Parliamentarian preachers depicted London as the site of an eschatological struggle and exhorted their congregations to pull down the rule of Antichrist to establish a new Jerusalem under the millennial rule of the saints. In their campaign against episcopacy and monarchical government they taxed Church and Crown with the typology of the Great Beast and the Whore of Babylon, turning the officially sanctioned rhetoric against their adversaries.[1] At first radical sectarians allegorized the Beast's seven heads and ten horns to represent the Established Church, and later to assail presbyterianism.

By the 1650s the metaphor of Babel-Babylon had lost much its polemical force as royalist reaction transformed it into an argument for social control and the preservation of traditional hierarchies. Sir Robert Filmer, for example, inveighed against democracy and popular government as 'this beast of many heads.'² Royalists treated Babel-Babylon as an emblem of the linguistic incomprehension at the root of civil strife, identifying it with sectarianism, social fragmentation, and the daily spawning of 'hard words' and political slogans. The trope had come to embody fears that sectarianism signalled the end of traditional social authority, indeed had already engendered a proliferation of discourses that could endlessly reproduce the internecine struggles of the interregnum. Babel never served any single use, and remained easily adjusted to various causes. Royalist co-optation, however, almost effected the trope's removal from the radical lexicon as revolutionary eschatology underwent parodic transformation. The monster from the bottomless pit becomes a comic bogeyman, like republicanism and congregationalism a living contradiction of the principle of rational dominance and the concentration of authority in elites.

Milton's many invocations of the Beast and Babylonian woe enact these polemical and figurative complexities. His early epigrams 'On the Gunpowder Plot' address the 'beast in ambush on the Seven Hills,' and assail Rome as 'the Latin monster' bearing a 'triple crown' and 'ten horns.' As late as 1673, he reaffirmed his view of the plot as an attempt to reimpose a *'Babylonish* Yoke' on English freedom. The eschatological drama of Babylonian luxuriousness also carried an anti-mercantile subtext in the sea merchants' cry at the destruction of Babylon: 'Alas alas, that great citie, wherein were made rich all that had ships in the sea, by reason of her costlinesse' (Rev. 18: 19). Milton draws on these associations in *The Reason of Church-Government*, where he attacks prelates as 'true merchants of Babylon' for their willingness to sell out liberties of conscience and plunge the freeborn nation into perpetual slavery. In *Eikonoklastes* (1650) he tauntingly rebuts King Charles's prophecy that God will not suffer his inquisitors 'to prosper in their *Babel*,' by equating monarchy with the Great Whore and the Beast of the Apocalypse. Ten years later, on the very brink of the Restoration, he remarks that a Babel 'not of tongues, but of factions' had undone the Protectorate and prevented the Commonwealth from erecting a tower 'to overshaddow kings and be another *Rome* in the west.'³

Michael McKeon has suggested that we should not assume 'a sectarian odor' to the apocalyptic rhetoric of Babylon and the Great Beast, since it was well within the boundaries of Protestant orthodoxy and the resurgence of anti-Catholicism after 1665.⁴ Yet the trope came down to the Restoration tightly imbricated with radical associations. Appropriations of it necessarily invoked a network of conflicting polemics. After the Restoration, Milton was accused of having used the metaphor as a vehicle of revolutionary meaning. An anonymous pamphleteer in the exchange growing out of *The Rehearsal Transpros'd* aimed a glance at the former Latin secretary for allying himself with reformers bent on suppressing the universities: 'doubtless at that time when *Latine* was the *Language of the Beast*, he might have kept in Office, because what he wrote differ'd much from what the *Beast* bellow'd.' The joke suggests an ironic resemblance between Miltonic polemic and papal edict at the same time that it ridicules the quality of Milton's Latinity. Earlier an anonymous respondent to Milton's *Readie and Easie Way* parodied his approach to the problem of church government as the view 'that the Church of Christ ought to have no Head upon Earth, but the Monster of many heads, the multitude.'[5] Milton's adversaries point to such phrases in order to discredit him by recalling his association with radicalism's watchword, Babylon.

As it undergoes parodic appropriation the apocalyptic rhetoric of Babylon loses much of its former effectiveness as a polemical weapon. John Cleveland identifies the Tower of Babel and the Whore of Babylon with the foes of the Established Church, personified by the five presbyterian divines who together made up the composite pseudonym 'Smectymnuus' (Stephen Marshall, Edmund Calamy, Thomas Young, Matthew Newcomen, William Spurstow): 'The Whore of *Babylon* left these brats behind, / Heires of Confusion by *Gavell-kind.*' Cleveland depicts Smectymnuus as at once the spiritual offspring of Rome and a cacophonous amalgam of heterogeneous doctrine. In a 1659 poem, Robert Wild retrospectively summed up the Protectorate as 'The seven years' Babel.' Cowley described England during this period as 'a *Chaos,* and Confusion ... A *Babel,* and a *Bedlam.*' William Uvedale's poem on Charles's Restoration proceeds in the same vein: 'What strange Babell have we seen of late! / Call it a larger Bedlam, not a State.' A poem in *Wit Restor'd* attacks the new fashion of shunning 'univocall' language, and worries over the social implications of unregulated discourse: 'fall wee upon / Another Babells Sub-confusion? / And in the selfe-same language must wee find, / A diverse faction of the wordes and mind?'[6] By the Restoration an explicit parallel had emerged between Babel as the precursor of Babylon's fall and linguistic and political instability as the cause of England's decline. The outcome of the proliferation of codes, customs, values is a penchant for controversy that threatens to bring the entire social fabric crashing to the ground. The typological completion of the destruction at Babel had become anarchic levelling and unbridled democracy. By placing the topos within a historical field constituted by the civil war and its aftermath, these writers emphasize the social coding of language and its inseparable relation to ideology and politics.

Throughout the miscellaneous prose and in *Hudibras* Butler confronts the contradictions of the Babel myth in relation to the advent of various religious and polemical discourses. For Butler Babel provided a powerful emblem of the linguistic and cultural diversity that first engendered conflict: 'The variation of Languages at the Building of Babell,' he writes, 'was but a 2d Curse upon the fall of man.' Butler carefully considered the theological implications of the pentecostal miracle, described in Acts 2, as antitype of Babel: 'The holy Ghost that first fell upon the Apostles in the Shape of Cloven Tongues, Did but tell them, that they should speak all Languages which before they never had been taught to understand, and by that miraculous meanes convert Some of all Sorts, to the Christian Faith, and disperse it over all the Face of the Earth, as the Division of Tongues had made all mankind to do at the Building of Babilon: so Punctuall is Divine Justice to cure the wounds it has inflicted, like the weapon-Salve, by the same way and method that it usd before to give them.' Although Butler regarded the pentecostal de-Babelization as demonstrating God's benevolence in releasing humanity from the second general curse, he could not reclaim the figure as long as it remained in the hands of adversaries. According to the Established Church, humanity's redemption from the Confusion is restricted to the first Whitsun, making the miracle of tongues a unique occurrence. In the *Characters*, Butler similarly maintains that the power conferred upon the apostles whereby they made themselves understood by every nation is irrecoverable: 'And therefore, as the *Apostles* made their divine Calling appear plainly to all the World by speaking Languages, which they never understood before; he [the 'hypocritical nonconformist'] endeavours to do the same Thing most preposterously by speaking that which is no Language at all, nor understood by any Body, but a Collection of affected and fantastic Expressions, wholly abstract from Sense, as *Nothingness, Soul Damningness and Savingness,* &c. in such a fustian Stile as the *Turks* and *Persians* use; that signify nothing but the Vanity and want of Judgment of the Speaker.' Butler ironically traces back contemporary fondness for neologism and lexical innovation to the tradition of pentecostalism. By identifying the puritans' 'insignificant' jargon with tongue-speaking he aims to discredit all such discourse as glossolalia, an agglomeration of meaningless expressions. He equates the discourses of puritanism with precipitous political decline and the fall of the Tower of Babel: 'As Confounding Languages Forerun / The Fall and slavery of Babilon, / So Canting brought the thorow-Reformation / T' inslave and over-run the English Nation.'[7] While much previous satire had dismissed 'cant' and doctrinal error as expressions of hypocrisy, Butler offers a subtler explanation, treating the waywardness of sectarianism as an inescapable consequence of Babel-Babylon. What begins as a trope in the arsenal of early Protestant polemic quickly becomes a conscious strategy to undermine the establishment's authority to preach and interpret Scripture.

In one of *Hudibras'* best-known passages, Butler describes Hudibras' rhetorical accomplishments in terms of the fragmentation and rupture for which Babylon was a byword:

> His ordinary Rate of Speech
> In loftiness of sound was rich,
> A *Babylonish* dialect,
> Which learned Pedants much affect.
> It was a particolour'd dress
> Of patch'd and pyball'd Languages:
> 'Twas *English* cut on *Greek* and *Latin*,
> Like Fustian heretofore on Sattin.
> It had an odde promiscuous Tone,
> As if h' had talk'd three parts in one.
> Which made some think, when he did gabble,
> Th' had heard three Labourers of *Babel*;
> Or *Cerberus* himself pronounce
> A Leash of Languages at once. (1.1.91–104)

Butler characterizes Hudibras' 'dialect' as 'Babylonish' in order to emphasize both its reliance on alien sources and its tendency to engender discord. The images of three labourers of Babel trying in vain to make themselves understood and of a trilingual Cerberus reinforce an atmosphere of strife and cacophony. The famous neologism 'Babylonish,' which fuses together the attributes of Romishness, polyglottism, and incomprehensibility, itself provides an example of what Butler implicitly rejects: a word not fully incorporated into the standard lexicon. Butler annotates 'A *Babylonish* dialect' as 'a confusion of Languages, such, as some of our Modern *Virtuosi* use to express themselves in.' The note directs us to connect Babylon to the Royal Society scientists who, ironically, put themselves in the van of linguistic progress.

If 'prophesying' was the main expression the desire for de-Babelization took among inspired sectarians, the intellectual elite looked towards a 'stylistic reformation' and the invention of a universal language and iconic character. Zachary Grey attempts to diffuse the anti-scientific subtext of

Butler's remark by aligning him with Thomas Sprat's *History*, which spoke out against the 'many *fantastical* Terms' introduced by sectarians and translators during the wars.[8] As much as he sides with plainness and linguistic reform, Butler explodes the contemporary dream of a perfectly transparent language, devoid of unruly metaphor. In *Hudibras* he mocks the futile scholarship expended on identifying the primal language; and in his notebooks he offers the opinion that those who traded in universals, including 'universall Characters[,] Languages, Medcins, and measures all met with the same success that is none at all' (1.1.175–8; *PO* 165–6). Replacing existing words or characters with new ones presented no solution to lexical overabundance, and the desire to remedy the harm of Babel would lead to further fragmentation. Such impracticable projects could only advance the very process they sought to reverse.

Hudibras exemplifies the principle that words can leave off being a tool for closing the gap between speakers and become instead a source of alienation. Verbal habits of the sort he indulges in have a deleterious effect on the health of society. Conforming to the character type of 'A Pedant,' Hudibras 'speaks in a different Dialect from other Men, and much affects forced Expressions, forgetting that *hard Words,* as well as *evil ones, corrupt good Manners*' (*Characters* 188). While many philosophers, including Descartes, thought that the gift of speech sets humanity apart from the beasts, Butler argues to the contrary that language has the inverse capacity to transform us into beasts. 'I am no *Horse*,' Hudibras responds to the Lady, who has been casting aspersions on his virility by comparing him to a gelding, 'I can argue, and discourse' (2.1.721–2). Hudibras' identification of discourse with argument, ironically enough, threatens to bring about his bestialization. Acrimonious verbal exchanges have already plunged England into civil war and the state of nature. When Butler's characters tire of controversy, they immediately fall to assailing their enemies tooth and nail. Butler localizes the source of discord in the organs of speech, using the beargarden as a symbol of the litigiousness and bitter controversy arising out of polemical exchange. Hudibras the polemicist does not engage in a dialogue to bring about clarification, but to vindicate a position held from the outset. He never deals with opponents as interlocutors but proceeds by identifying their transgressions, uncovering an ignoble motive, establishing guilt, and finally passing sentence. Hudibras' combination of prosecutorial zeal, theological dogmatism, rhetorical overkill, and predisposition for violent confrontation discloses an incapacity to acknowledge and accommodate political difference. Following the civil war and Glorious Revolution, as a recent study points out, diversity was legitimized in terms of an oppositional contract and the political mechanism of partisanship.⁹ With the emergence of party politics after 1688, the ideal of a unified commonweal gave way to something else. Controversy and fragmentation, once considered sources of social dysfunction, gradually became the normative conditions of English political life.

Butler persists in older habits of thinking, and associates diversity with the downward spiral of civilization attending the ascendancy of the sects. When any semblance of official order collapsed during the 'Year of Anarchy' before the Restoration of King Charles, the millennial saints considered themselves

> Deliver'd from th' *Ægyptian Awe*,
> Of *Justice, Government, and Law*.
> And free t' erect what *Spiritual Cantons*,
> Should be reveal'd, Or *Gospel Hans-Towns*,
> To Edify upon the Ruines
> Of *John* of *Leidens old out-goings*. (3.2.241–6)

Butler portrays the saints as master builders of chaos: they propose to subdivide the country into provinces or cantons, and establish new towns after the model of the Hanseatic League in Germany ('*Hans-Towns*'). The reign of the saints means perpetual 'edifying' and the setting up of new doctrines 'upon the Ruines' of old heresies. All this innovation works to the utter destruction of national unity. Butler fears nothing so much as dissent, multiplicity, and moral fragmentation. Under the cover of establishing order, the presbyterian mode of church governance has initiated a disintegrative process that moves England relentlessly towards collapse. The poem describes the Protectorate period as a time when both independent and presbyterian strove 'T'outcant the Babylonian Labourers, / At all their Dialects of Jabberers. / And tug at both ends of the Saw, / To tear down Government and Law' (3.2.151–4). After the death of Cromwell some independent factions pressed for pulling down 'th' High Places' of synods and classes, which oppressed them 'like Bloody *Nimrods*' (3.2.279–82). They cite Nimrod – the founder of Babylon and a conventional type of the tyrant – without realizing how well their application fits the breakdown of social order they themselves have engineered.

Through the sheer vehemence of their talk, Hudibras and his squire, Ralph, re-enact the polemically charged climate of public debate during the interregnum. Tensions between the two, as critics point out, parody tensions within the parliamentary party. Ralph never evinces Hudibras' compulsive need to triumph in controversy, to meet the challenge of debate with a fusillade of polemic. As the poem's chief representative of radical independency, Ralph continually appeals to egalitarian political and religious principles, including freedom of conscience and freedom to interpret Scripture according to his own 'light.' Of all the poem's characters, Ralph succumbs most often to the temptation of slinging the abusive epithets associated with Babylon at his ideological antagonists. As the poem's chief representative of 'adamicism,' moreover, he claims the authority of a 'primitive tradition' stretching back to Eden (1.1.525–6). His familiarity with a language that has escaped the penalty of Babel emerges in his ability to converse with 'subtlest *Parrots*,' a species that shares the human tendency to 'speak and think contrary clean' (1.1.543–4). Butler ironically supports this claim and attributes a deep Machiavellianism to chattering birds. Ralph's strategy for reconnecting polemic to the Edenic world becomes a measure of his fusion of politics and religion, and exemplifies sectarian readiness to vilify opponents by linking them with the Beast and the Whore. For Protestant reformers 'whoredom' meant a form of idolatry resulting from carnality, a worldliness that revels in money, bodies, and images. The mother of harlots appears throughout *Hudibras* in various guises, and several times *in propria persona*. When, for example, Hudibras encounters the carnival ritual of a skimmington he objects to the 'Idolatrous' practice, asking, 'Does not the Whore of *Babylon* ride / Upon her *Horned-Beast* astride, / Like this proud *Dame*?' (2.2.763–5). The Whore also takes the form of '*Semiramis* of *Babylon*,' the legendary queen (2.1.715), whose reputation for having 'receiv'd Horses into her embraces' Butler draws attention to in a note. His annotation explicitly identifies Semiramis with the Mother of Harlots, whose consort is the scarlet Beast she rides, and brings into play conventional associations of tyrannical rule with sexual depravity.

Ralph expertly capitalizes on all these sexual and apocalyptic associations in a long diatribe against synods in canto 3 of the first part. When Ralph equates bearbaitings with the presbyterian plan for church government by synods, he calls both a '*Babylonish* sport' (1.3.1098). Anything Ralph finds objectionable bears for him a dual affinity to the papacy and to presbyterianism. In this respect he is representative of sectarians who set about unfolding the mystery of Babylon in terms distinctly unflattering to their enemies. Ralph reveals the synod as an emblem of the beargarden and the presbyterian plan of church government as a type of the Beast: '*Synods* are mystical *Bear-gardens*, / Where *Elders, Deputies, Church-wardens*, / And other Members of the Court, / Manage the *Babylonish* sport'

(1.3.1095–8). Ralph embarks on a course of playful allegorizing that neatly parodies techniques of typology and applying biblical texts. Before he has finished we see the denunciatory language of Babylon that he hurls at adversaries stick to everyone and everything, including himself. Ralph develops his argument through an accretion of brilliant, if questionable, parallels, extended comparisons, and strained analogies.[10] His demonstration that presbyters are bears parodies the useful polemical strategy of redefining the term under discussion in a sense contrary to its ordinary acceptation. Butler specifically recalls the controversy over whether 'presbyter' and 'bishop' signify the same thing. In 1641 the Smectymnuans detected a world of difference between primitive and Caroline bishops, yet also maintained, on the authority of Saint Jerome, that episcopacy enjoyed no privileged status, 'that *Bishops* and *Presbyters* are originally the same; *Idem ergo est Presbyter qui Episcopus.*' Milton agreed that bishopdom did not constitute a legitimate ecclesiastical order. His famous pun on 'Presbyter' and 'Priest' deflates presbyterian pretensions to power by ironically supporting an assertion of identity.[11] Ralph's identification of presbyterianism with beargardens evolves from a similar detestation of improperly arrogated authority. Regarding such appeals to authority as a transparent cover for arbitrary behaviour, he exposes presbyterian claims to church governance by divine right as the grossest sort of ideological mystification.

Ralph's insight into presbyterian hierarchies, however, comes veiled in a mystifying hermeneutic that combines hermeticism, nominalism, and dark allegory. Typically, he concerns himself less with what verbal distinctions signify than what they conceal: 'For *Prolocutor, Scribe,* and *Bearward,* / Do differ onely in a mere word' (1.3.1099–100). Ralph assumes that one thing can be another without showing any sign of identicalness. Synods and beargardens, presbyterian officials and bear-wardens, presbytery and romanism are by nature the same. Only in arbitrary language, Ralph argues, are they considered different. The overarching equivalent to the synod, the grand equation to which all else conduces, is the papal See, which is itself revealed as the Great Beast:

Presbyterie does but translate
The Papacy to a *Free State,*
A *Common-wealth of Poperie,*
Where ev'ry Village is a *See*
As well as *Rome*
...
Such Church must (surely) be a Monster

With many heads: for if we conster
What in th'*Apocalyps* we find,
According to th'Apostle's mind,
'Tis that the *Whore of Babylon*
With many heads did ride upon;
Which Heads denote the sinful tribe
Of *Deacon, Priest, Lay-elder, Scribe*.   (1.3.1201–5; 1213–20)

Ralph has mastered an associative process whereby presbyterianism typologized is the horned Beast astride which the Great Harlot sits. Metaphor provides the means for circumventing artificial differences residing in names. Behind these false distinctions we see a unifying principle that makes diverse phenomena virtually indistinguishable. When Hudibras tries to parry Ralph's argument with a direct attack on his creation of a hybrid presbyter who is 'A strange *Chimæra* of Beasts and Men' (1.3.1317), he propagates an image of the talking red dragon of Revelation 13, with its seven heads, ten horns, and combined anatomy of leopard, bear, and lion. Thus he inadvertently bolsters Ralph's harangue by depicting presbyterianism as the Protestant Antichrist, a monster who speaks error in the tongues of all nations.

Butler's description of Hudibras' '*Babylonish* dialect' offers a complex appraisal of the use of polemic as an instrument of coercion. He uses the topos throughout Hudibras to bind politics to prophetic typology and ideology to language. When, for example, Butler identifies parliamentary rule with the hydra-headed Beast or describes an Independent politician's having 'more heads than a *Beast in Vision*, / And more Intrigues in ev'ry one, / Than all the Whores of Babylon,' he vicariously participates in the very process he denounces (3.2.352–4). Although he speaks in a register different from the sectarians', Butler occupies a site within a historical field where radical encodings were overlaid by royalist reaction. Resigning himself to the impossibility of escaping the consequences of political difference, he establishes a position both within and without the controversies following in the wake of English social conflict. While he may deride the typological treatment of the present in terms of biblical parallels, he cannot subject the Babel-Babylon trope, the common property of English Protestantism, to rigorous policing. Thus, the poem itself forms part of a polemic, and launches a critique of a system within whose limits it dwells.

Despite such contradictions (or perhaps because of them) *Hudibras* cannot erase the signs of its political engagement. Butler intended the poem to discredit the discourses of sectarianism, and, indeed, its popular success helped attain that goal. We can take one measure of the poem's political influence from the semi-official status its logomachical reading of the revolution achieved. After Butler, the Babel-Babylon trope retained less of its former usefulness among sectarians. It becomes inextricably linked with an ideological attack under the cover of stylistic and epistemological critique. Johnson's famous invocation of 'a Babylonish Dialect' to describe the diction and syntax of *Paradise Lost*, for example, closely correlates with his distaste for Milton's heterodoxy and republicanism.[12]

Hudibras' potential utility in providing a witness to civil strife necessitated the labours of a Zachary Grey to confine its author within the bounds of a carefully demarcated orthodoxy. Although Butler strained to disengage from topicality, continually moving towards origins and 'universal' human nature, his poem reaffirms its historical embeddedness and limitations as a product of language. The Babel-Babylon topos participates in a process of satiric appropriation that inevitably registers the pressure of the seventeenth-century quest to ground knowledge in an origin positioned outside of words.

11

By Equivocation Swear

Despite the considerable attention given to Butler's 'thought,' political readings of *Hudibras* have stood still with attempts to decode its topical allegory. As a result, we have inherited a strangely divided sense of Butler as a conservative poet whose work nevertheless bears traces of 'deism,' anti-rationalism, 'nihilism,' and 'protofeminism.'[1] Christopher Hill is among the few who have tried to explain this apparent contradiction, describing Butler as a 'radical royalist,' a thinker 'abreast of many modern ideas,' including those of Hobbes and the libertines, a proponent of a virulent anti-clericalism, and a writer who avoided publishing his prose manuscripts during his lifetime because of 'the very subversive nature of his ideas.' Hill argues that Butler's willingness to extend his animosity to almost every quarter has its roots in a view that mistrusts ideology in every form. Butler's experience of the revolution and Restoration led him to fear the legitimizing rationales used by various social groups and to distrust all totalizing systems.[2]

Hill reinforces what eighteenth- and nineteenth-century admirers of *Hudibras* overlooked: that Butler's satire participates in a historical process that brought to the fore a complex of basic social contradictions in the nation's political life. In *Hudibras* we see traces of the 'poetic disjunction' and 'persistent reiteration of contradiction' described by Laura Brown in relation to Dryden and other Restoration writers.[3] Although Butler may embrace an ideology that seeks to hide contradictions inherent in the interests it serves, he remains highly sceptical about the possibility of dissolving political difference in 'moderation' and the common good. His intensely political (and, for some modern readers, oppressively topical) poem is awash in contradictions – among them a desire to see the establishment of a methodically derived originary truth that might secure consensus.

Butler made the English epic unmistakably political in a way it had not been before, even while repudiating the frightening worlds of 'fierce contests' and 'stout polemic braul.' He probably began *Hudibras* in the 1640s, at a time when little possibility existed of bringing it before the public. Its open-ended structure may represent an accommodation to unpropitious historical conditions that could keep the poem from publication indefinitely. A significant portion of his writings appeared posthumously, and government censorship is probably among the factors that shaped his history of publication. The continually shifting political situation spurred him to cultivate a type of writing both polemical and oblique, formally constrained and oddly experimental.[4] Because Butler self-consciously strives to reproduce specific political positions, we should not neglect the poem's full range of meaning or ignore the powerful contradictions embedded within it. We need to recast the question of Butler's topicality in other terms, and develop a critical practice that avoids divorcing politics from genre and referentiality from form. We must avoid the trap of generalizing Butler's social critique to the point of toothlessness or shrugging off his unrelenting topicality as dross. When Milton ostensibly 'abandoned' politics for poetry he reoriented his writings to engage the struggle for reform in different terms. Butler's epic can also be read as political allegory, even though he explicitly discouraged the practice of seeking out point-by-point correspondences. Unable credibly to deny the poem's topicality, he claimed to have no specific allegorical design in mind, and encouraged an open-ended approach to its interpretation. In a letter to Sir George Oxenden, Butler acknowledged the existence of readers who 'pretend to discover ceartaine Psons of Quallity with whome they say those Characters agree,' and commented: 'every man should make what applications he pleases of it, either to himselfe or others.'[5]

In *Hudibras* we find Butler longing for the authorizing origin lost beneath strata of accumulated error. Butler viewed the civil war as a crisis of language and of legitimation. His placement of the poem within a sociohistorical field constituted by the revolution and its aftermath demonstrates the inseparable relation of knowledge to political life. Margaret Doody has written that 'the major literary implication of Civil War verse is that styles are not trustworthy,' and that words are generally inadequate for the purposes of their users.[6] Doody's generalization works well for Butler, whose writings give obsessive attention to the theme of verbal inadequacy. Style and language, however, form only part of the problem he delineates, one manifestation of the difficulty of representing origins. In Butler's hands, the philosophical counter-epic exposes how social conflict issues from obscured origins, how institutions for the exchange of ideas fail to contend with the problem, becoming instead a staging-place for polemic.

We can begin our philosophical-topical reading of Butler with an event that occurred when he was thirty-one years old and possibly in the service of Sir Samuel Luke, a presbyterian member of Parliament.

On 25 September 1643, hoping to cement a closer military and ecclesiastical alliance with the Scots, the English Parliament approved the Solemn League and Covenant. To make compliance as easy as possible the wording of the covenant was kept vague and free of any *jure divino* sanction. A pamphlet of October 1649 nevertheless referred to it as 'a long Oath, and abounding with ambiguous expressions.' Soon after, Edward Benlowes, taking a more aggressive stance, darkly warned: '*avant / With your six-hundred-sixtie-six-word*-Covenant.'[7] Subscribers to the oath swore to extirpate episcopacy and to undertake the reformation of religion 'according to the Word of God, and the example of the best reformed Churches.' The third article committed covenanters to safeguard the rights and privileges of the parliaments, and 'to preserve and defend the King's Majesty's person and authority, in the preservation and defence of the true religion and liberties of the kingdoms.' This article, originally intended as no more than a pro forma attestation of loyalty, took on tremendous importance in the course of later events. Subsequent debate revealed these words, and indeed the covenant as a whole, susceptible to widely divergent interpretations.

Six years later, at a time when the revolutionary government grew anxious to ensure its legitimacy and secure obedience, another oath was proposed: the engagement. At first required of the newly formed Council of State, in October 1649 it was extended by Parliament to soldiers, ministers, schoolmasters, clerks, and other public office-holders. In January 1650 it was demanded of all male citizens of eighteen years and over, making it a widespread concern, and – to borrow the title of a contemporary tract about it – a 'grand case of conscience.' Reluctant engagers raised various objections to the oath, but most often stressed two main stumbling blocks. First, the verbal formula itself: 'I do declare and promise, that I will be true and faithful to the Commonwealth of England, as it is now established, without a King or House of Lords.' The word *commonwealth* was subject to multiple constructions: did it mean a particular kind of government or just the nation as a whole? Similarly, did 'true and faithful' indicate mere passive obedience to authority or an active vigilance and zeal? Did the clause 'as it is now established, without a King or House of Lords' function as a simple description of the present government, or did it imply an obligation to uphold the present polity in the future? The second sticking point was the belief that the engagement was as contradictory to the covenant as the covenant was to the oath of allegiance. Since swearers could sidestep the issue of inconsistency by arguing for the engagement's nullification with changes of circumstance, some rationalized their reversals of allegiance on the basis of lawful submission to a de facto power.[8]

These two political crises had a decisive effect on the casuistry of oath-taking, projecting disputes over interpretive questions into the political arena. During a period when citizens subscribed to many oaths, some of which appeared in direct conflict with one another, interest in the politics of interpretation steadily mounted. *Hudibras* provides an example of how intensely self-conscious English writers had become about the political implications of such interpretive practices. As Butler represents them, the linguistic functions of equivocation and ambiguity have become integral to public forms of discourse, promoting the continuing degradation of the linguistic covenant upon which political life depends.

Butler's editor Zachary Grey represented the strategies of equivocation as characteristic of puritanism, quoting Robert Sanderson as a gloss on *Hudibras*. Grey recalls how many oath-takers hoped to absolve themselves of perjury by forcing 'some subtle Interpretation' upon the words of an oath.[9] Although Grey took for granted the importance of equivocation to sworn submission in *Hudibras*, the subject has all but escaped recent attention. One important exception, a chapter on 'Oaths and Vows' in Susan Staves's *Players' Scepters*, argues that Butler's satire on 'the Covenanters' slippery way with words' proceeds from a radical scepticism about language and the ontological status of universals. Although Staves concedes Butler's satire a kind of philosophic generality, she finds it at the same time fiercely (and hilariously) partisan, contending that Butler never spoke out against oaths imposed during the Restoration because he opposed social control only when enforced by presbyterians or independents. Under the Clarendon Code and related legislation, nonconformists faced fines, imprisonment, and other punishments for refusing sworn submission. Butler, however, did record his disapproval of the Test Act (1673), which excluded Catholics from public office by demanding sworn repudiation of Roman doctrine on transubstantiation. Whatever the official views of its authors, *Hudibras* cannot help but glance at Restoration abuses behind interregnum targets. Although the Cavalier Parliament ordered, among its first symbolic acts, the public burning of the Solemn League and Covenant, statutes such as the Corporation Act and the Quaker Act relied on oaths to police dissent. Published at a time when the interrogation of conscience had again become routine, the poem engrosses the new instruments of repression along with the old.[10]

Butler's habitual contradictoriness generally works against neat political alignments. The revisionist account of Commonwealth history in *Hudibras* portrays the Royalists, in marked contrast to the time-serving parliamentarians, as unwavering in principle: 'Their Duty never was defeated, / Nor from their Oaths and Faith Retreated' (3.2.171–2). Such praise, being at best half true, could as easily serve as a reprimand. Butler stands by the fiction of strict fidelity to monarchism in order to make convincing his excoriation of equivocators and other 'hypocrites.' Members of his own counter-revolutionary faction had as much to lose from a review of broken vows as their adversaries. Butler surely knew that the age's foremost authority on oaths and equivocation was Bishop Sanderson. Interest in Sanderson and in casuistry in general has revived over the past decade, and before turning to Butler we might consider Sanderson's writings on the covenant, the engagement, and oath-breaking in general. Although Butler makes no explicit reference to him, Sanderson provides us with a useful example of the sort of interpretive juggling we see parodied in *Hudibras*.[11]

Influential as both Regius professor of divinity at Oxford and adviser to the king, Sanderson considered the covenant's hazy language sufficient reason for its rejection, and refused to take it. In 1647, writing for the members of Oxford, he rejected as doctrinally erroneous the arguments that one could comply with the oath understood in some limited or special sense. Such practices, he argued, conflict with Christian doctrine and are contrary '*to the end of Speech*': 'God having given us the use of Speech for this end, that it might be the interpreter of the mind; it behoveth us as in all other our dealings and contracts, so especially where there is the intervention of an Oath, so to speake as that they, whom it concerneth, may clearly understand our meaning by our words.' A year later, according to Anthony à Wood, Sanderson 'was turned out of his Professorship of Divinity by the Parl. Visitors,' and retreated into obscurity to translate and conduct an extensive correspondence.[12]

By 1650, when he wrote 'The Case of the Engagement' (published 1668), Sanderson had evidently reconsidered his position. He now embraced what amounts to a sweeping principle of linguistic indeterminacy. This case came in response to a letter seeking his advice on whether one might take the engagement in good conscience. The letter's author, Thomas Washbourne, set before Sanderson eight questions, most of them variations on the 'de factoist' theory that justified obedience to an existing power. In a postscript he posed a final question, which Sanderson paraphrased thus: 'Whether upon supposition,' that the words of the Engagement will bear more constructions than one, the subscriber may take it in his own sense, or is bound to take it in the imposers sense?' The crux of the problem lay in the ethics of interpreting the engagement so as to make it reasonably consistent with the duty of a conscientious subject, without, however, invoking the noxious doctrine of equivocation. For Sanderson, rendering the engagement compatible with a binding allegiance to the king and his lawful heirs posed no great difficulty to anyone who considers 'that all expressions by words, are subject to such ambiguities, that scarce any thing can be said or expressed in any words, how cautelously soever chosen, which will not render the whole speech capable of more constructions than one.' For someone to take an oath in a private sense, or one manifestly different from the customary meaning, constitutes a gross abuse. Promises, Sanderson insists, must be understood according to the meaning of the person to whom the promise is tendered. But when an imposer of an oath fails to make his meaning clear, he himself opens he issue of multiple constructions. One could ask the imposer for clarification, but 'prudence' entitles the engager to interpret the words in their most favourable light. The promisor remains free to 'make use of that Latitude of sense' left 'undetermined' by the imposer, and thus to turn ambiguity to his advantage. The final burden of interpretive responsibility devolves upon the contriver.

Sanderson proceeds to demonstrate, clause by clause, the different ways in which the engagement can be read. Key phrases such as 'Commonwealth, as it is now established' and 'true and faithful' bear multiple constructions, which he expertly draws out. He finally settles on three readings of the oath: 1) I acknowledge that the sovereign power of this nation is vested in the House of Commons now sitting at Westminster without either king or Lords, and promise to maintain it to the utmost of my power; 2) I will not attempt any act of hostility against the government as presently established and will do what I can for the safety of my country and the maintenance of society; 3) I promise that for as long as the government continues without king and Lords, I 'will endeavor my self faithfully in my place and calling, to do what every good member of a Common-wealth ought to do for the safety of my Country, and preservation of Civil Society therein.' This last interpretation could be positively hostile to the existing power since it implies a distinction between the present government and the common good that no convinced parliamentarian would allow. A subscriber to the engagement understood in this sense could argue that the 'preservation of Civil Society' might best be achieved by overthrowing the government in power. Sanderson does not think that the gap between 'highest' and 'lowest' construction should much trouble the prospective engager: 'the Equivocation,' he judges, 'if there be any in that, must be put upon the Imposers, not on the Promisers score.'[13]

As a science of moral particulars that complicate choice, casuistry is notoriously sensitive to problems of intentionality and meaning. Sanderson's approach, however, amounts to an endorsement of equivocation, which he decries, under another name. Sanderson's formal repudiation hardly conceals the fact that he has resorted to equivocation to resolve his dilemma.[14]

Much of the resemblance of Sanderson's procedures to Roman casuistry lies in the transactional model of communication he adopts, his insistence, on one hand, that words should coincide with thoughts as their outward signs, and, on the other, a denial that perfect congruence is ever attainable.[15] Jesuits had traditionally justified equivocation by arguing that the verbal and mental parts of a sentence function together. To determine the truth of a statement we must consider both its mental and verbal aspects in conjunction. Jesuit defenders of equivocation, amphibology, and mental reservation appealed to the concept of a mixed proposition that combined verbal and mental components. Basing their discussion on Aristotelian proposition theory, they vindicated the truthfulness of a statement half-spoken and half-reserved in the mind.[16] Although English critics of Jesuit casuistry generally deplored such practices, they too considered instances where one might permissibly use an ambiguous phrase. Jeremy Taylor analysed various situations in which he considered lying lawful, and concluded that if 'the amphibology or equivocation be not insolent and strange, but such as is usual in forms of witty speech,' the person employing such usage 'does no more deceive his hearer, then he that speaks obscurely or profoundly is the cause of error in the ignorant people.' Taylor reaffirms the widely accepted theory that equivocation, or the near lie, is in practice less reprehensible than the lie direct, that it 'may upon less necessity and upon more causes be permitted then lying.'[17]

Butler upholds precisely the opposite view: 'Æquivocation is worse then plaine Lying in matters of Religion, for a lyer intends only to cheat another man, but he that aequivocat's do's at once design to deceive God, and his own Conscience and another man too.' Or again: 'Those that perjure themselves to delude others by æquivocation doe it (as they belive) to save their Consciences harmelesse, where the Sin is much greater, then if they forswore themselves plainly without any tricks, for in that they doe but deceive the world, and may be thought to make somewhat too bold with God's Mercy, which the other disclame and doe their Indevors to deceive God and the world, and their owne Consciences too' (*PO* 27, 234). Butler's violent reaction to equivocation procees from the belief that it overthrows the contractual basis of language, and that its applicability to oaths provides a compelling political reason for its rejection. In this respect, his ideas resemble those of Anthony Ascham, who bars all forms of equivocation as a contravention of linguistic custom and of the contractual obligation implied in speech. Toleration of equivocation and amphibology, Ascham writes, would make 'a martyrdome folly, and leagues and contracts of no assurance.'[18] Most English divines, however, avoided issuing blanket condemnations of the practice, even though they balked at the idea of mental reservation as a program for systematic tergiversation under oath. To Butler's mind such practices were the natural enemy of human society, its essential political and religious institutions. The doctrine of equivocation, he thought, had as its sole function the obscuring of ethical choices through deliberate and often crude exploitation of polysemy.

Butler's other principal objection to equivocation resides in its reduction of discourse to a form of verbal play, like punning, or foul play, like swearing. Casuists trivialize obligation by devaluing verbal contracts, exploding the inviolability of oaths, and subverting common assumptions about the nature of performative speech acts. In Butler's view, there is a natural progression from equivocation in the sense of punning or using words capable of double signification, to equivocation in the technical sense of expressing a virtual falsehood in a form that is verbally true. The equivocator bears a strong resemblance to the poet in that both trade in formulaic mouthings, and attempt to exploit the inescapable disjuncture between word and thought. Both are a type of the 'quibbler,' who talks 'nothing but Equivocation and mental Reservation, and mightily affects to give a Word a double Stroke, like a Tennis-Ball against two Walls at one Blow, to defeat the Expectation of his Antagonist' (*Characters* 132). The wordplay and equivocations of the poet-equivocator contribute to an elaborate game of frustrated expectations, which transforms speakers into antagonists, chips away at the linguistic and social contract upon which communication depends, and thereby throws into question the signifying power of words. Undecidability becomes an invaluable ally in the campaign to break down the basis of a vanishing feudal society – swearing one's bounden word and fealty in the presence of God.

The connection between devalued language and repudiated obligation becomes most explicit in the second part of *Hudibras,* where Hudibras' readiness to enter into engagements and other obligations proceeds from his considering promissory oaths no different from ordinary utterance. In canto 1 the Lady arrives to rescue Hudibras from the stocks, where he has been set by his adversaries, and to taunt him in his confinement. She argues that if, as Hudibras contends, defeat in battle is glorious, then a whipping would represent an even greater triumph, which might even move her to love. Hudibras, who has long desired to 'win and wear' the Lady's considerable property, immediately rises to the bait. He makes his matrimonial intentions plain, but is rebuffed. A debate on love and marriage ensues and the two strike a bargain. The Lady will release Hudibras from the stocks and receive him as a suitor on condition that he soundly whip himself: 'Bring me on *Oath,*' she demands, 'a fair account, / And *honor* too, when you have don't.' Hudibras readily accepts: 'I do *profess* and *swear,* / And will perform what you enjoyn' (2.1.835–6, 896–7). When set at large, however, Hudibras doubts the wisdom of his oath, and wonders whether he can break it with impunity. Deeply perplexed, he turns to his squire, Ralph, and initiates the longest of the poem's many exercises in mock-casuistry by asking:

Whether it be direct *infringing*
An *Oath,* if I should wave this *swinging,*
And what I've sworn to bear, forbear
And so b'*equivocation* swear;
Or whether't be a lesser *Sin*
To be forsworn then act the thing,
Are deep and subtle *points,* which must,
T'inform my conscience, be discust.
In which to *err* a tittle, may
To *errors* infinite make way.   (2.2.55–64)

The two embark on an excursus combining 'practical divinity' and contract law, which ends some four hundred lines later when Hudibras proclaims: 'It is enough ... Thou hast resolv'd, and clear'd the *Case*' (2.2.441–2). To Hudibras' immense satisfaction Ralph adjudicates the knight's case of conscience by freeing him from any obligation incurred by his oath. Ralph's disquisition parodies attempts to define legitimate compunctions out of existence with the aid of formal logic, paring scruples, and verbal guile.[19] From the whole manner in which Ralph sets about determining Hudibras' case of conscience, it is a foregone conclusion that he will employ his talent for twisting words to attain a satisfactory outcome.

Michel Foucault mentions casuistry as an example of a discursive system that has dropped from view. For Foucault, casuistry's disappearance – like the later appearance of disciplines such as economics or psychiatry – reveals the historical contingency of every discursive formation.[20] For Butler, the techniques of casuistry appear to exemplify the sort of dangerous indeterminacy that has contaminated modern life, particularly the rhetorical disciplines of poetry and law. Butler begins the canto with a play on the word *case,* and wordplay turns out to be an integral part of much that follows. Those who possess contentious dispositions 'keep their *Consciences* in Cases / As *Fidlers* do their *Crowds* and *Bases.* / Ne'r to be us'd but when they'r bent / To play a fit for *Argument*' (2.2.5–8). Such disputants keep their consciences in 'Cases' both in the sense that they lie dormant and unused until there is some controversy to exercise them in, and that they feel indifferent to moral matters not drawn up into formal cases. The ambiguity serves to put the reader on guard against Hudibras' and Ralph's seemingly inadvertent semantic shifts, and the verbal sleight of hand to follow. Consider, for example, Hudibras' words: 'And what I've sworn to bear, forbear / And so b' *equivocation* swear.' Anyone who phrases an ethical quandary in this manner has already committed a kind of verbal jury-rigging: 'forbear,' which has the contradictory meanings of 'endure' and 'dispense with,' is itself an evasion of verbal determinacy, and equivocation of sorts. As soon as Ralph launches into his reply it becomes obvious that he will enact an elaborate ritual designed to justify a predetermined course of action:

> Quoth *Ralpho,* since you do injoyn't
> I shall inlarge upon the *Point.*
> And for my own part do not doubt
> Th' *Affirmative* may be made out.
> But first to *state* the *Case* aright,
> For best advantage of our light;
> And thus 'tis: Whether 't be a *Sin*
> To *Claw* and *Curry* your own *skin*
> Greater, or less, then to forbear,
> And that you are forsworn, forswear.   (2.2.67–76)

Ralph casts the question in strongly relative terms: whether it is more sinful to whip oneself (a self-evident evil) than to forgo chastisement by swearing falsely (a possible evil). The 'forbear' of line 75 is not ambiguous in the present context, as 'forbear' is in line 57. Rather it is gathered into a nexus of like-sounding words — forsworn, forbear, forswear – which has the effect of suggesting a speaker in the midst of drawing fine distinctions, or weighing actions in balance. What Ralph means by the phrase 'And that you are forsworn, forswear' is that Hudibras risks perjuring himself twice by not performing the deed. When the knight breaks his initial promissory oath he puts himself in the position of possibly having to compound the original fault, which is exactly what he does in order to convince the sceptical Lady (3.1.199–200; 'The Ladies Answer to the Knight,' ll. 20–6).

One must recognize equivocation as verbal double-dealing in order to grasp the full implications of the following passage from part 3, where we observe the supposed consequences for oath-taking of divorcing public meaning from private 'sense':

> Was it to run away, we meant,
> Who taking of the *Covenant*,
> The lamest Cripples of the Brothers,
> Took Oaths, to run before all others;
> But in their own sense only swore
> To strive to run away before?
> And now would prove, the *Words*, and *Oath*,
> Ingage us to renounce them both?   (3.2.507–14)

This, as Butler's editors note, plays on a phrase from the Solemn League and Covenant, 'each one to go before another in the example of a real reformation,' a figure of speech hardly open to such egregious misconstrual. Butler recalls the covenant because he could not understand the scrupulousness applied to the engagement, 'though but a Civill Promise,' in comparison to the casual attitude taken towards the covenant, 'a solemne vow made to Almighty God' (*PO* 169). *Hudibras* draws a different parallel, equating the covenant with the vague and much maligned Etcetera Oath of 1640, which bound the swearer to resist alteration of church government by 'archbishops, bishops, deans, and archdeacons, etc.':

> For to subscribe, unsight unseen,
> T'an unknown Churches Discipline

> What is it else, but before-hand
> T'ingage, and after understand?
> For when we swore to carry on
> The present *Reformation*,
> According to the Purest mode
> Of Churches, best Reform'd abroad,
> What did we else but make a vow
> To doe we know not what, nor how?
> For no three of us will agree
> Where, or what Churches these should be.
> And is indeed the self-same case
> With theirs that swore *Et cæteras*. (1.2.637–50)

When confronted with their deceit, Butler claims, his contemporaries used every means at their disposal, including the equivocation of interpreting figurative language literally, to vindicate their freedom from the constraints of oaths and promises. Ralph's main point is that oaths have no more inherent value than the words they contain, and words, proverbially, are as wind.[21]

> *Oaths* are but *words*, and *words* but *wind*,
> Too feeble implements to *bind*;
> And hold with *deeds* proportion, so
> As *shadows* to a *substance* do. (2.2.107–10)

Ralph pulls this argument out of his sleeve as a kind of trump card: if ethics are contingent upon language and language is arbitrary noise, what allegiance do we then owe moral precepts? Hudibras may figure pre-eminently in the poem as the character most given to using 'unsignifying' words, but Ralph takes a far more radical stance when he claims that words are by nature unsignifying. To Ralph, promises have no special status as utterances invested with an assurances of veracity beyond normal expectations. Oaths are as insubstantial and non-binding as ordinary language, and as universally accessible as the air we breathe. The inevitable gap between intention and meaning renders oath-breaking or lying virtually impossible. Those who participated in the trials of King Charles before the High Court of Justice did 'nothing in their own sense, / But what they ought by *Oath* and *Conscience*.' Similarly, everyone acknowledges that the 'honor' which the peer calls to his defence in court is so much bluster, 'but a Word' (2.2.339–40, 389–90).

The third commandment presents no insurmountable obstacle to anyone who subjects the text to close reading:

> W' are not commanded to forbear,
> Indefinitely, at all to *swear*,
> But to *swear* idly, and in vain,
> Without self-interest, or gain.
> For, breaking of an *Oath* and *Lying*,
> Is but a kind of *Self-denying*.   (2.2.129–34)

With this reference to the Self-Denying Ordinance of 3 April 1645 – the law that enabled Cromwell ultimately to retain his military post while excluding the members of either house from public office and military command – Ralph initiates a historical review of the broken oaths and repudiated political measures of the interregnum. As Ralph establishes precedent and accumulates examples, a bitterly ironic hindsight swells up behind his voice:

> Was not the *Cause* at first begun
> With *Perjury*, and carry'd on?
> Was there an *Oath* the *Godly* took,
> But, in due time and place, they broke?
> Did we not bring our *Oaths* in first,
> Before our *Plate*, to have them burst,
> And cast in fitter *models*, for
> The present use of *Church* and *War*?
> Did not our *Worthies* of the *House*,
> Before they broke the *Peace*, break *Vows*?
> For having free'd us, first from both
> Th' *Allegeance*, and *Supremacy-Oath*;
> Did they not, next, compel the *Nation*,
> To take, and break the *Protestation*?
> To *swear*, and after to *recant*
> The *Solemn League and Covenant*?
> To take th' *Engagement*, and disclaim it,
> Enforc'd by those, who first did frame it?   (2.2.141–58)

The grand old cause, Butler maintains, was initiated and sustained by a sequence of broken oaths. In this passage oaths are no longer wind, but the more substantial plate, which can be melted down and formed into new moulds at will – an allusion to a request in 1642 for public contributions to maintain the parliamentary forces. Oaths have undergone a strange transformation, altered according to circumstances to serve the exigencies of warfare and achieve the destruction of adversaries. When Parliament absolved the nation of its obligation to abide by the oaths of allegiance and supremacy and compelled the people 'To take, and break the Protestation,' it set the stage for future strife, thrusting citizens into perjury. Butler provides a blunt answer to the consuming question of whether later oaths were compatible with earlier obligations. After the oaths of allegiance and supremacy were thrown out, oaths *qua* oaths could have no meaning or value. The Protestation's reversal with the Solemn League and Covenant constituted a completely foreseeable about-face, a logical consequence of a general low regard for oaths. Once started, the oath-breakers became literally unable to stop themselves.

We can compare these views to Milton's, who regarded the renunciation of the allegiance and supremacy oaths at watershed events. In *The Tenure of Kings and Magistrates* he argues that, with the abrogation of oaths in the 1640s, presbyterians irrevocably committed themselves to the principle of voluntary obedience:

Have they [presbyterians] not utterly broke the Oath of Allegeance, rejecting the Kings command and autority sent them from any part of the Kingdom whether in things lawful or unlawful? Have they not abjur'd the Oath of Supremacy by setting up the Parliament without the King, supreme to all thir obedience, and though thir Vow and Covnant bound them in general to the Parliament, yet sometimes adhering to the lesser part of Lords and Commons that remaind faithful, as they terme it, and eev'n of them, one while to the Commons without the Lords, another while to the Lords without the Commons? Have they not still declar'd thir meaning, whatever thir Oath were, to hold them onely for supreme whom they found at any time most yeilding to what they petiton'd? Both these Oaths which were the straitest bond of an English subject in reference to the King, being thus broke & made voide, it follows undenyably that the King from that time was by them in fact absolutely depos'd, and they no longer in reality to be thought his subjects, notwithstanding thir fine clause in the Covnant to preserve his person, Crown, and dignity, set there by som dodging Casuist with more craft then sincerity to mitigate the matter in case of ill success and not tak'n I suppose by any honest man, but as a condition subordinat to every the least particle that might more concerne Religion, liberty, or the public peace. (*CP* 3: 228–9)

While Butler suggests that the usurping government courted its own destruction in asking citizens to turn their backs on sworn obligations to king and country, Milton presents the original breach as a type of insurance against future backsliding. Both agree, however, that the conservative wing of the parliamentary party made use of 'dodging' and disengenuousness in order to create the appearance of a tolerable consistency. Both passages take the form of a series of confrontational, even overbearing, interrogations, designed to elicit a confession of duplicity from an adversary whose support may still possibly be enlisted. Both consider the implications of casuistical practices for a contractual model of government.

Butler's polemical strategy, however, rests on a convenient but fallacious lumping together of various shades of 'puritan' opinion, polarizing the multifarious forces of interregnum history into two camps – 'us' and 'them.' The 'they' who introduced the covenant were quite different from the 'they' responsible for the engagement. Butler himself acknowledges that after Pride's Purge in 1648, control of Parliament passed into sectarian hands, a group not especially well disposed towards presbyterian goals of continued adherence to the covenant and suppression of other forms of church organization (3.2.87–90). Those 'who first did frame' the engagement, in the midst of a constitutional crisis, were not directly responsible for Cromwell's ordinance of January 1654, which annulled the engagement as a burden to tender consciences. Rival factions introduced various oaths in their quest for domination and political consensus. Butler prefers, however, to treat the whole period in terms of a tightly unified narrative. In contrast to the theologian's or lawyer's highly technical treatment of the subject, he takes a deliberately broad view of what constitutes an oath. Butler considers all of the period's ordinances, petitions, declarations, resolutions, propositions, and other statements of intention to be 'oaths,' and any act of emphatic affirmation to be 'swearing.' Ralph reiterates the words *swear* and *vow* throughout his speech, debasing the act through repetition as the mechanical performance of a meaningless rite. Those who swear easily and frequently cannot be expected to stand by their pledges:

> Did they not *swear* to maintain *Law*,
> In which, that *swearing* made a *Flaw*?
> For *Protestant Religion* Vow,
> That did that *Vowing* disallow?
> For *Priviledg* of *Parliament*,
> In which that *swearing* made a *Rent*? (2.2.169–74)

Butler constructs a careful paradox: the swearers of recent history have betrayed exactly what they swore to preserve: the laws, religion, and parliamentary prerogatives. Broken oaths become a type of invective, a surrogate for physical abuse and a prelude to literal violence.

Oaths help explain Hudibras' tendency to go from fighting words to real violence. Political disputes, like street brawls, trace back to '*Oaths* and *Swearing*,' the root of civil strife: 'The *Solemn League and Covenant* / Will seem a meer *God-dam-me* Rant; / And we that took it, and have fought, / As lewd as Drunkards that fall out' (1.2.509–12).

In Ralph's capsule history of the interregnum, we find a similar conjunction of strong asseveration, invective, and violence arising in Cromwell's dealings with House:

> So *Crumwel* with deep *Oaths*, and *Vows*,
> Swore all the *Commons* out 'oth' *House*,
> Vow'd that the *Red-coats* would disband,
> I marry would they, at their Command.
> And trol'd 'em on, and *swore*, and *swore*,
> Till th' *Army* turn'd 'em out of *Dore*;
> This tells us plainly, what they thought,
> That *Oaths* and *swearing* go for nought.   (2.2. 181–8)

Butler's interpretation of Cromwell's troubled relations with the army in 1647 is, as we might expect, highly coloured. He alleges that Cromwell – here the consummate Machiavellian of Tory mythology – deliberately played the army against Parliament. It was commonly laid to Cromwell's charge that he reassured the House of the army's willing compliance while provoking the soldiery to rise up and purge that body. (The soldiers themselves swore in 'A Solemn Engagement of the Army' that they would 'cheerfully and readily disband when thereunto required by the Parliament.') It is true that in the summer of 1647 Cromwell made strong public declarations of his loyalty to the Commons. Sir William Waller claimed that Cromwell disavowed in the House any knowledge of the army's 'mutinous proceedings, and invoked the curse of God upon himself and his posterity if ever he should join or combine with them in any actings or attempts contrary to the orders of the House.' His account is supported by Sir Harbottle Grimston, who told Bishop Burnet that when Cromwell was accused in the House of planning to purge the Commons, he 'fell down upon his knees and made a solemn prayer to God, attesting his innocence and his zeal for the House.'[22] Whatever Cromwell's intentions, the army's part in the expulsion of dissidents from the Commons was viewed by many contemporaries as conclusive evidence of Cromwell's light regard for oaths.

In *Hudibras* Cromwell's abrogation of his solemn declarations is ironically counterpointed by verbal play. In colloquial speech 'to swear someone out of the house' means to expel someone with curses. As Butler uses the phrase, 'house' refers to the elective branch of English bicameral government, and 'swore' refers to Cromwell's unkept promises. These key words oscillate between two levels of meaning throughout the passage. Butler delights in the linguistic phenomenon that makes an 'oath' both 'solemn testimony' and 'impious profanation,' and 'to swear' both 'calling upon the deity as witness' and 'to curse and blaspheme.' Cromwell's affirmation by the name of the Virgin ('I marry') presents a mild example of a phrase that has left off being a pious interjection and become indistinguishable from profanation. Cromwell was hardly given to the use of profanity. In Butler's estimation, however, Cromwell's failed assurances approximate the splenetic ejaculations of a habitual curser. Butler charges the puritans with caring little about perjury, for all their conspicuous abhorrence of taking the name of the Lord in vain. Just as cursing figures as a type of ritual speech utterly devoid of significance, oath-breakers revert to a kind of unreflective sputtering. For them the covenant has become self-imprecation, 'a meer *God-dam-me* Rant.'

As Ralph continues, his view of oaths as meaningless rituals becomes increasingly obvious. An unkept oath, he insists, is not perjury, 'But a meer *Ceremony*, and a breach / Of nothing, but a form of speech' (2.2.207–8). In calling an oath 'a form of speech,' Ralph implies a relativistic and conventionalist view of grammatical and moral correctness. Because we possess the liberty either to depart altogether from sworn obligations, or to 'misinterpret them, by *private / Instructions*' (2.2.215–16), we can excuse any discrepancy between conventional standards and our own moral laxity under a charter of interpretive freedom. Ralph produces the Quakers as an example of such systematic deviation from social and linguistic norms. He alludes to the Quakers' refusal to take oaths, which he relates to other supposed eccentricities:

Quakers (that, like to *Lanthorns*, bear
Their light within 'em) will not *swear*.
Their *Gospel* is an *Accidence*,
By which they construe *Conscience*,
And hold no *sin* so deeply *red*,

> As that of breaking *Priscian*'s head
> (The *Head* and *Founder* of their *Order*,
> That stirring *Hats* held worse then murder)
> These thinking th' are oblig'd to *Troth*
> In *swearing*, will not take an *Oath*. (2.2.219–28)

Ralph associates the Quakers' refusal to swear with their unwillingness to doff their hats as a sign of respect, their literal-minded scripturalism, and their punctiliousness in forms of address – thou to one, you to many. He marvels at the sect's scrupulosity, particularly their naïve view that oaths actually obligate one. Behind Ralph's ironic disapproval lies a hint of Butler's own grudging admiration for any disinclination to treat oath-taking casually.[23] Yet for all the Quakers' strictness in following the dictates of conscience, Butler represents them as valuing the letter of Scripture and grammatical correctness at a higher rate than moral conduct. The divine Word becomes a grammatical primer that binds them to the letter of the law, a vehicle of legalism and moral indifference. Their aversion to oaths (based on Christ's injunction in the Sermon on the Mount, 'Swear not at all ... but let your communication be, Yea, yea; nay, nay') proceeds from literalism and legalistic quibbling, not from widespread abuses of oath-taking during the interregnum. The spiritual founder of Quakerism is not George Fox but the grammarian Priscian, who promotes a fear of committing solecisms ('breaking *Priscian*'s head') that supplants a capacity to make moral distinctions. Thus Butler's satire cuts both ways, mocking strict adherence to the letter of the Law at the same time as it skewers Ralph's moral relativism and metaphorical evasions of meaning.

Ralph presses his argument one step further, developing at length the point that 'saints' should be exempt from twinges of conscience that afflict the ungodly. Finally he lets off a devastating salvo, an unanswerable argument borrowed from the Jesuits. Both presbyterians and independents, he says, 'hold this for true, / *No Faith is to the wicked due*' (2.2.255–6). Hudibras seems perturbed that Ralph has spoken so openly, arguing that such '*Topical* Evasions / Of subtle *Turns*, and *Shifts* of sence' should be employed with discretion. Among these shifts he includes the following rationale: 'A breach of *Oath* is *Duple*, / And either way admits a *scruple*, / And may be *ex parte* of the *Maker*, / More criminal, then th'injured *Taker*' (2.2.262–3, 269–72). Placing the blame for breaking an oath upon its framer may seem outrageous, but is essentially in line with arguments, like Sanderson's, that made an oath's imposer responsible for its interpretation, and dismissed formulas tendered in general, 'undetermined' senses.

According to Hudibras, an oath is broken by 'he that made, and forc'd it,' not the swearer who 'for convenience took it' (2.2.275–6). He repeatedly takes advantage of the ambiguity inherent in the idiom 'to make an oath.' Whoever imposes an oath, he argues, 'makes' it, thus 'how can any man be said, / To break an *Oath* he never made?' Later he confesses that what motivated him to break vows, fear of poverty, encourages others to 'break a House' (2.2.377–80; 3.1.1237–40).

Although Hudibras never overtly defends the doctrine of equivocation, he embodies its essence in his everyday speech. A master of chop-logic and the strategic ambiguity, he can cloak mendacity in elaborate verbal subterfuges and intricate argumentation. Hudibras suggests that the answer to his dilemma might reside in a compromise: he will be whipped by proxy and thus satisfy his oath while sparing his back. Ralph judges the ruse permissible, but when Hudibras suggests that Ralph himself should act as surrogate, he rebels. As the two fall again to debating ways to avoid a whipping that will not invalidate the oath, Hudibras reveals his preference for equivocation over direct renunciation. Ralph contends that Hudibras' original plan will not work: 'For we must take our *Oaths* upon it, / You did the *deed*, when I have done it' (2.2.469–70). Hudibras, however, seems to have in mind some sort of equivocating verbal formula that would permit him to swear he had laid the whip on, without specifying the identities of the recipient and the administrator of the blows. Since Ralph will have none of this scheme, Hudibras ends up lying extravagantly about the events surrounding a fictitious self-flagellation. He sets aside verbal evasion to rely on a familiar standby: the direct lie.

If the engagement prodded Butler's contemporaries to theorize in new ways about government and the limits of power, it also pushed them to ponder the political implications of contemporary modes of interpretation. What Hudibras takes away from Ralph's arbitration is a simple maxim: 'an *Oath* obliges not, / Where any *thing* is to be got' (2.3.101–2). Yet this terse summary fails to do justice to the intricacies of the preceding arguments. Ralph relies on two main tactics to arrive at his conclusion. First, he rhymes off a number of well-known precedents for breaking oaths, which, taken together, outline the interregnum's principal crises of conscience; second, he attacks oaths at their very foundation, the evanescent and insubstantial words that comprise them. Although Ralph is unwilling to perform the part of Hudibras' whipping boy, he complaisantly releases the knight from his sworn obligation by demonstrating the malleability of meaning and the meaninglessness of language. Hudibras, whose great fear is being reduced to earning his living as a 'knight of the post,' a professional perjurer in the courts, has no qualms about taking on the role of equivocator.

For Butler, a widening proliferation of meaning, which first gained ground among philosophers, was successfully undermining verities in every sphere of life, and advancing to the practices of lawyers, controversialists, and politicians. The rationality he repeatedly (but gloomily) invokes represents a call to revive an original truth buried under layers of conflicting interpretation. Among the resources for binding the deeds of social subjects to their words were oaths, which play a central part in the political realm as figured in *Hudibras*. The old regime had failed to condition political behaviour by imposing oaths, and the commonwealth government fared no better. If the original intention of a founding agreement could not undergo alteration without equivocation, then beginnings would determine ends for the indefinite future. In the last analysis, the position of the unreliable subject could never be made secure. If the origin of government depended on oaths and civil society upon an achieved consensus, English society faced a future of endless debate and irreconcilable difference. Seeing the inevitable continuation of the problem, Butler's poem reveals more than its author can say.

In *Hudibras*, Butler wrote a comic version of the originary epic we have found in *Paradise Lost*. Despite his intense nostalgia for a sanctified origin, he concedes the impossibility of reaching back to an uninflected, ideologically neutral medium. Revivifying the heroic ideal of the indubitable origin began to look like a farcical enterprise. Butler could still, however, reinvent epic by standing the form on its head, reinscribing its scientific, historical, and encyclopaedic conventions to establish himself at the root of a new tradition. Despite an emphasis on the absurdity of post-Virgilian epic, he renews the form and becomes a sort of seminal figure, thus performing one of epic's traditional functions. He adjusts the loose assemblage of generic codes that constitute epic so that his poem might accommodate diverse and even incompatible materials. Once the poem has taken the measure of poetical tradition and found it wanting, it proclaims itself *sui generis* and constitutes itself as something other than 'literature.' In *Hudibras* the boundaries between poetry and other forms of cultural expression, between literary and political value, become increasingly unclear.

Butler's unfastidious immersion in the mire of topicality counterbalances his drive towards universality and satire on 'characters' rather than specific historical targets. *Hudibras* follows a program of depoliticization through the continual expansion of its intellectual contexts and polemical range. A writer who bases his entire conception of wit on the principles of contradiction and stylistic disruption has a ready-made defence against charges of narrow partisanship. Butler erects his political vision on the failure of 'humane learning' to ground knowledge in an empirically verifiable 'commonsense' truth. The common sense invoked in arguments such as his arises from an ideology of objective and unmediated experience. As Clifford Geertz explains: 'Religion rests its case on revelation, science on method, ideology on moral passion; but common sense rests its on the assertion that it is not a case at all, just life in a nutshell. The world is its authority.'[24] Butler offers a topical, but ostensibly depoliticized, diagnosis of the consequences of volatile speech and the civil war's explosion of competing meanings. His satire on the interregnum logomachy attaches blame to a force at loose in the culture at large, evident in the deficiencies found in contemporary law, in political theory, and in the first tentative efforts of the Royal Society.

As we have seen, the Restoration settlement undertook a political and ecclesiastical program with a pronounced epistemological objective: promoting the avoidance of dissension and dispute. To prevent reversion to the 'Babel' of the interregnum, the government imposed laws designed to regulate institutions for the production of knowledge. A concerted effort to reverse the politicization of language led to a program for 'reform,' which included the reimposition of censorship after 1660; the granting of a monopoly to the Stationers' Company and the universities; proposals for the rectification of prose style; and to various efforts to insulate public discourse from the deleterious effects of 'enthusiasm' and dissent. The Draconian measures brought in under the Clarendon Code, however, achieved only the outward semblance of conformity. They contributed nothing to resolving the root causes that produced the Restoration's factionalism of belief and value. Butler's poem contributed something less tangible but no less consequential: a way of understanding England's recent past, and a way of suppressing certain aspects of it. Butler's revisionist epic psychologizes and rationalizes the phenomenon of revolution, emphasizing its foundation in error and thus transforming it into the event Clarendon preferred to think of as the Great Rebellion. Butler's post-epic epic depoliticizes dissent through its use of epistemological explanation and a formula of systematic inversion that makes *arma* polemic, *vir* 'the Lady,' and *urbs* Babel. Butler's value to the eighteenth century rests, in part, on his ability to coordinate political and philosophical interests while demystifying the aesthetic dimension of poetic texts. As John Evelyn told Pepys, Clarendon himself was a great admirer of Butler. At his magnificent residence in St James, Clarendon furnished 'all the roomes of state and other apartments with the pictures of the most illustrious of our nation.' These included Bacon, Bishop Sanderson, and the poets 'Spenser, Mr. Waller, Cowley, Hudibras, which last he plac'd in the roome where he us'd to eate & dine in publiq.'[25] Clarendon, whose portrait collection associated England's national identity with its statesmen, clergy, and poets, clearly understood the uses Butler might serve in building a new and noncontroversial political order.

After the Restoration, the actual work of regulating the press fell to Roger L'Estrange and John Berkenhead. The first of these probably composed a 'Key' to *Hudibras,* and the latter was a hostile authority on puritanism quoted by Zachary Grey in his quasi-official edition of the poem. Such repressive measures did little to discourage nonconformists from using the press to disseminate their views, promote social change, and advance the Reformation.[26] Silencing their voices and barring them from publication, while possible, became increasingly less effective. Restoration critics of sectarianism often fixed the blame for the turmoil of the interregnum on tub-preachers and uncontrolled printing, which they considered responsible for sowing dissent and encouraging a war of words that eventually came to literal blows. The information explosion of the 1640s and 1650s (the period during which the bookseller George Thomason amassed his collection of more than 22,000 sermons, speeches, pamphlets, and other printed materials) effectively placed into circulation an unprecedented multiplicity of interpretations. While Butler on occasion speaks of the printing press as an engine of sedition, he generally avoids attaching blame to the specific conditions of textual production as agents of literary and political debasement. He bases his anti-puritanism instead on the failure of religion and philosophy to establish stable grounds for knowledge and to obviate the need for the sort of apparatuses of repression that only engendered more dissent and more repression.

Butler was hardly alone among his contemporaries in chalking up the crisis of the mid century to a crisis of style and meaning. Restoration writers often attributed contemporary political developments to the effects of ideology and language. If, as Hobbes and others suggested, political thinking was constituted in language, then the authorities would simply devise ways of monitoring forms of expression that seemed inimical to the state. The imprisonment of Anabaptists, Quakers, and other sectarians failed either to stifle dissent or preserve episcopacy unchallenged. Henceforth, politically or religiously charged debate would bear the stigma of 'fanaticism,' while a measured exchange on method takes centre stage under the imprimatur of a quasi-official Baconianism. Restricting the range and nature of matters suitable for public dispute constituted the principal aim of the Restoration ideology.[27]

I have argued that conceiving ideology as a cultural system, an outlook indispensable to life in society, rules out the possibility of imagining a world in which ideology has disappeared and science taken its place. Contemporary theory refuses to make science and ideology antithetical to one another. Butler, at an earlier stage of modernity, also appears doubtful about scientific rationality. Although he finds error and ideology everywhere and bemoans their consequences, he explicitly rejects the ideal of scientific objectivity. He consistently ridicules the concept of a scientific knowledge positioned outside of other forms of knowledge. 'The Original of Reason,' he wrote, emanates from a divine source that copies itself out upon nature. The natural world we perceive, however, is structured like language: individual elements or 'Characters' signify little before being placed in complex relations, when the 'become words and Sense' (*PO* 66). Given the inherent limitations of our perceptual apparatus and the deficiencies of language, we should not expect investigation of the natural world to yield certainty. We see the opposite assumption in the Royal Society scientists, who convince themselves they already know 'whats'ever's to be known,' and strive to atomize phenomena into their minutest components (2.3.297). Their attempt to study an unmediated nature results in perspectival delusion and cognitive absurdity. In the microscopy of Robert Hooke or the astronomy of Sidrophel we supposedly see the universal order reduced to the fallible subject's own psychic proportions. By failing to account for this phenomenal gap, they misrepresent (for gain or for self-aggrandizement) the nature of the 'original' they purport to study. For Butler, such claims to objective truth never actually connect to first-order concerns and unsuccessfully disguise their subordination to politics and 'interest.'

The discourse of origins was not invisible throughout the seventeenth century. Periodically it rose to a position where philosophers, theologians, and poets could inspect and discuss it. Along with its symbolic, mythical, and religious functions, systematically explored in *Paradise Lost*, it also could operate as a conscious system of belief, the basis for a philosophy of science and of knowledge. Although presented at times as self-evident, the doctrine of origins by no means went 'without saying' or unremarked. Ingrained but not unobserved, it inscribed itself within the poetry, philosophy, and social institutions of seventeenth-century England. We can describe it, as throughout this study, as an 'ideology' because it provided a medium through which people ordered their lives in language. It appears in contexts where it helps to legitimate the institutions of scientific research, kingship, and patriarchal rule. Origins provided a pre-understanding that made theories of truth, authority, and representation possible.

Almost at once, however, the discourse of origin faced the problem of how the mind can perceive a time literally 'out of memory,' a moment that resides beyond ordinary understanding. Original acts of foundation occur outside of history and custom, antedating language and writing. How does one begin at the beginning when language itself seems to condemn us to negotiating, transmitting, and revising the accumulated record of the past? How can philosophers critique the production of meaning within the constraints of existing structures if those structures remain indispensable for articulating their critiques? In 'Nietzsche, Genealogy, History,' Michel Foucault conceives the pursuit of origins as a kind of ideology, the positing of a metaphysical absolute in the place of historically determined subject positions. History and genealogy, he writes, expose the illusion of situating the origin at 'the point where the truth of things corresponded to a truthful discourse, the site of a fleeting articulation that discourse obscured and finally lost.' History, in Foucault's sense, condemns us to constructing discourses about discourse and abandoning the quest for origins.[28]

The discourse of origin provided a systematic order for articulating ideas about truth and representation in the seventeenth century. For Bacon, it furnished a method for conducting scientific inquiry and for attaining to a truth correspondent (more or less) to reality. More than a simple starting-point, that origin provided the basis for constructing new forms of intellectual authority. His work soon became embroiled in contradictions arising from the fact that origins were not obviously and immediately accessible. They had to be invented, constructed, interpreted. For Milton, origins provided a metaphysical legitimation of a particular form of belief. He authorized his aesthetic and political program by reference to an archaic tradition tied to a theological absolute. Butler remained more sceptical about such legitimations. He adopted a stance hostile to epic (and, covertly, to organized religion) while still maintaining an allegiance to an origin positioned on the other side of a cognitive gap occupied by language. Butler could not maintain, along with Restoration science, the utility of origins as a means for validating the testimony of the senses and the emergent notion of 'objectivity.' Naturalized as the best possible basis of knowledge, the origin offered an escape from an impasse where truth could never rest assured of itself or convince anyone of its meaning and power outside of language and ideology.

This general desire for rectification and unmediated access to an originary point found its most systematic institutional expression in the social and scientific programs of the Royal Society. But the authorizing trope of the origin crossed over many disciplinary and political boundaries. Tertullian's axiom, 'Verum quod primum, quod posterius adulterum est' [that which comes first is true, what comes after corrupt], could express a humanistic veneration of antiquity and the myth of a forfeited Golden Age. It could also serve to undergird innovative social or political programs. In the 1640s, presbyterian divines invoked it to contest episcopal supplements to Scripture, identifying themselves with the purity of the primitive church, and concurring 'with Tertullian ... whatsoever is first is true; but that which is latter is adulterous.'[29]

Butler followed and shaped contemporary opinion in seeing the civil war as a form of collective lunacy, mass hysteria induced by ideological thinking. If people went mad in the same way, Bacon wrote in an aphorism about 'anticipations of nature,' they still might agree well enough among themselves (*NO* 1: 27). To put it in other words, different people at different times arrive at discrepant conclusions about the same phenomena because they base their explanations on historically variable theories and presuppositions. If Bacon associated authoritative knowledge with origins, he nevertheless observed how particular knowers were socially and historically situated. Bacon suggests that interests outside of 'pure' rationality enter into the procedures of philosophy and science. If a general reconstruction of knowledge demanded the demolition of existing structures and rebuilding philosophy anew, how might one distinguish between new knowledge and madness? Could philosophers actually know whether an irrefutable originary truth had been properly applied in a given instance? By the end of the seventeenth century Butler might well wonder if the concept of rationality had slipped away altogether, if the ultimate truth of origins had either vanished or become inaccessible.

Butler considered the distinction between science and ideology barely worth drawing. The threat of a revived radical sectarianism gave questions of truth and certain knowledge a political immediacy. Science, for all the protestations of the Royal Society, appeared to take a position on the side of radical innovation. Butler rejected science's view of itself as engaged in a process of methodically recovering accurate representations of the world. During the Restoration claims to certain knowledge carried a tremendous weight of social authority; assertions of universal truth consigned social differences to insignificance. Yet the ideological articulation of origin, as I have argued, never bore a single political significance. It moved across formal and disciplinary boundaries, never reducing to an exclusive interest. We cannot 'read off' a single meaning from it, nor locate it in any one level of culture. *Hudibras* strives to sustain a particular social relation with its satirical unmasking of illusions and distorted language. It attempts to expose sectarianism as a force both psychologically motivated and historically determined. At the same time, the poem makes no attempt to conceal its own status as the product of particular historical forces, or its affinities with a subversive popular tradition. The discourse of origin provides Butler a trope for framing questions of truth and authority in terms that seemed independent of context. Nevertheless, the insistent modernizing of *Hudibras* contextualizes epic in the present, casting doubt on the possibility of achieving knowledge free from historical contingency. Epic becomes the site of complex interplay where the drive towards an absolute origin clashes with the principle of uncertainty. The archaic literary mode of epic falls before the modern heteroglot speech of the street, beargarden, and marketplace.

The general atmosphere of crisis and social disorder at mid century made the quest for foundations and originary truth seem especially pressing. Events before and after the Restoration, however, did little to blunt scepticism, to resolve theological dispute, to reconcile competing interests. All three of the writers treated in this study reflect, refract, and reproduce this climate of doubt and uncertainty. Their major works appeared at a time when traditional philosophies and poetic forms seemed at an impasse. The new science presented itself as a total reinvention of philosophy while writers of epic also searched for absolutes – in particular, absolute beginnings, founding myths, and privileged access to a world of meanings. The seemingly antithetical forms of post-Virgilian epic and Baconian aphorism both set out to investigate and represent the condition of origination. In different ways they performed important cultural work in seventeenth-century England.

Where Bacon is contradictory in his use of originating narratives and Milton ambiguous, Butler transforms origins into an occasion for satire. The opening up of a mock-epic paradigm proceeded from the desire to appropriate and reproduce narratives of origination. Butler recovered epic as satire, a delegitimation that became almost normative in the eighteenth century. What made epic so problematic, a genre 'of highest hope, and hardest attempting' was the difficulty of excavating through layers of accumulated error and falsehood to recover an absolute past. 'Time servs not now,' begins the famous account (from which I quote) of Milton's epic ambitions in *The Reason of Church-Government*: 'Time servs not now, and perhaps I might seem too profuse to give any certain account of what the mind at home in the spacious circuits of her musing hath liberty to propose to her self, though of highest hope, and hardest attempting ...' (*CP* 1: 812—14). The phrase suggests both the inappropriateness of the digression and the impossibility of writing a modern epic ('the fate of this age'). Yet poets did not abandon the genre altogether. In part under the influence of Milton's achievement, the form remained in high regard, even after conditions for its reproduction had all but disappeared.

In the triptych this book presents, Milton's position is perhaps the most difficult to describe. *Paradise Lost* considers the attainment of an origin constitutive of the paradisal state, but never places that state beyond the reach of doubt and inquiry. Milton does not consider the possibility of knowledge once having been unaffected by error. Where Butler emphasizes human fallibility, the potential wrongness of our perceptions and beliefs, Milton shows how distortions generated by language and the mind are inseparable from knowledge itself. Where Bacon dwells on obstructions of the understanding and outlines a typology of error, Milton treats knowledge as the product of an inescapably limited perspective. The pristine apprehension of nature sought by scientists, the recovery of a lost prototype, remained unattainable. The search for a paradisal origin occurs in an epic that eclipses certain origins and destabilizes the relation between truth and error.

I shall end this chapter, and the book, by returning to one of its recurrent concerns: the relationship between science and poetry. Throughout this study I have linked the discourse of origin to philosophy and to poetry, to a few celebrated and some half-forgotten texts. In this convergence of discursive types, both through explicit cross-referencing and through the juxtaposition of texts, I have argued for the continuity of scientific and literary interests. As we have seen, epic interacts with philosophy in the seventeenth century and together the two provide the structures through which the discourse of origin articulates itself. We cannot separate ideology from science because science makes use of the same historically conditioned system of representations. Ideology touches all human activities, working symbolically to join thought and language together. The claim that seizing an origin brings us closer to reality constitutes an outlook that has a profound impact on every domain of knowledge.

Philosophy often seems most persuasive when least visible, when theories pass over into the realm of indisputable knowledge or ideology. I have argued that we should not consider a desire for origins as being ideological in the sense of illusory or unreal, but as a mechanism for making sense of experience, as something indispensable and even valuable. Representing origins did not distort or falsify reality. Rather it established a way of thinking, a set of useful preconceptions for understanding the world and our experience of it. Origins wove themselves into the production of poetry, theology, philosophy, and into language itself.

The problem of ideology, like the question of origins, finally comes down to the problem of representation. Ideology would not exist, were it not for the processes of copying, imitating, and representing. The practice of basing poetic and scientific authority on locating origins without antecedents raised various issues, the most obvious being the apparent circularity of such thinking. What argument or notion (however clear and distinct) could possibly justify the conviction of having reached a point without antecedents?

The difficulty of recuperating origins produced many of the contradictions this study has explored. Once Bacon had called traditional verities into question, he had good reason to doubt the truth of the origin. The quest for something beyond doubt, for a bedrock certainty, brought him to consider the shifting terrain of language. In part 1 of this book I argued that Bacon viewed language as a self-reflective system, an order into which we are all inducted as children. The *Novum Organum* formulates the problem in terms of purging language of distortions, of returning thought to something pristine and irreducible. Bacon sought to identify truth with 'things in themselves,' a fixed origin undistorted by the peculiarities and standpoints of particular observers. At the same time, he saw no certain way to liberate science from the verbal-ideological world, from metaphor itself.

It has been my contention that the pervasive concern with truth and authority in the seventeenth century revolves the problem of referentiality, the apparent discontinuity between signifier and signified, between what Foucault calls the 'order of words' and the 'order of things.' As the focus of our inquiry has moved between epic and philosophy, we have seen how the desire for unambiguous reference produced increasingly complex, if finally unsatisfactory, theories of truth. The discourse of origin was constructed over time and in changing circumstances. Even after the retrievability of origins became the subject of debate, origins provided a grammar and repertoire of images sufficient to secure the grounding of Baconian science and the reconstruction of Virgilian epic.

Language has the power to order experience, to impose a relation. We cannot leave the circle of its influence, of being shaped and conditioned by the words that orient us to reality. In the seventeenth century, the quest for origins merged with a desire to achieve a unitary prelinguistic consciousness, free from error. Finding the relation between mind and world perpetually discrepant, Bacon, Milton, and Butler considered the possibility of devising a language that could adequately represent an authoritative origin. In all three we see an emphasis on foundations that cuts across literature, philosophy, and politics. Although their texts occupy a historical space that may seem removed from our concerns, they retain a power to speak in and of the world we inhabit.

Notes

INTRODUCTION: ORIGIN, ERROR, IDEOLOGY

1 David Quint, *Origin and Originality in Renaissance Literature: Versions of the Source* (New Haven: Yale UP 1983); John Guillory, *Poetic Authority: Spenser, Milton, and Literary History* (New York: Columbia UP 1983)
2 Edward W. Said, *Beginnings: Intention and Method* (New York: Basic 1975) 76. On the post-structuralist 'abandonment of all reference to a *center*, to a *subject*, to a privileged *reference*, to an origin, or to an absolute *archia*,' see Jacques Derrida's remarks on Lévi-Strauss in *Writing and Difference*, trans. Alan Bass (Chicago: U of Chicago P 1978) 286–7. A critique of the privileged origin informs much of Derrida's writings from the 1960s. See Jonathan Goldberg, 'Speculations: *Macbeth* and Source,' in *Shakespeare Reproduced: The Text in History and Ideology*, ed. Jean E. Howard and Marion F. O'Connor (New York: Methuen 1987) 242–64 for an attempt to appropriate Derrida's inquiry into the question of origin and a view of both authors and history as 'heterogeneous dispersal.'
3 Michel Foucault, 'Nietzsche, Freud, Marx,' *Cahiers de Royaumont – Philosophie* 6 (1967): 183–200, and 'Nietzsche, Genealogy, History,' *Language, Counter-Memory, Practice: Selected Essays and Interviews*, trans. Donald F. Bouchard, and Sherry Simon (Ithaca: Cornell UP 1977) 139–64, esp. 142; *The Archaeology of Knowledge* and *The Discourse on Language*, trans. A.M. Sheridan Smith (New York: Pantheon 1972) 137–40
4 Edward W. Said, 'Criticism between Culture and System,' *The World, the Text, and the Critic* (Cambridge: Harvard UP 1983) 187
5 Louis Althusser, 'Ideology and Ideological State Apparatuses (Notes towards an Investigation),' *Lenin and Philosophy and Other Essays*, trans. Ben Brewster (London: NLB 1971) 160–77, and his *Philosophy and the*

Spontaneous Philosophy of the Scientists and Other Essays, ed. Gregory Elliott (London: Verso 1990) 99. For versions of 'ideology,' see Raymond Williams, *Marxism and Literature* (Oxford: Oxford UP 1977) 55–71, and Terry Eagleton, *Ideology* (London: Verso 1991) 1–31.
6 E.P Thompson, 'The Poverty of Theory: Or an Orrery of Errors,' *The Poverty of Theory and Other Essays* (London: Merlin 1978) 214
7 Pierre Macherey, *A Theory of Literary Production*, trans. Geoffrey Wall (London: Routledge and Kegan Paul 1978)
8 See Louis A. Montrose, 'Professing the Renaissance: The Poetics and Politics of Culture,' in *The New Historicism*, ed. H. Aram Veeser (New York: Routledge 1989) 30: 'The possibility of political and institutional agency cannot be based upon the illusion of an escape from ideology. However, the very process of subjectively *living* the confrontations or contradictions within or among ideologies makes it possible to experience facets of our own subjection at shifting internal differences – to read, as in a refracted light, one fragment of our ideological inscription by means of another.'
9 Clifford Geertz, 'Ideology As a Cultural System,' *The Interpretation of Cultures* (New York: Basic 1973) 193–233
10 J.G.A. Pocock, *Politics, Language and Time* (1971; rpt. Chicago: U of Chicago P 1989) 17–21; see also the essays in *The Figural and the Literal: Problems of Language in the History of Science and Philosophy, 1630–1800*, ed. Andrew E. Benjamin, Geoffrey N. Cantor, and John R.R. Christie (Manchester: Manchester UP 1987).

1 'PURE AND UNCORRUPTED NATURAL KNOWLEDGE'

1 Karl R. Popper, *The Logic of Scientific Discovery*, rev. ed. (London: Hutchinson 1968) 278–81, 421–2, and *Conjectures and Refutations: The Growth of Scientific Knowledge* (New York: Basic 1962) 12–27, 46
2 Peter Urbach, *Francis Bacon's Philosophy of Science: An Account and a Reappraisal* (La Salle, IL: Open Court 1987), argues that both Popper and Bacon favour hypotheses that predict latent physical causes, advocate discarding theories undermined by 'factual' evidence, and oppose the conventionalism that values a theory's internal coherence over its plausibility.
3 Mary Hesse, *Revolutions and Reconstructions in the Philosophy of Science* (Bloomington: Indiana UP 1980) vii; cf. Hesse, 'Francis Bacon,' in *A Critical History of Western Philosophy*, ed. D.J. O'Connor (London: Collier-Macmillan 1964) 145–6. Thomas S. Kuhn, *The Structure of Scientific*

Revolutions, 2d ed. (Chicago: U of Chicago P 1970) 16, 18, cites the *Novum Organum* to demonstrate the shortcomings of pre-paradigmatic random fact-gathering, yet quotes Bacon's 'acute methodological dictum' (*NO* 2: 20) that truth 'will sooner come out from error than from confusion.' Kuhn turns to Bacon to make a point of his own: that variable and even erroneous judgments within a scientific community foster the paradigm shifts that yield 'normal' science.

4 Paul Feyerabend, *Against Method*, rev. ed. (London: Verso 1988) 170
5 Thomas S. Kuhn, *The Essential Tension: Selected Studies in Scientific Tradition and Change* (Chicago: U of Chicago P 1977) 43–4
6 Hans-Georg Gadamer, *Truth and Method*, trans. Garrett Barden and John Cumming (New York: Seabury 1975) 239–40, 241–53, 267–74
7 Victoria Kahn, 'Humanism and the Resistance to Theory,' in *Literary Theory / Renaissance Texts*, ed. Patricia Parker and David Quint (Baltimore: Johns Hopkins UP 1986) 381–6
8 Paolo Rossi, 'Truth and Utility in the Science of Francis Bacon,' in *Philosophy, Technology, and the Arts in the Early Modern Era*, ed. Benjamin Nelson, trans. Salvator Attanasio (New York: Harper and Row 1970) 173
9 Paolo Rossi, *Francis Bacon: From Magic to Science*, trans. Sacha Rabinovitch (London: Routledge and Kegan Paul 1968) 46; John Dewey, *Reconstruction in Philosophy, The Middle Works, 1899–1924*, ed. Jo Ann Boydston et al. 15 vols. (Carbondale: Southern Illinois UP 1976–83) 12: 100
10 Sir Francis Bacon, *The Essayes or Counsels, Civill and Morall*, ed. Michael Kiernan (Cambridge: Harvard UP 1985) 75–6 [hereafter *Essayes*]
11 Dewey 25. Theodore K. Rabb, 'Francis Bacon and the Reform of Society,' in *Action and Conviction in Early Modern Europe*, ed. Rabb and Jerrold E. Seigel (Princeton: Princeton UP 1969) 186 detects in Bacon's emphasis on innovation as restoration 'the paradox of an obsessive reformer who had serious reservations about reform.' Marshall McLuhan, 'Bacon: Ancient or Modern?' *Renaissance and Reformation* 10 (1974): 93–8 suggests that Bacon necessarily implemented his program for advancing knowledge 'within the traditional frame of patristic grammatica.' Lisa Jardine, *Francis Bacon: Discovery and the Art of Discourse* (Cambridge: Cambridge UP 1974) documents Bacon's indebtedness to numerous predecessors and contemporaries. Jean-Claude Margolin, 'L'idée de nouveauté et ses points d'application dans le *Novum Organum* de Bacon,' in *Francis Bacon: Science et méthode*, ed. Michel Malherbe and Jean-Marie Pousseur (Paris: Vrin 1985) 11–36 points out the 'dualité interne du concept de nouveauté,' especially when used adjectivally with words such as *via*.

Charles Whitney's *Francis Bacon and Modernity* (New Haven: Yale UP 1986) explores these antinomies at length, relating Bacon's apparent double-mindedness concerning tradition and innovation to discontinuities inherent in the modern condition. Bacon's instauration, in Whitney's view, anticipates post-modernism and the hopeless entanglement of modern culture in a past from which it cannot escape. Instauration becomes a strategy for negotiating the perils of novelty without discounting the shaping powers of tradition.

12 Cf. Bacon, *Works* 3: 290–1; on the iconographical tradition see D.J. Gordon, '*Veritas Filia Temporis:* Hadrianus Junius and Geoffrey Whitney,' in *The Renaissance Imagination: Essays and Lectures*, ed. Stephen Orgel (Berkeley: U of California P 1980) 220–32.

13 Bacon's use of the myth of instauration to underwrite science seems to contradict his goal of liberating natural philosophy from theological intervention. On the apparent gap between Bacon's program and the theological matrix in which it takes shape, see J. Samuel Preus, 'Religion and Bacon's New Learning: From Legitimation to Object,' in *Continuity and Discontinuity in Church History*, ed. F. Forrester Church and Timothy George (Leiden: Brill 1979) 284. Preus argues that when Bacon made religion the object of a separate knowledge, he maintained a methodological unity that transformed natural enquiry into a type of religion. Instead of subjecting religion to critical analysis, he let it remain 'the legitimating *context* of thought; he had not yet brought it into focus as an *object.*'

On Bacon's rhetoric of paradisal recovery as a form of 'linguistic secularization,' see Hans Blumenberg, *The Legitimacy of the Modern Age*, trans. Robert M. Wallace (Cambridge: MIT Press 1983) 105–6, 232–41.

14 Stephen H. Daniel, 'Myth and the Grammar of Discovery in Francis Bacon,' *Philosophy and Rhetoric* 15 (1982): 219–37 suggests that Bacon regards myth and metaphor in a manner parallel to 'claims of Derrida and Ricoeur that metaphors construct the text of the world.'

15 On the perfection of the *lingua adamica*, see Claude-Gilbert Dubois, *Mythe et langage au seizième siècle* (Bordeaux: Ducros 1970) 31–48; Gérard Genette, *Mimologiques: Voyage en cratylie* (Paris: Seuil 1976); David S. Katz, 'The Language of Adam in Seventeenth-Century England,' in *History and Imagination: Essays in Honor of H.R. Trevor-Roper*, ed. Hugh Lloyd-Jones, Valerie Pearl, and Blair Worden (New York: Holmes and Meier 1982) 132–45

16 John Donne, *Essays in Divinity*, ed. Evelyn M. Simpson (Oxford: Clarendon 1952) 23, 116n, taxes an anonymous contemporary suspiciously like Bacon (an 'enormous pretending Wit of our nation and age') for his

presumption in attempting to restore language to its original prelapsarian condition. This nameless projector, Donne says, aspired to surpass the primal language of Adam, in which individual names expressed 'natures and essences' with unfailing precision and exactitude.

17 Bacon 3: 265 (cf. 220); *GI* Plan (cf. 3: 224, 241, 287); 6: 714; Benjamin Farrington, *The Philosophy of Francis Bacon* (1964; rpt. Chicago: U of Chicago P 1966) 88–9

18 Michael McCanles, 'From Derrida to Bacon and Beyond,' in *Francis Bacon's Legacy of Texts: 'The Art of Discovery Grows with Discovery,'* ed. William A. Sessions (New York: AMS Press 1990) 38, and McCanles' *Dialectical Criticism and Renaissance Literature* (Berkeley: U of California P 1975) 24–43

2 WRITING ERROR IN THE *NOVUM ORGANUM*

1 Marta Fattori, *Lessico del 'Novum Organum' di Francesco Bacone*, 2 vols. (Rome: Edizioni dell'Ateneo 1980) 1: 85, 2: 447, records 49 occurrences of *error*.

2 Jonathan Goldberg, *James I and the Politics of Literature: Jonson, Shakespeare, Donne, and Their Contemporaries* (Baltimore: Johns Hopkins UP 1983) 21, shows how the poet-king James imposes the authority of his kingship upon texts, making them vehicles of authoritarian power. On Bacon as a servant of the absolutist state, see Robert E. Stillman, 'The Jacobean Discourse of Power: James I and Francis Bacon,' in *Renaissance Papers*, ed. Dale B.J. Randall and Joseph A. Porter (1989), 89–99, and Julian Martin, *Francis Bacon, the State, and the Reform of Natural Philosophy* (Cambridge: Cambridge UP 1992).

3 Joyce Oldham Appleby, *Economic Thought and Ideology in Seventeenth-Century England* (Princeton: Princeton UP 1978) 242–4 describes this process in a chapter titled 'An Ideological Triumph.' Oscar Kenshur, 'Demystifying the Demystifiers: Metaphysical Snares of Ideological Criticism,' *Critical Inquiry* 14 (1988): 335–53 positions Bacon at an early stage in the ideology of ideological demystification. Drawing a parallel between seventeenth-century and contemporary demystifications of ideology, Kenshur considers Bacon an early exponent of the view that regards science as a method for grasping an unmediated reality. See, however, Robert Markley's response in *Critical Inquiry* 15 (1989): 647–57.

4 Murray Cohen, *Sensible Words: Linguistic Practice in England, 1640–1785* (Baltimore: Johns Hopkins UP 1977) xxiv, 1–42; Martin Elsky, *Authorizing Words: Speech, Writing, and Print in the English Renaissance* (Ithaca:

Cornell UP 1989) 168–173. Hans Aarsleff, *From Locke to Saussure: Essays on the Study of Language and Intellectual History* (Minneapolis: U of Minnesota P 1982), argues that 'Adamicism' was the dominant linguistic paradigm of the seventeenth century, even though rejected by Bacon, Hobbes, and others.

5 Richard Waswo, *Language and Meaning in the Renaissance* (Princeton: Princeton UP 1987) 69, concludes: 'If it is true that the idea of language as an arbitrary "system" was by no means generally accepted in the sixteenth century, it is also true that this idea had been continuously advanced by different kinds of theorists since the middle of the fifteenth.' Waswo shows that given the multiplicity of views available to the period, we cannot embed seventeenth-century theories of reference in a cultural totality labelled 'resemblance.' Nor can the theory that conventionalism was a Lockean innovation withstand scrutiny, since few writers, within the traditions of late scholasticism and speculative grammar, debated the doctrine of conventionality.

6 Michel Foucault, *The Order of Things: An Archaeology of the Human Sciences* (New York: Random House 1970) 51

7 Timothy J. Reiss, *The Discourse of Modernism* (Ithaca: Cornell UP 1982) 208–9

8 Ian Hacking, *The Emergence of Probability: A Philosophical Study of Early Ideas about Probability, Induction and Statistical Inference* (Cambridge: Cambridge UP 1975) 80–1

9 *De Interpretatione* 16a in *The Complete Works of Aristotle*, ed. Jonathan Barnes, 2 vols. (Princeton: Princeton UP 1984) 1: 25: 'Now spoken sounds are symbols of affections in the soul, and written marks symbols of spoken sounds. And just as written marks are not the same for all men, neither are spoken sounds. But what these are in the first place signs of – affections of the soul – are the same for all; and what these affections are likenesses of – actual things – are also the same.' On interpretation of this text, see Elsky 11–17.

10 Henry King, *Two Sermons upon the Act Sunday* (Oxford 1625) 5

11 See, e.g., John Wilkins, *An Essay towards a Real Character and a Philosophical Language* (1668; facs. ed. Menston, England: Scolar 1968) 20. Although Bacon never actually devised an artificial language, passing remarks in the *Advancement* and *De Augmentis* provided a rationale for anyone who sought its advent. When Leibnitz later reoriented the search for the *lingua philosophica* towards mathematics, he drew on the language of Baconian instauration.

12 Stephen J. Greenblatt, 'Learning to Curse: Aspects of Linguistic

Colonialism in the Sixteenth Century,' *Learning to Curse: Essays in Early Modern Culture* (New York: Routledge 1990) 28; for Greenblatt, belief in the unity of mankind rests on a complex foundation of Edenic myth, the quest for universal linguistic structures, and a humanist ideology that regarded reality as 'constituted identically for all men at all times and in all places.'

13 Reiss 208
14 Vivian Salmon, *The Study of Language in 17th-Century England* (Amsterdam: Benjamins 1979) 108; and see the entry 'Notio' in Rudolph Goclenius [Gockel], *Lexicon Philosophicum* (Frankfurt 1613; facs. ed. Hildesheim: Olms 1964) 767–8 [misnumbered 778], for its specialized uses in logic, mathematics, and etymology.
15 *GI* Proem, Plan; cf. Bacon 3: 388: 'for Arguments consist of Propositions, and Propositions of Words; and Words are but the current tokens or marks of Popular Notions of things; which notions, if they be grossly and variably collected out of particulars, it is not the laborious examination either of consequences of arguments or of the truth of propositions, that can ever correct that error ... and therefore it was not without cause, that so many excellent philosophers became Sceptics and Academics, and denied any certainty of knowledge or comprehension, and held opinion that the knowledge of man extended only to appearances and probabilities.'
16 Ferruccio Rossi-Landi, *Marxism and Ideology*, trans. Roger Griffin (Oxford: Clarendon 1990) 29
17 Matteo Ricci, the Italian missionary to China, would, as a sort of mnemonic parlour trick, run through 500 randomly arranged Chinese ideograms and repeat them in reverse order: see Jonathan D. Spence, *The Memory Palace of Matteo Ricci* (New York: Penguin 1984) 9. Bacon attacked the techniques of place logic and vivid imaging that Ricci and others depended upon for such feats of memory, even though he allowed 'emblem' the power to reduce 'conceits intellectual to images sensible' (Bacon 3: 398–9).
18 Elsky 147–72
19 On the seventeenth-century word-thing split, see G.A. Padley, *Grammatical Theory in Western Europe, 1500–1700*, 3 vols. (Cambridge: Cambridge UP 1976–88) 1: 111–53, 2: 325–31.
20 John Webster, *Academiarum Examen* (London 1654) 34; see also Webster's remarks on 'that remarkable saying of the Lord Bacon,' that formal logic 'doth conduce to establish and fix errors (which are founded in vulgar notions) rather than to the inquisition of verity' (40; *NO* 1:12); George Herbert, 'In Honorem Illustr. D.D. Verulamii ... post editam ab eo

Instaurationem Magnam,' *The Latin Poetry of George Herbert*, trans. Mark McCloskey and Paul R. Murphy (Athens: Ohio UP 1965) 168. Joseph Glanvill, *Plus Ultra: or, The Progress and Advancement of Knowledge since the Days of Aristotle* (London 1668) 87; Robert Boyle, *A Discourse of Things above Reason* (London 1681) 57–8.

3 AUTHORIZING APHORISM

1 Roland Barthes, 'La Rochefoucauld: "Reflections or Sentences and Maxims,"' *New Critical Essays*, trans. Richard Howard (New York: Hill and Wang 1980) 3–22
2 On the syntactic schematics of the sixteenth-century *sententia*, see Janel M. Mueller, *The Native Tongue and the Word: Developments in English Prose Style, 1380–1580* (Chicago: U of Chicago P 1984) 260–303.
3 Theodor Adorno, *Minima Moralia: Reflections from Damaged Life*, trans. E.F.N. Jephcott (London: NLB 1974); Max Horkheimer, *Dawn and Decline*, trans. Michael Shaw (New York: Seabury 1978)
4 Desiderius Erasmus, *Adages Ii1 to Iv 100*, ed. R.A.B. Mynors, trans. Margaret Mann Phillips, *The Collected Works of Erasmus*, (Toronto: U of Toronto P 1982) 31: 3–4, 7–9
5 For another view see J.P. Stern, *Lichtenberg: A Doctrine of Scattered Occasions* (Bloomington: Indiana UP 1959), which traces aphorism's historical progression from science to literature.
6 Two partial exceptions are the 'Exemplum Tractatus de Justitia Universali ... in uno titulo, per Aphorismos' in book 8 of *De Augmentis Scientiarum* (1: 803–28), which paraphrases Roman law and arranges material under brief headings; and the conjoined *aphorisimi* and *explicationes* of the Hardwick ms: Graham Rees and Christopher Upton, eds. *Francis Bacon's Natural Philosophy: A New Source* (Chalfont St Giles: British Society for the History of Science 1984) 9–16, 103–73. Note, however, the difficulty Bacon experienced in ordering these manuscript 'aphorisms.'
7 Mikhail Bakhtin, *Problems of Dostoevsky's Poetics*, trans. Caryl Emerson (Minneapolis: U of Minnesota P 1984)
8 Michel Foucault, 'Politics and the Study of Discourse,' *Ideology and Consciousness* 3 (1978): 26; and *The Order of Things* (New York: Random House 1970) xiii–xiv. On the demise of authorship see Foucault, 'What Is an Author?' *Language, Counter-Memory, Practice* (Ithaca: Cornell UP 1977) 113–38, and Roland Barthes, 'The Death of the Author,' *Image Music Text*, trans. Stephen Heath (New York: Hill and Wang 1977) 142–8
9 On the politics of genre, see Stephen Greenblatt, ed., *The Forms of Power*

and the Power of Forms in the Renaissance, special issue of *Genre* 15 (1982): 1–242; and see the essays in part 3 of Barbara Kiefer Lewalski, ed., *Renaissance Genres; Essays on Theory, History, and Interpretation* (Cambridge: Harvard UP 1986) 189–298.

10 Edward Said, *Beginnings* (New York: Basic 1975) 83
11 Robert Dallington, To the Reader, *Aphorismes Civill and Militarie ... out of the First Quarterne of Fr[ancesco] Guicciardine* (London 1613) A4r; F.J. Levy, 'Francis Bacon and the Style of Politics,' *ELR* 16 (1986): 101–22
12 For Solomon's saying (slightly altered from Prov. 25: 2) see 3: 610 and *GI* Preface; and see the *Instauratio*'s Plan for formulation of the principle 'nor can nature be commanded except by being obeyed.'
13 Max Horkheimer and Theodor W. Adorno, *Dialectic of Enlightenment*, trans. John Cumming (New York: Seabury 1972) 3–5. See also William Leiss, *The Domination of Nature* (New York: Braziller 1972) 45–71, and James Holstun, *A Rational Millennium: Puritan Utopias of Seventeenth-Century England and America* (New York: Oxford UP 1987) 50–3, which detects in aphorism 129 a conflict between technology as the disinterested pursuit of universal knowledge and as an instrument of European colonialism. I am at work on this question in a book provisionally titled *'Replenish the Earth and Subdue It': Dominion over Nature in Early Modern England*.
14 On Bacon's words as seeds, see Stanley E. Fish, *Self-Consuming Artifacts: The Experience of Seventeenth-Century Literature* (Berkeley: U of California P 1972) 88, which stands on its ear the view of Bacon as an apostle of clarity and accessibility. Fish's Bacon addresses himself to the defects of human understanding by forging a complex didactic rhetorical practice designed to challenge the mind's complacency and self-confidence.
15 Hume is quoted in Francis Bacon, *Novum Organum*, ed. Thomas Fowler (Oxford: Clarendon 1889) 139; for Feuerbach, see the translation by Marx W. Wartofsky, *Feuerbach* (Cambridge: Cambridge UP 1977) 65: 'If Bacon had not so fragmented his life, if he had dedicated his whole life to the service of science, after the example of other great scholars, he would not have remained merely at the grandiose imperative, at superficial proposals concerning the great structure of science, without having worked out some of the details.' Thomas Babington Macaulay, *Critical and Historical Essays*, 3 vols. (Boston: Houghton Mifflin 1900) 2: 496–7
16 Thomas Tenison, 'An Account of All the Lord Bacon's Works,' *Baconiana: Or, Certain Genuine Remains* (London 1679) 12, 6–7. Oldenburg is quoted in Brian Vickers, 'Swift and Baconian Idol,' *The World of Jonathan Swift*, ed. Vickers (Cambridge: Harvard UP 1968) 90.

4 LEGITIMATION AND THE ORIGIN OF RESTORATION SCIENCE

1 Paolo Rossi, 'Ants, Spiders, Epistemologists,' *Francis Bacon: Terminologia e fortuna nel XVII secolo,* ed. Marta Fattori (Rome: Edizioni dell'Ateneo 1984) 245
2 Gerald Gillespie, 'Scientific Discourse and Postmodernity: Francis Bacon and the Empirical Birth of "Revision,"' *Boundary 2*, 7 (1979): 119–48; Dewey, *Reconstruction in Philosophy, Middle Works* vol. 12, (Carbondale: S. Illinois UP 1982) 100. Dewey also labels Bacon 'the real founder of modern thought,' and 'the father of induction' (95, 98). For an overview of Bacon's 'Followers and Critics,' see Anthony Quinton, *Francis Bacon* (New York: Hill and Wang 1980) 79–84.
3 On ideologies of order and recovery after 1660, see Nicholas Jose, *Ideas of the Restoration in English Literature, 1660–71* (Cambridge: Harvard UP 1984); see also Charles Whitney, 'Francis Bacon's *Instauratio*: Dominion of and over Humanity,' *JHI* 50 (1989): 371–90.
4 On the historically variable meaning of 'Baconianism,' see Antonio Pérez-Ramos, *Francis Bacon's Idea of Science and the Maker's Knowledge Tradition* (Oxford: Clarendon 1988) 7–31.
5 John Henry, 'The Origins of Modern Science: Henry Oldenburg's Contribution,' *British Journal for the History of Science* 21 (1988): 103–9
6 Hans Robert Jauss, *Toward an Aesthetic of Reception,* trans. Timothy Bahti (Minneapolis: U of Minnesota P 1982) 20, 52–3
7 Pierre Macherey, *A Theory of Literary Production* (London: Routledge 1978) 66–74; see also Terry Eagleton, 'Macherey and Marxist Literary Theory,' *Against the Grain: Essays 1975–1985* (London: Verso 1986) 9–21.
8 Susan Bordo, *The Flight to Objectivity: Essays on Cartesianism and Culture* (Albany: State U of New York P 1987) 97–118; Londa Schiebinger, *The Mind Has No Sex? Women in the Origins of Modern Science* (Cambridge: Harvard UP 1989) 137, 119–50. Evelyn Fox Keller, *Reflections on Gender and Science* (New Haven: Yale UP 1985) 43–54 presents the most complex picture of Bacon's masculinist bias. Keller shows that whereas hermeticism had treated knowledge in terms of sympathy and erotic 'merging,' post-Baconian science preferred the language of patriarchal domination. Bacon, who viewed knowledge as a union of mind and matter, acknowledged the necessarily dialectical and 'hermaphroditic' nature of scientific thinking. He portrays science as 'aggressive yet responsive, powerful yet benign, masterful yet subservient, shrewd yet innocent.' At the same time, his work reveals a denial of the feminine, which results in a

compensatory fantasy of virile self-generation and in turn produces increasingly hostile and emphatic gestures of repudiation.
9 *GI* Preface, Plan of Work; Farrington, *The Philosophy of Francis Bacon* (Chicago: U of Chicago P 1966) 72, 108; *NO* 1: 97; 3: 317–18, 222
10 Herbert, 'In Honorem ... Verulamii,' *Latin Poetry* (Athens: Ohio UP 1965), 168–70; Thomas Randolph, 'In Obitum Francisci Verulamii,' *Poetical and Dramatic Works,* ed. W. Carew Hazlitt, 2 vols. (London 1875) 2: 650–2
11 Thomas Forde, *Virtus Rediviva: A Panegyrick on Our Late King Charles the I* (London 1661) 154–5; Power is quoted by Richard Foster Jones, *Ancients and Moderns: A Study of the Rise of the Scientific Movement in Seventeenth-Century England,* 2d ed. (St Louis: Washington UP 1961) 191; Charles Webster, *The Great Instauration: Science, Medicine and Reform, 1626–1660* (London: Duckworth 1975) 335; C.H. Herford, Percy Simpson, and Evelyn Simpson, eds. *Ben Jonson,* 11 vols. (Oxford: Clarendon 1925–52) 8: 590–1
12 Robert Greville, Baron Brooke, *The Nature of Truth* (London 1641) 141–2; and William Rawley, 'Life' of Bacon (Bacon 1: 15–16); see also Ralph Austen, *Observations upon Some Part of Sr Francis Bacon's Naturall History* (Oxford 1658) A3, which excuses its boldness in departing 'from the Judgment of so *Eminent,* and *worthy an Author*' by noting that Bacon granted a charter for such revision and inquiry.
13 John Wilkins, *Mercury: Or, The Secret and Swift Messenger* (London 1641) 10; Herbert, 168–9; book 2 of John Wilkins, *A Discourse concerning a New World & Another Planet* (London 1640) 6–7, and see also Book 1, A3v; Alexander Ross, *The New Planet No Planet* (London 1646) 2–3, and *Arcana Microcosmi,* 2d ed. (London, 1652) A2r, 207, 263–7.
14 Beale is quoted by Michael Hunter, *Science and Society in Restoration England* (Cambridge: Cambridge UP 1981) 195. Robert Boyle, *A Discourse of Things above Reason* (London 1681) 57–8; on Boyle's latitudinarianism see Margaret C. Jacob, *The Cultural Meaning of the Scientific Revolution* (Philadelphia: Temple UP 1988) 73–104.
15 Thomas Sprat, *History of the Royal Society,* ed. Jackson I. Cope and Harold Whitmore Jones (facs. ed., St Louis: Washington UP, 1958) 35; subsequent citations are parenthetic. P.B. Wood, 'Methodology and Apologetics: Thomas Sprat's *History of the Royal Society,*' *British Journal for the History of Science* 13 (1980): 1–26. J.R. Jacob, 'Restoration, Reformation and the Origins of the Royal Society,' *History of Science* 13 (1975) 171 casts doubt on the claim that the Society strove to disengage itself from political or religious controversy, arguing that its self-proclaimed 'moderation' cloaked an 'aggressive, acquisitive, mercantilistic ideology

justified in the name of both Restoration and Reformation,' Margaret C. Jacob, *The Newtonians and the English Revolution, 1689–1720* (Ithaca: Cornell UP 1976) 36–9 argues that although Sprat represents science as a retreat from worldliness and political ideology, his 'understanding of the religious meaning of science was conditioned by the Revolution.'

16 Steven Shapin and Simon Schaffer, *Leviathan and the Air-Pump: Hobbes, Boyle, and the Experimental Life* (Princeton: Princeton UP 1985)

17 *Diary of John Evelyn*, ed. William Bray, 4 vols. (London 1879) 3: 351

18 Abraham Cowley, Preface to *Poems* (London 1656) sig. (b)2r. Pindaric imitation aligns Cowley with contemporaries who combined praise of a 'ruler' with advice, analysis, and even covert criticism: see David Norbrook, 'Marvell's "Horatian Ode" and the Politics of Genre,' in *Literature and the English Civil War*, ed. Thomas Healey and Jonathan Sawday (Cambridge: Cambridge UP 1990) 147–69.

19 Helen M. Burke, '*Annus Mirabilis* and the Ideology of the New Science,' *ELH* 57 (1990): 307–34

20 Antonio Pérez-Ramos, 'Francis Bacon and the Disputations of the Learned,' *British Journal for the Philosophy of Science* 42 (1991) 579; see also Hans Aarsleff, 'Thomas Sprat,' *From Locke to Saussure* (Minneapolis: U of Minnesota P 1982) 248. Hunter 194–7 and Shapin and Schaffer 32–5 discuss the frontispiece.

21 Abraham Cowley, *A Proposition for the Advancement of Experimental Philosophy* in *Essays, Plays and Sundry Verses*, ed. A.R. Waller (Cambridge: Cambridge UP 1906) 258

22 Peter Dear, '*Totius in Verba*: Rhetoric and Authority in the Early Royal Society,' *Isis* 76 (1985): 145–61 argues that the scientific program promoted by Sprat embodies 'a fundamental change in concepts of experience and authority in natural philsophy.' See also Robert Markley, 'Objectivity as Ideology: Boyle, Newton, and the Languages of Science,' *Genre* 16 (1983): 355–72, for the Restoration's attempted reconciliation of revolutionary science and theology within the metaphysic of objectivity.

23 Henry Stubbe, *The Plus Ultra Reduced to a Non Plus* (London 1670) second t.p.; also 'To the Reader,' 43, 55.

24 James R. Jacob, *Henry Stubbe: Radical Protestantism and the Early Enlightenment* (Cambridge: Cambridge UP 1983) views Stubbe as consistently radical after 1660, and interprets his attacks on the Royal Society as the reaction of a crypto-secularist to the latitudinarian linkage of science and the established church. While Jacob presents a counter-argument to R.F. Jones, his analysis refuses to admit the possibility of historical ruptures in Restoration authorship: Anthony à Wood, *Athenae*

Oxonienses, 2d ed., 2 vols. (London 1721) 1: 563, thought Stubbe brilliant but 'a Person of no fix'd Principles.'

25 *A Further Discovery of M. Stubbe* (1671), quoted in Jones 256-7
26 Henry Stubbe, 'A Reply, by way of Preface to the Calumnies of *Eccebolius Glanvile*,' *The Lord Bacons Relation of the Sweating-Sickness Examined* (London 1671) 3, 6; the existence of copies with the alternative title is reported by Jackson I. Cope, *Joseph Glanvill, Anglican Apologist* (St. Louis: Washington UP 1956) 27n. For a preliminary and comparatively mild swipe at Bacon, see Stubbe's 'Mistakes about the Sweating-Sicknes, and its Cure,' in *Legends No Histories: Or, A Specimen of Some Animadversions upon the 'History of the Royal Society'* (London 1670) 23-34. Like Stubbe, Swift regarded Bacon's overvaluation of novelty as a vehicle for promoting revolutionary action and a direct forerunner of the interregnum. In the *Battle of the Books* he deflects Bacon's judgment of Aristotelian arrogance and *libido dominandi* onto Bacon himself, transforming the advancement of learning into the advance of an army: see *A Tale of a Tub and Other Works*, ed. Angus Ross and David Woolley (Oxford: Oxford UP 1986) 117.
27 Agricola Carpenter, *Pseuchographia Anthropomagica* (London, 1652) 23-5.
28 Elizabeth Hanson, 'Torture and Truth in Renaissance England,' *Representations* 34 (1991): 63-6 connects Bacon's epistemology of discovery to his legitimation of torture in English juridical practice. John Evelyn, interestingly, considered Bacon's method less inquisitorial than Robert Boyle's: 'Never did stubborn matter come under his [Boyle's] inquisition but he extorted a confession of all that lay in her most intimate recesses; and what he discover'd he as faithfully register'd, and frankly com'unicated; in this, exceeding my Lord Verulam, who (tho' never to be mention'd without honor and admiration) was us'd to tell all that came to hand without much examination': Evelyn 3: 482 [letter to Wotton dated 1696].
29 Timothy Reiss, *Discourse of Modernism* (Ithaca: Cornell UP 1982), 214

5 BEGINNING LATE

1 Edward Said, *Beginnings* (New York: Basic 1975) 315
2 Dryden, who loaded the poem with superlatives in his preface to *The State of Innocence* ('undoubtedly one of the greatest, most noble, and most sublime poems which either this age or nation has produced') later eulogized its author for achieving an English hybridization of Homer and Virgil: John T. Shawcross, *Milton: The Critical Heritage* (New York: Barnes and Noble 1970) 97. In the Dedication of the *Æneis*, however, Dryden relegates him to secondary status along with Pierre Le Moyne, de

Scudéry, Chapelain, and Spenser: *The Works of John Dryden,* ed. Edward Niles Hooker, H.T. Swedenberg, Jr, et al. (Berkeley: U of California P 1956–) 5: 275–6. On Barrow, see Michael Lieb, 'S.B.'s *"In Paradisum Amissam"*: Sublime Commentary,' *Milton Quarterly* 19 (1985) 71–8.

3 'To the Unknown Authour of this Excellent Poem,' 'To Mr. Dryden, on his Poem of Paradice,' *The Works of Nathaniel Lee,* ed. Thomas B. Stroup and Arthur L. Cooke, 2 vols. (New Brunswick, NJ: Scarecrow P 1955) 2: 559, 557–8.

4 Christopher Hill, *Milton and the English Revolution* (New York: Viking 1977) 348 argues that the message of the last three poems 'is not resignation, but a different type of political action from those which have failed so lamentably'; David Loewenstein, *Milton and the Drama of History: Historical Vision, Iconoclasm, and the Literary Imagination* (Cambridge: Cambridge UP 1990), sees in the closing books of *Paradise Lost* the same emphasis on historical causes and explanation that informs the revolutionary polemics.

5 Sir William Davenant, 'The Author's Preface,' *Gondibert,* ed. David F. Gladish (Oxford: Clarendon 1971) 3

6 Cowley, *Davideis, Poems* (London 1656) 13; cf. Torquato Tasso, *Discourses on the Heroic Poem,* trans. Mariella Cavalchini and Irene Samuel (Oxford: Clarendon 1991) 77–8

7 Harold Bloom, *Ruin the Sacred Truths: Poetry and Belief from the Bible to the Present* (Cambridge: Harvard UP 1989) 111, 96, calls *Paradise Lost* 'the most resolutely archaic of literary works,' and speaks of a process of poetic 'transumption' whereby Milton stations himself 'with radical originality, in an anxiously emptied-out present time.' Milton's poem, according to Bloom, offers us access to an absolute origin and utterly transforms and regenerates the past. Bloom's version of Miltonic originality hoists him aloft into a literary pantheon and endows him with God-like self-possession. 'Milton' becomes an allegory of psychic and poetic strength engaged in a timeless dialogue with the Bible, Homer, and other sacred texts.

8 Francis C. Blessington, *'Paradise Lost' and the Classical Epic* (Boston: Routledge and Kegan Paul 1979) xiii. Among the many studies of Milton's 'revision' of epic convention, see John M. Steadman, *Milton and the Renaissance Hero* (Oxford: Clarendon 1967), and T.J.B. Spencer, *'Paradise Lost:* The Anti-Epic,' in *Approaches to 'Paradise Lost,'* ed. C.A. Patrides (Toronto: U of Toronto P 1968) 89, which emphasizes the problematic relation between 'revision' and repudiation.

9 A.S.P. Woodhouse, *The Heavenly Muse: A Preface to Milton,* ed. Hugh MacCallum (Toronto: U of Toronto P 1972) 182; Mary Ann Radzinowicz,

Milton's Epics and the Book of Psalms (Princeton: Princeton UP 1989). On the epic-scriptural nexus see also Leland Ryken, 'Paradise Lost and Its Biblical Epic Models,' in *Milton and Scriptural Tradition: The Bible into Poetry*, ed. James H. Sims and Leland Ryken (Columbia: U of Missouri P 1984) 43–81

10 Northrop Frye, *The Return of Eden: Five Essays on Milton's Epics* (Toronto: U of Toronto P 1965) 7, 14–15
11 Barbara Kiefer Lewalski, *Milton's Brief Epic: The Genre, Meaning, and Art of 'Paradise Regained'* (Providence: Brown UP 1966) 10, 54–5
12 J.B. Broadbent, *Some Graver Subject: An Essay on 'Paradise Lost'* (New York: Barnes and Noble 1960) 55
13 Christopher Kendrick, *Milton: A Study in Ideology and Form* (New York: Methuen 1986) 83–4. Classicists might not share Kendrick's view in all its paticulars: they are divided on the importance of slavery to the Roman imperial economy, and on Virgil's relation to the Augustan ideology of *res gestae*. Also see G.K. Hunter, *Paradise Lost* (London: Allen and Unwin 1980) 14–16, who describes Milton's epic as encompassing 'his two abiding passions, patriotism and religion,' but traces his retreat from the 'explicitly political' to internal conditions of the heroic.
14 When *Lusiads* foretells the future triumphs of the Portuguese in the east, it transposes the Virgilian model into a modern register that lays bare the whole imperial ethos. On Camoens' relation to *Paradise Lost*, see Louis L. Martz, *Milton: Poet of Exile*, rev. ed. (New Haven: Yale UP 1986) 155–68, and David Quint, 'Epic and Empire,' *Comparative Literature* 41 (1989): 1–32. Andrew Fichter, *Poets Historical: Dynastic Epic in the Renaissance* (New Haven: Yale UP 1982) 207–9, considers Milton's poem a contribution to 'Christian dynastic epic,' a form in which Ariosto, Spenser, and Tasso succeed where Milton cannot because of his distaste for monarchy and his foregrounding of theology.
15 Balachandra Rajan, '*Paradise Lost*: The Uncertain Epic,' *The Form of the Unfinished: English Poetics from Spenser to Pound* (Princeton: Princeton UP, 1985) 104–27. Rajan puts a deconstructive spin on traditional views of Miltonic self-dividedness. For a recent attempt to reinstate Christian humanism as the primary context for reading Milton, see Joan S. Bennett, *Reviving Liberty: Radical Christian Humanism in Milton's Great Poems* (Cambridge: Harvard UP, 1989). Thomas O. Sloane, *Donne, Milton, and the End of Humanist Rhetoric* (Berkeley: U of California P 1985) finds the collapse of humanist rhetorical theory (and of humanism itself) in Milton and the later seventeenth century.
16 Barbara Kiefer Lewalski, '*Paradise Lost*' *and the Rhetoric of Literary Forms*

(Princeton: Princeton UP 1985) 3–24. Herman Rapaport, *'Paradise Lost* and the Novel,' in *Approaches to Teaching Milton's 'Paradise Lost,'* ed. Galbraith M. Crump (New York: MLA 1986) 136 suggests that the desire to distance *Paradise Lost* from the novel and Restoration England insulates it 'from criticisms that call its authenticity as a genre into question and that therefore problematize the usual uncritical assumptions concerning Milton's relation to his appropriation of texts from the epic tradition.'

17 Mikhail Bakhtin, 'Epic and Novel,' *The Dialogic Imagination: Four Essays,* ed. Michael Holquist, trans. Caryl Emerson and Michael Holquist (Austin: U of Texas 1981) 13ff; see also the lucid account by Tzvetan Todorov, *Mikhail Bakhtin: The Dialogical Principle,* trans. Wlad Godzich (Minneapolis: U of Minnesota P 1984) 80–93, esp 89, on the central opposition between novel and epic coming down to 'possible or impossible continuity between the time of the (represented) utterance and the time of (representing) uttering.'

18 Georg Lukács, *The Theory of the Novel,* trans. Anna Bostock (Cambridge: MIT Press 1971) 46, 55, 60, 68, 88, 126. On Milton in relation to Lukács, see Leopold Damrosch, Jr, *God's Plot & Man's Stories: Studies in the Fictional Imagination from Milton to Fielding* (Chicago: U of Chicago P 1985) 78–9, and Andrew Milner, *John Milton and the English Revolution: A Study in the Sociology of Literature* (Totawa, NJ: Barnes and Noble 1981) 141–9.

19 Harold E. Toliver, 'Milton's Household Epic,' *Milton Studies* 9 (1976): 106, 119; see also Catherine Belsey, *John Milton: Language, Gender, Power* (Oxford: Blackwell 1988) 60, 36, 85–6, 89, which treats the humanist emphasis on inwardness and inviolable subjectivity as mechanisms for the dissemination of a universal and unitary truth. The ideology of subjectivity, Belsey contends, finds a home within the unitary master-narrative of epic prior to its migration to the novel.

20 De Scudéry, *Ibrahim: Or, the Illustrious Bassa,* trans. Henry Cogan (London 1674) preface, sig. A3v; on the use of classical models in romance and their relation to epic, see Lennard J. Davis, *Factual Fictions: The Origins of the English Novel* (New York: Columbia UP 1983) 25–41.

21 Stella P. Revard, 'Vergil's *Georgics* and *Paradise Lost,*' in *Vergil at 2000: Commemorative Essays on the Poet and His Influence,* ed. John D. Bernard (New York: AMS Press 1986) 259–60 remarks that Vergil's epic 'has universally been recognized as an important model for Milton,' particularly in relation to 'its twelve-book epic structure, its scenes of council and war, and its famous description of the underworld.' See, *inter alia,* Davis P. Harding, *The Club of Hercules: Studies in the Classical Background of 'Paradise Lost'* (Urbana: U of Illinois P 1962) 1–39.

22 Gian Biagio Conte, *The Rhetoric of Imitation: Genre and Poetic Memory in Virgil and Other Latin Poets*, trans. Charles Segal (Ithaca: Cornell UP 1986) 142
23 Richard Waswo, 'The History that Literature Makes,' *New Literary History* 19 (1988): 546
24 Frederick Morgan Padelford, *Select Translations from Scaliger's 'Poetics'* (New York: Henry Holt 1905) 73-81, 54; cf. Julius Caesar Scaliger, *Poetices Libri Septem* (1561; facs. ed. Stuttgart: Frommann 1964) 144 [book 3, chap. 96]
25 Davenant 4-6; on 'the obsolescence of epic,' see Brooks Otis, *Virgil: A Study in Civilized Poetry* (Oxford: Clarendon 1964) 5-40.
26 *Juvenal's Sixteen Satyrs*, trans. Sir Robert Stapylton (London 1647), 95; *The Institutio Oratoria of Quintilian*, trans. H.E. Butler, 4 vols. (London: Heinemann; Cambridge: Harvard UP 1922) [X.i.86]
27 Marco Girolamo Vida, *The De Arte Poetica*, trans. Ralph G. Williams (New York: Columbia UP 1976); J.C. Scaliger, *Poetices* 5, chaps. 2, 3; see also François Rigolot, 'Homer's Virgilian Authority: Ronsard's Counterfeit Epic Theory,' in *Discourses of Authority in Medieval and Renaissance Literature*, ed. Kevin Brownlee and Walter Stephens (Hanover, NH: UP of New England 1989) 65, 73, on Pierre de Ronsard's simultaneous appeal to both Virgilian and Homeric authority in *La Franciade* (1572), and his use of the primal Homeric ur-text to position his work in a liminal space that defined the concepts of truth and literary originality.
28 René Rapin, *Comparaison des poëmes d'Homère et Virgile* (1664; facs. ed. Hildesheim: Olms 1973) 165; Thomas Hobbes, *The English Works*, ed. Sir William Molesworth (London: J. Bohn 1839-45) 11 vols (1839-45) 10: x; cf. Gerardus Joannes Vossius, *Poeticarum Institutionum libri tres* (Amsterdam 1647), book 3, p. 10, which treats Virgil and Cicero as the fount of eloquence.
29 'Vindiciae Virgilianae Sive Iulii Caesaris Scaligeri Virgilium Homero praenponentis contrà I. Lips. Apologia,' in George Hakewill, *An Apologie or Declaration of the Power and Providence of God*, 3d ed. (Oxford 1635) 290, 57
30 Merritt Y. Hughes, gen. ed., *A Variorum Commentary on the Poems of John Milton*, 3 vols. to date (New York: Columbia UP 1970–) 1: 214; I quote the 1604 translation by Sir John Harington, *The Sixth Book of Virgil's Aeneid*, ed. Simon Cauchi (Oxford: Clarendon 1991) 37, 116.
31 William Kerrigan, *The Prophetic Milton* (Charlottesville: UP of Virginia 1974) 78-9; *CP* 1: 814, n94 also supports such a reading.
32 Anthony Low, *The Georgic Revolution* (Princeton: Princeton UP 1985) 3-4, 310-28. Low considers *Paradise Regained*, with its four-book

13 Edward Reynolds, *A Treatise of the Passions and Faculties of the Soule of Man* (1640; facs. ed. Gainesville FL: Scholars' Facsimiles 1971) 457–8; Hugh MacCallum, *Milton and the Sons of God: The Divine Image in Milton's Epic Poetry* (Toronto: U of Toronto P 1986) 122–34 shows that Adam does not have the divine nature forcibly stamped upon him at his birth. Instead Milton expresses Adam's relation to the deity through the metaphorics of reflection and the trope of sonship, a partial likeness that distances him from the divine nature and suggests the possibility of future growth.

14 Translation in Leslie George Whitbread, *Fulgentius the Mythographer* (Columbus: Ohio State UP 1971) 124, 126. Bernardus Silvestris, *Commentary on the First Six Books of Virgil's 'Aeneid,'* trans. Earl Schreiber and Thomas E. Maresca (Lincoln: U of Nebraska P 1979)

15 Michael Murrin, *The Allegorical Epic: Essays in Its Rise and Decline* (Chicago: U of Chicago P 1980) 27–38, 197–201, detects the influence of Academic scepticism on Virgil's presentation of visionary states and emphasis on dreams, deception, and uncertainty. On *labor, labyrinthus,* and *inextricabilis error* in the *Aeneid*, see Penelope Reed Doob, *The Idea of the Labyrinth from Classical Antiquity through the Middle Ages* (Ithaca: Cornell UP 1990) 227–53.

16 Debora K. Shuger, 'The Temptation of Eve,' in *Traditions and Innovations: Essays on British Literature of the Middle Ages and the Renaissance*, ed. David G. Allen and Robert A. White (Newark: U of Delaware P 1990) 188–9; Dennis H. Burden, *The Logical Epic: A Study of the Argument of 'Paradise Lost'* (London: Routledge and Kegan Paul 1967) 97–123 and esp. 106–7 compares Milton to Bacon, quoting the *Advancement* (3: 264–5) on the distinction between knowledge 'of nature and universality,' and presumptuous knowledge of good and evil.

17 *CP* 6: 303, 133–52, 299–300; on the beginning of eternity see also Margaret Cavendish, Duchess of Newcastle, *CCXI Sociable Letters* (1664; facs. ed. Menston, England: Scolar 1969) sig. Tt: 'God was the First Producer of the Matter that made the World, yet the Power that God Had, and Hath, to make the Matter, was Infinite and Eternal, and the Matter being in the Infinite and Eternal Power, is also Infinite and Eternal, without Beginning or Ending.'

18 John Leonard, *Naming in Paradise: Milton and the Language of Adam and Eve* (Oxford: Clarendon 1990); and Leonard Mustazza, *'Such Prompt Eloquence': Language as Agency in Milton's Epics* (Lewisburg PA: Bucknell UP 1988) 71: 'Edenic words are not arbitrary labels assigned to things but sounds that are themselves intimately bound up with the things' natures or essences.' See also Robert L. Entzminger, *Divine Word: Milton and the*

Redemption of Language (Pittsburgh: Duquesne UP 1985) 30–5; and Michael Lieb, *Poetics of the Holy: A Reading of 'Paradise Lost'* (Chapel Hill: U of North Carolina P 1981) 171–84, on traditions of glorifying the holy name.
19 Giovanni Francesco Loredano, *The Life of Adam*, trans. J.S. (London 1659) 1, 85
20 Stein is quoted in Mustazza 17; Edward Said, *Beginnings* (New York: Basic 1975) 43–4, 279–80
21 Isaac La Peyrère, *Men before Adam* (London 1656) 54–8; Bruno is translated by Richard H. Popkin, *Isaac La Peyrère 1596–1676: His Life, Work and Influence* (Leiden: Brill 1987) 35.
22 Edward Stillingfleet, *Origines Sacrae: or, A Rational Account of the Grounds of the Christian Faith* (London 1662) 534, 2–7; and see p. 4 on Adam's naming: 'where there was a true knowledge, the *conceptions* must agree with the *things*; and *words* being to *express* our *conceptions*, none are so fit to do it, as those which are *expressive* of the several *natures* of the things they are used to *represent*.' See also Sir Matthew Hale, *The Primitive Origination of Mankind* (London 1677), who rejects arguments for the eternity of the world, the pre-Adamite thesis, and for humanity's having no point of origination or termination.
23 *Monsieur Pascall's Thoughts, Meditations, and Prayers, Touching Matters Moral and Divine*, trans. Joseph Walker (London 1688) 137–8 [in modern editions this *pensée* is numbered Brunschvicg 434, Lafuma 131, or Sellier 164].

7 THE FIGURE IN THE MIRROR

1 Edward Said, *Beginnings* (New York: Basic 1975) 46
2 Regina Schwartz, 'Rethinking Voyeurism and Patriarchy: The Case of *Paradise Lost*,' *Representations* 34 (1991) 102–3 n33; John Guillory, 'From the Superfluous to the Supernumerary: Reading Gender into *Paradise Lost*,' in *Soliciting Interpretation: Literary Theory and Seventeenth-Century English Poetry*, ed. Elizabeth D. Harvey and Katharine Eisaman Maus (Chicago: U of Chicago P 1990) 68–88
3 Catherine Belsey, *John Milton* (Oxford: Blackwell 1988) 64; James Grantham Turner, *One Flesh: Paradisal Marriage and Sexual Relations in the Age of Milton* (Oxford: Clarendon 1987) 123. Joseph Wittreich, *Feminist Milton* (Ithaca: Cornell UP 1987) argues that women writers between 1680 and 1830 enlisted Milton on behalf of a 'feminist' ethos and radical critique of masculinist interpretations.

4 Christine Froula, 'When Eve Reads Milton: Undoing the Canonical Economy,' in *Canons*, ed. Robert von Hallberg (Chicago: U of Chicago P 1984) 149–75; Mary Nyquist, 'The Genesis of Gendered Subjectivity in the Divorce Tracts and in *Paradise Lost*,' in *Re-membering Milton: Essays on the Texts and Traditions*, ed. Nyquist and Margaret W. Ferguson (New York: Methuen 1987) 120; for Schwartz, 'Rethinking Voyeurism,' 98, Eve's desire for her own image is an attempt to regain the spectatorial position, the power of the gaze that male desire denies her.

  Marshall Grossman, 'Servile/Sterile/Style: Milton and the Question of Woman,' in *Milton and the Idea of Woman*, ed. Julia M. Walker (Urbana: U of Illinois P 1988) 151–2, finds in the Narcissus episode an originary moment that initiates Eve's discovery of 'the necessary interplay between subjectification and subjection' that attends 'collateral love.' Eve, Grossman concludes, surrenders her desire and autonomy in exchange for the deferred promise of motherhood and the 'multitudinous repetition of an originary image.'

5 Ester Sowernam, *Ester Hath Hang'd Haman: or, An Answere to a Lewde Pamphlet* (London 1617) 5. Isotta Nogarola's 'Of the Equal or Unequal Sin of Adam and Eve' (1451–3) mobilizes the argument of Eve's imperfect creation in woman's 'defence': 'When God created man, from the beginning he created him perfect, and the powers of his soul perfect, and gave him a greater understanding and knowledge of truth as well as a greater depth of widom. Thus it was that the Lord led to Adam all the animals of the earth and the birds of heaven, so that Adam could call them by their names': see Margaret L. King and Albert Rabil, Jr, eds., *Her Immaculate Hand: Selected Works by and about the Women Humanists of Quattrocento Italy* (Binghamton, NY: MRTS 1983) 63

6 Turner 25–7; Elaine Pagels, *Adam, Eve, and the Serpent* (New York: Random 1988) 15–17, 25, 91–7

7 James Holstun, '"Will You Rent Our Ancient Love Asunder?": Lesbian Elegy in Donne, Marvell, and Milton,' *ELH* 54 (1987): 854–62

8 Janet E. Halley, 'Female Autonomy in Milton's Sexual Poetics,' in Walker, ed., *Milton and the Idea of Woman* 230–53, surveys feminist criticism of Milton, finding it divided between 'critics who see Eve as the object of Milton's patriarchal imagination' and critics 'to whom she is the image of genuine female subjectivity not created but recognized by a progressive, liberal Milton.' For the latter see Diane Kelsey McColley, *Milton's Eve* (Urbana: U of Illinois P 1983).

9 James W. Earl, 'Eve's Narcissism,' *Milton Quarterly* 19 (1985): 13–16 reads Milton's lines in conjunction with Jacques Lacan's account of the 'mirror

stage' in the formation of personal identity among children. The mirror stage, which Earl follows Lacan in thinking normative and universal, thus presents a description of the experience Eve undergoes when she perceives her body as Other and passes from primary narcissism to the constitution of a unified self; see also Richard Halpern, 'The Great Instauration: Imaginary Narratives in Milton's "Nativity Ode,"' in Nyquist and Ferguson ed., *Re-membering Milton* 3–24.

10 William G. Madsen, *From Shadowy Types to Truth: Studies in Milton's Symbolism* (New Haven: Yale UP 1968) 87–113

11 Umberto Eco, *Semiotics and the Philosophy of Language* (Bloomington: Indiana UP 1984) 204–7

12 See Herbert Grabes, *The Mutable Glass: Mirror-Imagery in Titles and Texts of the Middle Ages and English Renaissance*, trans. Gordon Collier (Cambridge: Cambridge UP 1982), a vast compendium of medieval and Renaissance mirror imagery, which includes a bibliographic survey of *speculum*, mirror, glass, looking-glass, and 'prospective-glass' titles from Augustine to the 1690s.

13 Peter Charron, *Of Wisdome*, trans. Samson Lennard (London [1612]), and *Of Wisdome* (London 1670); the engraving (by Gaultier and later copied by William Hole) comes from *De la Sagesse*, 2d ed. (Paris 1604). *De la sagesse* (Amsterdam 1662) modifies the engraving, and explains it in a sonnet and prose 'Explanation de la Figure,' 3–5, which provides the basis of the English explication.

14 Scipio du Plesis [Scipion Du Pleix], *The Resolver: or, Curiosities of Nature* (London 1635) 284–5, s.v. 'Looking-glasses or Mirrours'

15 Richard Rorty, *Philosophy and the Mirror of Nature* (Princeton: Princeton UP 1979); John W. Yolton, 'Mirrors and Veils, Thoughts and Things: The Epistemological Problematic,' *Reading Rorty: Critical Responses to 'Philosophy and the Mirror of Nature' (and Beyond)* ed. Alan R. Malachowski (Oxford: Basil Blackwell 1990) 70 argues that the use of mirror imagery by Descartes and Locke does not necessarily commit them to crudely mentalistic theories of knowledge-as-representation. Yolton concludes that 'if this metaphor of a veil of ideas involves holding that (1) ideas are special objects, (2) we can only be aware of ideas, (3) ideas are modelled on retinal images and (4) these ideas inhabit an inner space, I do not think the majority of writers in the way of ideas tradition (and certainly neither Descartes nor Locke) held to, or were committed to, this metaphor.'

16 John Locke, *An Essay Concerning Human Understanding*, ed. John W. Yolton, 2 vols. (New York: Dutton 1961) 1: 89 [2.1.2–25]

17 McCanles, *Dialectical Criticism* (Berkeley: U of California P 1975) 151–2; Grossman, *'Authors to Themselves'* (New York: Cambridge UP 1987) 83 offers a similar argument: 'Eve's interaction with her own image in the water, although it raises the specter of narcissism, also emphasizes the dialectical nature of God's creation.'

18 Geoffrey H. Hartman, 'Adam on the Grass with Balsamum,' *Beyond Formalism: Literary Essays, 1958–1970* (New Haven: Yale UP 1970) 124–50

19 Kathleen M. Swaim, *Before and After the Fall: Contrasting Modes in 'Paradise Lost'* (Amherst: U of Massachusetts P 1986) 227–31 comments: 'When the higher faculties are inoperative, mimic fancy undertakes the work of either fancy itself or reason (the "her" of line 111 is ambiguous) and puts together errant connections of sensory data.'

20 Edmund Spenser, *The Faerie Queene*, ed. A.C. Hamilton (London: Longman 1977) 256; see also *Paradise Lost* 6.42–3; 9.113; 12.86; 7.9–10; 8.563–4.

21 Nyquist, 120. Fish, *Surprised by Sin* (London: Macmillan; New York: St Martin's 1967, 216–19) describes the dynamic of a subtle didacticism at work, contending that Milton raises the possibility of Eve's mistake prefiguring a fatal character flaw only to retract it: once we register the allusion, we cannot let it compromise the principle of prelapsarian freedom.

22 Belsey, *Milton* 61

23 William Kerrigan and Gordon Braden, *The Idea of the Renaissance* (Baltimore: Johns Hopkins UP 1989) 201, 203 connect this description of Edenic sexuality, particularly the detail of Eve's flowing tresses, to seventeenth-century love poetry. They contend that the Renaissance's erotic fixation on scenes of women fleeing from men, preliminary to capitulation, figures as a means for prolonging desire and keeping its object from decay. Combining Ovidianism and psychological realism, Milton places 'the first first time' in implicit opposition to the unrequited love and failed consummation of the Narcissus scene. See also David Aers and Bob Hodge, 'Rational Burning: Milton on Sex and Marriage,' *Literature, Language and Society in England, 1580–1680* (Totowa, NJ: Barnes and Noble 1981) 149 for tensions within the passage.

24 Hill, *Milton and the English Revolution* (New York: Viking 1977) 346

25 Sir Robert Filmer, *Patriarcha and Other Writings*, ed. Johann P. Sommerville (Cambridge: Cambridge UP 1991) 138: 'Here we have the original grant of government, and the fountain of all power, placed in the father of all mankind'; cf. 6–7; John Locke, *Two Treatises of Government*, ed. Peter Laslett, 3d ed. (Cambridge: Cambridge UP 1988) 174; see also Gordon J. Schochet, *The Authoritarian Family and Political Attitudes in*

God,' *The Works of John Locke*, 10 vols. (London 1823) 9: 250, 212 Locke criticizes Malebranche for suggesting that we know the world by matching mental phantasms to extra-mental phenomena. 'How can I know,' he asks, 'that the picture of any thing is like that thing, when I never see that which it represents?' That an 'idea' can 'be the true representation of any thing that exists ... neither our author nor any body else can know.' In the *Essay* 4.4.3–4, however, Locke argues that 'simple ideas' are not fictions but the product of genuine conformity.

2 See Wilders, Introduction, *Hudibras* xxiv, and de Quehen, Introduction, *PO* xxx–xxxiv.

3 Dewey, *Reconstruction in Philosophy*, Middle Works vol. 12 (Carbondale: Southern Illinois UP 1982) 126–7

4 Nicolas Malebranche, *Malebranch's Search after Truth: or A Treatise of the Nature of the Humane Mind*, 2 vols. (London 1694, 1695) 1: 24ff; 2: 129, 131 [book 6, chap. 1]; see also George Rust, *A Discourse of Truth* in Joseph Glanvill, *Two Choice and Useful Treatises* (London 1682) 165–8, 194–5, who distinguishes objective truth ('Truth in the Object') from 'Truth in the Subject.' A strict representationalist, Rust thinks it self-evident that the truth 'is nothing but the conformity of its conceptions or *Ideas* with the natures and relations of things.'

5 Grey, *Hudibras*, in a note to lines 138–9, refers us to book 3 of Locke's *Essay*: 'This Satire is against those *Philosophers*, who took their Ideas of Substances, to be the Combinations of Nature, and not the arbitrary Workmanship of the Human mind; and that the Essence of each sort is more than the *Abstract Idea.*' Butler, however, stops short of Lockean conceptualism, considering certain distinctions 'so plaine, that they make themselves' (*PO* 69).

6 *Characters* 100, 54, 69, 122, 124, and *PO* 168; William C. Horne, 'Hard Words in *Hudibras*,' *Durham University Journal* 75 (1983): 31–44 shows how tedious oratory, metaphysical wit, difficult terminology, and physical violence all converge in the formula 'hard words.'

7 *Characters* 55; see also Holstun, *Rational Millennium* (New York: Oxford UP 1987) 269–70 on Butler's anti-utopianism and the character book's invitation to readers 'to analyze and control the mob by identifying themselves with some preexistent and so presumably non-"charactered" ideal of custom and permanence.'

8 Thomas Stanley, *The History of Philosophy*, 2 vols. (London 1655), pt. 8, chap. 8, p. 27

9 John W. Yolton, 'Locke and the Seventeeth-Century Logic of Ideas,' *JHI* 16 (1955): 433. For 'notions' as unfounded beliefs, see, e.g., Edward, Lord

Townshend, WA: Bay P 1983): I would disagree with Jameson that eighteenth-century irony is, in Wayne Booth's terms, 'stable.'
12 Michael McKeon, *The Origins of the English Novel, 1600–1740* (Baltimore: Johns Hopkins UP 1987)
13 James Smith, John Mennes, et al. *Wit Restor'd* (1658; facs. ed. Delmar NY: Scholars' Facsimiles 1985) 141, 142
14 *Certain Verses Written by Severall of the Authors Friends,* in Davenant, *Gondibert,* ed. Gladish. (Oxford: Clarendon 1971) 273–6
15 Paul Scarron, *Typhon: or, The Gyants War with the Gods. A Mock-Poem in Five Cantos,* trans. John Phillips (London 1665) 144–6
16 Charles Cotton, *Scarronides: or, Virgile Travestie, A Mock Poem* (London 1664) 2
17 John Boys, Preface, *Æneas his Descent into Hell* (London 1661) A2r. Book 4 was attempted by Ben Jonson (1601), and Giles Fletcher (1610), Sir Dudley Digges (1622), Richard Stapylton (1634), Richard Fanshawe (1648), Godolphin and Waller (1658), Sir Robert Howard (1660), Sir John Denham (1668).
18 *Works of Publius Virgilius Maro,* trans. John Ogilby (London 1649) and *Works of Publius Virgilius Maro: Translated, Adorn'd with Sculpture, and Illustrated with Annotations* (London 1654); *Homer His Iliads* (London 1660); *Homer His Odysses* (London 1665)
19 Annabel Patterson, *Pastoral and Ideology: Virgil to Valéry* (Berkeley: U of California P 1987) 169
20 Raymond A. Anselment, *Loyalist Resolve: Patient Fortitude in the English Civil War* (Newark: U of Delaware P 1988)
21 Voltaire 27, 69; see also William Frost's Commentary on Dryden's Vergil, *Works of John Dryden,* vol. 6, esp. 862–76.
22 Francis Cairns, *Virgil's Augustan Epic* (Cambridge: Cambridge UP 1989) 92–108, and 5–6, 71
23 'An Horatian Ode upon Cromwel's Return from Ireland,' *The Poems and Letters of Andrew Marvell* ed. H.M. Margoliouth, 3d ed. 2 vols. (Oxford: Clarendon 1971) 1: 91–4
24 Hobbes, *Works* 10: iv
25 Abraham Cowley, *The Collected Works of Abraham Cowley,* ed. Thomas O. Calhoun, Laurence Heyworth, and Allan Pritchard, 1 vol. to date (Newark: U of Delaware P 1989–) 1: 376–7
26 Raymond Williams, *Marxism and Literature* (Oxford: Oxford UP 1977) 122

9 METAPHYSICK WIT

1 In 'An Examination of P. Malebranche's Opinion of Seeing All Things in

Herbert of Cherbury, *De Veritate*, trans. Meyrick H. Carré (Bristol: U of Bristol 1937).
10 Sir Kenelm Digby, *Two Treatises* (Paris 1644) 2
11 Alexander Ross, *The Philosophical Touch-stone: or, Observations upon Sir Kenelm Digbie's Discourses of the Nature of Bodies, and of the Reasonable Soul* (London 1645) 2 takes exception to Digby's conventionalism: 'If there can be no *adequation* of our conceptions with the things we conceive, there can be no *metaphysicall* truth in us; which consisteth in the agreement of our thoughts with the things.' Ross's attacks on Bacon, Harvey, Copernicus, and others who challenged orthodoxy inspired Butler's 'There was an ancient sage *Philosopher*, / That had read *Alexander Ross* over' (1.2.1–2), which makes the modern interpreter Ross superior in authority to antiquity.
12 *To Sir Kenelme Digby upon His Two Incomparable Treatises of Philosophy* (London 1653); John W. Yolton, *John Locke and the Way of Ideas* (London: Oxford UP 1956) 109–10, 77 observes that Sergeant, like Digby himself, 'belongs to that tradition in epistemology which explains knowing in the Aristotelian fashion as an absorption of the form of objects by the mind, the form constituting the essential features of the object which is known.' Yolton regards Digby and Sergeant as contributors to a pre-Kantian critique of empiricism based on the insight that the reports of the senses cannot yield knowledge of the world without the supplement (or foundation) of basic rational principles.
13 John Sergeant, *Solid Philosophy Asserted against the Fancies of the Ideists* (London 1697) A3v–A4v, A5v
14 Digby 345–6; *PO* 15, cf. p. 21. Butler recorded another version of this in his notebook: 'Truth is Scarse so much as a Notion, for it is but the Putting of those Notions of things (in the understanding of Man) into the same order that their Originals are in Nature.'
15 *Satires* 39; cf. the Lawyer of the Characters, who behaves as if 'Right and Wrong were only notional, and had no Relation at all to practice ... or Reason and Truth did wholly consist in the right Spelling of Letters, when, as the subtler Things are, the nearer they are to nothing; so the subtler Words and Notions are, the nearer they are to Nonsense' (112).
16 François Rabelais, *The Works of F. Rabelais*, trans. Sir Thomas Urquhart and Pierre Le Motteux, 5 vols. (London 1693–4) 4: 219–20 (book 4, chapter 56 [misnumbered XLVI]): 'Here, here, said *Pantagruel*, here are some that are not yet thaw'd. He then throw'd us on the Deck whole handfulls of frozen Words, which seem'd to us like your rough Sugar-Plumbs, of many Colours ... and we really heard them, but could not understand them, for it was a Barbarous Gibberish.'

17 Richard Baxter, *Reliquiae Baxterianae* (London 1696) 6, for example, numbers '*Aquinas, Scotus, Durandus, Ockham,* and their Disciples' among the favourite reading materials of Baxter's youth, second only to works of practical divinity.

18 Thomas Edwards, *Gangræna: or, A Catalogue and Discovery of Many of the Errours, Heresies, Blasphemies and Pernicious Practices of the Sectaries of This Time* (London 1646) 4–5, 18, 15; see also *The Second Part of Gangraena* (London 1646), and *The Third Part of Gangraena* (London 1646).

10 A BABYLONISH DIALECT

1 See Paul Christianson, *Reformers and Babylon: English Apocalpytic Visions from the Reformation to the Eve of the Civil War* (Toronto: U of Toronto P 1978), and Christopher Hill, *Antichrist in Seventeenth-Century England*, rev. ed. (London: Verso 1990). Bacon translated Psalm 137 ('By the waters of Babylon'), a fantasy of rebellion and apocalyptic revenge under foreign yoke, in 1624:

> And thou, O Babylon, shalt have thy turn
>   By just revenge, and happy shall he be,
> That thy proud walls and tow'rs shall waste and burn,
>   And as thou didst by us, so do by thee.
>   Yea, happy he, that takes thy children's bones,
>   And dasheth them against the pavement stones.   (7: 284–5)

2 Filmer, *Patriarcha*, ed. Sommerville (Cambridge: Cambridge UP 1991) 28. Christopher Hill, 'The Many-Headed Monster,' *Change and Continuity in Seventeenth-Century England*, 2d ed. (New Haven: Yale UP 1991) 181–204, 296–324, and Postscript 288–90, relates the many-headed Beast to class conflict, and to the 'masterless men' for whom no authority answered.

3 Milton, *CP* 8: 430, 3: 598, 7: 357; see also 7: 308 on the many-headed beast as setting anyone other than Christ at the head of the 'ecclesiastical bodie.'

4 Michael McKeon, *Politics and Poetry in Restoration England: The Case of Dryden's 'Annus Mirabilis'* (Cambridge: Harvard UP 1975) 217

5 [Henry Stubbe? Sir Roger L'Estrange?], *A Common-place-Book out of 'The Rehearsal Transpros'd'* (London 1673) 36; [Richard Leigh], *The Censure of the Rota upon Mr Miltons Book, Entituled 'The Ready and Easie Way to Establish a Free Common-wealth'* (London 1660) B2r

6 'Smectymnuus, or the Club-Divines,' *The Poems of John Cleveland*, ed. Brian Morris and Eleanor Withington (Oxford: Clarendon 1967) 24; Robert

Wild, 'Iter Boreale,' George de F. Lord, ed. *Poems on Affairs of State,* 7 vols. (New Haven: Yale UP 1963–75) 1: 6; Abraham Cowley, 'A Discourse by Way of Vision, concerning the Government of Oliver Cromwell,' *Essays, Plays and Sundry Verses,* ed. A.R. Waller (Cambridge: Cambridge UP 1906) 344; William Uvedale, 'Welcome, Dread Sir ...' *Britannia Rediviva* (Oxford 1660); [William Strode] 'On a Disembler,' in James Smith, John Mennes, et al. *Wit Restor'd* (1658; facs. ed. Delmar NY: Scholars' Facsimiles 1985) 100

7 *PO* 257, 156; *Characters* 49–50; *Satires* 445

8 Zachary Grey, *Critical, Historical, and Explanatory Notes upon 'Hudibras'* (London 1752) 19, persuades himself of Butler's favourable disposition towards the Royal Society against much evidence to the contrary: see *PO* 155, on 'The Historian of Gresham Colledge,' and *Hudibras* 2.3.1024–6.

9 Kevin Sharpe and Steven N. Zwicker, 'Politics of Discourse: Introduction,' *Politics of Discourse: The Literature and History of Seventeenth-Century England,* ed. Sharpe and Zwicker (Berkeley: U of California P 1987) 6; on the religio-juridical foundations of polemic see Michel Foucault, 'Polemics, Politics, and Problemizations: An Interview,' in *The Foucault Reader,* ed. Paul Rabinow (New York: Pantheon 1984) 382

10 Paul J. Korshin, *Typologies in England, 1650–1820* (Princeton: Princeton UP 1982) 277

11 *An Answer to a Book Entituled 'An Humble Remonstrance'* ([London] 1641) 27–8; [Joseph Hall], *A Defence of the 'Humble Remonstrance'* (London 1641) 56–66; see also 139: 'None but the *Babylonian* note sounds well in your eare, Downe with it, downe with it even to the grownd'; and Milton, *CP* 1: 650, 2: 539–40.

12 Samuel Johnson, *Lives of the English Poets,* ed. George Birbeck Hill, 3 vols. (Oxford: Clarendon 1905) 1: 191

11 BY EQUIVOCATION SWEAR

1 [Sir Roger L'Estrange?], 'An Alphabetical Key to *Hudibras,*' in Samuel Butler, *Posthumous Works in Prose and Verse,* 2 vols. (London 1715); Hardin Craig, '*Hudibras,* Part I, and the Politics of 1647,' *Manly Anniversary Studies* (Chicago: U of Chicago P 1923); Ward S. Miller, 'The Allegory in Part I of *Hudibras,*' *Huntington Library Quarterly* 21 (1958): 323–43. George Wasserman, *Samuel 'Hudibras' Butler,* 2d ed. (Boston: Twayne 1989) 45, 79, 92

2 Christopher Hill, 'Samuel Butler (1613–80),' *The Collected Essays,* 3 vols. (Brighton: Harvester 1985–6) 1: 277–97, which was originally a review of

Wilders' edition of *Hudibras* titled 'The End of Ideology.' Christopher Hill, *Some Intellectual Consequences of the English Revolution* (Madison: U of Wisconsin P 1980) 21 explains the vogue for 'de factoist' political theories: 'In the early sixteen-fifties there seems to have been a weariness, a suspicion of ideological politics, a desire to escape from previous commitments and loyalties, a willingness to withdraw from opposition to the all-powerful Army even if not giving its rule enthusiastic support.'
3 Laura Brown, 'The Ideology of Restoration Poetic Form: John Dryden,' *PMLA* 97 (1982): 395–407
4 Annabel Patterson, *Censorship and Intepretation: The Conditions of Writing and Reading in Early Modern England* (U of Wisconsin P 1984), shows how ambiguity and other forms of literary encryption served seventeenth-century authors and readers in negotiating the perils of censorship.
5 *Hudibras*, pp. 450–1; on 'application' as interpretive technique, see John M. Wallace, '"Examples Are Best Precepts": Readers and Meanings in Seventeenth-Century Poetry,' *Critical Inquiry* 1 (1974): 273–90.
6 Margaret Anne Doody, *The Daring Muse: Augustan Poetry Reconsidered* (Cambridge: Cambridge UP 1985) 55
7 *Some Considerations about the Nature of an Oath, More Particularly Relating to Our Nationall Covenant* (London 1649) 1; Edward Benlowes, *Theophila: or, Loves Sacrifice* (London 1652) 47; for the text of the covenant, see S.R. Gardiner ed. *The Constitutional Documents of the Puritan Revolution, 1625–1660* 3d ed. (Oxford: Clarendon 1906) 267–71.
8 On the political theory of the engagement controversy, see Glenn Burgess, 'Usurpation, Obligation and Obedience in the Thought of the Engagement Controversy,' *Historical Journal* 29 (1986): 515–36; Quentin Skinner, 'Conquest and Consent: Thomas Hobbes and the Engagement Controversy,' in *The Interregnum: The Quest for Settlement, 1646–1660*, ed. G.E. Aylmer (Hamden, CT: Archon 1972) 79–98; John M. Wallace, *Destiny His Choice: The Loyalism of Andrew Marvell* (Cambridge: Cambridge UP 1968) 43–68
9 *Hudibras*, ed. Grey 1: 360–3, and 2: 4
10 Susan Staves, *Players' Scepters: Fictions of Authority in the Restoration* (Lincoln: U of Nebraska P 1979) 24–7, 191–251; for Butler's objections to the first Test Act, see PO 6.
11 The best recent studies of casuistry are Perez Zagorin, *Ways of Lying: Dissimulation, Persecution, and Conformity in Early Modern Europe* (Cambridge: Harvard UP 1990); Albert R. Jonsen and Stephen Toulmin,

The Abuse of Casuistry: A History of Moral Reasoning (Berkeley: U of California P 1988); and Camille Wells Slights, *The Casuistical Tradition in Shakespeare, Donne, Herbert, and Milton* (Princeton: Princeton UP 1981).
12 *Reasons of the Present Judgement of the University of Oxford* (Oxford 1647) 22; Wood, *Athenae Oxonienses* 2d ed., 2 vols. (London 1721) 2: 319
13 Robert Sanderson, *Eight Cases of Conscience* (London 1674) 114, 113, 119–20, 124–5
14 Slights 43–59; Jonsen and Toulmin 195–215; Zagorin 244–8
15 Robert Sanderson, *De Juramento: Seven Lectures Concerning the Obligation of Promissory Oaths* (London 1655) 31–6
16 Frank L. Huntley, 'Macbeth and the Background of Jesuitical Equivocation,' *PMLA* 79 (1964): 393; on Aristotle's theory of homonymous equivocation, see Heather A.R. Asals, *Equivocal Predication: George Herbert's Way to God* (U of Toronto P 1981) 9–14.
17 Jeremy Taylor, *Ductor Dubitantium* (London 1660), book 3, 101, 103, in answer to the question 'whether it be lawfull to equivocate, or use words of doubtfull signification ...'
18 Anthony Ascham, *Of the Confusions and Revolutions of Goverments* (London 1649) 65; and note Taylor, book 3, 83, on the 'universal contract' implied in all discourse.
19 A version of 2.2.103–382 (with interpolations from 1.2.) appeared in broadsheet: *The Priviledge of Our Saints in the Business of Perjury. Useful for Grand-Juries* (London 1681); James L. Thorson, 'A Broadside by Samuel Butler (1612–1680),' *Bodleian Library Record* 9 (1974): 178–86 dates the pamphlet in early July, when interest in grand juries swelled in the wake of those convened after the Popish plot.
20 Michel Foucault, 'Politics and the Study of Discourse,' *Ideology and Consciousness* 3 (1978): 9
21 Edward Hyde, *A Brief View and Survey of the Dangerous and Pernicious Errors to Church and State in Mr. Hobbes's Book, Entitled 'Leviathan'* (Oxford 1676) 255 wonders why Hobbes, who supposedly endorses prevarication of principle, 'did not make use of a Text of *Euripides* englisht in *Hudibras*, who is much a graver writer, and far better Casuist, as an autority to support his doctrine, *Oaths are but words, and words but wind, / Too feeble instruments to bind. &c*' Butler's oaths-as-wind trope reappears in *Characters* 32–3.
22 For the army's engagement see A.S.P. Woodhouse ed. *Puritanism and Liberty*, 2d ed. (Chicago: U of Chicago P 1974) 402; Waller and Grimston are quoted by Wilbur Cortez Abbott ed. *The Writings and Speeches*

of Oliver Cromwell, 3 vols. (Cambridge: Harvard UP 1937–47) 1: 461–2.
23 For a half-sympathetic account of the Quakers' refusal to swear, see John Gauden, *A Discourse Concerning Publick Oaths* (London 1662); see also Richard Bauman, *Let Your Words Be Few: Symbolism of Speaking and Silence among Seventeenth-Century Quakers* (Cambridge: Cambridge UP 1983) 95–119, and Barry Reay, *The Quakers and the English Revolution* (New York: St Martins 1985 62–78.
24 'Common Sense as a Cultural System,' *Local Knowledge: Further Essays in Interpretive Anthropology* (New York: Basic 1983) 75
25 *Diary of John Evelyn*, ed. William Bray, 4 vols. (London 1879) 3: 443–4 [letter dated 12 August 1689]
26 See N.H. Keeble, *The Literary Culture of Non-Conformity in Later Seventeenth-Century England* (Leicester: Leicester UP 1987) 83, 82–135.
27 Shapin and Schaffer, *Leviathan and the Air-Pump* (Princeton: Princeton UP 1985) 283–331
28 Foucault, *Language, Counter-Memory, Practice* (Ithaca: Cornell UP 1977) 143; Derrida, *Writing and Difference* (Chicago: U of Chicago P 1979) 36, writing specifically of *Madness and Civilization* but thinking of Foucault's archaeological method in general, comments: 'A history, that is, an archaeology against reason doubtless cannot be written, for, despite all appearances to the contrary, the concept of history has always been a rational one. It is the meaning of "history" or *archia* that should have been questioned first, perhaps. A writing that exceeds, by questioning them, the values "origin," "reason," and "history" could not be contained within the metaphysical closure of an archaeology.'
29 Smectymnuus [Thomas Young et al.] *An Answer to a Book Entituled, 'An Humble Remonstrance'* (n.p. 1641) 26–7; cf. Tertullian, *Treatise against Praxeas*, trans. Ernest Evans (London: S.P.C.K. 1948) 132: 'against all heretics let it from now on be taken as already proven that whatever is earliest is true and whatever is later is counterfeit.'

Index

Aarsleff, Hans 250 n4
Adam 164, 186; and creation 114, 125–35; language of 31–2, 42–4, 88, 119–37, 201, 210, 248 nn15, 16, 249 n4, 264 n18; and nature 82, 186; as prototype 70, 86; and reason 152–4
Adorno, Theodor 64
Aesop 50
Alexander of Hales 196
Alfonso II 111
Althusser, Louis 9–11
Andrewes, Lancelot 83, 111
Anselment, Raymond A. 271 n20
aphorism 8, 13, 46, 50, 53, 55–68
Appleby, Joyce 40–1
Aristippus 73
Aristotle 22, 24–5, 40, 57, 75, 83–5, 127, 143, 175, 185, 187, 190, 191, 196, 221, 277 n16; *De interpretatione* 44–5, 51, 250 n9; *Metaphysics* 120, 194. See also scholasticism.
Ascham, Anthony 222
Aubrey, John 69
Augustine, Saint 143

Babel and Babylon. *See under* Bible.

Bacon, Francis 142, 160, 184, 190, 197–8, 202, 236, 238–40, 242–3; and cultural authority 7–9, 13–14, 39, 53, 60–8, 74–86, 91, 249 n2; and innovation 28–31, 41–2, 46–7, 51, 68–70, 77, 78–9, 87, 247 n11, 255 n12, 257 n26; and nature 62–5, 74, 81–3, 149, 253 n12, 264 n16; and religion 30–3, 133, 248 n13, 274 n1. Works: *Advancement of Learning* 10, 28, 44, 46, 58–9, 91; *Apophthegmes New and Old* 60; *De Augmentis Scientiarum* 59, 75; *De Interpretatione Naturae* 59; *De Sapientia Veterum* 34, 74, 84, 149; *Essayes* 28, 61, 87, 147; *Great Instauration (GI)* 25, 26, 32, 38–40, 61, 70, 73, 86, 91; *Letters* 28, 39; *Maxims of the Law* 59; *New Atlantis* 28, 49, 75; *Novum Organum (NO)* 8, 29, 31–3, 37–41, 43, 46–8, 51–2, 55, 60–4, 66, 70, 74, 85, 88, 91, 239, 242, 246 n3; *On Principles and Origins* 33; *Sylva Sylvarum* 74, 76, 84; *Temporus Partus Masculus* 72; *Valerius Terminus* 65

Bakhtin, Mikhail 14, 60, 101–3, 169
Bale, John 203
Barber, John 270 n6
Barrow, Samuel (S.B.) 93–4, 110
Du Bartas, Guillaume de Saluste, Sieur 42, 99
Barthes, Roland 56
Baxter, Richard 274 n17
Beale, John 77
Belsey, Catherine 139, 154, 260 n19
Benlowes, Edward 217
Berkenhead, Sir John 236
Bernardus Silvestris 124
Berry, Boyd M. 269 n2
Bible 22, 30, 98, 135, 198; Babel and Babylon 16, 31–2, 43, 44, 49, 133, 186, 202–13, 235, 274 n1, 275 n11. Books: Acts 49, 201, 206; 1 Corinthians 65, 143, 150; Ephesians 144; Genesis 32, 88, 117, 124, 130–1, 140, 143, 158; Isaiah 121; Matthew 31; Proverbs 63, 253 n12; Psalms 99; Revelation 203–4, 212, 274 nn2, 3; 1 Timothy 143
Bloom, Harold 97, 258 n7
Blumenberg, Hans 248 n13
Boileau-Despréaux, Nicolas 164, 166, 270 n7
Bordo, Susan 73
Boyle, Robert 52, 77, 255 n14
Braden, Gordon 155, 268 n23
Brooke, Robert Greville, baron 75, 255 n12
Brouncker, William, viscount (president of Royal Society) 80
Brown, Laura 215
Browne, Sir Thomas 75, 83
Bruno, Giordano 134
Burke, Kenneth 11

Burnet, Gilbert 230
Butler, Samuel 15–17, 94, 113, 144, 160; and controversy 189, 206–13; *Hudibras* 8, 16, chapters 8, 9, 10, 11 passim; reputation of 164–70; on the reliability of the senses 184–6, 189; and social conflict 183, 202, 208–12. *See also under* error; notions.

Caesar, Julius 177
Camoens (Camões), Luis de 259 n14
Cardan, Jerome (Girolamo Cardano) 24, 65
Casaubon, Isaac 28
casuistry 16, 192, 218–34. *See also* oaths and vows.
Cavendish, Margaret, duchess of Newcastle 264 n17
censorship 216, 218–19, 235–6, 276 n4
Cervantes Saavedra, Miguel de 170, 179
Charles II 70, 80, 94, 204–5, 209, 226
Charron, Pierre 148, 267 n13
Cicero, Marcus Tullius 75, 189, 261 n28
Clarendon, Edward Hyde, earl of 277 n21
Cleveland, John 205
Cohen, Murray 41–2
Columbus, Christopher 64
Congreve, William 168
Conte, Gian Biagio 105
Copernicus, Nicolaus 67
Cotton, Charles 173
Cowley, Abraham 78–84, 94–6, 167, 173, 175, 178–9, 236
Cromwell, Oliver 176–7, 230
Cyprian, Saint 108

Dallington, Sir Robert 61
Dante Alighieri 103, 124
Davenant, Sir William 14, 94–5, 100, 106, 167, 171–3, 175
Davis, Lennard 260 n20
Dear, Peter 256 n22
Denham, Sir John 175
Dennis, John 270 n6
de Quehen, A.H. 270 n8, 272 n2
Derrida, Jacques 34, 119, 245 n2, 248 n14, 278 n28
Descartes, René 65, 78, 136; and Cartesianism 26, 73, 88, 135, 186, 190–1, 198
Destutt de Tracy, Antoine 8
Dewey, John 27–8, 69, 184, 254 n2
Diderot, Denis 170
Digby, Sir Kenelm 190–3, 273 nn11, 12
Diogenes Laertius 73
Donne, John 109, 144, 248 n16
Doody, Margaret 216
Dostoyevsky, Fyodor 103
Downe, John 108
Drogheda, capture of 176
Dryden, John 94, 173, 215, 257 n2
Dubois, Claude-Gilbert 120, 248 n15
Duns Scotus, John 196–7

Eagleton, Terry 245 n5, 254 n7
Eco, Umberto 146
Edwards, Thomas 198
Elsky, Martin 42
empire 62, 83, 100, 105, 175–7, 179–80, 259 nn13, 14
epic poetry: and allegory 105, 124–5; and creation 95–6; and domesticity 139–42, 164; form of 117–20, 234; and mock epic 8, 15, 93, 163–81, 269 n1; and modernity 4, 95–9, 106–14, 169, 240; and the novel 101–4; and romance 166–7, 260 n20; prestige of 88, 94–5; and topicality 164–5, 215–17, 235–6
Epicureanism 64, 66, 135
Erasmus, Desiderius 57
error 4, 13–16; in Bacon 21–2, 25–9, 38–40, 87, 241; and Bacon's idols 41, 43, 46–53, 70, 151–2; in *Hudibras* 183–99, 201, 216; in *Paradise Lost* 121–4, 137, 142, 145, 263 n10; as wandering 37–8. *See also* ideology; language.
Eve 114, 121, 132, 150, 160, 164, 268 nn17, 21; and gender identity 139–46, 151–9
Evelyn, John 77–8, 235, 257 n28

Fanshawe, Sir Richard 175
Feuerbach, Ludwig 67, 253 n15
Feyerabend, Paul 22–3
Filmer, Sir Robert 158, 203, 268 n25
Fish, Stanley 123, 253 n14, 263 nn10, 12, 268 n21
Foucault, Michel 6–7, 10, 42, 60, 224, 238, 252 n8, 275 n9, 278 n28
Fox, George 232
Foxe, John 203
Frankfurt school 57
Freud, Sigmund 6, 119
Froula, Christine 141, 145
Frye, Northrop 99, 119
Fulgentius, Fabius Planciades 124, 130

Gadamer, Hans-Georg 25
Galilei, Galileo 67
Gassendi, Pierre 78, 191
Gauden, John 278 n23

Geertz, Clifford 11, 235, 278 n24
Genette, Gérard 248 n15
Gilbert, William 67
Glanvill, Joseph 52, 84
Goclenius, Rudolph 251 n14, 263 n7
Godwin, William 168
Goldberg, Jonathan 158, 245 n2, 249 n2
Grabes, Herbert 267 n12
Greenblatt, Stephen 45, 250 n12
Grey, Zachary 165, 207, 213, 218, 236, 272 n5, 275 n8
Grimston, Sir Harbottle 230
Grossman, Marshall 119, 145, 262 n4, 268 n17
Guicciardini, Francesco 61
Guillory, John 3-4, 139
Gwynne, Nell 147

Hacking, Ian 44
Hakewill, George 108-9
Hale, Sir Matthew 265 n22
Halifax, George Savile, marquis of 58
Hall, Joseph 150, 275 n11
Halley, Janet E. 266 n8
Hanseatic League 209
Hanson, Elizabeth 257 n28
Harington, Sir John 261 n30
Harrington, James 174-5, 189
Harriot, Thomas 135
Hartman, Geoffrey 152
Harvey, William 67, 69
Heraclitus 56
Herbert, George 52, 74, 75
Hesse, Mary 22-3
Heywood, Thomas 118
Hill, Christopher 164, 215, 258 n4, 274 n2, 275 n2
Hippocrates 58, 59

Hobbes, Thomas 78, 108, 177, 191, 192, 198, 215, 236, 277 n21
Hollar, Wenceslaus 80, 174
Holstun, James 144, 253 n13, 272 n7
Homer 88, 93, 98, 101, 103, 114, 167, 170; rivalry with Virgil 106-9, 261 nn27, 28
Hooke, Robert 237
Horace 84, 113-14, 164, 165
Horkheimer, Max 64
Horne, William C. 272 n6
humanism 4, 21, 97-100, 108, 189, 196, 235, 250 n12, 259 n15, 260 n19
Hume, David 21, 66
Hunter, Michael 255 n14

ideology 8, 37, 41, 46-7, 53, 142-5, 275 n2; and language 87, 100, 101, 139, 165, 166, 176, 180, 202-5, 211-13, 215-16, 234-5, 239-43; and science 9-12, 91, 109, 236-7. *See also* error; language.

Jacob, James R. 255 n15, 256 n24
Jacob, Margaret C. 255 nn14, 15
James I 27, 39, 67, 85, 249 n2
Jameson, Fredric 169, 270 n11
Jardine, Lisa 247 n11
Jauss, Hans Robert 71-2
Jerome, Saint 211
Johnson, Samuel 213
Jonsen, Albert R. 276 n11
Jonson, Ben 74, 113
Juvenal 107

Kahn, Victoria 26
Keller, Evelyn Fox 254 n8
Kendrick, Christopher 100, 259 n13

Kenshur, Oscar 249 n3
Kerrigan, William 111, 118, 155, 268 n23
King, Henry 44
Kuhn, Thomas 22, 24–5, 246 n3

Lalli, Jean Baptiste 168
Landino, Cristoforo 125
language 25, 150–1, 157, 187–8, 242; and agency 7–8, 60, 130–2; and equivocation 183, 195, 217–34; and metaphor 29–30, 37, 43, 56, 197–8; and money 50; and naming 130–3; and nominalism 34, 191; and reference 24, 48–53, 134, 136, 156, 159, 242; as *'res and verba'* 35, 42–5, 51, 82–3, 189; and style 42, 68, 82–3, 216–17. *See also* error; ideology.
La Peyrère, Isaac 135
La Rochefoucauld, François, duc de 58
Le Bossu, René 175–6
Lee, Nathaniel 94
Leibnitz, Gottfried Wilhelm 192, 250 n11
Leigh, Richard 167
L'Estrange, Sir Roger 236
Lévi-Strauss, Claude 245 n2
Levy, F.J. 61
Lewalski, Barbara Kiefer 101
Lewes, George Henry 69
Lichtenberg, Georg Christoph 58
Locke, John 45, 130, 149, 183, 185, 190, 191–2, 271 n1, 272 n5
Loewenstein, David 258 n4, 263 n12
Loredano, Giovanni Francesco 133
Low, Antony 261 n32
Lucan 106, 114, 178–9, 270 n7

Lucretius 63, 108
Lukács, Georg 103, 260 n18
Luke, Sir Samuel 217
Lyotard, Jean-François 169

Macaulay, Thomas Babington, baron 67, 69
MacCallum, Hugh 264 n13
McCanles, Michael 34, 151, 249 n18
Macherey, Pierre 11, 72, 254 n7
Machiavelli, Niccolò 58, 61, 176, 210, 230
McKeon, Michael 170, 204
MacLean, Gerald M. 270 n7
McLuhan, Marshall 247 n11
Maistre, Joseph Marie, comte de 69
Malebranche, Nicolas 186, 192, 271 n1
Margolin, Jean-Claude 247 n11
Markley, Robert 249 n3, 256 n22
Marlowe, Christopher 135
Martin, Julian 249 n2
Marvell, Andrew 93, 94, 167, 177–8, 205
Marx, Karl, and Marxism 6, 9, 72
Massinger, Philip 171
Mennes, John 168
method: and the discourse of origins 3–8, 12–17, 26–35, 37–40, 88, 158–9; and hypothesis 21–5, 84; and induction 33, 52–3, 55, 66; and modernity 69–71, 75–84. *See also* science.
Milton, John 4, 9, 163–4, 168, 173, 213, 238, 240; and knowledge 91–3, 117–30, 137, 142–54, 160; and society 95, 101, 158–9, 216. Works: *Apology against a Pamphlet* 150; *Areopagitica* 111, 123,

150, 197; *Christian Doctrine* 131; divorce tracts 132; *Eikonoklastes* 204; *History of Britain* 96, 179; 'In Proditionem Bombardicam' 204; *Of Education* 201; *Paradise Lost* 8, 14–15, 88; chapters 5, 6, 7 passim, 163, 167, 234, 237, 241; *Paradise Regained* 98, 112, 261 n32; *Prolusions* 91, 109; *Readie and Easie Way* 205; *Reason of Church-Government* 101, 111, 204, 241; *Tenure of Kings and Magistrates* 228–9. See also Adam; epic poetry; Eve.
Miner, Earl 121, 269 n4
mirrors and mirroring 34, 52, 139, 145–60, 185, 191, 266 n9, 267 n15; as metaphor 14, 33–4, 41, 88, 142
Montaigne, Michel Eyquem de 61
Montrose, Louis A. 246 n8
Mueller, Janel M. 252 n2

Nash, Treadway Russel 270 n6
Newton, Sir Isaac 80
Nietzsche, Friedrich 6, 57–8, 136
Nogarola, Isotta 266 n5
notions 13, 16, 33; in Bacon 41, 45–7, 49–53, 86–7, 251 nn14, 15; in Butler 183–9, 191–7, 271 n1, 273 nn14, 15; in Milton 128, 136, 149
Nyquist, Mary 142, 145, 154

oaths and vows: and polysemy 221–31; and Quakers 231–2, 278 n23; the Engagement 217–21, 233; Solemn Engagement of the Army 230; Solemn League and Covenant 217, 219, 225; Test Act 218. See also casuistry; language.

objectivity 3, 12–14, 16, 26, 40, 86, 88, 149; and perception 31, 148–9, 160, 273 n12; and social order 27, 86–7, 120, 135–6, 216–17, 237–43; as unitary rationality 183, 202
Ockham, William of 187, 196
Octavian (Augustus) 176
Ogilby, John 173–4, 271 n18
Oldenburg, Henry 67–8
Ovid 144
Oxenden, Sir George 216

Pascal, Blaise 136
Patterson, Annabel 174–5, 271 n19, 276 n4
Paul, Saint 65, 143, 144
Pepys, Samuel 235
Pérez-Ramos, Antonio 80, 254 n4
Phillips, John 168, 172, 271 n15
Plato: and Platonism 22, 34, 47, 125, 136–7, 146, 188, 199; *Cratylus* 44, 130; *Republic* 75
Pliny the Elder 108
Pocock, J.G.A. 12
Popper, Karl 21–2
Pordage, Samuel 164
Power, Henry 74
presbyterians 199, 203, 209–12, 217, 218, 228, 239
Preus, J. Samuel 248 n13
Pride's Purge 229
Priscian 232
Protestantism 98, 133, 165; and Catholicism 79, 100, 203–4, 210, 218, 221, 232, 277 n19; and episcopacy 217; and idolatry 210; and Judaism 109; and the Reformation 5, 30, 109, 236; and sectarianism 9, 15, 112, 198, 201, 204, 206, 209–13, 218, 229, 231, 236, 239

Quilligan, Maureen 263 n11
Quint, David 3–4, 118, 259 n14
Quintilian 107

Rabb, Theodore K. 247 n11
Rabelais, François 170, 179, 195, 273 n16
Radzinowicz, Mary Ann 99
Ralegh, Sir Walter 117, 135
Ramus, Peter 24, 40
Randolph, Thomas 74
Rapaport, Herman 259 n16
Rapin, René 107
Rawley, William 75
Reiss, Timothy 43, 45, 87
representation 3, 11, 13, 23–4, 34, 37, 41–3, 53, 102–3, 130, 137, 148–50, 158, 183–99
Restoration 8, 42, 75, 77–8, 80, 86, 91, 135, 165, 175, 191, 204–5, 209, 215, 236; and Baconianism 8, 15, 69–88, 70, 123, 172, 184, 185–6, 243; and the reception of Milton 94, 167
Revard, Stella P. 260 n21
revolution, English 8, 13, 111, 164, 176, 178–9, 204–5, 208, 209, 216, 239; Bacon as cause of 85
Reynolds, Edward 124
Ricci, Matteo 251 n17
Ricks, Christopher 263 n10
Ricoeur, Paul 248 n14
Rigolot, François 261 n27
Rochester, John Wilmot, earl of 166
Ronsard, Pierre de 261 n27
Rorty, Richard 148–9, 267 n15
Ross, Alexander 75–6, 273 n11
Rossi, Paolo 27, 69
Rust, George 272 n4

Said, Edward 6–7, 61, 92, 134, 139, 159
Salmon, Vivian 45
Sanderson, Robert 218–21, 232, 236
Scaliger, Julius Caesar 45, 106–8
Scarron, Paul 166, 168, 170, 172–4
scepticism 3, 16, 27, 38, 123, 135, 136, 184, 192
Schaffer, Simon 78
Schiebinger, Londa 73
scholasticism 5, 27, 30, 32, 42, 65, 75, 78, 91, 184–9, 191–7. See also Aristotle.
Schwartz, Regina 119, 139, 266 n4
science: and astrology 237; and atomism 46, 93, 135; and causation 3–4, 92, 120; and cosmology 125–8, 135; and empiricism 22–5, 42, 73, 170, 184, 273 n12; and gender 72–86, 139, 254 n8; and materialism 10–11, 93; as narrative 169, 241–2; and nature 3, 25, 62, 91; and the Royal Society 13, 68, 71, 77–88, 207, 235, 237, 239, 255 n15, 256 nn22, 24, 275 n8; and teleology 6–7, 22, 38. See also method.
Scudamore, James 168
Scudéry, Georges de 104, 257 n2
Scudéry, Madeleine de 104, 260 n20
Seidel, Michael 164, 269 nn3, 4
Self-Denying Ordinance 227
Sergeant, John 191–3, 273 n12
Shapin, Steven 78
Sharpe, Kevin 275 n9
Smectymnuus 205, 211
Smith, James 168, 171
Sowernam, Ester 143
Spenser, Edmund 4, 93, 95, 106, 111,

122, 179, 197, 236, 257 n2; *Faerie Queene* 153, 263 n11
Sprat, Thomas 77–9, 82, 84, 208
Stanley, Thomas 189
Statius 106
Staves, Susan 218
Stein, Arnold 134
Stillingfleet, Edward 135, 191, 265 n22
Stone, Lawrence 145
Stubbe, Henry 84–5, 256 n24, 257 n26
Swaim, Kathleen M. 268 n19
Swift, Jonathan 257 n26

Tasso, Torquato 100, 106, 111
Tayler, Edward 114, 263 n10
Taylor, Jeremy 191, 221, 277 n17
Tenison, Thomas 67–8
Tertullian 143, 239, 262 n2, 278 n29
Teskey, Gordon 119, 122, 262 n6
Thomas Aquinas, Saint 24, 193–4, 196–7
Thompson, E.P. 10
Tillotson, John 191
Todorov, Tzvetan 260 n17
Toliver, Harold 103
Toulmin, Stephen 276 n11
Turner, James G. 140, 144, 263 n12

Urbach, Peter 245 n2

Vicars, John 173–5, 177
Vico, Giambattista 92
Vida, Marco Girolamo 107, 114
Virgil 4, 15, 74, 88, 93, 99–101, 166, 167, 170–2, 234, 243, 257 n2, 260 n21, 264 n15; imitation of 173–4, 178; *Aeneid* 98, 104–8, 110, 112–14, 124–5, 154, 168, 174–80
Voltaire 269 n1
Vossius, Gerardus Joannes 261 n28

Wallace, John M. 276 nn5, 8
Waller, Edmund 175, 236
Waller, Sir William 230
Washbourne, Thomas 220
Wasserman, George 169
Waswo, Richard 105, 250 n5
Webster, Charles 74
Webster, John 52, 251 n20
Whitney, Charles 247 n11
Whorf, Benjamin 23
Wild, Robert 205
Wilders, John 184, 275 n2
Wilding, Michael 164
Wilkins, John 75–6, 250 n11
Williams, Raymond 180–1, 245 n5
Wittgenstein, Ludwig 58
Wittreich, Joseph 139, 265 n3
Wolseley, Robert 166
Wood, Anthony à 219, 256 n24
Wood, P.B. 77
Woodhouse, A.S.P. 258 n9
Woolf, Virginia 139
Wordsworth, William 159
writing (ideograms, hieroglyphics, 'real character') 44, 49–51, 55, 250 n11

Yolton, John W. 190, 267 n15, 272 n9, 273 n12

Zagorin, Perez 276 n11
Zwicker, Steven N. 275 n9